THE LIFE

OF

MICHELANGELO BUONARROTI

VOLUME 1

MICHELANGELO BUONARROTI.

THE LIFE OF
MICHELANGELO BUONARROTI

BASED ON STUDIES IN THE ARCHIVES OF THE
BUONARROTI FAMILY AT FLORENCE

JOHN ADDINGTON SYMONDS

Introduction by Creighton E. Gilbert

Volume 1

University of Pennsylvania Press

Philadelphia

Originally published by J.C. Nimmo and Charles Scribner's Sons
Third Edition 1911

Introduction copyright © 2002 University of Pennsylvania Press

Published 2002 by
University of Pennsylvania Press
Philadelphia, Pennsylvania 19104-4011

10 9 8 7 6 5 4 3 2 1

Library of Congress Cataloging-in-Publication Data

Symonds, John Addington, 1840–1893.
    The life of Michelangelo Buonarroti : based on studies in the archives of
the Buonarroti family at Florence / by John Addington Symonds ; introduction by Creighton E. Gilbert.—
        p.cm
    Originally published: 3rd ed. New York : J.C. Nimmo and C. Scribner's
Sons, 1911. With new introd.
    Includes bibliographical references and index.
    ISBN 0-8122-3611-4 (cloth : alk. paper)—ISBN 0-8122-1761-6 (pbk. :
alk. paper)
    1. Michelangelo Buonarroti, 1475–1564. 2. Artists—Italy—Biography. I.
Michelangelo Buonarroti, 1475–1564. II. Title.
N6923.B9 S9 2001
709'.2—dc21
[B]   2001043629

CONTENTS

INTRODUCTION

Creighton E. Gilbert

The title page of this book presents three names, in rapidly descending order of importance, and together they embody its promises to the reader. As to the first name, nothing need be said here, as it is so familiar as to be the reason why the book was picked up at all, and the hoped-for benefit of reading it would be to enrich one's knowledge of him. The second name identifies our guide here to such enrichment and implies a claim that he is highly qualified to provide it. Readers may well not be familiar with him, and when they learn that this book was first published in 1892 they may understandably doubt its claims. We can provisionally give credence to reports about Michelangelo by his contemporaries in the sixteenth century as well as to the latest research results of today or to interpretations in tune with our culture. Here, however, we have neither. Books remote both from their subjects and from us can hardly ever gain acceptance in the way that both the earliest and the latest readily may.

This book thus has to overcome extraordinarily high odds against the author to merit attention from a new audience in approximately the same way it was received when new, which is what it asks in being reis-

sued. Yet it has over the decades garnered more
approval than most of its more recent rivals, often written with the intent to crowd it out. Nonfiction books of
a century ago are usually found of interest, if at all,
solely as documents of historiography, whether they
address their own period (as most do) or an earlier one.
In the latter case, the interest is the extremely narrow
one of showing what their epoch thought about the earlier one discussed, and when we find that out, our most
frequent reaction is that we do not agree with it. Thus
this introduction, all that is allotted to the third name
on the title page, must ask why Symonds is a spectacu-
lar exception who usually receives this approval without explanation, sometimes indeed without noticing
how distant the book's origins are. It will be my concern also to record some particulars in which the book
does indeed require updating, but even these will suggest by their slightness why its claim to continued
respect is warranted.

Symonds's success seems to me to result from the
confluence of two major factors. The first involves the
raw materials he used, the information about
Michelangelo he digests and presents. Michelangelo
had from early in his career been recorded to a degree
unique among artists of his time or earlier, because he
stimulated such awe and honor. Among such writings of
his time the bulkiest and the most unusual were two
biographies by people who knew him, both published

while he was living. No other artist had been or for generations would be the theme of more than one contemporary biography, even unpublished ones. Symonds, of course, like all other writers on the artist, quotes a great deal, even solid paragraphs, from both of them in his own English translation. Symonds also agrees with other writers in his characterization of both these writings, first the one by Giorgio Vasari that concludes his long series of lives of artists, and then the one by Michelangelo's studio assistant Ascanio Condivi, which is widely accepted as virtually a dictated autobiography. Condivi's book has mainly attracted specialist interest, but Vasari's remains a lively object of fascination like his whole set of lives, frequently translated and continuously in print.

Biographical information about Michelangelo was thus exceptionally easy to obtain from the beginning. The artist's life from start to finish was recounted, and there would seem to be no pressure to ask for more. That situation did not change until the mid-nineteenth century. Vast further materials then emerged, the most important for Symonds being the publication of hundreds of the artist's letters. In 1875 a well-edited volume presented 495 of them. More of Michelangelo's letters exist than by any other artist up to recent eras, a result of several contingencies such as his very long life and the tendency of the addressees, mainly his family, to save the famous man's words as relics. Most of the letters to the family, which are more than half the total, still belonged to their descendants until shortly before they were published. The last heir willed them to the city of Florence in 1858. Two other similar major sources also emerged. Michelangelo's 300 poems, previously known in bowdlerized editions, were first printed accurately in Italian in 1863, also mainly from family papers. Letters to Michelangelo were also chiefly among the family papers, and in 1890 a small volume of 36 of them to the painter Sebastiano del Piombo appeared. They were only a small fraction of the material, which emerged gradually until a complete set of five volumes with almost 1,400 letters to and from the artist was finally completed in 1983. One of Symonds's most notable, if less noted, contributions was to have arranged to study these unpublished letters in Florence and to make full use of their evidence.

This great shift in the availability of raw materials reflects typical patterns of nineteenth-century intellectual culture. It is a special product of the large scale emergence of scholarly philology, most fully seen in the newly strong German universities with their doctoral training. In relation to Michelangelo, however, the chief German product was the two-volume life by the literary man Herman Friedrich Grimm, first published in 1862–63, just as the letters were moving into public ownership. Grimm at first was able to utilize only a few of them, but in later editions of his book up to the tenth in 1901 introduced more and more, with exemplary attentiveness. His book was still being reprinted at least up to the 1940s, and was the chief rival to Symonds's success. Its English translation of 1865 was also successful, with a fifteenth printing in 1896 but none after that, clearly superseded by Symonds's appearance in 1892.

The broader nineteenth-century development generating this enhancement of materials was the force of nationalism, in particular the Italian version leading to the unification of the country, the risorgimento. Pervasive patriotism, among its many effects, made scholars opt to study past Italian heroes of culture, most obviously Dante. Typically, the important edition of Michelangelo's letters was issued on the fourth centennial of the artist's birth with an introduction arguing at length that he had been a great patriot. That point, common at the time, today may perhaps be best seen as a token of the way most books reflected their own age better than that of their theme, reducing them to the historiographic interest suggested above.

All this new information was available for Symonds to profit by in a way that made earlier books on Michelangelo entirely obsolete, but it calls for emphasizing here for a different reason. It was so effective that very little was to be added afterward so far as the artist's human biography is concerned. That was simply a lucky gift to Symonds, but it certainly is basic to its continuing validity. It is still true that a few important details have appeared, and the most important ones call for notice here in the context of offering the biography to today's readers. One is the date when Michelangelo's father died, 1531, aged eighty-eight or a few months less. (Michelangelo himself died just short of eighty-nine.) The date of 1534 had been usually given, on a fairly vague basis, and indeed the new one got itself established in the literature only gradually and with some muddle. Symonds accepted 1534 like everyone else, but should be credited with having pointed out that the date was shaky. As with his labor on the unpublished letters, we see him here helping to make his luck.

Most of the additions since Symonds naturally refer to the artist's early years, when there were fewer records than those clustering later around the famous man. A number of these are owing to the work of the scholar Michael Hirst, though not the earliest of all. That is from 1487, when the twelve-year-old Michelangelo was an apprentice to the painter Ghirlandaio. Vasari had cited a contract of 1488 of apprenticeship to the same artist, thus famously refuting Condivi's account of Michelangelo's self-teaching. The new record seems puzzling; how could the apprenticeship precede the contract? A plausible explanation lies in the fact that apprentices might get paid only in the later stages of their work, which would match the

The complication is that an Entombment altarpiece in London had been argued by some scholars, long before these records were known, to be an early Michelangelo. Some kind of connection with him is certain, for a drawing by him, a profile of a young woman, is an exact preparatory sketch for a head in the London picture. That work is not the one Andrea delivered, since it had to have been finished, whereas the London work has the peculiarity, perhaps even unique, of showing a plain plaster area untouched by any paint or even drawn line, bounded by what suggests the outline of a figure, among the five totally completed figures that otherwise fill the surface. Like everyone else at the time, Michelangelo regularly applied himself to each stage of the working process, both in painting and sculpture, over a whole surface, before proceeding to the next, so that in an unfinished work any area is at most only one step less developed than the rest. The opinion that the London picture is by him seems not to address the other puzzle of the returned money; if he had got as far as what we see, it is really baffling that he did not hold on to the commission. It would also be entirely unique as a work by him of somewhat ambitious scale never to have been mentioned by writers of the time; his fame saw to it that all his work was pointed out. A possible solution may be offered. He might have started work on the London panel before returning the money, using the profile drawing and others to start laying out a composition in sketch form, but then have left it. Someone else would then have used this base to do the painting, and the blank segment would reflect Michelangelo's not having worked at all on that area and the imitator's not attempting it on his own. This formulation is happily compatible with Symonds's judgment of the panel, that it is by a close imitator of Michelangelo. He seems to have been the first to say this, and has been followed by a few other observers. Symonds was less fortunate in claiming Michelangelo's authorship for the sculpture of a kneeling youth in the Victoria and Albert Museum, London. This was usual at the time, but the idea has been completely abandoned today.

Of all the pieces of raw data added to our stock since Symonds's time, the most fascinating is a series of notes in the margins of a copy of Condivi's book. The writer, it is agreed, here wrote down points that Michelangelo made to him orally, often beginning: "He said that. . . ." We here obtain an unexpected check on Condivi's accuracy, as judged by the artist. Although one might at first assume that he wanted to correct mistakes, in fact most of the notes reinforce Condivi, with some added details. The one most explicit denial of what Condivi said, and the only point made in two of the notes, concerns Michelangelo's attitude to Bramante. He denies the statement that he complained or said anything bad about the older architect. Michelangelo's annoyed feeling about Bramante, as reported by Condivi, has always been a famous detail about him. Do we now infer that Condivi was mistaken? That does not seem likely, both because such annoyance would have been natural under the circumstances at the time, and because it is hard to see how Condivi would have got this idea otherwise. Michelangelo, instead, may here have tuned out any memory of his own inappropriate behavior and reconstructed his earlier self as courteous. Something similar seems to have been involved in the only other note denying a statement by Condivi, one in which he says he had not spoken ill of one of the Medici.

Just as this scattering of additional material is to be interfiled with Symonds's narrative, a few things need to be removed from it. The most important is the material obtained from the dialogues of Francisco da Hollanda. Symonds like some others gives it much space and credence, which is understandable, for in them the artist is shown as an interlocutor making broad statements about aesthetic preferences, such as are not otherwise on record anywhere. Other scholars, however, have rejected the authenticity of the dialogues as accurate accounts of the artist's words or ideas, since such statements as calling painting superior to sculpture are just the opposite of Michelangelo's views as found in all other sources. Fictional dialogues, assigning the names of real people to the discussants, form a standard literary type of the period, and these opinions are ones that one may consider natural as those of Francisco da Hollanda himself. He was not only a painter, but at home in Portugal had to compete with an established taste for Flemish style in painting. Thus, when the dialogue makes Michelangelo attack Flemish painting, an aspect of it frequently noticed, it brings up a subject that Michelangelo very likely would not oppose, but which seems never to have been of special interest for him, as it would very much be for Francisco da Hollanda.

In benefiting from the great growth of nineteenth-century scholarship, Symonds was among many other authors of his era. Some of them also shared his luck, of being able to write biographies or other books of history that have remained valid for similar reasons. Though each case shows significant differences, a few examples of this kind seem of interest in suggesting Symonds's cultural context. William Prescott's books about the Spanish empire of the sixteenth century, especially his *Conquest of Mexico*, remain standard assignments today for students in courses. They are even more astonishing than Symonds, being fifty years older and also not having attracted many later competing efforts. This may be explained in part in that their theme has a less wide popular audience than Michelangelo, and also in part in that Prescott drew to a much greater extent on unpublished archives, more difficult for others to mine than most of Symonds's materials. It is the more

extraordinary that Symonds has maintained his position in the face of the easier access to his sources, to a
large extent already in print in his time and more so
since.

The second case involves Leonardo da Vinci,
Michelangelo's closest analogue as a great artist of his
time with wide-ranging areas of activity. The great
materials about him are his quantities of notebooks,
virtually unknown to all until 1883. The texts in the
two massive volumes of that year, edited by the
German scholar Jean Paul Richter in the original and
also with an English translation, have been added to
only slightly since then. The most special use of this
data was in the strange work of Dimitri Merezkowski,
The Romance of Leonardo da Vinci, published in 1902
and soon translated into many languages. It appeared
in English in that very year and remained popular for
decades, as suggested in the 1920s and up to the 1950s
by its inclusion, like Symonds's *Michelangelo*, in the
culturally important Modern Library of the World's
Best Books. Its single most remarkable impact was as
the chief source for Sigmund Freud's account of
Leonardo. Its oddity was that the author presented it
as a novel, and moreover as part of a series embodying
his scheme of world history. Only when one reads it
does one see that it is solidly based on Richter's data.
Yet the factor of being a novel no doubt accounts for its
having vanished today even from studies of the historiography of Leonardo, an outcome so different from the
case of Symonds's book.

The case of Titian is an instructive variant. He too was the .theme of a biography in the late nineteenth century, *Life and Times of Titian*, so good that it is still often recommended as the best, and it too introduced archival material in quantity that has been little super-seded. Yet today no one cares to read it. It strikes us as hopelessly Victorian, especially in its aesthetic descrip-tions. Paradoxically, its misfortune is to have focused so much on the actual art, clearly involving a taste that we cannot share. This focus was the contribution of one of its two coauthors, G. B. Cavalcaselle, probably the finest art historian of his time, while the other, J. A. Crowe, an accomplished journalist, provided the smooth prose.

The eventual rejection of the content of Caval-caselle's art critical analysis clarifies another basis for Symonds's success over the long haul. Along with the luck of first using all his materials, Symonds gained negatively, so to speak, by his choice of emphasis. He wrote a biography of a human person, with only minor forays into discussion of works of art. The works are the events in Michelangelo's life and the reason for our interest in him. Yet, though a biography has to be about the main events of its subject, Symonds gives this aspect oddly little wordage. The reader's implied demand to have a guide who will support claims for the greatness of the works, by descriptions, is not much answered here. Symonds explicitly noted that, of his fifteen chapters, two were about the work of the artist and twelve about the man, a psychological portrait.

(The one other chapter will be discussed below.) If today's readers ought to be alerted to this before plunging into the book, they benefit, for they will not be confronted to any great extent by Victorian aesthetic.

Indeed, when such points do appear, they have the mainly historiographic interest of most writings on art of that era. A striking case is the scolding of the architecture of the Medici chapel for several pages. Today, its design is admired for its inventiveness and paradoxical approach to classical tradition and labeled as a key pioneering example of the phase of art history called mannerism. This became widely admired in the 1920s, and it has been usual to remark that before then it was disliked, but illustrations of such dislike are rarely offered. Symonds provides a splendid one. He is more specific about architecture than in his treatment of the artist's sculpture and painting, where he tends to turn quickly to abstract universal theories of art. Or he shifts to descriptions of figural gestures and the like, not unlike many unsophisticated writers and lecturers on Renaissance art. Or, taking advantage of his literary base, he climaxes his survey of the Last Judgment by quoting what Stendhal had said about it, and this is among his most effective lines.

Thus one of Symonds's happy qualities is the minor role he gives to this aspect of his theme. We cannot look to him for everything any more than we can to any author, but we can depend on him most in what he emphasizes at greatest length. If it is correct, as has been recently argued, that Vasari's formula of subsuming people in their work has regularly recurred since, leading to a "tedious Michelangelism," Symonds is the desirable exception.

Yet Symonds's involvement with the works of art led him to some results that specialist art historians may need to respect. His judgment about the London Entombment has been mentioned. In a quite different case, the late Pietà in Florence, he was long alone judging that the involvement of Tiberio Calcagni in finishing up Michelangelo's work was slight, but this idea has very recently been argued with strong bases. Unexpectedly, we may contemplate Symonds the connoisseur.

If we assign Symonds's continuing value to his having had the use of most of the raw material, the obvious question becomes: Why have later books that use it not put him in the shade? This brings up what seems to me the second major factor in his success. Unlike most later rivals, he was a professional writer with a command of prose. Today well written biographical and similar nonfiction books appear regularly, but are more often than not understood not to show fresh scholarship. It is normal for them to popularize previous academic research that had been presented in dry volumes, ones that we will only struggle through if we are strongly motivated to be taught.

In Symonds's world of Victorian culture, on the other hand, original scholarship was encouraged to merge with the polished writing of belles lettres. A distinguished group of such books survives along with his, initiated perhaps with Gibbon's *Decline and Fall of the Roman Empire*. Prescott's writing mentioned above extends the pattern to America, as does Motley's *Rise of the Dutch Republic*. Carlyle's *French Revolution* (also included in the Modern Library in the 1930s) was followed by his multi-volume *Frederick the Great*. The pattern is memorably extended into the treatment of art by Ruskin's *Stones of Venice* and many other books. Every one of these books was an instant best-seller, as were numerous others hazily remembered today. Macaulay's *History of England* may serve as a prime example. The chief professional skill for them all, well honed, was as writers.

A pattern emerges in their background and training, if it can be called training, along with variations in some respects in each case. Most went to the most admired schools and then to universities, usually Oxford. They could do so because there was some family money, and thus they shared the education of the upper class, the landowning peerage. (Here a notable exception is the poverty of Carlyle, whose hard work gave him an entree.) The chief school subject was Latin literature, from which they had to produce endless translations, along with translations into Latin. Oxford's most conspicuous specialty, "greats," was about classical literature, including at the time an increasing portion of Greek, especially Plato. Modern humanities were a slightly less distinguished option. It is often wryly noted that the British empire at its height at the time depended on this system to produce its colonial administrators as well as its domestic political leaders. Yet it can well be added that this was a splendid basis for producing such writers, even if Ruskin's Latin remained weak.

The family money usually derived from business a generation or so earlier, as with Ruskin's father the wine merchant. Symonds's great-grandfather did well selling navy supplies during the Napoleonic wars. The writers themselves, however, were understood to belong to the "professional classes," like Symonds's father, a prominent surgeon. Symonds was expected to be a lawyer, one of the few other usual options. But when he, like the others, turned to a literary career, it was socially quite acceptable, and was expected to be financially practical, if after some early efforts that the family would cover as it would a law career. Easy contact with the peers who had been schoolmates could continue, combined with a factor of exchange of attractive benefits. The other qualification besides education for the writers usually involved much travel to suitable places, such as Italy, and much reading of source texts and previous books, usually along with unpublished archives. This was enough. There was not, as there would be today, and then was already in Germany, systematic study of the special subject with its professors.

George Wilhelm Friedrich Hegel at the University of Berlin and Jacob Burckhardt at Basel are perhaps the most conspicuous of a series of teachers in philosophy and art history whose students developed their topics further. The older system is still recognizable in America in the education of Bernard Berenson in the 1890s and in England in that of John Pope-Hennessy in the 1930s, though it would be unthinkable today in art history or any similar specialty.

Symonds's focus on the Renaissance, chiefly in Italy, which would produce most of his books, was at first in tandem with the aim of being a poet. After his college days when he won a prize his poetry was never admired, but he never gave it up. His first intensive study of Michelangelo emerged from the combination of the two interests, with an article about the artist's poems published when he was thirty-two. It included some twenty translations. In 1878 he brought out a volume of translations of all Michelangelo's sonnets. In the same lucky way as mentioned above, this was the first translation based on the accurate original texts. His book bracketed them with the sonnets of Tommaso Campanella, another Renaissance personality, who today is recalled if at all for his little book *The City of the Sun*, a Utopia somewhat similar to Thomas More's. The two poets do not have much in common beyond having produced sonnets in some quantity while mainly active in quite other areas to which they owe their fame.

Symonds's version remained the standard one of Michelangelo's for some seventy-five years. This standing is still reflected in the frequent use of the phrase "Michelangelo's sonnets" by speakers clearly taking them to be all his poetry, though they actually are fewer than his madrigals. It was thus reasonable that they were incorporated in numerous cases in the biography, so that they reappear here. Otherwise they have come to seem glaringly obsolete because of their artificial poetic language, so unlike the author's prose. Symonds evidently felt entitled to adopt such forms, as most translators of poetry from Homer's on then did, because of his own credentials as a poet. Their lack of fidelity to the originals similarly contrasts with his approach to the letters and other prose sources that he translated.

His combined focus on the two sonneteers has its obvious background in the seven-volume *Renaissance in Italy* that he brought out from 1875 to 1886, with major units on political-social history, humanism, art, literature, and the counter-reformation. None of his other twenty-five books were even close to such a scale, even while their publication in twenty-two years shows him to be such an efficient writer. The big work naturally established Symonds as an authority, in England at any rate, as suggested in his contribution of the article "Renaissance" to the *Encyclopædia Britannica*. But the remark in the same encyclopedia's entry on

Symonds that it was "the work by which he would be longest remembered" proved a poor prophecy. In contrast to Burckhardt's *Civilization of the Renaissance in Italy*, the succinct essay to which it was long compared, it has not survived the obliteration of its viewpoint by later information and attitudes.

His greatest success, as measured by continuity in print up to the present, has been his translation of the autobiography of Benvenuto Cellini. Its first edition in 1887 sold out at once; its recent incarnation as a mass paperback is shared, among writings of the Italian Renaissance, only with Macchiavelli's *Prince* and Castiglione's *Courtier*, which benefit from heavy use in schools. It has had no trouble in outlasting rival translations. Its most recent and diverting token of life has been through the play *Cellini*, by John Patrick Shanley, performed in New York in 2001. The author, best known for writing the film *Moonstruck*, has told of coming across the *Autobiography* while browsing in a bookstore, not having known of it at all before. His never having heard of Cellini evinces the thinning out of general humanistic education, which in this instance was compensated for by the book's vast circulation, so that one could run into it by a natural chance. "Reading," Shanley reports, "I started laughing right in the bookstore," and he then found himself identifying with the author. Yet here Symonds survives only in a submerged way, performing his professional writer's job as the conveyer of the story. Thus it is not the work by which he is remembered, even if it is a pleasure to see him get a credit line in newspaper reviews of the play and so a bit of renewal.

This translation was done on the suggestion of the publisher, who paid £210. After its success the same publisher proposed a life of Michelangelo for a fee of £525 (a fee referred to more elegantly as 500 guineas; elsewhere the sum is reported as £300, plus £100 for any reprints). The transition to this book from the Cellini would certainly be natural and easy. The sculptor Cellini may well have originally been stimulated to dictate his own life to an assistant in his shop by Condivi's *Life of Michelangelo*, which can likewise be thought of figuratively as dictated, resulting from the sculptor's conversations with the author. Symonds's *Life* is also in great part translation. If the encyclopedia writer failed in choosing which work of Symonds would last, he did better in his relative judgments about the various genres of his writing. He gave the poetry the lowest mark, calling it rather "that of a student than of an inspired singer," and provided a balanced estimate of his prose ("rich in description," "vivid and concentrated," if without the "harmony and unity" required in philosophical argument), but called his translations "among the finest in the language."

Symonds worked on the *Life* rapidly, producing in the three summer months of 1891, as he reported in a

letter, all but one of the twelve belonging to "the biographical part," leaving only the briefer "critical part,"
single chapters on architecture, on painting and sculpture, and on the artist's poetry and "feelings." Not sur-
prisingly in a commissioned task, he could at times
regret it as drudgery, complaining that he was "recook-
ing the jaded cabbage" of a carver. He wondered
whether he had been stupid to undertake it, since he
did not need the money and was doing it because he
had promised. He doubts that a new book is needed
after the others he is reading, and dislikes having to
spend time in Florence, with four hours daily in the
archives and inspecting Michelangelo's "ugly architecture."

All this may indeed inform our view of what
Symonds wrote, but not, I suggest, in the most obvious
way. The clue is not the implication of a chore, with
deadened results, but in the lively expression of his feeling about it. The book shows us Symonds the writing
professional, like the best of reporters, concerned to
keep the reader engaged by both the validity and the
expressiveness of his account. The most prestigious of
the original book reviews, by Andrew Lang, noted that
Symonds's style, once floridly rhetorical, now uses
"plain and simple words." (Lang was another prominent literary author, whose books ranged from a history of Scotland to a collaboration with linguists on a
translation of Homer, long standard.) The early florid

Symonds is visible here in his translations of the sonnets.

Symonds died a few months after the Michelangelo
biography appeared. The firm survival of this and the
Cellini, his two last books, may be matched with that of
novelists of the same years, like Hardy, but, as already
suggested, jumps out when compared with his peers in
nonfiction. He has recently acquired, besides, a totally
different importance, as a unique analyst and docu-
menter in his time of homosexuality. Unlike his contemporary Oscar Wilde or anyone else, he addressed
this theme too from a base as a professional writer of
nonfiction and in particular of biography. He did this in
his own memoirs, which chiefly are about his own sexual attitudes and, to a lesser extent, experiences.
Concerned, of course, to keep this all secret, he
arranged for the manuscript to be inaccessible, and his
executor stipulated that it could not be published until
1976—a date that made more luck for the author.

Three aspects of homosexual concern emerge from it
and from letters to a few similarly oriented friends. The
first is the experience of a boys' boarding school, in this
case the elite Harrow. Compared with others',
Symonds's report is unusually plain and full, making
the point that it was pervasive. His own reaction was
that it was ghastly and he avoided it. The reason, at
least as he later thought about it, was its exclusive
physicality. The second phase belongs to Oxford and

shortly thereafter. It presents idealized love of physically beautiful young men, often in poems and other
writings, with vigorous denial of "vice" or any sexual
factors. Certainly the importance of Plato in Oxford
education is relevant, while the newly popular term
"Platonic love" was being reflected in a Gilbert and
Sullivan operetta in 1881. In a letter to Walt Whitman,
Symonds adopted from him the formulation that "the
'adhesiveness' of comradeship has no interblending
with the 'amativeness' of sexual love." He could pass a
night naked in bed with a man with kissing and
embracing but deem it "not licentious." He could
record this in his diary and in letters, but tended to do
so in Latin. He married at twenty-four and had six children; his wife had some partial awareness of the situation, it seems, but there is no specific record.

At thirty-seven he seems to have entered a third
phase, when he accepted, from "curiosity," a friend's
suggestion to go to a male brothel. He found his partner
there businesslike but "comradely," leading him to conclude that "some of the deepest problems might be
solved by fraternity." From this evidently there derived
a few years later, in Venice where he spent the summers,
a permanent employment of a sex partner, in public his
gondolier, and a similar arrangement in Switzerland
where he and his family had their main home. He found
both relationships to be mutually affectionate and
arranged trips to England for both men, where he

introduced them to friends. For the gondolier, who had an established girlfriend and children, he subsidized marriage, with a sense of kindness and comfortable feeling. Unlike the first two phases, this one is reported in its details but without any reflection on a broader context of psychology or theory.

Symonds was writing the memoir and the life of Michelangelo at the same time. His emphasis on the artist's personal life thus led him to think about his sexuality, a quite new topic. In the biography he presents it as idealizing; his preference for male beauty did not "degenerate into vice." He mounts an attack on unnamed others who would so claim, and thus sets up a correspondence with the second phase of his own experience. Indeed, his description of Michelangelo's dying slave is almost identical with his report of his own gaze at a beautiful sleeping naked man. His letters offer a rather different view, that "if Michelangelo had any sexual energy at all (which is doubtful), he was a U"— short for the period's term "Urning" for homosexual. Elsewhere, he judges that "the artist was certainly born with innate sexual inversion." A chapter in the book devoted to the matter, along with the poetry, was for him its most original and most difficult.

The idea of a homosexual Michelangelo had previously been suggested only glancingly. The one most cited case, because the only one of his own era, was by Pietro Aretino, whose fame actually is mainly based on his maliciousness to people who did not do him favors when he asked, as Michelangelo did not. Symonds's chapter coincided with the larger emergence of the topic, and since then a homosexual Michelangelo has for some seemed axiomatic, not requiring to be evidenced. He has been a major homosexual hero, first perhaps in Oscar Wilde's speech at his trial, where the sonnets are cited, of course from Symonds's translation. The basis for this view is in a small number of poems and letters that express love for several men. The counterargument is to suggest that there is a leap from this to sexual desire; in the Renaissance, for a heterosexual man to say he loves a man is commonplace, as indeed in many cultures other than the Victorian and post-Victorian middle class.

The subject remains too charged with the agenda of those discussing it to be easily explored. A recent writer who perhaps is the best credentialed is Robert Liebert, a psychoanalyst who also shows solid grounding in the sources, in his book of 1983, *Michelangelo: A Psychoanalytic Study of His Life and Images.* He concluded that most probably Michelangelo had stronger emotional leanings toward the male but did not engage in sex at all. This statement is strikingly similar to one of Symonds's remarks quoted above, and also to a source not available until recently: one of the marginal notes in a copy of Condivi mentioned earlier. Commenting on Condivi's statement that the artist was healthy into old age "because of bodily exercise and his continence both in intercourse and eating," the marginal note reads: "I have always practiced this, and if you want to prolong your life, practice it not at all or in the least you can." With muddled syntax, quite likely derived from hasty jotting of words heard, the writer first picks up the earlier antecedent, continence, as what Michelangelo always does, but then the later one, intercourse, as what he does not do. The context excludes the ambiguity that a modern reader might initially presume. To be sure, neither this nor any other text settles the debate, but this must become one of the main items to consider.

Symonds's chapter on the subject was the point of origin for subsequent discussion until today, which has been a powerful factor in notions about the artist even if it seems to have been the more powerful the more distant and generalized these notions were from the source data and the work. Yet the actual content of Symonds's chapter today seems oddly irrelevant, perhaps more Victorian than any other part of his book. What survives from it is, happily, on its merits, its much larger and through account of Michelangelo.

PREFACE TO SECOND EDITION.

THE first edition of this work having been exhausted in a space of little over three months, I take this opportunity of saying that the critical notices which have hitherto appeared do not render it necessary to make any substantial changes in the text. A few points of difference between my reviewers and myself, concerning opinion rather than fact, are now briefly discussed in a series of notes printed at the end of Vol. II.

J. A. S.

DAVOS PLATZ, *Jan.* 9, 1893.

PREFACE.

THE biographer of Michelangelo Buonarroti, who is bold enough to attempt a new Life after the many which have been already published, must introduce his work by a critical survey of the sources he has drawn from. These may be divided into five main categories : original documents in manuscript or edited; contemporary Lives; observations by contemporaries; Lives written during the present century ; criticisms. I do not intend to classify the whole mass of Michelangelo literature. This would imply a volume in itself, and to perform the task exhaustively would entail a vast expenditure of time and labour.[1] It is possible, however, to indicate the leading features of the five grand divisions I have mentioned in the order of their value.

I. By far the most important of these sources is the large collection of manuscripts preserved in the Casa Buonarroti at Florence. These consist of authentic contracts, and of letters, poems, and memoranda, mostly in Michelangelo's own

---

[1] A fairly sufficient basis for the undertaking is supplied by Passerini's *Bibliografia*, &c.

autograph; copies made by his grand-nephew, Michelangelo the younger, and autograph letters addressed by persons of all qualities to the great sculptor during his lifetime. The papers in question were preserved among other family archives until the middle of this century, rarely inspected even by the curious, and used by no professed biographers. Only a few specimens found their way by special privilege into the collections of Gaye, Piot, Bottari-Ticozzi, and others. In 1858 the Commendatore Cosimo Buonarroti bequeathed them, together with the house and its art treasures, to the city of Florence, placing them under the trusteeship of the Syndic, the Director of the Galleries, and the Prefect of the Laurentian Library. This gentleman's wife, Rosina Vendramin, of Venice, the widow of Thomas Grant, Esq., had devoted herself to classifying and arranging the precious documents, so that the whole collection passed over to the town in a fair state of preservation. By the Commendatore's will, access to the Buonarroti archives, and the right to divulge them, were strictly refused even to the learned; but this prohibition has in certain cases been set aside, as I shall presently describe.

Next in importance to the Buonarroti archives is a large collection of Michelangelo's letters, purchased by the British Museum in 1859 from the

painter Cavaliere Michelangelo Buonarroti, nephew
of the Commendatore Cosimo above mentioned.
The majority of these were first introduced to the
public by Hermann Grimm. It remains to mention
a set of personal memoranda in Michelangelo's
handwriting, with letters addressed to him or
written about him to his nephew Lionardo, published in a semi-private manner by Daelli of Milan
in 1865. Finally, there exist in private libraries
and public museums scattered letters, most of which
have found their way into various printed works.

On the occasion of Michelangelo's fourth cen-
tenary, in 1875, it was decided to give as complete
an edition as possible of his own letters to the public.
The Commendatore Gaetano Milanesi, Curator of the
Florentine State Archives, undertook the responsibility of this work, and was allowed to throw open the
treasures of the Museo Buonarroti. The result is a
handsome volume, containing 495 documents, drawn
from all sources, which, however it may be criticised,
remains a monument of respectable scholarship and
industry. It forms the principal existing basis for
exact studies in the illustrious artist's life-history.

Some years before the issue of this complete
epistolary—that is to say, in 1863—similar license
had been granted to Signor Cesare Guasti for the
publication of Michelangelo's poems from the texts

preserved in the Museo Buonarroti. These texts he collated, but not completely, with a codex in the Vatican Library. Guasti's volume, although it also has been subjected to severe criticism, remains the classical edition, to which every student must have recourse.[1] It did nothing less than to revolutionise previous conceptions of Michelangelo as poet and as man of feeling. Up to the date 1863, his sonnets, madrigals, and longer lyric compositions were only known to the world in the falsified and garbled form which Michelangelo the younger chose to give them when he published the first edition of the "Rime" in 1623. The history of what may be called this pious fraud by a grand-nephew, over-anxious for his illustrious ancestor's literary and personal reputation, will be found in the twelfth chapter of my book. Suffice it here to say, that all earlier translations from the poems, and all deductions drawn from them regarding their author's psychology, were deprived of value by Guasti's publication of the originals. Michelangelo's life had to be studied afresh and rewritten upon new and truer data.

Milanesi, while preparing his edition of Michelangelo's letters, used the opportunities he enjoyed

---

[1] The most severe attacks upon Milanesi and Guasti have been made by Hermann Grimm in the later editions of his *Leben Michelangelo's*.

in the Archivio Buonarroti to make a complete copy of the voluminous correspondence addressed by persons of different degrees and qualities to the illustrious Florentine. Part of this valuable manuscript he placed at the disposal of the Bibliothèque Internationale des Beaux-Arts, and in 1890 there appeared an elegant small quarto volume entitled " Les Correspondants de Michel-Ange. I. Sebastiano del Piombo. Paris: Librairie de l'Art." It is, in fact, the first instalment of Milanesi's transcript above mentioned, containing the Italian text of Sebastiano's letters, with a French translation by Dr. A. Le Pileur. By what I must regard as an error of judgment, the editors omitted from their collection those letters of Sebastiano—one of them of great importance—which had previously appeared in Gaye and Gotti. In spite of this omission, the utility of the publication cannot be called in question, and I am grateful to it for important assistance in the composition of my present work. Still, there are many reasons why this piecemeal and unauthoritative divulgation of the Buonarroti Archives should be regarded as unsatisfactory. Scholars are debarred from collating the printed matter with the autographs; and as long as documents appear without the sanction of the Italian Government or that of the trustees of the Museo Buonarroti, it is always open to critics to dispute their textual validity. I am, therefore, glad to be able to announce the fact that arrangements have recently been made between the Government and the so-called "Ente Buonarroti" for a complete official edition of the correspondence in question. The value of these private letters for Michelangelo's biography was proved in 1875, when Aurelio Gotti produced the new Italian Life, of which I shall make mention farther down. Nevertheless, it is obvious that specimens selected from a huge mass of documents by a few privileged students, and used to support their own theories, can never carry the same weight or inspire the same confidence as an authorised edition of the whole. Without disputing the accuracy of Milanesi, Guasti, and Gotti, and without impugning their good faith, I am bound to say that a personal inspection of the manuscripts led me to conclusions upon some points very different from those which they have drawn. It is, therefore, greatly to be hoped that the project of the "Ente Buonarroti" will be carried out, and that their edition of the correspondence will receive the support it deserves from public libraries and amateurs of art throughout the world.

This leads me to mention the fact that, by special favour of the Italian Government, I was allowed to examine the Archivio Buonarroti, and to make copies of documents. The results of my researches will appear in the notes to this work, and in a certain number of hitherto inedited letters printed at its close. Study of the original sources enabled me to clear up some points of considerable interest regarding Michelangelo's psychology, and to dispel some erroneous theories which had been invented to explain the specific nature of his personal relations with the Marchioness of Pescara and Messer Tommaso Cavalieri.[1]

Before concluding this section on original documents, it is necessary to include the miscellaneous correspondence, Papal briefs, contracts, minutes, and memoranda of all kinds, brought together by Gaye in the "Carteggio d'Artisti," by Bottari and Ticozzi in the "Lettere Pittoriche," and by Milanesi in the "Prospetto Cronologico" appended to Vasari's "Life of Michelangelo," ed. Le Monnier, 1855. Minor material of the same kind, collected by Campori, Frediani, Zolfanelli, Fea, and others, for the illustration of special episodes in Buonarroti's life, will be noticed in the proper places.

2. We possess two biographies composed by contemporaries, both of them friends, admirers, and pupils of Michelangelo—Condivi and Vasari. The earliest of these is a short Life included by Giorgio Vasari

[1] See Chapter XII. of this book.

in his first edition of the "Lives of Italian Artists,"
1550. This brief sketch, though highly flattering,
was tainted with inaccuracies and hasty statements.
Ascanio Condivi, at that time an inmate of Buonarroti's house, felt impelled to produce a more exact
and truthful portrait of his revered master. This
task he executed while enjoying the privilege of
daily converse with Michelangelo; and the little
book, pregnant with valuable information, saw the
light in 1553, while its subject was still living.
Written with obvious simplicity and candour,
it takes rank after original documents as our
most important authority, embalming, as it does,
the old artist's own memories of his past career.
Vasari, though he was not directly alluded to by
Condivi, seems to have bitterly resented the implied
censure of his own inaccuracy. Four years after
Michelangelo's death he published a second and
greatly enlarged edition of his Life, which incorporated all that was valuable in the memoir of his
Roman critic. The wide fame of Vasari's comprehensive work extinguished Condivi for the next
two centuries. With regard to the comparative
authority of these two biographies, I have already
pronounced a decided opinion. It must, however,
be remembered that Vasari's second Life is a source
of the highest importance on its own account. It

supplies a large quantity of authentic information which we do not find in Condivi, communicates some interesting letters and poems, and abounds in vivid anecdotes collected during a long and intimate friendship with Buonarroti. In all that relates to Michelangelo's later years it is invaluable and indispensable.

3. Next in importance to contemporary biographies are the notes preserved to us by personal friends who enjoyed Michelangelo's familiarity. The Dialogues of Francesco d'Olanda and Donato Giannotti offer a vivid picture of his habits and opinions in old age. Varchi's commentary on one of his sonnets and the panegyrics spoken at his obsequies deserve consideration. Varchi's Florentine history, and the letters addressed to him by Busini, must also be mentioned here. Nor is Cellini's autobiography without importance. Even more valuable is the side-light thrown upon Michelangelo's habits and character by correspondents. In this respect the letters of Sebastiano del Piombo, Vittoria Colonna, Tommaso Cavalieri, Lionardo Sellajo, Giovan Francesco Fattucci, Bartolommeo Angelini, Cornelia degli Amadori, Pietro Aretino, Daniele da Volterra, and Tiberio Calcagni, possess peculiar interest, flashing, as it were, from divers facets the reflection of one physiognomy. It would

be tedious to mention all the letter-writers who have helped me to round the great man's portrait.

4. I come now to consider the Lives which have been written during the last hundred years, and in doing so I must omit several included in encyclopædias and histories of art, as well as numerous sketches which do not claim more than a literary or appreciative merit. At the end of the last century a purer taste for what is really great in Italian art began to revive; men of feeling and culture professed a special devotion to the sublime. In England, the lectures of Sir Joshua Reynolds, of Fuseli, and of Opie diffused an enthusiasm for Michelangelo which became the special note of intellectual breeding. Under these influences Richard Duppa published his Life in 1806, accompanied by a very useful atlas of engravings selected from various portions of Buonarroti's works. The next Life of importance was Quatremère de Quincy's, in 1835. John Samuel Harford, inspired by the study of Roscoe's books upon the Renaissance, shot far ahead of these pioneers in his two-volumed Life, which was published in the year 1857, together with an atlas of engravings by Gruner. The latter portion of his work retains its value to the present day, especially in what concerns the architecture of S. Peter's. Hermann Grimm, who had been engaged in the same field

simultaneously with Harford, produced the first edition of his famous Life in 1860. Though the biography of the hero is so much embedded in the history of Italian dynasties and wars and revolutions as to be almost submerged, yet this book marked a new departure in the treatment of Michelangelo. It introduced a sound critical and scientific method, and added large stores of documentary material. The fifth edition, of 1875, will remain as a standard authority upon the subject. Charles Clement's Life, which appeared in 1861, does not need the same consideration, although it is a refined specimen of French critical intelligence. Peculiar importance attaches to Aurelio Gotti's "Vita di Michelangelo," published at Florence in 1875. Here, for the first time, the treasures of the Museo Buonarroti were used freely, letters of Michelangelo's correspondents being copiously employed to illustrate the events of his life and social surroundings. As literature, it does not reach a very high standard, nor yet can it be maintained that Gotti added much of true or penetrative to the study of his hero's temperament. Nevertheless, Mr. Heath Wilson was well advised in partly translating this Life, the documentary importance of which he fully realised, and in grafting his own original observations upon its stock. Heath Wilson's Life,

printed in Florence, but published by Murray in
London, 1876, contains a great deal that is highly
valuable in the region of research into Michelangelo's technical methods and the present conditions of his frescoes. It has not yet received the
public recognition which it amply deserves. The
book is distinguished by modesty of tone, simplicity
of style, and sterling contributions to our knowledge
of facts. In the same year, 1876, the editor of the
Gazette des Beaux-Arts issued a volume of seven
essays, composed by seven eminent French artists
and archæologists, which must be rated among the
most happily conceived and admirably executed
studies which have yet appeared in Michelangelo
literature. "L'Œuvre et la Vie de Michel-Ange"
is a striking monument of the lively and incisive
Parisian spirit, presenting a many-sided view of its
complex subject. Without the unity of a biography,
it combines under one cover the appreciations of
several experts, all of them competent judges in
their own departments. Special mention must
finally be made of Anton Springer's second edition
of his "Raffael und Michelangelo" (1883). For
fulness of learning, for concision, and for critical
acumen, this is a very noticeable performance. It
combines all that is needful of historical, biographical, archæological, and æsthetical information.

Large masses of literature have been absorbed and condensed by the author, who does not sacrifice his own originality, and who presents the results of his extensive studies with ingenuous modesty.

5. To speak of purely critical work in this field would carry me beyond the scope of a preface. Kugler, Burckhardt, De Stendhal, Charles Perkins, and countless other writers on the fine arts, have given excellent appreciations of the great man's artistic genius. Ruskin has shown how far a gifted writer can miss the mark through want of sympathy.[1] Pater has touched upon the poems with his usual delicacy; Niccolini, in his treatise on the Sublime, has written fiery passages of impassioned eloquence; Michelet has sought to connect the prophecy of Michelangelo's art with the political and moral death-throes of his age. I mention only a few of the more distinguished authors, in whose work penetrative acumen of one sort or another is combined with a real literary talent. Of late another school of critics has arisen, who, passing lightly over Michelangelo as artist, seek to explain his personal character by the methods of morbid psychology. These will be duly considered in the proper place; but, for obvious reasons, it is impossible for me to render due

[1] See the lecture on Michelangelo and Tintoretto.

account here of all the fugitive essays and critical
expositions which have saturated my mind during
thirty years of sustained interest in Michelangelo.
My own previous work in this department will be
found in the third volume of the "Renaissance
in Italy," and in the preface to my translation of
"Sonnets of Michael Angelo and Campanella."

In writing the biography which follows, I have
striven to exclude extraneous matter, so far as this
was possible. I have not, therefore, digressed into
the region of Italian history and comparative artistic
criticism. My purpose was to give a fairly complete
account of the hero's life and works, and to concentrate attention on his personality. Wherever I
could, I made him tell his own tale by presenting
original letters and memoranda; also, whenever the
exigencies of the narrative permitted, I used the
language of his earliest biographers, Condivi and
Vasari. While adopting this method, I was aware
that my work would suffer in regard to continuity
of style; but the compensating advantages of veracity, and direct appeal to authoritative sources,
seemed to justify this sacrifice of form.

I must finally record my obligations to many
friends and scholars who have rendered me important assistance during the composition of this
book. First and foremost comes the Cavaliere

Professor Guido Biagi, Prefect of the Laurentian Library at Florence, to whom I am in great measure indebted for access to the manuscripts of the Museo Buonarroti, who has spared no pains in furnishing me with exact information upon several intricate questions, and who copied documents for me with his own hand. To Professor J. Henry Middleton, of Cambridge, are due my sincere thanks, both for placing his reconstruction of the Tomb of Julius at my disposal, and also for reading a large portion of the proof-sheets as they passed through the press, and making many valuable suggestions. Lieut.-Col. Alfred Pearson and Mrs. Ross of Poggio Gherardo performed the same kind office of reading proofs and offering hints upon points of literary style. To Dr. Fortnum I am indebted for permission to reproduce his wax model and Leone's medal of Michelangelo in old age. Professor Sidney Colvin, of the British Museum, allowed me to photograph eight original drawings existing in that national collection. To Mr. Edward Prioleau Warren I owe much interesting information, collected by him from old authors, upon difficult points connected with the Cupola of S. Peter's. Mr. Stillman of Rome helped me finally to arrive at the truth about Michelangelo's model for the Dome. To his untiring kindness, and to Dr. Josef Durm, whose work is cited in my List of

LIST OF SOME OF THE PRINCIPAL BOOKS
REFERRED TO IN THESE VOLUMES.

Le Lettere di Michelangelo Buonarroti, publicate coi Ricordi ed i Contratti artistici. Per cura di Gaetano Milanesi. Firenze : Le Monnier, 1875. Cited, *Lettere.*

Le Rime di Michelangelo Buonarroti, cavate dagli Autografi e pubblicate da Cesare Guasti. Firenze : Le Monnier, 1863. Cited, *Rime.*

Carte Michelangiolesche inedite. Milano : Autografia, G. Daelli, 1865. Cited, *Carte Mich.*

Les Correspondants de Michel-Ange. No. 1. Sebastiano del Piombo. Texte italien publié pour la première fois par Gaetano Milanesi, avec trad. fr. par A. Le Pileur. Paris : Librairie de l'Art, 1890. Cited, *Les Correspondants.*

Carteggio d'Artisti. Giovanni Gaye. 3 vols. Firenze : Molini, 1840. Cited, *Gaye.*

Lettere Pittoriche raccolte dal Bottari e Ticozzi. Milano : Silvestri, 1822. Cited, *Lett. Pitt.*

Les Arts en Portugal. A. Raczynski. Paris : Renouard, 1846. Cited, *Raczynski.*

Vita di Michelangelo Buonarroti, Scritta da Ascanio Condivi. Pisa : N. Capurro, 1823. Cited, *Condivi.*

Le Vite de' piu eccellenti Pittori Scultori e Architetti, di Giorgio Vasari. 14 vols. Firenze : Le Monnier, 1855. Cited, *Vasari.*

The Life of Michel Angelo Buonarroti. By John S. Harford. 2 vols. London : Longmans, 1857. Cited, *Harford.*

Illustrations of the Genius of Michael Angelo. Published for John S. Harford. London : Colnaghi & Longmans, 1857. Cited, *Harford Illustrations.*

Leben Michelangelo's. Von Hermann Grimm. 2 vols. 5th edit.
Berlin : W. Hertz, 1879. Cited, *Grimm.*

Vita di Michelangelo Buonarroti, Narrata con l'aiuto di nuovi
Documenti da Aurelio Gotti. Firenze : Tip. della Gazzetta
d'Italia, 1875. 2 vols. Cited, *Gotti.*

Life and Works of Michelangelo Buonarroti. By C. Heath
Wilson. London : John Murray, 1876. Cited, *Heath Wilson.*

Raffael und Michelangelo. Von Anton Springer. 2 vols.
Leipzig : Seemann, 1883. Cited, *Springer.*

L'Œuvre et la Vie de Michel-Ange. Paris : Gazette des Beaux-
Arts, 1876. Cited, *L' Œuvre et la Vie.*

La Bibliografia di Michelangelo Buonarroti, e gli Incisori delle
sue Opere. Luigi Passerini. Firenze : Cellini, 1875. Cited,
La Bibliografia.

Le Rime di Vittoria Colonna, con la Vita della Medesima da
P. E. Visconti. Roma : Salviucci, 1840. Cited, *Visconti.*

A Critical Account of the Drawings of Michelangelo and
Raffaello in the Univ. Gall., Oxford. By J. C. Robinson.
Oxford : Clarendon Press, 1870. Cited, *Robinson.*

The Sonnets of M. A. Buonarroti and T. Campanella, translated
by John Addington Symonds. London : Smith, Elder, &
Co., 1878. Cited, *English Version.*

The Renaissance in Italy. By John Addington Symonds. 7 vols.
London : Smith, Elder, & Co. Cited, *Renaissance in Italy.*

Michelangelo's Entwurf zu dem Karton der Schlacht bei Cascina.
Von Moriz Thausing. Leipzig : Seemann, 1878. Cited,
Thausing.

Tuscan Sculptors : their Lives, Works, and Times. By C. C.
Perkins. 2 vols. London : Longmans, 1864. Cited,
Perkins.

Ragionamento Storico su le diverse gite fatte a Carrara da
Michelangielo Buonarroti. Massa, pei Fratelli Frediani,
1837. Cited, *Frediani.*

La Lunigiana e le Alpi Apuane. Studii del Professore Cesare
Zolfanelli. Firenze : Barbèra, 1870. Cited, *Zolfanelli.*

Lettera di M. A. Buonarroti, pubblicata ed illustrata dal Professore Sebastiano Ciampi. Firenze: Passigli, 1834. Cited, *Ciampi*.

Michelangelo Buonarroti (Il Vecchio): Studio di Carlo Parlagreco. Napoli: Fratelli Orfeo, 1888. Cited, *Parlagreco*.

The Life of Benvenuto Cellini. Translated by John Addington Symonds. London: John C. Nimmo. Cited, *Cellini*.

Storia Fiorentina di Benedetto Varchi. 3 vols. Firenze: Le Monnier, 1857. Cited, *Varchi*.

Lettere di Giambattista Busini a Benedetto Varchi. Firenze: Le Monnier, 1861. Cited, *Busini*.

La Scrittura di Artisti Italiani. Firenze: Pini, 1869. Cited, *Pini*.

The Art of Michelangelo Buonarroti in the British Museum. By Louis Fagan. London: Dulau, 1883. Cited, *Fagan*.

South Kensington Museum. Italian Sculpture of the Middle Ages, &c. By J. C. Robinson. London: Chapman & Hall, 1862. Cited, *Sculpture, S.K.M.*

Michelangelo: eine Renaissancestudie. Von Ludwig von Scheffler. Altenberg: S. Geibel, 1892. Cited, *Von Scheffler*.

Carteggio di Vittoria Colonna Marchesa di Pescara. Raccolto e pubblicato da Ermanno Ferrero e Giuseppe Müller. Torino: E. Loescher, 1889. Cited, *Ferrero and Müller*.

Die Domkuppel in Florenz, und die Kuppel der Petruskirche in Rom. Von Josef Durm. Berlin: Ernst & Korn, 1887. Cited, *Durm*.

LIFE OF MICHELANGELO.

CHAPTER I.

I.

THE Buonarroti Simoni, to whom Michelangelo
belonged, were a Florentine family of ancient burgher
nobility. Their arms appear to have been originally "azure two bends or." To this coat was
added "a label of four points gules enclosing three
fleur-de-lys or." That augmentation, adopted from
the shield of Charles of Anjou, occurs upon the
scutcheons of many Guelf houses and cities. In
the case of the Florentine Simoni, it may be ascribed

to the period when Buonarrota di Simone Simoni held office as a captain of the Guelf party (1392). Such, then, was the paternal coat borne by the subject of this Memoir. His brother Buonarroto received a further augmentation in 1515 from Leo X., to wit: "upon a chief or, a pellet azure charged with fleur-de-lys or, between the capital letters L. and X." At the same time he was created Count Palatine. The old and simple bearing of the two bends was then crowded down into the extreme base of the shield, while the Angevine label found room beneath the chief.

According to a vague tradition, the Simoni drew their blood from the high and puissant Counts of Canossa. Michelangelo himself believed in this pedigree, for which there is, however, no foundation in fact, and no heraldic corroboration. According to his friend and biographer Condivi, the sculptor's first Florentine ancestor was a Messer Simone dei Conti di Canossa, who came in 1250 as Podestà to Florence.[1] "The eminent qualities of this man gained for him admission into the burghership of the city, and he was appointed captain of a Sestiere; for Florence in those days was divided into Sestieri, instead of Quartieri, as according to the present usage." Michelangelo's contemporary, the Count Alessandro da Canossa, acknowledged this relationship. Writing on the 9th of October 1520, he addresses the then famous sculptor as "honoured

[1] Condivi, p. 1.

kinsman," and gives the following piece of information : [1] "Turning over my old papers, I have discovered that a Messere Simone da Canossa was
Podestà of Florence, as I have already mentioned
to the above-named Giovanni da Reggio." Nevertheless, it appears now certain that no Simone da
Canossa held the office of Podestà at Florence in
the thirteenth century. The family can be traced
up to one Bernardo, who died before the year 1228.
His grandson was called Buonarrota, and the fourth
in descent was Simone.[2] These names recur frequently in the next generations. Michelangelo
always addressed his father as " Lodovico di Lionardo
di Buonarrota Simoni," or " Louis, the son of
Leonard, son of Buonarrota Simoni ; " and he used
the family surname of Simoni in writing to his
brothers and his nephew Lionardo. Yet he preferred to call himself Michelangelo Buonarroti ;
and after his lifetime Buonarroti became fixed
for the posterity of his younger brother. " The
reason," says Condivi, " why the family in Florence
changed its name from Canossa to Buonarroti was
this : Buonarroto continued for many generations
to be repeated in their house, down to the time of
Michelangelo, who had a brother of that name ;
and inasmuch as several of these Buonarroti held
rank in the supreme magistracy of the republic,

[1] Gotti, i. 4.
[2] He died probably in 1314, after playing a considerable part in the
history of his native town. From him the family derived their surname of Simoni.

especially the brother I have just mentioned, who filled the office of Prior during Pope Leo's visit to Florence, as may be read in the annals of that city, this baptismal name, by force of frequent repetition, became the cognomen of the whole family; the more easily, because it is the custom at Florence, in elections and nominations of officers, to add the christian names of the father, grandfather, great-grandfather, and sometimes even of remoter ancestors, to that of each citizen. Consequently, through the many Buonarroti who followed one another, and from the Simone who was the first founder of the house in Florence, they gradually came to be called Buonarroti Simoni, which is their present designation."[1] Excluding the legend about Simone da Canossa, this is a pretty accurate account of what really happened. Italian patronymics were formed indeed upon the same rule as those of many Norman families in Great Britain. When the use of Di and Fitz expired, Simoni survived from Di Simone, as did my surname Symonds from Fitz-Symond.

On the 6th of March 1475, according to our present computation, Lodovico di Lionardo Buonarroti Simoni wrote as follows in his private notebook: "I record that on this day, March 6, 1474, a male child was born to me. I gave him the name of Michelangelo, and he was born on a Monday morning four or five hours before daybreak,

[1] Condivi, p. 2.

and he was born while I was Podestà of Caprese, and he was born at Caprese; and the godfathers were those I have named below. He was baptized on the eighth of the same month in the Church of San Giovanni at Caprese. These are the godfathers :—

> Don Daniello di ser Buonaguida of Florence, Rector of San Giovanni at Caprese;
> Don Andrea di . . . . of Poppi, Rector of the Abbey of Diasiano (*i.e.* Dicciano) ;
> Jacopo di Francesco of Casurio (?) ;
> Marco di Giorgio of Caprese ;
> Giovanni di Biagio of Caprese ;
> Andrea di Biagio of Caprese ;
> Francesco di Jacopo del Anduino (?) of Caprese ;
> Ser Bartolommeo di Santi del Lanse (?), Notary.

Note that the date is March 6, 1474, according to Florentine usage *ab incarnatione,* and according to the Roman usage, *a nativitate,* it is 1475."[1]

Vasari tells us that the planets were propitious at the moment of Michelangelo's nativity: "Mercury and Venus having entered with benign aspect into the house of Jupiter, which indicated that marvellous and extraordinary works, both of manual art and intellect, were to be expected from him."[2]

---

[1] Gotti, vol. i. p. 3. [2] Vasari, xii. 158.

II.

Caprese, from its beauty and remoteness, deserved to be the birthplace of a great artist. It is not improbable that Lodovico Buonarroti and his wife Francesca approached it from Pontassieve in Vald-arno, crossing the little pass of Consuma, descending on the famous battle-field of Campaldino, and skirting the ancient castle of the Conti Guidi at Poppi. Every step in the romantic journey leads over ground hallowed by old historic memories. From Poppi the road descends the Arno to a richly cultivated district, out of which emerges on its hill the prosperous little town of Bibbiena. High up to eastward springs the broken crest of La Vernia, a mass of hard millstone rock (*macigno*) jutting from desolate beds of lime and shale at the height of some 3500 feet above the sea. It was here, among the sombre groves of beech and pine which wave along the ridge, that S. Francis came to found his infant Order, composed the Hymn to the Sun, and received the supreme honour of the stigmata. To this point Dante retired when the death of Henry VII. extinguished his last hopes for Italy. At one extremity of the wedge-like block which forms La Vernia, exactly on the water-shed between Arno and Tiber, stands the ruined castle of Chiusi in Casentino. This was one of the

two chief places of Lodovico Buonarroti's podes-
teria. It may be said to crown the valley of the
Arno ; for the waters gathered here flow downwards
toward Arezzo, and eventually wash the city walls
of Florence. A few steps farther, travelling south,
we pass into the valley of the Tiber, and, after
traversing a barren upland region for a couple of
hours, reach the verge of the descent upon Caprese.
Here the landscape assumes a softer character. Far
away stretch blue Apennines, ridge melting into
ridge above Perugia in the distance. Gigantic
oaks begin to clothe the stony hillsides, and little
by little a fertile mountain district of chesnut-woods
and vineyards expands before our eyes, equal in
charm to those aërial hills and vales above Pontre-
moli. Caprese has no central commune or head-
village. It is an aggregate of scattered hamlets and
farmhouses, deeply embosomed in a sea of greenery.
Where the valley contracts and the infant Tiber
breaks into a gorge, rises a wooded rock crowned
with the ruins of an ancient castle. It was here,
then, that Michelangelo first saw the light. When
we discover that he was a man of more than usually
nervous temperament, very different in quality from
any of his relatives, we must not forget what a
fatiguing journey had been performed by his mother,
who was then awaiting her delivery. Even supposing that Lodovico Buonarroti travelled from Florence
by Arezzo to Caprese, many miles of rough mountain-
roads must have been traversed by her on horseback.

III.

Lodovico, who, as we have seen, was Podestà òf Caprese and of Chiusi in the Casentino, had already one son by his first wife, Francesca, the daughter of Neri di Miniato del Sera and Bonda Rucellai. This elder brother, Lionardo, grew to manhood, and became a devoted follower of Savonarola. Under the influence of the Ferrarese friar, he determined to abjure the world, and entered the Dominican Order in 1491. We know very little about him, and he is only once mentioned in Michelangelo's correspondence. Even this reference cannot be considered certain. Writing to his father from Rome, July 1, 1497, Michelangelo says: "I let you know that Fra Lionardo returned hither to Rome. He says that he was forced to fly from Viterbo, and that his frock had been taken from him, wherefore he wished to go there (*i.e.* to Florence). So I gave him a golden ducat, which he asked for; and I think you ought already to have learned this, for he should be there by this time."[1] When Lionardo died is uncertain. We only know that he was in the convent of S. Mark at Florence in the year 1510. Owing to this brother's adoption of the religious life, Michelangelo became, early in his youth, the eldest son of Lodovico's family. It

[1] Lettere, No. i. p. 3.

will be seen that during the whole course of his long career he acted as the mainstay of his father, and as father to his younger brothers. The strength and the tenacity of his domestic affections are very remarkable in a man who seems never to have thought of marrying. "Art," he used to say, "is a sufficiently exacting mistress." Instead of seeking to beget children for his own solace, he devoted himself to the interests of his kinsmen.

The office of Podestà lasted only six months, and at the expiration of this term Lodovico returned to Florence. He put the infant Michelangelo out to nurse in the village of Settignano, where the Buonarroti Simoni owned a farm. Most of the people of that district gained their livelihood in the stone-quarries around Settignano and Maiano on the hillside of Fiesole. Michelangelo's foster-mother was the daughter and the wife of stone-cutters. "George," said he in after-years to his friend Vasari, "if I possess anything of good in my mental constitution, it comes from my having been born in your keen climate of Arezzo; just as I drew the chisel and the mallet with which I carve statues in together with my nurse's milk."[1]

When Michelangelo was of age to go to school, his father put him under a grammarian at Florence named Francesco da Urbino. It does not appear, however, that he learned more than reading and writing in Italian, for later on in life we find him

[1] Vasari, xii. p. 159.

complaining that he knew no Latin.[1] The boy's
genius attracted him irresistibly to art. He spent
all his leisure time in drawing, and frequented the
society of youths who were apprenticed to masters
in painting and sculpture. Among these he contracted an intimate friendship with Francesco
Granacci, at that time in the workshop of Domenico
Ghirlandajo. Granacci used to lend him drawings
by Ghirlandajo, and inspired him with the resolution to become a practical artist. Condivi says that
"Francesco's influence, combined with the continual
craving of his nature, made him at last abandon
literary studies. This brought the boy into disfavour with his father and uncles, who often used
to beat him severely; for being insensible to the
excellence and nobility of Art, they thought it
shameful to give her shelter in their house. Nevertheless, albeit their opposition caused him the
greatest sorrow, it was not sufficient to deter him
from his steady purpose. On the contrary, growing
even bolder, he determined to work in colours."[2]
Condivi, whose narrative preserves for us Michelangelo's own recollections of his youthful years,
refers to this period the painted copy made by the
young draughtsman from a copper-plate of Martin
Schöngauer. We should probably be right in sup-

---

[1] This we gather from Donato Giannotti's Dialogue *De' giorni che
Dante consumò*, etc. Firenze, Tip. Gal., 1859. Also in 1518, when
the members of the Florentine Academy sent a petition to Leo X. about
the bones of Dante, he alone signed in Italian.

[2] Condivi, p. 4.

posing that the anecdote is slightly antedated. I give it, however, as nearly as possible in the biographer's own words. "Granacci happened to show him a print of S. Antonio tormented by the devils. This was the work of Martino d'Olanda, a good artist for the times in which he lived; and Michelangelo transferred the composition to a panel.[1] Assisted by the same friend with colours and brushes, he treated his subject in so masterly a way that it excited surprise in all who saw it, and even envy, as some say, in Domenico, the greatest painter of his age. In order to diminish the extraordinary impression produced by this picture, Ghirlandajo went about saying that it came out of his own workshop, as though he had some part in the performance. While engaged on this piece, which, beside the figure of the saint, contained many strange forms and diabolical monstrosities, Michelangelo coloured no particular without going first to Nature and comparing her truth with his fancies. Thus he used to frequent the fish-market, and study the shape and hues of fishes' fins, the colour of their eyes, and so forth in the case of every part belonging to them; all of which details he reproduced with the utmost diligence in his painting."[2] Whether this transcript from Schöngauer was made as early as Condivi reports may, as I

[1] See Grimm, vol. i. p. 542, for notes upon the pictures from Schöngauer's copper-plate, now in the possession of the Bianconi family at Bologna and Baron Triqueti in Paris.
[2] Condivi, p. 5.

have said, be reasonably doubted. The anecdote is interesting, however, as showing in what a naturalistic spirit Michelangelo began to work. The unlimited mastery which he acquired over form, and which certainly seduced him at the close of his career into a stylistic mannerism, was based in the first instance upon profound and patient interrogation of reality.

IV.

Lodovico perceived at length that it was useless to oppose his son's natural bent. Accordingly, he sent him into Ghirlandajo's workshop. A minute from Ghirlandajo's ledger, under the date 1488, gives information regarding the terms of the apprenticeship. " I record this first of April how I, Lodovico di Lionardo di Buonarrota, bind my son Michelangelo to Domenico and Davit di Tommaso di Currado[1] for the next three ensuing years, under these conditions and contracts: to wit, that the said Michelangelo shall stay with the above-named masters during this time, to learn the art of painting, and to practise the same, and to be at the orders of the above-named ; and they, for their part, shall give to him in the course of these three years

[1] That was the family name of the famous Ghirlandajo, so called because he made the garlands of golden leaves which Florentine women wore.

twenty-four florins (*fiorini di suggello*) : to wit, six florins in the first year, eight in the second, ten in the third ; making in all the sum of ninety-six pounds (*lire*)." A postscript, dated April 16th of the same year, 1488, records that two florins were paid to Michelangelo upon that day.[1]

It seems that Michelangelo retained no very pleasant memory of his sojourn with the Ghirlandajo brothers. Condivi, in the passage translated above, hints that Domenico was jealous of him. He proceeds as follows : " This jealousy betrayed itself still more when Michelangelo once begged the loan of a certain sketch-book, wherein Domenico had portrayed shepherds with their flocks and watch-dogs, landscapes, buildings, ruins, and such-like things. The master refused to lend it ; and indeed he had the fame of being somewhat envious ; for not only showed he thus scant courtesy toward Michelangelo, but he also treated his brother like-wise, sending him into France when he saw that he was making progress and putting forth great promise ; and doing this not so much for any profit to David, as that he might himself remain the first of Florentine painters. I have thought fit to men-tion these things, because I have been told that

---

[1] The *Ricordo* translated above was published by Vasari (xii. 160). He says that it was shown him by Ghirlandajo's heirs, in order to prove that the master was not envious or unhelpful to his pupil. Of course it does not prove anything of the kind. It is only a common record of apprenticeship. Gotti (p. 6, note) reckons the pay promised at fr. 206.40 of present value.

Domenico's son is wont to ascribe the genius and divinity of Michelangelo in great part to his father's teaching, whereas the truth is that he received no assistance from that master. I ought, however, to add that Michelangelo does not complain : on the contrary, he praises Domenico both as artist and as man."[1]

This passage irritated Vasari beyond measure. He had written his first Life of Michelangelo in 1550. Condivi published his own modest biography in 1553, with the expressed intention of correcting errors and supplying deficiencies made by " others," under which vague word he pointed probably at Vasari. Michelangelo, who furnished Condivi with materials, died in 1564 ; and Vasari, in 1568, issued a second enlarged edition of the Life, into which he cynically incorporated what he chose to steal from Condivi's sources. The supreme Florentine sculptor being dead and buried, Vasari felt that he was safe in giving the lie direct to this humble rival biographer. Accordingly, he spoke as follows about Michelangelo's relations with Domenico Ghirlandajo : " He was fourteen years of age when he entered that master's service,[2] and inasmuch as one (Condivi), who composed his biography after 1550, when I had published these Lives for the first time, declares that certain persons, from want of familiarity

[1] Condivi, pp. 5, 6.
[2] As Michelangelo was born March 6, 1475, and as the indenture of apprenticeship proves that he went to Ghirlandajo, April 1, 1488, he must have been rather less than thirteen years and one month old.

with Michelangelo, have recorded things that did not happen, and have omitted others worthy of relation ; and in particular has touched upon the point at issue, accusing Domenico of envy, and saying that he never rendered Michelangelo assistance."——Here Vasari, out of breath with indignation, appeals to the record of Lodovico's contract with the Ghirlandajo brothers. "These minutes," he goes on to say, "I copied from the ledger, in order to show that everything I formerly published, or which will be published at the present time, is truth. Nor am I acquainted with any one who had greater familiarity with Michelangelo than I had, or who served him more faithfully in friendly offices ; nor do I believe that a single man could exhibit a larger number of letters written with his own hand, or evincing greater personal affection, than I can." [1]

This contention between Condivi and Vasari, our two contemporary authorities upon the facts of Michelangelo's life, may not seem to be a matter of great moment for his biographer after the lapse of four centuries. Yet the first steps in the art-career of so exceptional a genius possess peculiar interest. It is not insignificant to ascertain, so far as now is possible, what Michelangelo owed to his teachers. In equity, we acknowledge that Lodovico's record on the ledger of the Ghirlandajo brothers proves their willingness to take him as a prentice, and their payment to him of two florins in advance;

[1] Vasari, xii. p. 160.

but the same record does not disprove Condivi's statement, derived from his old master's reminiscences, to the effect that Domenico Ghirlandajo was in no way greatly serviceable to him as an instructor. The fault, in all probability, did not lie with Ghirlandajo alone. Michelangelo, as we shall have occasions in plenty to observe, was difficult to live with; frank in speech to the point of rudeness, ready with criticism, incapable of governing his temper, and at no time apt to work harmoniously with fellow-craftsmen. His extraordinary force and originality of genius made themselves felt, undoubtedly, at the very outset of his career; and Ghirlandajo may be excused if, without being positively jealous of the young eagle settled in his homely nest, he failed to do the utmost for this gifted and rough-natured child of promise. Beethoven's discontent with Haydn as a teacher offers a parallel; and sympathetic students of psychology will perceive that Ghirlandajo and Haydn were almost superfluous in the training of phenomenal natures like Michelangelo and Beethoven.

Vasari, passing from controversy to the gossip of the studio, has sketched a pleasant picture of the young Buonarroti in his master's employ. "The artistic and personal qualities of Michelangelo developed so rapidly that Domenico was astounded by signs of power in him beyond the ordinary scope of youth. He perceived, in short, that he not only surpassed the other students, of whom Ghirlandajo had a large number under his tuition, but also that he often competed on an equality with the master. One of the lads who worked there made a pen-drawing of some women, clothed, from a design of Ghirlandajo. Michelangelo took up the paper, and with a broader nib corrected the outline of a female figure, so as to bring it into perfect truth to life. Wonderful it was to see the difference of the two styles, and to note the judgment and ability of a mere boy, so spirited and bold, who had the courage to chastise his master's handiwork! This drawing I now preserve as a precious relique, since it was given me by Granacci, that it might take a place in my Book of Original Designs, together with others presented to me by Michelangelo. In the year 1550, when I was in Rome, I Giorgio showed it to Michelangelo, who recognised it immediately, and was pleased to see it again, observing modestly that he knew more about the art when he was a child than now in his old age.

" It happened then that Domenico was engaged upon the great Chapel of S. Maria Novella ;[1] and being absent one day, Michelangelo set himself to draw from nature the whole scaffolding, with some easels and all the appurtenances of the art, and

---

[1] The frescoes in the choir. These excellent works of Florentine design formed Michelangelo's earliest school in art, and what he after-wards achieved in fresco must have mainly been learned there.

a few of the young men at work there. When
Domenico returned and saw the drawing, he exclaimed : 'This fellow knows more about it than
I do,' and remained quite stupefied by the new
style and the new method of imitation, which a
boy of years so tender had received as a gift from
heaven."[1]

Both Condivi and Vasari relate that, during his
apprenticeship to Ghirlandajo, Michelangelo demonstrated his technical ability by producing perfect
copies of ancient drawings, executing the facsimile
with consummate truth of line, and then dirtying
the paper so as to pass it off as the original of
some old master.[2] "His only object," adds Vasari,
"was to keep the originals, by giving copies in
exchange; seeing that he admired them as specimens of art, and sought to surpass them by his
own handling; and in doing this he acquired great
renown." We may pause to doubt whether at the
present time—in the case, for instance, of Shelley
letters or Rossetti drawings—clever forgeries would
be accepted as so virtuous and laudable. But it
ought to be remembered that a Florentine workshop
at that period contained masses of accumulated
designs, all of which were more or less the common
property of the painting firm. No single specimen
possessed a high market value. It was, in fact,
only when art began to expire in Italy, when Vasari
published his extensive necrology and formed his

[1] Vasari, xii. p. 161   [2] Condivi, p. 6 ; Vasari, p. 162.

famous collection of drawings, that property in a sketch became a topic for moral casuistry.

Of Michelangelo's own work at this early period we possess probably nothing except a rough scrawl on the plaster of a wall at Settignano. Even this does not exist in its original state. The Satyr which is still shown there may, according to Mr. Heath Wilson's suggestion, be a *rifacimento* from the master's hand at a subsequent period of his career.[1]

V.

Condivi and Vasari differ considerably in their accounts of Michelangelo's departure from Ghirlandajo's workshop. The former writes as follows : " So then the boy, now drawing one thing and now another, without fixed place or steady line of study, happened one day to be taken by Granacci into the garden of the Medici at San Marco, which garden the magnificent Lorenzo, father of Pope Leo, and a man of the first intellectual distinction, had adorned with antique statues and other reliques of plastic art. When Michelangelo saw these things and felt their beauty, he no longer frequented Domenico's shop, nor did he go elsewhere, but, judging the Medicean gardens to be the best school, spent all his time and faculties in working there."[2]

[1] Heath Wilson, p. 10.   [2] Condivi, p. 7.

Vasari reports that it was Lorenzo's wish to raise the art of sculpture in Florence to the same level as that of painting; and for this reason he placed Bertoldo, a pupil and follower of Donatello, over his collections, with a special commission to aid and instruct the young men who used them. With the same intention of forming an academy or school of art, Lorenzo went to Ghirlandajo, and begged him to select from his pupils those whom he considered the most promising. Ghirlandajo accordingly drafted off Francesco Granacci and Michelangelo Buonarroti.[1] Since Michelangelo had been formally articled by his father to Ghirlandajo in 1488, he can hardly have left that master in 1489 as unceremoniously as Condivi asserts. Therefore we may, I think, assume that Vasari upon this point has preserved the genuine tradition.

Having first studied the art of design and learned to work in colours under the supervision of Ghirlandajo, Michelangelo now had his native genius directed to sculpture. He began with the rudiments of stone-hewing, blocking out marbles designed for the Library of San Lorenzo,[2] and acquiring that practical skill in the manipulation of the chisel which he exercised all through his life. Condivi and Vasari agree in relating that a copy he made

[1] Vasari, xii. 162.

[2] Condivi, p. 7. Lorenzo very likely intended to build a house for his own and his father Cosimo's unrivalled collection of manuscripts. The design was carried out in after-years by Pope Clement VII., who selected a spot at San Lorenzo for the purpose.

for his own amusement from an antique Faun first brought him into favourable notice with Lorenzo. The boy had begged a piece of refuse marble, and carved a grinning mask, which he was polishing when the Medici passed by. The great man stopped to examine the work, and recognised its merit. At the same time he observed with characteristic geniality: "Oh, you have made this Faun quite old, and yet have left him all his teeth! Do you not know that men of that great age are always wanting in one or two?" Michelangelo took the hint, and knocked a tooth out from the upper jaw. When Lorenzo saw how cleverly he had performed the task, he resolved to provide for the boy's future and to take him into his own household. So, having heard whose son he was, "Go," he said, "and tell your father that I wish to speak with him."

A mask of a grinning Faun may still be seen in the sculpture-gallery of the Bargello at Florence, and the marble is traditionally assigned to Michelangelo. It does not exactly correspond to the account given by Condivi and Vasari; for the mouth shows only two large tusk-like teeth, with the tip of the tongue protruding between them. Still there is no reason to feel certain that we may not have here Michelangelo's first extant work in marble.

"Michelangelo accordingly went home, and delivered the message of the Magnificent. His father, guessing probably what he was wanted for, could only be persuaded by the urgent prayers of Granacci and other friends to obey the summons. Indeed, he complained loudly that Lorenzo wanted to lead his son astray, abiding firmly by the principle that he would never permit a son of his to be a stone-cutter. Vainly did Granacci explain the difference between a sculptor and a stone-cutter : all his arguments seemed thrown away. Nevertheless, when Lodovico appeared before the Magnificent, and was asked if he would consent to give his son up to the great man's guardianship, he did not know how to refuse. ' In faith,' he added, ' not Michelangelo alone, but all of us, with our lives and all our abilities, are at the pleasure of your Magnificence ! ' When Lorenzo asked what he desired as a favour to himself, he answered : ' I have never practised any art or trade, but have lived thus far upon my modest income, attending to the little property in land which has come down from my ancestors ; and it has been my care not only to preserve these estates, but to increase them so far as I was able by my industry.' The Magnificent then added : ' Well, look about, and see if there be anything in Florence which will suit you. Make use of me, for I will do the utmost that I can for you.' It so happened that a place in the Customs, which could only be filled by a Florentine citizen, fell vacant shortly afterwards. Upon this Lodovico returned to the Magnificent, and begged for it in these words : ' Lorenzo, I am good for nothing but reading and writing. Now, the mate of Marco Pucci in the Customs having died, I should like to enter into this office, feeling myself able to fulfil its duties decently.' The Magnificent laid his hand upon his shoulder, and said with a smile: 'You will always be a poor man;' for he expected him to ask for something far more valuable. Then he added: 'If you care to be the mate of Marco, you can take the post, until such time as a better becomes vacant.' It was worth eight crowns the month, a little more or a little less."[1] A document is extant which shows that Lodovico continued to fill this office at the Customs till 1494, when the heirs of Lorenzo were exiled; for in the year 1512, after the Medici returned to Florence, he applied to Giuliano, Duke of Nemours, to be reinstated in the same.[2]

If it is true, as Vasari asserts, that Michelangelo quitted Ghirlandajo in 1489, and if Condivi is right in saying that he only lived in the Casa Medici for about two years before the death of Lorenzo, April 1492, then he must have spent some twelve months working in the gardens at San Marco before the Faun's mask called attention to his talents. His whole connection with Lorenzo, from the spring of 1489 to the spring of 1492, lasted three years; and, since he was born in March 1475, the space of his life covered by this patronage extended from the commencement of his fifteenth to the commencement of his eighteenth year.

[1] Condivi, pp. 8-10.
[2] The original is given by Gotti, vol. ii. p. 31.

These three years were decisive for the development of his mental faculties and special artistic genius. It is not necessary to enlarge here upon Lorenzo de' Medici's merits and demerits, either as the ruler of Florence or as the central figure in the history of the Italian Renaissance. These have supplied stock topics for discussion by all writers who have devoted their attention to that period of culture. Still we must remember that Michelangelo enjoyed singular privileges under the roof of one who was not only great as diplomatist and politician, and princely in his patronage, but was also a man of original genius in literature, of fine taste in criticism, and of civic urbanity in manners. The palace of the Medici formed a museum, at that period unique, considering the number and value of its art treasures —bas-reliefs, vases, coins, engraved stones, paintings by the best contemporary masters, statues in bronze and marble by Verocchio and Donatello. Its library contained the costliest manuscripts, collected from all quarters of Europe and the Levant. The guests who assembled in its halls were leaders in that intellectual movement which was destined to spread a new type of culture far and wide over the globe. The young sculptor sat at the same board as Marsilio Ficino, interpreter of Plato; Pico della Mirandola, the phœnix of Oriental erudition; Angelo Poliziano, the unrivalled humanist and melodious Italian poet; Luigi Pulci, the humorous inventor of burlesque romance—with artists, scholars, students innumer-

able, all in their own departments capable of satisfy-
ing a youth's curiosity, by explaining to him the
particular virtues of books discussed, or of antique
works of art inspected. During those halcyon years,
before the invasion of Charles VIII., it seemed as
though the peace of Italy might last unbroken. No
one foresaw the apocalyptic vials of wrath which
were about to be poured forth upon her plains and
cities through the next half-century. Rarely, at
any period of the world's history, perhaps only in
Athens between the Persian and the Peloponnesian
wars, has culture, in the highest and best sense of
that word, prospered more intelligently and pacific-
ally than it did in the Florence of Lorenzo, through
the co-operation and mutual zeal of men of eminence, inspired by common enthusiasms, and labouring in diverse though cognate fields of study and
production.

Michelangelo's position in the house was that of
an honoured guest or adopted son. Lorenzo not
only allowed him five ducats a month by way of
pocket-money, together with clothes befitting his
station, but he also, says Condivi, "appointed him
a good room in the palace, together with all the
conveniences he desired, treating him in every respect, as also at his table, precisely like one of his
own sons. It was the custom of this household,
where men of the noblest birth and highest public
rank assembled round the daily board, for the guests
to take their places next the master in the order

of their arrival; those who were present at the beginning of the meal sat, each according to his degree, next the Magnificent, not moving afterwards for any one who might appear. So it happened that Michelangelo found himself frequently seated above Lorenzo's children and other persons of great consequence, with whom that house continually flourished and abounded. All these illustrious men paid him particular attention, and encouraged him in the honourable art which he had chosen. But the chief to do so was the Magnificent himself, who sent for him oftentimes in a day, in order that he might show him jewels, cornelians, medals, and such-like objects of great rarity, as knowing him to be of excellent parts and judgment in these things."[1] It does not appear that Michelangelo had any duties to perform or services to render. Probably his patron employed him upon some useful work of the kind suggested by Condivi. But the main business of his life in the Casa Medici was to make himself a valiant sculptor, who in after-years should confer lustre on the city of the lily and her Medicean masters. What he produced during this period seems to have become his own property, for two pieces of statuary, presently to be described, remained in the possession of his family, and now form a part of the collection in the Casa Buonarroti.

[1] Condivi, p. 9.

VI.

Angelo Poliziano, who was certainly the chief scholar of his age in the new learning, and no less certainly one of its truest poets in the vulgar language, lived as tutor to Lorenzo's children in the palace of the Medici at Florence. Benozzo Gozzoli introduced his portrait, together with the portraits of his noble pupils, in a fresco of the Pisan Campo Santo. This prince of humanists recommended Michelangelo to treat in bas-relief an antique fable, involving the strife of young heroes for some woman's person.[1] Probably he was also able to point out classical examples by which the boyish sculptor might be guided in the undertaking. The subject made enormous demands upon his knowledge of the nude. Adult and youthful figures, in attitudes of vehement attack and resistance, had to be modelled; and the conditions of the myth required that one at least of

---

[1] Condivi tells us that this composition represented "the rape of Deianeira and the battle of the Centaurs." Critics have attempted to find in it the legend of the Centaurs and the Lapithæ, also the story of Herakles and Eurytion. The subject has been ably discussed by Josef Strzygowski in *Jahrbuch der K. Pr. Kunstsammlungen*, vol. xii. Heft 4, 1891. It may be assumed, I think, that the central figure in the group of combatants is meant for a woman. Obeying some deep instinct of his nature, the youthful Michelangelo gave to this female form attributes which render it scarcely distinguishable from the adolescent male. The details of the bas-relief, however, are such as to make it uncertain what particular episode of the Heraklean myth he chose to represent.

them should be brought into harmony with equine forms. Michelangelo wrestled vigorously with these difficulties. He produced a work which, though it is imperfect and immature, brings to light the specific qualities of his inherent art-capacity. The bas-relief, still preserved in the Casa Buonarroti at Florence, is, so to speak, in fermentation with powerful half-realised conceptions, audacities of foreshortening, attempts at intricate grouping, violent dramatic action and expression. No previous tradition, unless it was the genius of Greek or Græco-Roman antiquity, supplied Michelangelo with the motive force for this prentice-piece in sculpture. Donatello and other Florentines worked under different sympathies for form, affecting angularity in their treatment of the nude, adhering to literal transcripts from the model or to conventional stylistic schemes. Michelangelo discarded these limitations, and showed himself an ardent student of reality in the service of some lofty intellectual ideal. Following and closely observing Nature, he was also sensitive to the light and guidance of the classic genius. Yet, at the same time, he violated the æsthetic laws obeyed by that genius, displaying his Tuscan proclivities by violent dramatic suggestions, and in loaded, over-complicated composition. Thus, in this highly interesting essay, the horoscope of the mightiest Florentine artist was already cast. Nature leads him, and he follows Nature as his own star bids. But that star is double, blending classic influence with Tuscan instinct. The roof of the Sistine was destined to exhibit to an awe-struck world what wealths of originality lay in the artist thus gifted, and thus swayed by rival forces. For the present, it may be enough to remark that, in the geometrical proportions of this bas-relief, which is too high for its length, Michelangelo revealed imperfect feeling for antique principles; while, in the grouping of the figures, which is more pictorial than sculpturesque, he already betrayed, what remained with him a defect through life, a certain want of organic or symmetrical design in compositions which are not rigidly subordinated to architectural framework or limited to the sphere of an *intaglio*.[1]

Vasari mentions another bas-relief in marble as belonging to this period, which, from its style, we may, I think, believe to have been designed earlier than the Centaurs. It is a seated Madonna with the Infant Jesus, conceived in the manner of Donatello, but without that master's force and power over the lines of drapery. Except for the interest attaching to it as an early work of Michelangelo, this piece would not attract much attention. Vasari praises it for grace and composition above the scope of Donatello; and certainly we may trace here the first germ of that sweet and winning majesty which Buonarroti was destined to develop in his Pietà of S. Peter, the

[1] What I mean will be felt after a due consideration of the cartoon for the Battle of Pisa in the extant copy of that work. It appears in the frescoes of the Pauline Chapel of the Vatican, as well as in a large variety of original drawings.

Madonna at Bruges, and the even more glorious Madonna of S. Lorenzo. It is also interesting for the realistic introduction of a Tuscan cottage stair-case into the background. This bas-relief was pre-sented to Cosimo de' Medici, first Grand-Duke of Tuscany, by Michelangelo's nephew Lionardo. It afterwards came back into the possession of the Buonarroti family, and forms at present an ornament of their house at Florence.

VII.

We are accustomed to think of Michelangelo as a self-withdrawn and solitary worker, living for his art, avoiding the conflict of society, immersed in sublime imaginings. On the whole, this is a correct concep-tion of the man. Many passages of his biography will show how little he actively shared the passions and contentions of the stirring times through which he moved. Yet his temperament exposed him to sudden outbursts of scorn and anger, which brought him now and then into violent collision with his neighbours. An incident of this sort happened while he was studying under the patronage of Lorenzo de' Medici, and its consequences marked him physically for life. The young artists whom the Magnificent gathered round him used to practise drawing in the Brancacci Chapel of the

Carmine. There Masaccio and his followers bequeathed to us noble examples of the grand style upon the frescoed panels of the chapel walls. It was the custom of industrious lads to make transcripts from those broad designs, some of which Raphael deigned in his latest years to repeat, with altered manner, for the Stanze of the Vatican and the Cartoons. Michelangelo went one day into the Carmine with Piero Torrigiano and other comrades. What ensued may best be reported in the narration which Torrigiano at a later time made to Benvenuto Cellini.

"This Buonarroti and I used, when we were boys, to go into the Church of the Carmine, to learn drawing from the chapel of Masaccio. It was Buonarroti's habit to banter all who were drawing there; and one day, when he was annoying me, I got more angry than usual, and, clenching my fist, I gave him such a blow on the nose that I felt bone and cartilage go down like biscuit beneath my knuckles; and this mark of mine he will carry with him to the grave."[1] The portraits of Michelangelo prove that Torrigiano's boast was not a vain one. They show a nose broken in the bridge. But Torrigiano, for this act of violence, came to be regarded by the youth of Florence with aversion, as one who had laid sacrilegious hands upon the sacred ark. Cellini himself would have wiped out the insult with blood. Still Cellini knew that personal violence was not in the line of Michelangelo's character; for Michelangelo,

[1] *Memoirs of Cellini*, Book i. chap. xiii.

according to his friend and best biographer, Condivi, was by nature, " as is usual with men of sedentary and contemplative habits, rather timorous than otherwise, except when he is roused by righteous anger to resent unjust injuries or wrongs done to himself or others, in which case he plucks up more spirit than those who are esteemed brave; but, for the rest, he is most patient and enduring." [1]   Cellini, then, knowing the quality of Michelangelo's temper, and respecting him as a deity of art, adds to his report of Torrigiano's conversation : " These words begat in me such hatred of the man, since I was always gazing at the masterpieces of the divine Michelangelo, that, although I felt a wish to go with him to England, I now could never bear the sight of him."

VIII.

The years Michelangelo spent in the Casa Medici were probably the blithest and most joyous of his lifetime. The men of wit and learning who surrounded the Magnificent were not remarkable for piety or moral austerity. Lorenzo himself found it politically useful " to occupy the Florentines with shows and festivals, in order that they might think of their own pastimes and not of his designs, and, growing unused to the conduct of the common-

[1] Condivi, p. 83.

wealth, might leave the reins of government in his hands."[1]   Accordingly he devised those Carnival triumphs and processions which filled the sombre streets of Florence with Bacchanalian revellers, and the ears of her grave citizens with ill-disguised obscenity.   Lorenzo took part in them himself, and composed several choruses of high literary merit to be sung by the masqueraders.   One of these carries a refrain which might be chosen as a motto for the spirit of that age upon the brink of ruin :—

> Youths and maids, enjoy to-day :
> Naught ye know about to-morrow !

He caused the triumphs to be carefully prepared by the best artists, the dresses of the masquers to be accurately studied, and their chariots to be adorned with illustrative paintings.   Michelangelo's old friend Granacci dedicated his talents to these shows, which also employed the wayward fancy of Piero di Cosimo and Pontormo's power as a colourist.   " It was their wont," says Il Lasca, " to go forth after dinner ; and often the processions paraded through the streets till three or four hours into the night, with a multitude of masked men on horseback following, richly dressed, exceeding sometimes three hundred in number, and as many on foot with lighted torches. Thus they traversed the city, singing to the accompaniment of music arranged for four, eight, twelve,

---

[1] Adapted from Savonarola's *Trattato circa il Reggimento*, &c., Florence, 1847.

or even fifteen voices, and supported by various
instruments."[1] Lorenzo represented the worst as
well as the best qualities of his age. If he knew
how to enslave Florence, it was because his own
temperament inclined him to share the amusements
of the crowd, while his genius enabled him to in-
vest corruption with charm. His friend Poliziano
entered with the zest of a poet and a pleasure-
seeker into these diversions. He helped Lorenzo
to revive the Tuscan Mayday games, and wrote
exquisite lyrics to be sung by girls in summer even-
ings on the public squares. This giant of learning, who filled the lecture-rooms of Florence with
students of all nations, and whose critical and
rhetorical labours marked an epoch in the history
of scholarship, was by nature a versifier, and a versifier of the people. He found nothing easier than
to throw aside his professor's mantle and to im-
provise *ballate* for women to chant as they danced
their rounds upon the Piazza di S. Trinità. The
frontispiece to an old edition of such lyrics represents Lorenzo surrounded with masquers in quaint
dresses, leading the revel beneath the walls of the
Palazzo. Another woodcut shows an angle of the
Casa Medici in Via Larga, girls dancing the *carola*
upon the street below, one with a wreath and
thyrsus kneeling, another presenting the Magnificent with a book of love-ditties.[2] The burden

---

[1] Preface to *Tutti i Trionfi*, Firenze, 1559.
[2] See my *Renaissance in Italy*, vol. iv. p. 386.

of all this poetry was: "Gather ye roses while ye may, cast prudence to the winds, obey your instincts."

There is little doubt that Michelangelo took part in these pastimes; for we know that he was devoted to poetry, not always of the gravest kind. An anecdote related by Cellini may here be introduced, since it illustrates the Florentine customs I have been describing. "Luigi Pulci was a young man, who possessed extraordinary gifts for poetry, together with sound Latin scholarship. He wrote well, was graceful in manners, and of surpassing personal beauty. While he was yet a lad and living in Florence, it was the habit of folk in certain places of the city to meet together during the nights of summer on the open streets, and he, ranking among the best of the improvisatori, sang there. His recitations were so admirable, that the divine Michelangelo, that prince of sculptors and of painters, went, wherever he heard that he would be, with the greatest eagerness and delight to listen to him. There was a man called Piloto, a goldsmith, very able in his art, who, together with myself, joined Buonarroti upon these occasions."[1] In like manner, the young Michelangelo probably attended those nocturnal gatherings upon the steps of the Duomo which have been so graphically described

[1] Cellini, Book i. chap. xxxii. This Luigi Pulci must not be confounded with the famous author of the *Morgante*. The period referred to here by Cellini may have been about 1520.

by Doni:[1] "The Florentines seem to me to take more pleasure in summer airings than any other folk; for they have, in the square of S. Liberata, between the antique temple of Mars, now the Baptistery, and that marvellous work of modern architecture, the Duomo: they have, I say, certain steps of marble, rising to a broad flat space, upon which the youth of the city come and lay themselves full-length during the season of extreme heat. The place is fitted for its purpose, because a fresh breeze is always blowing, with the blandest of all air, and the flags of white marble usually retain a certain coolness. There then I seek my chiefest solace, when, taking my aërial flights, I sail invisibly above them; see and hear their doings and discourses: and forasmuch as they are endowed with keen and elevated understanding, they always have a thousand charming things to relate; as novels, intrigues, fables; they discuss duels, practical jokes, old stories, tricks played off by men and women on each other: things, each and all, rare, witty, noble, decent and in proper taste. I can swear that during all the hours I spent in listening to their nightly dialogues, I never heard a word that was not comely and of good repute. Indeed, it seemed to me very remarkable, among such crowds of young men, to overhear nothing but virtuous conversation."

At the same period, Michelangelo fell under very different influences; and these left a far more lasting

---

[1] *I Marmi.* Firenze: Barbèra, 1863, vol. i. p. 8.

impression on his character than the gay festivals
and witty word-combats of the lords of Florence.
In 1491 Savonarola, the terrible prophet of coming
woes, the searcher of men's hearts, and the remorse-
less denouncer of pleasant vices, began that Florentine career which ended with his martyrdom in 1498.
He had preached in Florence eight years earlier,
but on that occasion he passed unnoticed through
the crowd. Now he took the whole city by storm.
Obeying the magic of his eloquence and the mag-
netism of his personality, her citizens accepted this
Dominican friar as their political leader and moral
reformer, when events brought about the expulsion
of the Medici in 1494. Michelangelo was one of his
constant listeners at S. Marco and in the Duomo.
He witnessed those stormy scenes of religious revival
and passionate fanaticism which contemporaries have
impressively described. The shorthand-writer to
whom we owe the text of Savonarola's sermons at
times breaks off with words like these: "Here I was
so overcome with weeping that I could not go on."
Pico della Mirandola tells that the mere sound
of the monk's voice, startling the stillness of the
Duomo, thronged through all its space with people,
was like a clap of doom ; a cold shiver ran through
the marrow of his bones, the hairs of his head stood
on end while he listened. Another witness reports :
"Those sermons caused such terror, alarm, sobbing,
and tears, that every one passed through the streets
without speaking, more dead than alive."

One of the earliest extant letters of Michelangelo, written from Rome in 1497 to his brother Buonarroto, reveals a vivid interest in Savonarola.[1] He relates the evil rumours spread about the city regarding his heretical opinions, and alludes to the hostility of Fra Mariano da Genezzano ; adding this ironical sentence : " Therefore he ought by all means to come and prophesy a little in Rome, when afterwards he will be canonised; and so let all his party be of good cheer." In later years, it is said that the great sculptor read and meditated Savonarola's writings together with the Bible. The apocalyptic thunderings and voices of the Sistine Chapel owe much of their soul-thrilling impressiveness to those studies. Michelet says, not without justice, that the spirit of Savonarola lives again in the frescoes of that vault.

On the 8th of April 1492, Michelangelo lost his friend and patron. Lorenzo died in his villa at Careggi, aged little more than forty-four years. Guicciardini implies that his health and strength had been prematurely broken by sensual indulgences. About the circumstances of his last hours there are some doubts and difficulties ; but it seems clear that he expired as a Christian, after a final interview with Savonarola. His death cast a gloom over Italy. Princes and people were growing uneasy with the presentiment of impending disaster ; and now the only man who by his diplomatical sagacity could maintain the balance of power, had been taken from

---

[1] Lettere, xlvi. p. 59

them. To his friends and dependants in Florence the loss appeared irreparable. Poliziano poured forth his sorrow in a Latin threnody of touching and simple beauty.[1] Two years later both he and Pico della Mirandola followed their master to the grave. Marsilio Ficino passed away in 1499; and a friend of his asserted that the sage's ghost appeared to him.[2] The atmosphere was full of rumours, portents, strange premonitions of revolution and doom. The true golden age of the Italian Renaissance may almost be said to have ended with Lorenzo de' Medici's life.

[1] See *Carmina Quinque Ill.: Poetarum*, Bergomie, Lancellotus, 1753, p. 283. Monodia in Laur. Med. Intonata per Arrighum Isac.

> Quis dabit capiti meo
> Aquam ? quis oculis meis
> Fontem lacrymarum dabit ?
> Ut nocte fleam,
> Ut luce fleam.

Compare (*op. cit.*, p. 38) Bembo's fine elegy on the almost contemporary deaths of Lorenzo and Poliziano, which closes with these lines :—

> Heu sic tu raptus, sic te mala fata tulerunt,
> Arbiter Ausoniæ Politiane lyræ.

[2] Ficino and Michele Mercato had frequently discussed the immortality of the soul together. They also agreed that whichever of the two died first should, if possible, appear to the other, and inform him of the life beyond the grave. Michele, then, was studying at an early hour one morning, when a horseman stopped beneath his window, and Marsilio's voice exclaimed : "Michele, Michele, it is all true !" The scholar rose and saw his friend upon a white horse vanishing into the distance. He afterwards discovered that Ficino died precisely at the time when the apparition came to him. Harford, i. 71.

CHAPTER II.

I.

AFTER the death of Lorenzo de' Medici, Michelangelo returned to his father's home, and began to work upon a statue of Hercules, which is now lost. It used to stand in the Strozzi Palace until the siege of Florence in 1530, when Giovanni Battista della Palla bought it from the steward of Filippo Strozzi, and sent it into France as a present to the king.

The Magnificent left seven children by his wife

Clarice, of the princely Roman house of the Orsini. The eldest, Piero, was married to Alfonsina, of the same illustrious family. Giovanni, the second, had already received a cardinal's hat from his kinsman, Innocent VIII. Giuliano, the third, was destined to play a considerable part in Florentine history under the title of Duke of Nemours. One daughter was married to a Salviati, another to a Ridolfi, a third to the Pope's son, Franceschetto Cybò. The fourth, Luisa, had been betrothed to her distant cousin, Giovanni de' Medici; but the match was broken off, and she remained unmarried.

Piero now occupied that position of eminence and semi-despotic authority in Florence which his father and grandfather had held; but he was made of different stuff, both mentally and physically. The Orsini blood, which he inherited from his mother, mixed but ill in his veins with that of Florentine citizens and bankers. Following the proud and insolent traditions of his maternal ancestors, he began to discard the mask of civil urbanity with which Cosimo and Lorenzo had concealed their despotism. He treated the republic as though it were his own property, and prepared for the coming disasters of his race by the overbearing arrogance of his behaviour. Physically, he was powerful, tall, and active; fond of field-sports, and one of the best pallone-players of his time in Italy. Though he had been a pupil of Poliziano, he displayed but little of his father's interest in learning, art, and literature. Chance brought Michelangelo into personal relations with this man. On the 20th of January 1494 there was a heavy fall of snow in Florence, and Piero sent for the young sculptor to model a colossal snow-man in the courtyard of his palace. Critics have treated this as an insult to the great artist, and a sign of Piero's want of taste ; but nothing was more natural than that a previous inmate of the Medicean household should use his talents for the recreation of the family who lived there. Piero upon this occasion begged Michelangelo to return and occupy the room he used to call his own during Lorenzo's lifetime. "And so," writes Condivi, "he remained for some months with the Medici, and was treated by Piero with great kindness ; for the latter used to extol two men of his household as persons of rare ability, the one being Michelangelo, the other a Spanish groom, who, in addition to his personal beauty, which was something wonderful, had so good a wind and such agility, that when Piero was galloping on horseback he could not outstrip him by a hand's-breadth." [1]

II.

At this period of his life Michelangelo devoted himself to anatomy. He had a friend, the Prior of

[1] Condivi, p. 12.

S. Spirito, for whom he carved a wooden crucifix of nearly life-size. This liberal-minded churchman put a room at his disposal, and allowed him to dissect dead bodies. Condivi tells us that the practice of anatomy was a passion with his master. " His prolonged habits of dissection injured his stomach to such an extent that he lost the power of eating or drinking to any profit. It is true, however, that he became so learned in this branch of knowledge that he has often entertained the idea of composing a work for sculptors and painters, which should treat exhaustively of all the movements of the human body, the external aspect of the limbs, the bones, and so forth, adding an ingenious discourse upon the truths discovered by him through the investigations of many years. He would have done this if he had not mistrusted his own power of treating such a subject with the dignity and style of a practised rhetorician. I know well that when he reads Albert Dürer's book, it seems to him of no great value ; his own conception being so far fuller and more useful. Truth to tell, Dürer only treats of the measurements and varied aspects of the human form, making his figures straight as stakes ; and, what is more important, he says nothing about the attitudes and gestures of the body. Inasmuch as Michelangelo is now advanced in years, and does not count on bringing his ideas to light through composition, he has disclosed to me his theories in their minutest details. He

also began to discourse upon the same topic with
Messer Realdo Colombo, an anatomist and surgeon
of the highest eminence. For the furtherance of
such studies this good friend of ours sent him the
corpse of a Moor, a young man of incomparable
beauty, and admirably adapted for our purpose. It
was placed at S. Agata, where I dwelt and still
dwell, as being a quarter removed from public
observation. On this corpse Michelangelo demonstrated to me many rare and abstruse things, which
perhaps have never yet been fully understood, and
all of which I noted down, hoping one day, by
the help of some learned man, to give them to
the public." [1] Of Michelangelo's studies in anatomy we have one grim but interesting record in
a pen-drawing by his hand at Oxford. A corpse
is stretched upon a plank and trestles. Two men
are bending over it with knives in their hands ;
and, for light to guide them in their labours, a
candle is stuck into the belly of the subject.

As it is not my intention to write the political
history of Michelangelo's period, I need not digress
here upon the invasion of Italy by Charles VIII.,
which caused the expulsion of the Medici from
Florence, and the establishment of a liberal government under the leadership of Savonarola. Michelangelo appears to have anticipated the catastrophe
which was about to overwhelm his patron. He
was by nature timid, suspicious, and apt to foresee

[1] Condivi, p. 73.

disaster. Possibly he may have judged that the haughty citizens of Florence would not long put up with Piero's aristocratical insolence. But Condivi tells a story on the subject which is too curious to be omitted, and which he probably set down from Michelangelo's own lips. "In the palace of Piero a man called Cardiere was a frequent inmate. The Magnificent took much pleasure in his society, because he improvised verses to the guitar with marvellous dexterity, and the Medici also practised this art; so that nearly every evening after supper there was music. This Cardiere, being a friend of Michelangelo, confided to him a vision which pursued him, to the following effect. Lorenzo de' Medici appeared to him barely clad in one black tattered robe, and bade him relate to his son Piero that he would soon be expelled and never more return to his home. Now Piero was arrogant and overbearing to such an extent that neither the good-nature of the Cardinal Giovanni his brother, nor the courtesy and urbanity of Giuliano, was so strong to maintain him in Florence as his own faults to cause his expulsion. Michelangelo encouraged the man to obey Lorenzo and report the matter to his son; but Cardiere, fearing his new master's temper, kept it to himself. On another morning, when Michelangelo was in the courtyard of the palace, Cardiere came with terror and pain written on his countenance. Last night Lorenzo had again appeared to him in the same garb of woe; and while he was awake and gazing with his eyes, the spectre dealt him a blow on the cheek, to punish him for omitting to report his vision to Piero. Michelangelo immediately gave him such a thorough scolding that Cardiere plucked up courage, and set forth on foot for Careggi, a Medicean villa some three miles distant from the city. He had travelled about halfway, when he met Piero, who was riding home; so he stopped the cavalcade, and related all that he had seen and heard. Piero laughed him to scorn, and, beckoning the running footmen, bade them mock the poor fellow. His Chancellor, who was afterwards the Cardinal of Bibbiena, cried out: 'You are a madman! Which do you think Lorenzo loved best, his son or you? If his son, would he not rather have appeared to him than to some one else?' Having thus jeered him, they let him go; and he, when he returned home and complained to Michelangelo, so convinced the latter of the truth of his vision, that Michelangelo after two days left Florence with a couple of comrades, dreading that if what Cardiere had predicted should come true, he would no longer be safe in Florence."[1]

This ghost-story bears a remarkable resemblance to what Clarendon relates concerning the apparition of Sir George Villiers. Wishing to warn his son, the Duke of Buckingham, of his coming murder at the hand of Lieutenant Felton, he did not appear to the Duke himself, but to an old man-

[1] Condivi, p. 13.

servant of the family; upon which behaviour of Sir George's ghost the same criticism has been passed as on that of Lorenzo de' Medici.

Michelangelo and his two friends travelled across the Apennines to Bologna, and thence to Venice, where they stopped a few days. Want of money, or perhaps of work there, drove them back upon the road to Florence. When they reached Bologna on the return journey, a curious accident happened to the party. The master of the city, Giovanni Bentivoglio, had recently decreed that every foreigner, on entering the gates, should be marked with a seal of red wax upon his thumb. The three Florentines omitted to obey this regulation, and were taken to the office of the Customs, where they were fined in fifty Bolognese pounds. Michelangelo did not possess enough to pay this fine; but it so happened that a Bolognese nobleman called Gianfrancesco Aldovrandi was there, who, hearing that Buonarroti was a sculptor, caused the men to be released. Upon his urgent invitation, Michelangelo went to this gentleman's house, after taking leave of his two friends and giving them all the money in his pocket. With Messer Aldovrandi he remained more than a year, much honoured by his new patron, who took great delight in his genius; "and every evening he made Michelangelo read aloud to him out of Dante or Petrarch, and sometimes Boccaccio, until he went to sleep." [1] He also worked upon the tomb of San

[1] Condivi, p. 15.

Domenico during this first residence at Bologna.[1] Originally designed and carried forward by Nicola Pisano, this elaborate specimen of mediæval sculpture remained in some points imperfect. There was a San Petronio whose drapery, begun by Nicolo da Bari, was unfinished. To this statue Michelangelo put the last touches; and he also carved a kneeling angel with a candelabrum, the workmanship of which surpasses in delicacy of execution all the other figures on the tomb.

III.

Michelangelo left Bologna hastily. It is said that a sculptor, who had expected to be employed upon the *arca* of S. Domenic, threatened to do him some mischief if he stayed and took the bread out of the mouths of native craftsmen.[2] He returned to Florence some time in 1495. The city was now quiet again, under the rule of Savonarola. Its burghers, in obedience to the friar's preaching, began to assume that air of pietistic sobriety which contrasted strangely with the gay licentiousness encouraged by their former master. Though the reigning branch of the Medici remained in exile,

---

[1] It is an *arca* or sarcophagus of Gothic design, adorned with bas-reliefs and a great number of detached statuettes. It stands in a chapel on the south side of the nave of the Church of S. Domenico.

[2] Condivi, p. 16.

their distant cousins, who were descended from Lorenzo, the brother of Cosimo, Pater Patriæ, kept their place in the republic. They thought it prudent, however, at this time, to exchange the hated name of de' Medici for Popolano. With a member of this section of the Medicean family, Lorenzo di Pierfrancesco, Michelangelo soon found himself on terms of intimacy. It was for him that he made a statue of the young S John, which was perhaps rediscovered at Pisa in 1874.[1] For a long time this S. Giovannino was attributed to Donatello; and it certainly bears decided marks of resemblance to that master's manner, in the choice of attitude, the close adherence to the model, and the treatment of the hands and feet. Still it has notable affinities to the style of Michelangelo, especially in the youthful beauty of the features, the disposition of the hair, and the sinuous lines which govern the whole composition.[2] It may also be remarked that those peculiarities in the hands and feet which I have mentioned as reminding us of Donatello—a remarkable length in both extremities, owing to the elongation of the metacarpal and metatarsal bones and of the spaces dividing these from the forearm and tibia—

[1] It had been bought in 1817, and placed in the palace of the Counts Gualandi Rosselmini at Pisa. The Berlin Museum acquired it in 1880, and Professor Bode strongly maintained its genuineness as a work of Michelangelo.

[2] The face is formed upon a type which Donatello used for his S. George, and which Michelangelo adhered to afterwards in many of his works. Not much can be based upon this detail. Botticelli's type of face corresponds in the same way to that of Filippino Lippi.

are precisely the points which Michelangelo retained through life from his early study of Donatello's work. We notice them particularly in the Dying Slave of the Louvre, which is certainly one of his most characteristic works. Good judges are therefore perhaps justified in identifying this S. Giovannino, which is now in the Berlin Museum, with the statue made for Lorenzo di Pierfrancesco de' Medici.[1]

The next piece which occupied Michelangelo's chisel was a Sleeping Cupid. His patron thought this so extremely beautiful that he remarked to the sculptor: "If you were to treat it artificially, so as to make it look as though it had been dug up, I would send it to Rome; it would be accepted as an antique, and you would be able to sell it at a far higher price."[2] Michelangelo took the hint. His Cupid went to Rome, and was sold for thirty ducats to a dealer called Messer Baldassare del Milanese, who resold it to Raffaello Riario, the Cardinal di S. Giorgio, for the advanced sum of 200 ducats. It appears from this transaction that Michelangelo did not attempt to impose upon the first purchaser, but that this man passed it off upon the Cardinal as an antique. When the Cardinal

[1] Grimm, vol. i. p. 546, hazards a conjecture that both this statue and the Adonis of the Bargello are works by some follower of Michelangelo. This suggestion does not seem to me probable. The reason for not assigning the little S. John to Michelangelo is that it does not exhibit his peculiar manner. But this peculiar quality a follower would have certainly aimed at acquiring. The choice lies between Donatello himself, and Buonarroti refining on that sculptor's mannerism.

[2] Condivi, p. 16.

began to suspect that the Cupid was the work of a modern Florentine, he sent one of his gentlemen to Florence to inquire into the circumstances. The rest of the story shall be told in Condivi's words.

"This gentleman, pretending to be on the look-out for a sculptor capable of executing certain works in Rome, after visiting several, was addressed to Michelangelo. When he saw the young artist, he begged him to show some proof of his ability; whereupon Michelangelo took a pen (for at that time the crayon [*lapis*] had not come into use), and drew a hand with such grace that the gentleman was stupefied. Afterwards, he asked if he had ever worked in marble, and when Michelangelo said yes, and mentioned among other things a Cupid of such height and in such an attitude, the man knew that he had found the right person. So he related how the matter had gone, and promised Michelangelo, if he would come with him to Rome, to get the difference of price made up, and to introduce him to his patron, feeling sure that the latter would receive him very kindly. Michelangelo, then, partly in anger at having been cheated, and partly moved by the gentleman's account of Rome as the widest field for an artist to display his talents, went with him, and lodged in his house, near the palace of the Cardinal."[1] S. Giorgio compelled Messer Baldassare to refund the 200 ducats, and to take the Cupid back. But Michelangelo got nothing

[1] Condivi, p. 17.

beyond his original price; and both Condivi and Vasari blame the Cardinal for having been a dull and unsympathetic patron to the young artist of genius he had brought from Florence. Still the whole transaction was of vast importance, because it launched him for the first time upon Rome, where he was destined to spend the larger part of his long life, and to serve a succession of Pontiffs in their most ambitious undertakings.

Before passing to the events of his sojourn at Rome, I will wind up the story of the Cupid. It passed first into the hands of Cesare Borgia, who presented it to Guidobaldo di Montefeltro, Duke of Urbino. On the 30th of June 1502, the Marchioness of Mantua wrote a letter to the Cardinal of Este, saying that she should very much like to place this piece, together with an antique statuette of Venus, both of which had belonged to her brother-in-law, the Duke of Urbino, in her own collection. Apparently they had just become the property of Cesare Borgia, when he took and sacked the town of Urbino upon the 20th of June in that year. Cesare Borgia seems to have complied immediately with her wishes; for in a second letter, dated July 22, 1502, she described the Cupid as " without a peer among the works of modern times." [1]

---

[1] See Gaye, vol. ii. pp. 53, 54. After writing the above paragraph, I thought it worth while to go to Mantua expressly for the purpose of tracing out the Cupid. At one end of the long gallery of the Liceo there

IV.

Michelangelo arrived in Rome at the end of June 1496. This we know from the first of his extant letters, which is dated July 2, and addressed to Lorenzo di Pierfrancesco de' Medici. The superscription, however, bears the name of Sandro Botticelli, showing that some caution had still to be observed in corresponding with the Medici, even with those who latterly assumed the name of Popolani. The young Buonarroti writes in excellent spirits : " I only write to inform you that last

is a little marble figure, about four feet long, of a Cupid stretched upon his back asleep, short wings spread out beneath his shoulders, arms laid along his sides, the bow and quiver close to the left flank, the head crowned with a wreath of leaves and conventional flowers. Two snakes, their tails coiled loosely round each of the boy's wrists, are creeping with open mouths as though they mean to come together above his navel. The marble seems to be Carrara, and has stains of faint blue traceable upon the surface. The finish of the statuette is exquisite where there has been no injury. It shines like polished ivory. But deep scratches, livid discolorations, and bruised extremities point to the action of violence and time. The style is that of Græco-Roman decadence, not differing in any important respect from that of two marble Cupids in the Uffizi, one of which, supposing it to have come down from Lorenzo de' Medici's collection, may have supplied Michelangelo with his subject. Neither in type nor in handling would any one recognise a work of Buonarroti. Yet this does not invalidate its genuineness, since we know that the lost Cupid was sold as an antique. We are told that the sculptor added marks of injury and earth-stains, " so that," as Condivi says, " it seemed to have been fashioned many years before, there being no sleight of ingenuity hidden from his talent." Before we reject this statuette on the score of its classic style, we must remember that Michelangelo in his youth

Saturday we arrived safely, and went at once to visit the Cardinal di San Giorgio; and I presented your letter to him. It appeared to me that he was pleased to see me, and he expressed a wish that I should go immediately to inspect his collection of statues. I spent the whole day there, and for that reason was unable to deliver all your letters. Afterwards, on Sunday, the Cardinal came into the new house, and had me sent for. I went to him, and he asked what I thought about the things which I had seen. I replied by stating my opinion, and certainly I can say with sincerity that there are many fine things in the collection. Then he asked me whether I had the courage to make some beautiful work of art.

amused himself with making exact copies of old drawings, which he passed off as originals, while the mask of the Faun shows what he could do in imitation of the antique. One notable peculiarity of the statuette is the addition of the two snakes to the sleeping figure. Some allegory, not wholly in the spirit of classic art, but very much in the line of fifteenth-century thought, seems to have been intended. Condivi says that Michelangelo's Cupid existed at his time in the Palazzo Gonzaga at Mantua. De Thou (quoted in the notes to Condivi, p. 179) saw it there in 1573. The sleeping Cupid now in the Liceo was brought there from the palace of the Dukes of Mantua. At the same time we should remember that several of the Mantuan marbles were transferred to Venice after the sack of the town in 1630; and among the antique statues in the Ducal Palace of S. Mark there are two Sleeping Cupids, both obviously of the latest Roman decadence. It seems impossible, therefore, to decide either affirmatively or negatively upon the question of the genuineness of this work. The mere fact that Buonarroti planned a mystification places it, in the absence of external evidence, beyond the sphere of criticism. I must add, finally, that Springer (vol. i. p. 306) regards the Mantuan Cupid as not to be identified with Michelangelo's, on the ground that Niccola d'Arca in an epigram mentions a torch at the boy's side.

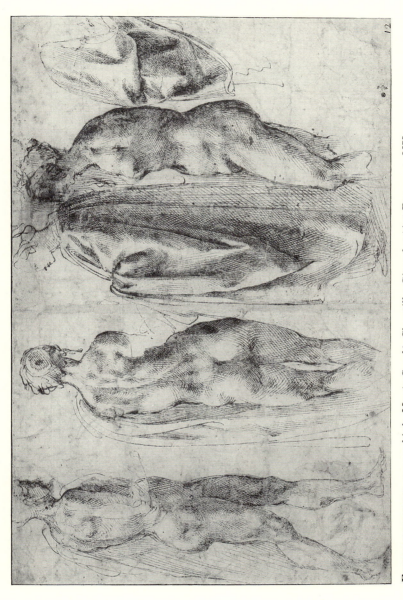

FIGURE SKETCHES, pen and ink. Musée Condé, Chantilly. Giraudon/Art Resource, NY.

I answered that I should not be able to achieve anything so great, but that he should see what I could do. We have bought a piece of marble for a life-size statue, and on Monday I shall begin to work."[1]

After describing his reception, Michelangelo proceeds to relate the efforts he was making to regain his Sleeping Cupid from Messer Baldassare : " Afterwards, I gave your letter to Baldassare, and asked him for the child, saying I was ready to refund his money. He answered very roughly, swearing he would rather break it in a hundred pieces ; he had bought the child, and it was his property ; he possessed writings which proved that he had satisfied the person who sent it to him, and was under no apprehension that he should have to give it up. Then he complained bitterly of you, saying that you had spoken ill of him. Certain of our Florentines sought to accommodate matters, but failed in their attempt. Now I look to coming to terms through the Cardinal ; for this is the advice of Baldassare Balducci. What ensues I will report to you." It is clear that Lorenzo di Pierfrancesco, being convinced of the broker's sharp practice, was trying to recover the Sleeping Cupid (the child) at the price originally paid for it, either for himself or for Buonarroti. The Cardinal is mentioned as being the most likely person to secure the desired result.

Whether Condivi is right in saying that S. Giorgio

[1] Lettere, No. cccxlii. p. 375.

neglected to employ Michelangelo may be doubted.
We have seen from this letter to Lorenzo that the
Cardinal bought a piece of marble and ordered a
life-size statue. But nothing more is heard about
the work. Professor Milanesi, however, has pointed
out that when the sculptor was thinking of leaving
Rome in 1497 he wrote to his father on the 1st of
July as follows : " Most revered and beloved father,
do not be surprised that I am unable to return, for
I have not yet settled my affairs with the Cardinal,
and I do not wish to leave until I am properly paid
for my labour; and with these great patrons one
must go about quietly, since they cannot be compelled. I hope, however, at any rate during the
course of next week, to have completed the transaction." [1]

Michelangelo remained at Rome for more than
two years after the date of the letter just quoted.
We may conjecture, then, that he settled his accounts
with the Cardinal, whatever these were, and we
know that he obtained other orders. In a second
letter to his father, August 19, 1497, he writes thus :
" Piero de' Medici gave me a commission for a
statue, and I bought the marble. But I did not
begin to work upon it, because he failed to perform
what he promised. Wherefore I am acting on my
own account, and am making a statue for my own
pleasure. I bought the marble for five ducats, and
it turned out bad. So I threw my money away.

[1] Lettere, No. i. p. 3, and editor's note.

Now I have bought another at the same price, and the work I am doing is for my amusement. You will therefore understand that I too have large expenses and many troubles." [1]

During the first year of his residence in Rome (between July 2, 1496, and August 19, 1497) Michelangelo must have made some money, else he could not have bought marble and have worked upon his own account. Vasari asserts that he remained nearly twelve months in the household of the Cardinal, and that he only executed a drawing of S. Francis receiving the stigmata, which was coloured by a barber in S. Giorgio's service, and placed in the Church of S. Pietro a Montorio. [2] Benedetto Varchi describes this picture as having been painted by Buonarroti's own hand. [3] We know nothing more for certain about it. How he earned his money is, therefore, unexplained, except upon the supposition that S. Giorgio, unintelligent as he may have been in his patronage of art, paid him for work performed. I may here add that the Piero de' Medici who gave the commission mentioned in the last quotation was the exiled head of the ruling family. Nothing had to be expected from such a man. He came to Rome in order to be near the Cardinal Giovanni, and to share this brother's better fortunes; but his days and nights were spent in debauchery among the companions and accomplices of shameful riot.

[1] Lettere, No. ii. p. 4.   [2] Vasari, p. 169.
[3] *Orazione in Morte di M. A.*, cap. 16.

V.

Michelangelo, in short, like most young artists, was struggling into fame and recognition. Both came to him by the help of a Roman gentleman and banker, Messer Jacopo Gallo. It so happened that an intimate Florentine friend of Buonarroti, the Baldassare Balducci mentioned at the end of his letter to Lorenzo di Pierfrancesco, was employed in Gallo's house of business.[1] It is probable, therefore, that this man formed the link of connection between the sculptor and his new patron. At all events, Messer Gallo purchased a Bacchus, which now adorns the sculpture-gallery of the Bargello, and a Cupid, which may possibly be the statue at South Kensington.

Condivi says that this gentleman, "a man of fine intelligence, employed him to execute in his own house a marble Bacchus, ten palms in height, the form and aspect of which correspond in all parts to the meaning of ancient authors. The face of the youth is jocund, the eyes wandering and wanton, as is the wont with those who are too much addicted to a taste for wine. In his right hand he holds a cup, lifting it to drink, and gazing at it like one

---

[1] There are two letters from Giovanni Balducci to Michelangelo preserved in the Archivio Buonarroti, Cod. vi. Nos. 45, 46. Both belong to the summer of 1506.

who takes delight in that liquor, of which he was the first discoverer. For this reason, too, the sculptor has wreathed his head with vine-tendrils. On his left arm hangs a tiger-skin, the beast dedicated to Bacchus, as being very partial to the grape. Here the artist chose rather to introduce the skin than the animal itself, in order to hint that sensual indulgence in the pleasure of the grape-juice leads at last to loss of life. With the hand of this arm he holds a bunch of grapes, which a little satyr, crouched below him, is eating on the sly with glad and eager gestures. The child may seem to be seven years, the Bacchus eighteen of age." [1] This description is comparatively correct, except that Condivi is obviously mistaken when he supposes that Michelangelo's young Bacchus faithfully embodies the Greek spirit. The Greeks never forgot, in all their representations of Dionysos, that he was a mystic and enthusiastic deity. Joyous, voluptuous, androgynous, he yet remains the god who brought strange gifts and orgiastic rites to men. His followers, Silenus, Bacchantes, Fauns, exhibit, in their self-abandonment to sensual joy, the operation of his genius. The deity descends to join their revels from his clear Olympian ether, but he is not troubled by the fumes of intoxication. Michelangelo has altered this conception. Bacchus, with him, is a terrestrial young man, upon the verge of toppling over into drunkenness. The value of the

[1] Condivi, p. 18.

work is its realism. The attitude could not be sustained in actual life for a moment without either the goblet spilling its liquor or the body reeling side-ways. Not only are the eyes wavering and wanton, but the muscles of the mouth have relaxed into a tipsy smile ; and, instead of the tiger-skin being suspended from the left arm, it has slipped down, and is only kept from falling by the loose grasp of the trembling hand. Nothing, again, could be less godlike than the face of Bacchus. It is the face of a not remarkably good-looking model, and the head is too small both for the body and the heavy crown of leaves. As a study of incipient intoxication, when the whole person is disturbed by drink, but human dignity has not yet yielded to a bestial impulse, this statue proves the energy of Michelangelo's imagination. The physical beauty of his adolescent model in the limbs and body redeems the grossness of the motive by the inalienable charm of health and carnal comeliness. Finally, the technical merits of the work cannot too strongly be insisted on. The modelling of the thorax, the exquisite roundness and fleshiness of the thighs and arms and belly, the smooth skin-surface expressed throughout in marble, will excite admiration in all who are capable of appreciating this aspect of the statuary's art. Michelangelo produced nothing more finished in execution, if we except the Pietà at S. Peter's. His Bacchus alone is sufficient to explode a theory favoured by some critics, that, left to work unhindered, he would still have preferred a certain vagueness, a certain want of polish in his marbles.

Nevertheless, the Bacchus leaves a disagreeable impression on the mind—as disagreeable in its own way as that produced by the Christ of the Minerva. That must be because it is wrong in spiritual conception—brutally materialistic where it ought to have been noble or graceful. In my opinion, the frank, joyous naturalism of Sansovino's Bacchus (also in the Bargello) possesses more of true Greek inspiration than Michelangelo's. If Michelangelo meant to carve a Bacchus, he failed; if he meant to imitate a physically desirable young man in a state of drunkenness, he succeeded.

What Shelley wrote upon this statue may here be introduced,[1] since it combines both points of view in a criticism of much spontaneous vigour.

"The countenance of this figure is the most revolting mistake of the spirit and meaning of Bacchus. It looks drunken, brutal, and narrow-minded, and has an expression of dissoluteness the most revolting. The lower part of the figure is stiff, and the manner in which the shoulders are united to the breast, and the neck to the head, abundantly inharmonious. It is altogether without unity, as was the idea of the deity of Bacchus in the conception of a Catholic. On the other hand, considered merely as a piece of workmanship, it has great merits. The arms are executed in the most perfect and manly beauty; the

---

[1] Forman's edition of the Prose Works, vol. iii. p. 71.

body is conceived with great energy, and the lines which describe the sides and thighs, and the manner in which they mingle into one another, are of the highest order of boldness and beauty. It wants, as a work of art, unity and simplicity ; as a representation of the Greek deity of Bacchus, it wants everything."

Jacopo Gallo is said to have also purchased a Cupid from Michelangelo. It has been suggested, with great plausibility, that this Cupid was the piece which Michelangelo began when Piero de' Medici's commission fell through, and that it therefore preceded the Bacchus in date of execution. It has also been suggested that the so-called Cupid at South Kensington is the work in question. We have no authentic information to guide us in the matter.[1] But the South Kensington Cupid is certainly a production of the master's early manhood. It was discovered some forty years ago, hidden away in the cellars of the Gualfonda (Rucellai) Gardens at Florence, by Professor Miliarini and the famous Florentine sculptor Santarelli. On a cursory inspection they both declared it to be a genuine Michelangelo.[2]

---

[1] Springer (vol. i. p. 22) points out that while Condivi mentions a Cupid, Ulisse Aldovrandi, who also saw the statue in Messer Gallo's house at Rome, talks of an Apollo, quite naked, with a quiver at his side and an urn at his feet.

[2] Heath Wilson, p. 33. *Catalogue of the Italian Sculpture at the South Kensington Museum*, by J. C. Robinson, pp. 134, 135. The want of finish in certain portions of the marble is the only sign which makes me doubt its attribution to Michelangelo's first Roman visit.

The left arm was broken, the right hand damaged, and the hair had never received the sculptor's final touches. Santarelli restored the arm, and the Cupid passed by purchase into the possession of the English nation. This fine piece of sculpture is executed in Michelangelo's proudest, most dramatic manner. The muscular young man of eighteen, a model of superb adolescence, kneels upon his right knee, while the right hand is lowered to lift an arrow from the ground. The left hand is raised above the head, and holds the bow, while the left leg is so placed, with the foot firmly pressed upon the ground, as to indicate that in a moment the youth will rise, fit the shaft to the string, and send it whistling at his adversary. This choice of a momentary attitude is eminently characteristic of Michelangelo's style; and, if we are really to believe that he intended to portray the god of love, it offers another instance of his independence of classical tradition. No Greek would have thus represented Erôs. The lyric poets, indeed, Ibycus and Anacreon, imaged him as a fierce invasive deity, descending like the whirlwind on an oak, or striking at his victim with an axe. But these romantic ideas did not find expression, so far as I am aware, in antique plastic art. Michelangelo's Cupid is therefore as original as his Bacchus. Much as critics have written, and with justice, upon the classical tendencies of the Italian Renaissance, they have failed

What else of certain he wrought there, shows a most scrupulous seeking after completion.

to point out that the Paganism of the Cinque Cento rarely involved a servile imitation of the antique or a sympathetic intelligence of its spirit. Least of all do we find either of these qualities in Michelangelo. He drew inspiration from his own soul, and he went straight to Nature for the means of expressing the conception he had formed. Unlike the Greeks, he invariably preferred the particular to the universal, the critical moment of an action to suggestions of the possibilities of action. He carved an individual being, not an abstraction or a generalisation of personality. The Cupid supplies us with a splendid illustration of this criticism. Being a product of his early energy, before he had formed a certain manneristic way of seeing Nature and of reproducing what he saw, it not only casts light upon the spontaneous working of his genius, but it also shows how the young artist had already come to regard the inmost passion of the soul. When quite an old man, rhyming those rough platonic sonnets, he always spoke of love as masterful and awful. For his austere and melancholy nature, Erôs was no tender or light-winged youngling, but a masculine tyrant, the tamer of male spirits. Therefore this Cupid, adorable in the power and beauty of his vigorous manhood, may well remain for us the myth or symbol of love as Michelangelo imagined that emotion. In composition, the figure is from all points of view admirable, presenting a series of nobly varied line-harmonies. All we have to regret is that time, exposure to weather, and vulgar outrage should have spoiled the surface of the marble.[1]

V.

It is natural to turn from the Cupid to another work belonging to the English nation, which has recently been ascribed to Michelangelo. I mean the Madonna, with Christ, S. John, and four attendant male figures, once in the possession of Mr. H. Labouchere, and now in the National Gallery. We have no authentic tradition regarding this tempera painting, which in my judgment is the most beautiful of the easel pictures attributed to Michelangelo. Internal evidence from style renders its genuineness in the highest degree probable. No one else upon the close of the fifteenth century was capable of producing a composition at once so complicated, so harmonious, and so clear as the group formed by Madonna, Christ leaning on her knee to point a finger at the book she holds, and the young S. John turned round to combine these figures with the exquisitely blended youths behind him. Unfortunately the two angels or genii upon the left hand are unfinished; but had the picture been completed, we should probably have been able

[1] There is reason to think that it stood some two hundred years in the open air, and that it was once used as a mark for pistol-shooting.

to point out another magnificent episode in the
composition, determined by the transverse line carried from the hand upon the last youth's shoulder,
through the open book and the upraised arm of
Christ, down to the feet of S. John and the last
genius on the right side.   Florentine painters had
been wont to place attendant angels at both sides
of their enthroned Madonnas.   Fine examples might
be chosen from the work of Filippino Lippi and
Botticelli.   But their angels were winged and
clothed like acolytes ; the Madonna was seated on
a rich throne or under a canopy, with altar-candles,
wreaths of roses, flowering lilies.   It is characteristic
of Michelangelo to adopt a conventional motive, and
to treat it with brusque originality.   In this picture
there are no accessories to the figures, and the
attendant angels are Tuscan lads half draped in
succinct tunics.   The style is rather that of a flat
relief in stone than of a painting ; and though we
may feel something of Ghirlandajo's influence, the
spirit of Donatello and Luca della Robbia are more
apparent.   That it was the work of an inexperienced
painter is shown by the failure to indicate pictorial
planes.   In spite of the marvellous and intricate
beauty of the line-composition, it lacks that effect
of graduated distances which might perhaps have
been secured by execution in bronze or marble.
The types have not been chosen with regard to ideal
loveliness or dignity, but accurately studied from
living models.   This is very obvious in the heads

of Christ and S. John. The two adolescent genii
on the right hand possess a high degree of natural
grace. Yet even here what strikes one most is
the charm of their attitude, the lovely interlacing
of their arms and breasts, the lithe alertness of
the one lad contrasted with the thoughtful leaning
languor of his comrade. Only perhaps in some
drawings of combined male figures made by Ingres
for his picture of the Golden Age, have lines of
equal dignity and simple beauty been developed.
I do not think that this Madonna, supposing it to
be a genuine piece by Michelangelo, belongs to the
period of his first residence in Rome. In spite of
its immense intellectual power, it has an air of
immaturity. Probably Heath Wilson was right in
assigning it to the time spent at Florence after
Lorenzo de' Medici's death, when the artist was
about twenty years of age.[1]

I may take this occasion for dealing summarily
with the Entombment in the National Gallery.
The picture, which is half finished, has no pedigree.
It was bought out of the collection of Cardinal
Fesch, and pronounced to be a Michelangelo by

[1] I am indebted to Prof. Middleton for some observations on this picture. He points out the hesitating brush-work, timid use of hatched
lines, and so forth, in the technique. We know so little about Michelangelo's first essays at painting, and he so strenuously asserted that
painting was not his trade, that I do not feel the indecision noticeable
in the workmanship of this panel to be stringent evidence against its
genuineness. At any rate, if we refuse to acknowledge it as a piece of
his own handiwork, we must accept it as a careful transcript from his
design by one who, like himself, was not by trade a painter.

the Munich painter Cornelius.[1]   Good judges have
adopted this attribution, and to differ from them
requires some hardihood.   Still it is painful to
believe that at any period of his life Michelangelo
could have produced a composition so discordant,
so unsatisfactory in some anatomical details, so
feelingless and ugly.   It bears indubitable traces
of his influence; that is apparent in the figure of
the dead Christ.   But this colossal nude, with the
massive chest and attenuated legs, reminds us of
his manner in old age; whereas the rest of the
picture shows no trace of that manner.   I am
inclined to think that the Entombment was the
production of a second-rate craftsman, working
upon some design made by Michelangelo at the
advanced period when the Passion of our Lord
occupied his thoughts in Rome.   Even so, the spirit
of the drawing must have been imperfectly assimilated; and, what is more puzzling, the composition
does not recall the style of Michelangelo's old age.
The colouring, so far as we can understand it, rather
suggests Pontormo.

[1] Mr. Robert Macpherson found it in a dealer's shop at Rome in
1846, completely painted over.   He had it cleaned, and the under surface was assigned to Michelangelo.

VI.

Michelangelo's good friend, Jacopo Gallo, was again helpful to him in the last and greatest work which he produced during this Roman residence. The Cardinal Jean de la Groslaye de Villiers François, Abbot of S. Denys, and commonly called by Italians the Cardinal di San Dionigi,[1] wished to have a specimen of the young sculptor's handiwork. Accordingly articles were drawn up to the following effect on August 26, 1498 : "Let it be known and manifest to whoso shall read the ensuing document, that the most Rev. Cardinal of S. Dionigi has thus agreed with the master Michelangelo, sculptor of Florence, to wit, that the said master shall make a Pietà of marble at his own cost; that is to say, a Virgin Mary clothed, with the dead Christ in her arms, of the size of a proper man, for the price of 450 golden ducats of the Papal mint, within the term of one year from the day of the commencement of the work." Next follow clauses regarding the payment of the money, whereby the Cardinal agrees to disburse sums in advance. The contract concludes with a guarantee and surety given by Jacopo Gallo. "And I, Jacopo Gallo, pledge my word to his most Rev. Lordship that

[1] He came in 1493 as ambassador from Charles VIII. to Alexander VI., when the Borgia gave him the scarlet hat.

the said Michelangelo will finish the said work within one year, and that it shall be the finest work in marble which Rome to-day can show, and that no master of our days shall be able to produce a better. And, in like manner, on the other side, I pledge my word to the said Michelangelo that the most Rev. Card. will disburse the payments according to the articles above engrossed. To witness which, I, Jacopo Gallo, have made this present writing with my own hand, according to date of year, month, and day as above." [1]

The Pietà raised Michelangelo at once to the highest place among the artists of his time, and it still remains unrivalled for the union of sublime æsthetic beauty with profound religious feeling. The mother of the dead Christ is seated on a stone at the foot of the cross, supporting the body of her son upon her knees, gazing sadly at his wounded side, and gently lifting her left hand, as though to say, " Behold and see ! " She has the small head and heroic torso used by Michelangelo to suggest immense physical force. We feel that such a woman has no difficulty in holding a man's corpse upon her ample lap and in her powerful arms. Her face, which differs from the female type he afterwards preferred, resembles that of a young woman. For this he was rebuked by critics who thought that her age should correspond more natur- ally to that of her adult son. Condivi reports that

[1] Gotti, ii. p. 33.

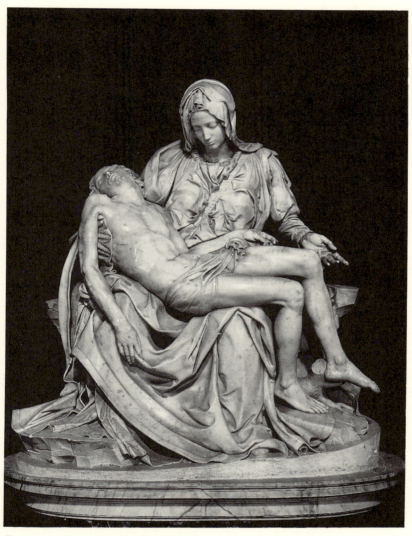

PIETÀ, marble, 1498. Basilica of St. Peter, Rome. Alinari/Art
Resource, NY.

Michelangelo explained his meaning in the following words: "Do you not know that chaste women maintain their freshness far longer than the unchaste? How much more would this be the case with a virgin, into whose breast there never crept the least lascivious desire which could affect the body? Nay, I will go further, and hazard the belief that this unsullied bloom of youth, beside being maintained in her by natural causes, may have been miraculously wrought to convince the world of the virginity and perpetual purity of the Mother. This was not necessary for the Son. On the contrary, in order to prove that the Son of God took upon himself, as in very truth he did take, a human body, and became subject to all that an ordinary man is subject to, with the exception of sin; the human nature of Christ, instead of being superseded by the divine, was left to the operation of natural laws, so that his person revealed the exact age to which he had attained. You need not, therefore, marvel if, having regard to these considerations, I made the most Holy Virgin, Mother of God, much younger relatively to her Son than women of her years usually appear, and left the Son such as his time of life demanded."[1] "This reasoning," adds Condivi, "was worthy of some learned theologian, and would have been little short of marvellous in most men, but not in him, whom God and Nature fashioned, not merely to be peerless in his

[1] Condivi, p. 20.

handiwork, but also capable of the divinest con-
cepts, as innumerable discourses and writings which
we have of his make clearly manifest."

The Christ is also somewhat youthful, and
modelled with the utmost delicacy; suggesting no
lack of strength, but subordinating the idea of
physical power to that of a refined and spiritual
nature. Nothing can be more lovely than the
hands, the feet, the arms, relaxed in slumber.
Death becomes immortally beautiful in that recumbent figure, from which the insults of the
scourge, the cross, the brutal lance have been
erased. Michelangelo did not seek to excite pity
or to stir devotion by having recourse to those
mediæval ideas which were so passionately expressed
in S. Bernard's hymn to the Crucified. The æsthetic
tone of his dead Christ is rather that of some sweet
solemn strain of cathedral music, some motive from
a mass of Palestrina or a Passion of Sebastian Bach.
Almost involuntarily there rises to the memory that
line composed by Bion for the genius of earthly
loveliness bewailed by everlasting beauty—

E'en as a corpse he is fair, fair corpse as fallen aslumber.

It is said that certain Lombards passing by and
admiring the Pietà ascribed it to Christoforo Solari
of Milan, surnamed Il Gobbo. Michelangelo,
having happened to overhear them, shut himself
up in the chapel, and engraved the belt upon

Madonna's breast with his own name. This he never did with any other of his works.[1]

This masterpiece of highest art combined with pure religious feeling was placed in the old Basilica of S. Peter's, in a chapel dedicated to Our Lady of the Fever, Madonna della Febbre. Here, on the night of August 19, 1503, it witnessed one of those horrid spectacles which in Italy at that period so often intervened to interrupt the rhythm of romance and beauty and artistic melody. The dead body of Roderigo Borgia, Alexander VI., lay in state from noon onwards in front of the high altar; but since " it was the most repulsive, monstrous, and deformed corpse which had ever yet been seen, without any form or figure of humanity, shame compelled them to partly cover it." " Late in the evening it was transferred to the chapel of Our Lady of the Fever, and deposited in a corner by six hinds or porters and two carpenters, who had made the coffin too narrow and too short. Joking and jeering, they stripped the tiara and the robes of office from the body, wrapped it up in an old carpet, and then with force of fists and feet rammed it down into the box, without torches, without a ministering priest, without a single person to attend and bear a consecrated candle." [2] Of such sort was the vigil kept by this solemn

[1] Vasari, p. 171.

[2] *Dispacci di Antonio Giustinian*, ed. P. Villari, Firenze, Le Monnier, 1876, vol. ii. pp. 124, 458.

statue, so dignified in grief and sweet in death, at the ignoble obsequies of him who, occupying the loftiest throne of Christendom, incarnated the least erected spirit of his age. The ivory-smooth white corpse of Christ in marble, set over against that festering corpse of his Vicar on earth, " black as a piece of cloth or the blackest mulberry," what a hideous contrast ! [1]

VII.

It may not be inappropriate to discuss the question of the Bruges Madonna here. This is a marble statue, well placed in a chapel of Notre Dame, relieved against a black marble niche, with excellent illumination from the side. The style is undoubtedly Michelangelesque, the execution careful, the surface-finish exquisite, and the type of the Madonna extremely similar to that of the Pietà at S. Peter's. She is seated in an attitude of almost haughty dignity, with the left foot raised upon a block of stone. The expression of her features is marked by something of sternness, which seems inherent in the model. Between her knees stands, half reclining, half as though wishing to

[1] Industrious and unimaginative scholars may do what they choose to whitewash Alexander VI., and excuse him on the score of his being a child of the age ; but they cannot annul the fact that this man, in all his appetites, acts, and ambitions, directly contradicted the principles for which Christ lived and died.

step downwards from the throne, her infant Son.
One arm rests upon his mother's knee ; the right
hand is thrown round to clasp her left. This
attitude gives grace of rhythm to the lines of his
nude body. True to the realism which controlled
Michelangelo at the commencement of his art
career, the head of Christ, who is but a child,
slightly overloads his slender figure. Physically
he resembles the Infant Christ of our National
Gallery picture, but has more of charm and sweetness. All these indications point to a genuine
product of Michelangelo's first Roman manner ; and
the position of the statue in a chapel ornamented
by the Bruges family of Mouscron renders the attribution almost certain.[1] However, we have only two
authentic records of the work among the documents
at our disposal. Condivi, describing the period
of Michelangelo's residence in Florence (1501–
1504), says : " He also cast in bronze a Madonna
with the Infant Christ, which certain Flemish
merchants of the house of Mouscron, a most noble
family in their own land, bought for two hundred
ducats, and sent to Flanders." [2] A letter addressed

[1] The external evidence in favour of its genuineness is also strong.
See *L'Œuvre et la Vie*, p. 253. Albert Dürer in 1521, and Marcus von
Waernewyck in 1560, both ascribe a Madonna in Notre Dame to
Michelangelo. We have, moreover, an original drawing by Michel-
angelo in the Taylor Gallery at Oxford, which was clearly made for it.
See Robinson's *Critical Account*, &c., p. 18.

[2] Condivi, p. 23. Vasari, following and altering Condivi's text,
alludes negligently to "a Madonna of bronze in a round, cast for
certain Flemish merchants of the Mouscron family" (Vasari, p. 176).

under date August 4, 1506, by Giovanni Balducci
in Rome to Michelangelo at Florence, proves that
some statue which was destined for Flanders remained among the sculptor's property at Florence.
Balducci uses the feminine gender in writing about
this work, which justifies us in thinking that it
may have been a Madonna. He says that he has
found a trustworthy agent to convey it to Viareggio,
and to ship it thence to Bruges, where it will be
delivered into the hands of the heir of John and
Alexander Mouscron and Co., "as being their property."[1] This statue, in all probability, is the
"Madonna in marble" about which Michelangelo
wrote to his father from Rome on the 31st of
January 1507, and which he begged his father to
keep hidden in their dwelling.[2] It is difficult to
reconcile Condivi's statement with Balducci's letter.
The former says that the Madonna bought by the
Mouscron family was cast in bronze at Florence.
The Madonna in the Mouscron Chapel at Notre
Dame is a marble. I think we may assume that
the Bruges Madonna is the piece which Michelangelo executed for the Mouscron brothers, and
that Condivi was wrong in believing it to have
been cast in bronze. That the statue was sent
some time after the order had been given, appears

[1] Gotti, ii. 51.
[2] Lettere, No. iii. Milanese conjectures that the "Madonna in
marble" was the little early bas-relief. But I do not see what reason
Michelangelo had for wishing that not to be seen.

from the fact that Balducci consigned it to the
heir of John and Alexander, "as being their property;" but it cannot be certain at what exact date
it was begun and finished.

VIII.

While Michelangelo was acquiring immediate
celebrity and immortal fame by these three statues,
so different in kind and hitherto unrivalled in
artistic excellence, his family lived somewhat
wretchedly at Florence. Lodovico had lost his
small post at the Customs after the expulsion of the
Medici ; and three sons, younger than the sculptor,
were now growing up. Buonarroto, born in 1477,
had been put to the cloth-trade, and was serving
under the Strozzi in their warehouse at the Porta
Rossa.[1] Giovan-Simone, two years younger (he was
born in 1479), after leading a vagabond life for
some while, joined Buonarroto in a cloth-business
provided for them by Michelangelo. He was a
worthless fellow, and gave his eldest brother much
trouble. Sigismondo, born in 1481, took to soldier-
ing ; but at the age of forty he settled down upon

---

[1] This actual engagement in trade was not considered unworthy of a
noble family at Florence. The mediæval ordinances of the Republic
even compelled burghers to enroll themselves under one or other of the
Guilds, to buy and sell, as a condition of their right to share in the
government.

the paternal farm at Settignano, and annoyed his brother by sinking into the condition of a common peasant.[1] The constant affection felt for these not very worthy relatives by Michelangelo is one of the finest traits in his character. They were continually writing begging letters, grumbling and complaining. He supplied them with funds, stinting himself in order to maintain them decently and to satisfy their wishes. But the more he gave, the more they demanded; and on one or two occasions, as we shall see in the course of this biography, their rapacity and ingratitude roused his bitterest indignation. Nevertheless, he did not swerve from the path of filial and brotherly kindness which his generous nature and steady will had traced. He remained the guardian of their interests, the cus-

[1] Up to the present date considerable uncertainty has rested upon the circumstances of Lodovico Buonarroti's two marriages. It did not seem clear whether Giovan-Simone and Sigismondo were not the sons of the second wife. Litta, in the *Famiglie Celebri*, throws no light on the point. Passerini, in the pedigree published by Gotti, vol. ii., represents the first wife, Francesca, as having died in 1497, while he assigns the marriage of Lucrezia, the second wife, to the year 1485—a gross and obvious blunder. Heath Wilson fixes 1497 as the date of Francesca's death, but is discreetly silent about the time of Lucrezia's marriage. Springer (vol. i. p. 7) adheres to 1485 as the date of the second marriage; but in the pedigree (ibid. p. 303) he represents the two younger sons, born in 1479 and 1481, as the children of the second wife, Lucrezia—also a gross and obvious blunder. I am now in a position to state upon documentary evidence that Francesca was married in 1472, and was the mother of all the five sons. Lucrezia was married in 1485, had no children, died in 1497, and was buried on July 9 in the Church of S. Croce. The registration of this burial in the Libro dei Morti (Archivio di Stato) was wrongly referred by Passerini to Francesca, the first wife. See documents in Appendix, No. I.

todian of their honour, and the builder of their fortunes to the end of his long life. The correspondence with his father and these brothers and a nephew, Lionardo, was published in full for the first time in 1875. It enables us to comprehend the true nature of the man better than any biographical notice ; and I mean to draw largely upon this source, so as gradually, by successive stipplings, as it were, to present a miniature portrait of one who was both admirable in private life and incomparable as an artist.

This correspondence opens in the year 1497. From a letter addressed to Lodovico under the date August 19, we learn that Buonarroto had just arrived in Rome, and informed his brother of certain pecuniary difficulties under which the family was labouring. Michelangelo gave advice, and promised to send all the money he could bring together. " Although, as I have told you, I am out of pocket myself, I will do my best to get money, in order that you may not have to borrow from the Monte, as Buonarroto says is possible.[1] Do not wonder if I have sometimes written irritable letters ; for I often suffer great distress of mind and temper, owing to matters which must happen to one who is away from home. . . . In spite of all this, I will send you what you ask for, even should I have to sell myself into slavery."[2]

[1] The Monte di Pietà was established as a state institution to lend money on security.
[2] Lettere, No. ii. p. 4.

Buonarroto must have paid a second visit to Rome; for we possess a letter from Lodovico to Michelangelo, under date December 19, 1500, which throws important light upon the latter's habits and designs. The old man begins by saying how happy he is to observe the love which Michelangelo bears his brothers. Then he speaks about the cloth business which Michelangelo intends to purchase for them. Afterwards, he proceeds as follows : "Buonarroto tells me that you live at Rome with great economy, or rather penuriousness. Now economy is good, but penuriousness is evil, seeing that it is a vice displeasing to God and men, and moreover injurious both to soul and body. So long as you are young, you will be able for a time to endure these hardships; but when the vigour of youth fails, then diseases and infirmities make their appearance; for these are caused by personal discomforts, mean living, and penurious habits. As I said, economy is good; but, above all things, shun stinginess. Live discreetly well, and see you have what is needful. Whatever happens, do not expose yourself to physical hardships; for in your profession, if you were once to fall ill (which God forbid), you would be a ruined man. Above all things, take care of your head, and keep it moderately warm, and see that you never wash : have yourself rubbed down, but do not wash."[1] This

[1] Gotti, p. 23. This advice is so peculiar that I will copy the original : "E non ti lavare mai ; fatti stropicciare e non ti lavare."

sordid way of life became habitual with Michelangelo. When he was dwelling at Bologna in 1506,
he wrote home to his brother Buonarroto: "With
regard to Giovan-Simone's proposed visit, I do not
advise him to come yet awhile, for I am lodged here
in one wretched room, and have bought a single
bed, in which we all four of us (i.e., himself and his
three workmen) sleep."[1] And again: "I am impatient to get away from this place, for my mode of
life here is so wretched, that if you only knew what
it is, you would be miserable."[2] The summer was
intensely hot at Bologna, and the plague broke out.
In these circumstances it seems miraculous that the
four sculptors in one bed escaped contagion. Michelangelo's parsimonious habits were not occasioned by
poverty or avarice. He accumulated large sums of
money by his labour, spent it freely on his family,
and exercised bountiful charity for the welfare of his
soul. We ought rather to ascribe them to some
constitutional peculiarity, affecting his whole temperament, and tinging his experience with despond-
ency and gloom. An absolute insensibility to merely
decorative details, to the loveliness of jewels, stuffs,
and natural objects, to flowers and trees and pleasant
landscapes, to everything, in short, which delighted
the Italians of that period, is a main characteristic
of his art. This abstraction and aridity, this ascetic
devotion of his genius to pure ideal form, this almost
mathematical conception of beauty, may be ascribed,

[1] Lettere, No. xlviii. p. 61.   [2] Lettere, No. lxxiv. p. 90.

I think, to the same psychological qualities which determined the dreary conditions of his home-life. He was no niggard either of money or of ideas; nay, even profligate of both. But melancholy made him miserly in all that concerned personal enjoyment; and he ought to have been born under that leaden planet Saturn rather than Mercury and Venus in the house of Jove. Condivi sums up his daily habits thus : " He has always been extremely temperate in living, using food more because it was necessary than for any pleasure he took in it ; especially when he was engaged upon some great work ; for then he usually confined himself to a piece of bread, which he ate in the middle of his labour. However, for some time past, he has been living with more regard to health, his advanced age putting this constraint upon his natural inclination. Often have I heard him say : ' Ascanio, rich as I may have been, I have always lived like a poor man.' And this abstemiousness in food he has practised in sleep also ; for sleep, according to his own account, rarely suits his constitution, since he continually suffers from pains in the head during slumber, and any excessive amount of sleep deranges his stomach. While he was in full vigour, he generally went to bed with his clothes on, even to the tall boots, which he has always worn, because of a chronic tendency to cramp, as well as for other reasons. At certain seasons he has kept these boots on for such a length of time, that when he drew them off the skin came away together with the leather, like that of a sloughing snake. He was never stingy of cash, nor did he accumulate money, being content with just enough to keep him decently ; wherefore, though innumerable lords and rich folk have made him splendid offers for some specimen of his craft, he rarely complied, and then, for the most part, more out of kindness and friendship than with any expectation of gain." [1] In spite of all this, or rather because of his temperance in food and sleep and sexual pleasure, together with his manual industry, he preserved excellent health into old age.

I have thought it worth while to introduce this general review of Michelangelo's habits, without omitting some details which may seem repulsive to the modern reader, at an early period of his biography, because we ought to carry with us through the vicissitudes of his long career and many labours an accurate conception of our hero's personality. For this reason it may not be unprofitable to repeat what Condivi says about his physical appearance in the last years of his life. "Michelangelo is of a good complexion ; more muscular and bony than fat or fleshy in his person : healthy above all things, as well by reason of his natural constitution as of the exercise he takes, and habitual continence in food and sexual indulgence. Nevertheless, he was a weakly child, and has suffered two illnesses in manhood. His

[1] Condivi, p. 81.

countenance always showed a good and wholesome colour. Of stature he is as follows: height middling; broad in the shoulders; the rest of the body somewhat slender in proportion. The shape of his face is oval, the space above the ears being one sixth higher than a semicircle. Consequently the temples project beyond the ears, and the ears beyond the cheeks, and these beyond the rest; so that the skull, in relation to the whole head, must be called large. The forehead, seen in front, is square; the nose, a little flattened—not by nature, but because, when he was a young boy, Torrigiano de' Torrigiani, a brutal and insolent fellow, smashed in the cartilage with his fist. Michelangelo was carried home half dead on this occasion; and Torrigiano, having been exiled from Florence for his violence, came to a bad end. The nose, however, being what it is, bears a proper proportion to the forehead and the rest of the face. The lips are thin, but the lower is slightly thicker than the upper; so that, seen in profile, it projects a little. The chin is well in harmony with the features I have described. The forehead, in a side-view, almost hangs over the nose; and this looks hardly less than broken, were it not for a trifling protuberance in the middle. The eyebrows are not thick with hair; the eyes may even be called small, of a colour like horn, but speckled and stained with spots of bluish yellow. The ears in good proportion; hair of the head black, as also the beard, except that both are now grizzled by old age ; the beard double-forked, about five inches long, and not very bushy, as may partly be observed in his portrait."

We have no contemporary account of Michelangelo in early manhood; but the tenor of his life was so even, and, unlike Cellini, he moved so constantly upon the same lines and within the same sphere of patient self-reserve, that it is not difficult to reconstruct the young and vigorous sculptor out of this detailed description by his loving friend and servant in old age. Few men, notably few artists, have preserved that continuity of moral, intellectual, and physical development in one unbroken course which is the specific characterisation of Michelangelo. As years advanced, his pulses beat less quickly and his body shrank. But the man did not alter. With the same lapse of years, his style grew drier and more abstract, but it did not alter in quality or depart from its ideal. He seems to me in these respects to be like Milton : wholly unlike the plastic and assimilative genius of a Raphael.

CHAPTER III.

I.

Michelangelo returned to Florence in the spring of 1501. Condivi says that domestic affairs compelled him to leave Rome, and the correspondence with his father makes this not improbable. He brought a heightened reputation back to his native city. The Bacchus and the Madonna della Febbre had placed him in advance of any sculptor of his time. Indeed, in these first years of the sixteenth century he may be said to have been the only Tuscan sculptor of commanding eminence.[1] Ghiberti, Della Quercia, Brunelleschi, Donatello, all had joined the majority before his birth. The second group of distinguished craftsmen—Verocchio, Luca della Robbia, Rossellino, Da Maiano, Civitali, Desiderio da Settignano—expired at the commencement of the century. It seemed as though a gap in the ranks of plastic artists had purposely been made for the entrance of a predominant and tyrannous personality. Jacopo Tatti, called Sansovino, was the only man who might have disputed the place of pre-eminence with Michelangelo, and Sansovino chose Venice for the theatre of his life-labours. In these circumstances, it is not singular that commissions speedily began to overtax the busy sculptor's power of execution. I do not mean to assert that the Italians, in the year 1501, were conscious of Michelangelo's unrivalled qualities, or sensitive to the corresponding limitations which rendered these qualities eventually baneful to the evolution of the arts; but they could not help feeling that in this young man of twenty-six they possessed a first-rate craftsman, and one who had no peer among contemporaries.

The first order of this year came from the Cardinal

[1] What his contemporaries thought of him may be seen from a letter of Piero Soderini to the Marchese Alberigo Malaspina of Massa (Gaye, ii. 107) : " Non essendo homo in Italia apto ad expedire una opera di cotesta qualità, è necessario che lui solo, e non altro," &c.

Francesco Piccolomini, who was afterwards elected
Pope in 1503, and who died after reigning three
weeks with the title of Pius III.   He wished to
decorate the Piccolomini Chapel in the Duomo of
Siena with fifteen statues of male saints.   A contract
was signed on June 5, by which Michelangelo agreed
to complete these figures within the space of three
years.   One of them, a S. Francis, had been already
begun by Piero Torrigiano; and this, we have some
reason to believe, was finished by the master's hand.
Accounts differ about his share in the remaining
fourteen statues; but the matter is of no great
moment, seeing that the style of the work is conventional, and the scale of the figures disagreeably
squat and dumpy.   It seems almost impossible that
these ecclesiastical and tame pieces should have
been produced at the same time as the David and
by the same hand.   Neither Vasari nor Condivi
speaks about them, although it is certain that Michelangelo was held bound to his contract during several
years.   Upon the death of Pius III., he renewed it
with the Pope's heirs, Jacopo and Andrea Piccolomini, by a deed dated September 15, 1504; and in
1537 Anton Maria Piccolomini, to whom the inheritance succeeded, considered himself Michelangelo's
creditor for the sum of a hundred crowns, which had
been paid beforehand for work not finished by the
sculptor.[1]

[1] The documents upon which these transactions rest will be found in
G. Milanesi's *Documenti per la Storia dell' Arte Senese.*   Siena : Porri,

A far more important commission was intrusted to Michelangelo in August of the same year, 1501. Condivi, after mentioning his return to Florence, tells the history of the colossal David in these words: " Here he stayed some time, and made the statue which stands in front of the great door of the Palace of the Signory, and is called the Giant by all people. It came about in this way. The Board of Works at S. Maria del Fiore owned a piece of marble nine cubits in height, which had been brought from Carrara some hundred years before by a sculptor insufficiently acquainted with his art. This was evident, inasmuch as, wishing to convey it more conveniently and with less labour, he had it blocked out in the quarry, but in such a manner that neither he nor any one else was capable of extracting a statue from the block, either of the same size, or even on a much smaller scale. The marble being, then, useless for any good purpose, Andrea del Monte San Savino thought that he might get possession of it from the Board, and begged them to make him a present of it, promising that he would add certain pieces of stone and carve a statue from it. Before they made up their minds to give it, they sent for Michelangelo; then, after explaining the wishes and the views of Andrea, and considering his own opinion that it would be

1856, vol. iii. A drawing of a bearded saint, heavily draped, cowled, and holding a book in his left hand, now at the British Museum, is ascribed to Michelangelo. It may have been made for one of the Piccolomini statues.

possible to extract a good thing from the block, they finally offered it to him. Michelangelo accepted, added no pieces, and got the statue out so exactly, that, as any one may see, in the top of the head and at the base some vestiges of the rough surface of the marble still remain. He did the same in other works, as, for instance, in the Contemplative Life upon the tomb of Julius; indeed, it is a sign left by masters on their work, proving them to be absolute in their art. But in the David it was much more remarkable, for this reason, that the difficulty of the task was not overcome by adding pieces; and also he had to contend with an ill-shaped marble. As he used to say himself, it is impossible, or at least, extraordinarily difficult, in statuary to set right the faults of the blocking out. He received for this work 400 ducats. and carried it out in eighteen months."

The sculptor who had spoiled this block of marble is called "Maestro Simone" by Vasari; but the abundant documents in our possession, by aid of which we are enabled to trace the whole history of Michelangelo's David with minuteness, show that Vasari was misinformed.[1] The real culprit was Agostino di Antonio di Duccio, or Guccio, who had succeeded with another colossal statue for the Duomo.[2] He is honourably known in the history of Tuscan sculpture by his reliefs upon the façade of

[1] These documents will be found in Gaye, vol. ii. pp. 454–464.
[2] See Gaye, vol. ii. pp. 465–468.

the Duomo at Modena, describing episodes in the life of S. Gemignano, by the romantically charming reliefs in marble, with terracotta settings, on the Oratory of S. Bernardino at Perugia, and by a large amount of excellent surface-work in stone upon the chapels of S. Francesco at Rimini.[1] We gather from one of the contracts with Agostino that the marble was originally blocked out for some prophet.[2] But Michelangelo resolved to make a David; and two wax models, now preserved in the Museo Buonarroti, neither of which corresponds exactly with the statue as it exists, show that he felt able to extract a colossal figure in various attitudes from the damaged block. In the first contract signed between the Consuls of the Arte della Lana, the Operai del Duomo, and the sculptor, dated August 16, 1501, the terms are thus settled : " That the worthy master Michelangelo, son of Lodovico Buonarroti, citizen of Florence, has been chosen to fashion, complete, and finish to perfection that male statue called the

---

[1] Agostino was born in 1418. He worked at Modena in 1442, and in 1446 was banished on a charge of theft from Florence. Yriarte conjectures that after this date he laboured at Rimini, ascribing to him the bas-reliefs of the planets and the zodiac in the Chapel of the S. Sacrament, together with the *stiacciato* decorations of the Chapel of S. Sigismond and those of the Chapel of S. Gaudenzio, all in the Temple of the Malatesta family. Between 1459 and 1461 he worked at Perugia. The Operai del Duomo at Florence commissioned the Colossus in 1464, and withdrew their order in 1466. He died after 1481. See Yriarte, *Rimini*. Paris : Rothschild, 1882, p. 407, &c.

[2] "Locaverunt Aghostino Ghucci, scultori, cit. flor., unam figuram di marmo bianclo a chavare a Charara di braccia nove, a ghuisa di guglante, in vece e nome di . . . profeta."

Giant, of nine cubits in height,[1] now existing in the workshop of the cathedral, blocked out aforetime by Master Agostino of Florence, and badly blocked; and that the work shall be completed within the term of the next ensuing two years, dating from September, at a salary of six golden florins per month;[2] and that what is needful for the accomplishment of this task, as workmen, timbers, &c., which he may require, shall be supplied him by the Operai; and when the statue is finished, the Consuls and Operai who shall be in office shall estimate whether he deserve a larger recompense, and this shall be left to their consciences."

II.

Michelangelo began to work on a Monday morning, September 13, in a wooden shed erected for the purpose, not far from the cathedral. On the 28th of February 1502, the statue, which is now called for the first time " the Giant, or David," was brought so far forward that the judges declared it to be half finished, and decided that the sculptor should be paid in all 400 golden florins, including the stipulated salary. He seems to have laboured assidu-

---

[1] The Florentine *braccio* is said to be fifty-nine centimètres. The English cubit is eighteen inches.

[2] Gotti estimates six florins at 57.60 in francs, or about £2, 6s.

DAVID, marble, 1504. Galleria dell'Accademia,
Florence. Alinari/Art Resource, NY.

ously during the next two years, for by a minute of the 25th of January 1504 the David is said to be almost entirely finished.   On this date a solemn council of the most important artists resident in Florence was convened at the Opera del Duomo to consider where it should be placed.

We possess full minutes of this meeting, and they are so curious that I shall not hesitate to give a somewhat detailed account of the proceedings.[1] Messer Francesco Filarete, the chief herald of the Signory, and himself an architect of some pretensions, opened the discussion in a short speech to this effect : "I have turned over in my mind those suggestions which my judgment could afford me. You have two places where the statue may be set up : the first, that where the Judith stands; the second, in the middle of the courtyard where the David is.[2]   The first might be selected, because the Judith is an omen of evil, and no fit object where it stands, we having the cross and lily for our ensign ; besides, it is not proper that the woman should kill the male ; and, above all, this statue was erected under an evil constellation, since you have gone continually from bad to worse since then.   Pisa has been lost too.   The David of the courtyard is imperfect in the right leg ; and so I should counsel you to put the Giant in one of these places, but I

[1] Gaye, ii. 455.

[2] Donatello's Judith used to stand outside the great door of the Palazzo Vecchio, where the David was eventually placed. A bronze David by Donatello stood in the court of the Palazzo.

give the preference myself to that of the Judith."
The herald, it will be perceived, took for granted
that Michelangelo's David would be erected in the
immediate neighbourhood of the Palazzo Vecchio.
The next speaker, Francesco Monciatto, a wood-
carver, advanced the view that it ought to be placed
in front of the Duomo, where the Colossus was
originally meant to be put up. He was immediately
followed, and his resolution was seconded, by no less
personages than the painters Cosimo Rosselli and
Sandro Botticelli. Then Giuliano da San Gallo, the
illustrious architect, submitted a third opinion to
the meeting. He began his speech by observing
that he agreed with those who wished to choose the
steps of the Duomo, but due consideration caused
him to alter his mind. "The imperfection of the
marble, which is softened by exposure to the air,
rendered the durability of the statue doubtful. He
therefore voted for the middle of the Loggia dei
Lanzi, where the David would be under cover."
Messer Angelo di Lorenzo Manfidi, second herald
of the Signory, rose to state a professional objection.
"The David, if erected under the middle arch of the
Loggia, would break the order of the ceremonies
practised there by the Signory and other magis-
trates. He therefore proposed that the arch facing
the Palazzo (where Donatello's Judith is now)
should be chosen." The three succeeding speakers,
people of no great importance, gave their votes in
favour of the chief herald's resolution. Others

followed San Gallo, among whom was the illustrious
Lionardo da Vinci. He thought the statue could
be placed under the middle arch of the Loggia
without hindrance to ceremonies of state. Salvestro,
a jeweller, and Filippino Lippi, the painter, were
of opinion that the neighbourhood of the Palazzo
should be adopted, but that the precise spot should
be left to the sculptor's choice. Gallieno, an em-
broiderer, and David Ghirlandajo, the painter, suggested a new place—namely, where the lion or
Marzocco stood on the Piazza. Antonio da San
Gallo, the architect, and Michelangelo, the goldsmith, father of Baccio Bandinelli, supported Giuliano da San Gallo's motion. Then Giovanni Piffero—
that is, the father of Benvenuto Cellini—brought the
discussion back to the courtyard of the palace. He
thought that in the Loggia the statue would be
only partly seen, and that it would run risks of
injury from scoundrels. Giovanni delle Corniole,
the incomparable gem-cutter, who has left us the
best portrait of Savonarola, voted with the two San
Galli, " because he hears the stone is soft." Piero
di Cosimo, the painter, and teacher of Andrea del
Sarto, wound up the speeches with a strong recommendation that the choice of the exact spot should
be left to Michelangelo Buonarroti. This was eventually decided on, and he elected to have his David
set up in the place preferred by the chief herald—
that is to say, upon the steps of the Palazzo Vecchio,
on the right side of the entrance.

The next thing was to get the mighty mass of sculptured marble safely moved from the Duomo to the Palazzo. On the 1st of April, Simone del Pollajuolo, called Il Cronaca, was commissioned to make the necessary preparations; but later on, upon the 30th, we find Antonio da San Gallo, Baccio d'Agnolo, Bernardo della Ciecha, and Michelangelo associated with him in the work of transportation. An enclosure of stout beams and planks was made and placed on movable rollers. In the middle of this the statue hung suspended, with a certain liberty of swaying to the shocks and lurches of the vehicle. More than forty men were employed upon the windlasses which drew it slowly forward. In a contemporary record we possess a full account of the transit:[1] "On the 14th of May 1504, the marble Giant was taken from the Opera. It came out at 24 o'clock, and they broke the wall above the gateway enough to let it pass. That night some stones were thrown at the Colossus with intent to harm it. Watch had to be kept at night; and it made way very slowly, bound as it was upright, suspended in the air with enormous beams and intricate machinery of ropes. It took four days to reach the Piazza, arriving on the 18th at the hour of 12. More than forty men were employed to make it go; and there were fourteen rollers joined beneath it, which were changed from hand to hand. Afterwards, they worked until the 8th of June

[1] Gaye, vol. ii. p. 464.

1504 to place it on the platform (*ringhiera*) where the Judith used to stand. The Judith was removed and set upon the ground within the palace. The said Giant was the work of Michelangelo Buonarroti." [1]

Where the masters of Florence placed it, under the direction of its maker, Michelangelo's great white David stood for more than three centuries uncovered, open to all injuries of frost and rain, and to the violence of citizens, until, for the better preservation of this masterpiece of modern art, it was removed in 1873 to a hall of the Accademia delle Belle Arti.[2]   On the whole, it has suffered very little.   Weather has slightly worn away the extremities of the left foot; and in 1527, during a popular tumult, the left arm was broken by a huge stone cast by the assailants of the palace.   Giorgio Vasari tells us how, together with his friend Cecchino Salviati, he collected the scattered pieces, and brought them to the house of Michelangelo Salviati, the father of Cecchino.[3]   They were subsequently put together by the care of the Grand Duke Cosimo, and restored to the statue in the year 1543.[4]

[1] In a note to Gotti, vol. i. p. 29, there is another interesting account of this transit of the David, from the MS. *Stor. Fior.* of Pietro Parenti.

[2] For a full account of this transaction, see Gotti, vol. ii. pp. 35–51.

[3] Vasari, vol. xii. p. 49.   [4] Gotti, vol. i. p. 31.

III.

In the David Michelangelo first displayed that quality of *terribilità,* of spirit-quailing, awe-inspiring force, for which he afterwards became so famous. The statue imposes, not merely by its size and majesty and might, but by something vehement in the conception. He was, however, far from having yet adopted those systematic proportions for the human body which later on gave an air of monotonous impressiveness to all his figures. On the contrary, this young giant strongly recalls the model; still more strongly indeed than the Bacchus did. Wishing perhaps to adhere strictly to the Biblical story, Michelangelo studied a lad whose frame was not developed. The David, to state the matter frankly, is a colossal hobbledehoy. His body, in breadth of the thorax, depth of the abdomen, and general stoutness, has not grown up to the scale of the enormous hands and feet and heavy head. We feel that he wants at least two years to become a fully developed man, passing from adolescence to the maturity of strength and beauty. This close observance of the imperfections of the model at a certain stage of physical growth is very remarkable, and not altogether pleasing in a statue more than nine feet high. Both Donatello and Verocchio had treated their Davids in the same realistic manner, but they were working on a small scale and in bronze. I insist upon this point, because students of Michelangelo have been apt to overlook his extreme sincerity and naturalism in the first stages of his career.

Having acknowledged that the head of David is too massive and the extremities too largely formed for ideal beauty, hypercriticism can hardly find fault with the modelling and execution of each part. The attitude selected is one of great dignity and vigour. The heroic boy, quite certain of victory, is excited by the coming contest. His brows are violently contracted, the nostrils tense and quivering, the eyes fixed keenly on the distant Philistine. His larynx rises visibly, and the sinews of his left thigh tighten, as though the whole spirit of the man were braced for a supreme endeavour. In his right hand, kept at a just middle point between the hip and knee, he holds the piece of wood on which his sling is hung. The sling runs round his back, and the centre of it, where the stone bulges, is held with the left hand, poised upon the left shoulder, ready to be loosed. We feel that the next movement will involve the right hand straining to its full extent the sling, dragging the stone away, and whirling it into the air; when, after it has sped to strike Goliath in the forehead, the whole lithe body of the lad will have described a curve, and recovered its perpendicular position on the two firm legs. Michelangelo invariably chose some decisive moment in the action he had to represent; and though he was working here under difficulties, owing to the limitations of the damaged block at his disposal, he contrived to suggest the imminence of swift and sudden energy which shall disturb the equilibrium of his young giant's pose. Critics of this statue, deceived by its superficial resemblance to some Greek athletes at rest, have neglected the candid realism of the momentary act foreshadowed. They do not understand the meaning of the sling. Even Heath Wilson, for instance, writes: "The massive shoulders are thrown back, the right arm is pendent, and *the right hand grasps resolutely the stone* with which the adversary is to be slain."[1] This entirely falsifies the sculptor's motive, misses the meaning of the sling, renders the broad strap behind the back superfluous, and changes into mere plastic symbolism what Michelangelo intended to be a moment caught from palpitating life.

It has often been remarked that David's head is modelled upon the type of Donatello's S. George at Orsanmichele. The observation is just; and it suggests a comment on the habit Michelangelo early formed of treating the face idealistically, however much he took from study of his models. Vasari, for example, says that he avoided portraiture, and composed his faces by combining several individuals. We shall see a new ideal type of the male head

---

[1] Heath Wilson, p. 51. Springer, and indeed all critics, make the same mistake.

emerge in a group of statues, among which the most distinguished is Giuliano de' Medici at San Lorenzo. We have already seen a female type created in the Madonnas of S. Peter's and Notre Dame at Bruges. But this is not the place to discuss Michelangelo's theory of form in general. That must be reserved until we enter the Sistine Chapel, in order to survey the central and the crowning product of his genius in its prime.

We have every reason to believe that Michelangelo carved his David with no guidance but drawings and a small wax model of about eighteen inches in heig'ht. The inconvenience of this method, which left the sculptor to wreak his fury on the marble with mallet and chisel, can be readily conceived. In a famous passage, disinterred by M. Mariette from a French scholar of the sixteenth century, we have this account of the fiery master's system :[1] " I am able to affirm that I have seen Michelangelo, at the age of more than sixty years, and not the strongest for his time of life, knock off more chips from an extremely hard marble in one quarter of an hour than three young stone-cutters could have done in three or four—a thing quite incredible to one who has not seen it. He put such impetuosity and fury into his work, that I thought the whole must fly to pieces; hurling to the ground at one blow great fragments three or

[1] Condivi, p. 188. Mariette quotes from Blaise de Vigenere's annotations to the Images of Philostratus.

four inches thick, shaving the line so closely, that if he had overpassed it by a hair's-breadth, he ran the risk of losing all, since one cannot mend a marble afterwards or repair mistakes, as one does with figures of clay and stucco." It is said that, owing to this violent way of attacking his marble, Michelangelo sometimes bit too deep into the stone, and had to abandon a promising piece of sculpture. This is one of the ways of accounting for his numerous unfinished statues. Accordingly a myth has sprung up representing the great master as working in solitude upon huge blocks, with nothing but a sketch in wax before him. Fact is always more interesting than fiction ; and, while I am upon the topic of his method, I will introduce what Cellini has left written on this subject. In his treatise on the Art of Sculpture, Cellini lays down the rule that sculptors in stone ought first to make a little model two palms high, and after this to form another as large as the statue will have to be.[1] He illustrates this by a critique of his illustrious predecessors. "Albeit many able artists rush boldly on the stone with the fierce force of mallet and chisel, relying on the little model and a good design, yet the result is never found by them to be so satisfactory as when they fashion the model on a large scale. This is proved by our Donatello, who was a Titan in the art, and afterwards by

[1] *I Trattati dell' Oreficeria, etc., di Benvenuto Cellini.* Firenze : Le Monnier, 1857, p. 197.

the stupendous Michelangelo, who worked in both ways. Discovering latterly that the small models fell far short of what his excellent genius demanded, he adopted the habit of making most careful models exactly of the same size as the marble statue was to be. This we have seen with our own eyes in the Sacristy of S. Lorenzo. Next, when a man is satisfied with his full-sized model, he must take charcoal, and sketch out the main view of his figure on the marble in such wise that it shall be distinctly traced; for he who has not previously settled his design may sometimes find himself deceived by the chiselling irons. Michelangelo's method in this matter was the best. He used first to sketch in the principal aspect, and then to begin work by removing the surface stone upon that side, just as if he intended to fashion a figure in half-relief; and thus he went on gradually uncovering the rounded form."

Vasari, speaking of four rough-hewn Captives, possibly the figures now in a grotto of the Boboli Gardens, says:[1] "They are well adapted for teaching a beginner how to extract statues from the marble without injury to the stone. The safe method which they illustrate may be described as follows. You first take a model in wax or some other hard material, and place it lying in a vessel full of water. The water, by its nature, presents a level surface; so that, if you gradually lift the model, the higher parts are first exposed, while the

[1] Vasari, xii. 273.

lower parts remain submerged ; and proceeding thus, the whole round shape at length appears above the water.　Precisely in the same way ought statues to be hewn out from the marble with the chisel; first uncovering the highest surfaces, and proceeding to disclose the lowest.　This method was followed by Michelangelo while blocking out the Captives, and therefore his Excellency the Duke was fain to have them used as models by the students in his Academy."　It need hardly be remarked that the ingenious process of "pointing the marble" by means of the "pointing machine" and "scale-stones," which is at present universally in use among sculptors, had not been invented in the six-teenth century.

IV.

I cannot omit a rather childish story which Vasari tells about the David.[1]　After it had been placed upon its pedestal before the palace, and while the scaffolding was still there, Piero Soderini, who loved and admired Michelangelo, told him that he thought the nose too large.　The sculptor immediately ran up the ladder till he reached a point upon the level of the giant's shoulder.　He then took his hammer and chisel, and, having concealed some dust of marble in the hollow of his

[1] Vasari, xii. 174.

hand, pretended to work off a portion from the surface of the nose. In reality he left it as he found it;
but Soderini, seeing the marble dust fall scattering
through the air, thought that his hint had been
taken. When, therefore, Michelangelo called down
to him, "Look at it now!" Soderini shouted up in
reply, "I am far more pleased with it; you have
given life to the statue."

At this time Piero Soderini, a man of excellent
parts and sterling character, though not gifted with
that mixture of audacity and cunning which impressed the Renaissance imagination, was Gonfalonier of the Republic. He had been elected to
the supreme magistracy for life, and was practically
Doge of Florence. His friendship proved on more
than one occasion of some service to Michelangelo;
and while the gigantic David was in progress he
gave the sculptor a new commission, the history of
which must now engage us.[1] The Florentine envoys
to France had already written in June 1501 from
Lyons, saying that Pierre de Rohan, Maréchal de
Gié, who stood high in favour at the court of Louis
XII., greatly desired a copy of the bronze David by
Donatello in the courtyard of the Palazzo Vecchio.
He appeared willing to pay for it, but the envoys
thought that he expected to have it as a present.
The French alliance was a matter of the highest

---

[1] The documents relating to this bronze David will be found in Gaye,
vol. ii. pp. 52, 55, 58–61, &c., down to 109. The whole series of events
is well described in *L'Œuvre et la Vie*, pp. 242 et seq.

importance to Florence, and at this time the Republic was heavily indebted to the French crown. Soderini, therefore, decided to comply with the Marshal's request, and on the 12th of August 1502 Michelangelo undertook to model a David of two cubits and a quarter within six months.[1] In the bronze-casting he was assisted by a special master, Benedetto da Rovezzano.[2] During the next two years a brisk correspondence was kept up between the envoys and the Signory about the statue, showing the Marshal's impatience. Meanwhile De Rohan became Duke of Nemours in 1503 by his marriage with a sister of Louis d'Armagnac, and shortly afterwards he fell into disgrace. Nothing more was to be expected from him at the court of Blois. But the statue was in progress, and the question arose to whom it should be given. The choice of the Signory fell on Florimond Robertet, secretary of finance, whose favour would be useful to the Florentines in their pecuniary transactions with the King. A long letter from the envoy, Francesco Pandolfini, in September 1505, shows that Robertet's mind had been sounded on the subject; and we gather from a minute of the Signory, dated November 6, 1508,

---

[1] There is every reason to suppose that this David was an original work ; but whether Donatello's bronze David was also copied does not appear. Condivi (p. 22) says : " At the request of his great friend Piero Soderini he cast a life-size statue, which was sent to France, and also a David with Goliath beneath his feet. That which one sees in the courtyard of the Palazzo de' Signori is by the hand of Donatello."

[2] See Vasari, xii. 350.

that at last the bronze David, weighing about 800 pounds, had been "packed in the name of God" and sent to Signa on its way to Leghorn. Robertet received it in due course, and placed it in the courtyard of his chateau of Bury, near Blois. Here it remained for more than a century, when it was removed to the chateau of Villeroy. There it disappeared. We possess, however, a fine pen-and-ink drawing by the hand of Michelangelo, which may well have been a design for this second David.[1] The muscular and naked youth, not a mere lad like the colossal statue, stands firmly posed upon his left leg with the trunk thrown boldly back. His right foot rests on the gigantic head of Goliath, and his left hand, twisted back upon the buttock, holds what seems meant for the sling. We see here what Michelangelo's conception of an ideal David would have been when working under conditions more favourable than the damaged block afforded. On the margin of the page the following words may be clearly traced: "Davicte cholla fromba e io chollarcho Michelagniolo,"—David with the sling, and I with the bow.[2]

Meanwhile Michelangelo received a still more

---

[1] In the Louvre. Part of the drawing is engraved on p. 243 of *L'Œuvre et la Vie.*

[2] What is meant by *the bow* I cannot guess. It seems, however, that Michelangelo was meditating verses, for lower down we read *Roct' è lalta cholonna* (first words of Petrarch's sonnet, 2, In M. di M. L.) The Italians say *Con l'arco della schiena* when they wish to express "with all one's might."

important commission on the 24th of April 1503. The Consuls of the Arte della Lana and the Operai of the Duomo ordered twelve Apostles, each 4¼ cubits high, to be carved out of Carrara marble and placed inside the church. The sculptor undertook to furnish one each year, the Board of Works defraying all expenses, supplying the costs of Michelangelo's living and his assistants, and paying him two golden florins a month. Besides this, they had a house built for him in the Borgo Pinti after Il Cronaca's design.[1] He occupied this house free of charges while he was in Florence, until it became manifest that the contract of 1503 would never be carried out. Later on, in March 1508, the tenement was let on lease to him and his heirs. But he only held it a few months; for on the 15th of June the lease was cancelled, and the house transferred to Sigismondo Martelli.

The only trace surviving of these twelve Apostles is the huge blocked-out S. Matteo, now in the court-yard of the Accademia. Vasari writes of it as follows: "He also began a statue in marble of S. Matteo, which, though it is but roughly hewn, shows perfection of design, and teaches sculptors how to extract figures from the stone without exposing them to injury, always gaining ground by removing the superfluous material, and being able to withdraw or change in case of need."[2] This stupendous sketch or shadow of a mighty form is

[1] Gaye, vol. ii. pp. 92, 473–478.   [2] Vasari, xii. 177.

indeed instructive for those who would understand Michelangelo's method. It fully illustrates the passages quoted above from Cellini and Vasari, showing how a design of the chief view of the statue must have been chalked upon the marble, and how the unfinished figure gradually emerged into relief. Were we to place it in a horizontal position on the ground, that portion of the rounded form which has been disengaged from the block would emerge just in the same way as a model from a bath of water not quite deep enough to cover it. At the same time we learn to appreciate the observations of Vigenere while we study the titanic chisel-marks, grooved deeply in the body of the stone, and carried to the length of three or four inches. The direction of these strokes proves that Michelangelo worked equally with both hands, and the way in which they are hatched and crossed upon the marble reminds one of the pen-drawing of a bold draughtsman. The mere surface-handling of the stone has remarkable affinity in linear effect to a pair of the master's pen-designs for a naked man, now in the Louvre. On paper he seems to hew with the pen, on marble to sketch with the chisel. The saint appears literally to be growing out of his stone prison, as though he were alive and enclosed there waiting to be liberated. This recalls Michelangelo's fixed opinion regarding sculpture, which he defined as the art " that works by force of taking away." [1] In

[1] Lettere, No. cdlxii.

his writings we often find the idea expressed that a statue, instead of being a human thought invested with external reality by stone, is more truly to be regarded as something which the sculptor seeks and finds inside his marble—a kind of marvellous discovery. Thus he says in one of his poems:[1] "Lady, in hard and craggy stone the mere removal of the surface gives being to a figure, which ever grows the more the stone is hewn away." And again[2]—

> The best of artists hath no thought to show
> Which the rough stone in its superfluous shell
> Doth not include: to break the marble spell
> Is all the hand that serves the brain can do.

S. Matthew seems to palpitate with life while we scrutinise the amorphous block; and yet there is little there more tangible than some such form as fancy loves to image in the clouds.

To conclude what I have said in this section about Michelangelo's method of working on the marble, I must confirm what I have stated about his using both left and right hand while chiselling. Raffaello da Montelupo, who was well acquainted with him personally, informs us of the fact:[3] "Here I may mention that I am in the habit of drawing with my left hand, and that once, at Rome,

---

[1] Madrigale xii., *Rime*, p. 37.　　[2] Sonnet xv., *Rime*, p. 173.

[3] This passage occurs in Montelupo's autobiography, the original of which may be found in Barbèra's diamond edition of Italian classics. *Autobiografie*, ed. A. D'Ancona, 1859. I have borrowed the above translation from Perkins's *Tuscan Sculptors*, vol. ii. p. 74.

while I was sketching the Arch of Trajan from the Colosseum, Michelangelo and Sebastiano del Piombo, both of whom were naturally left-handed (although they did not work with the left hand excepting when they wished to use great strength), stopped to see me, and expressed great wonder, no sculptor or painter ever having done so before me, as far as I know."

V.

If Vasari can be trusted, it was during this residence at Florence, when his hands were so fully occupied, that Michelangelo found time to carve the two *tondi*, Madonnas in relief enclosed in circular spaces, which we still possess. One of them, made for Taddeo Taddei, is now at Burlington House, having been acquired by the Royal Academy through the medium of Sir George Beaumont. This ranks among the best things belonging to that Corporation.[1] The other, made for Bartolommeo Pitti, will be found in the Palazzo del Bargello at Florence. Of the two, that of our Royal Academy is the more ambitious in design, combining singular grace and dignity in the Madonna with action playfully suggested in the infant Christ and little S. John. That of the Bargello is simpler, more tranquil, and more

---

[1] The bas-relief has been cast, and used to be on sale at Brucciani's, but I know of no photographic reproduction from the original.

stately. The one recalls the motive of the Bruges Madonna, the other almost anticipates the Delphic Sibyl. We might fancifully call them a pair of native pearls or uncut gems, lovely by reason even of their sketchiness. Whether by intention, as some critics have supposed,[1] or for want of time to finish, as I am inclined to believe, these two reliefs are left in a state of incompleteness which is highly suggestive. Taking the Royal Academy group first; the absolute roughness of the groundwork supplies an admirable background to the figures, which seem to emerge from it as though the whole of them were there, ready to be disentangled. The most important portions of the composition—Madonna's head and throat, the drapery of her powerful breast, on which the child Christ reclines, and the naked body of the boy—are wrought to a point which only demands finish. Yet parts of these two figures remain undetermined. Christ's feet are still imprisoned in the clinging marble ; his left arm and hand are only indicated, and his right hand is resting on a mass of broken stone, which hides a portion of his mother's drapery, but leaves the position of her hand uncertain. The infant S. John, upright upon his feet, balancing the chief group, is hazily subordinate. The whole of his form looms blurred through the veil of stone, and what his two hands and arms are doing with the hidden right arm and hand of the

[1] Mr. Pater, *Studies in the History of the Renaissance*, and M. Guillaume, *L'Œuvre et la Vie*, for instance.

Virgin may hardly be conjectured.   It is clear that on this side of the composition the marble was to have been more deeply cut, and that we have the highest surfaces of the relief brought into prominence at those points where, as I have said, little is wanting but the finish of the graver and the file.   The Bargello group is simpler and more intelligible.   Its composition by masses being quite apparent, we can easily construct the incomplete figure of S. John in the background.   What results from the study of these two circular sketches in marble is, that although Michelangelo believed all sculpture to be imperfect in so far as it approached the style of painting,[1] yet he did not disdain to labour in stone with various planes of relief which should produce the effect of chiaroscuro.   Furthermore, they illustrate what Cellini and Vasari have already taught us about his method.   He refused to work by piece-meal, but began by disengaging the first, the second, then the third surfaces, following a model and a drawing which controlled the cutting.   Whether he preferred to leave off when his idea was sufficiently indicated, or whether his numerous engagements prevented him from excavating the lowest surfaces, and lastly polishing the whole, is a question which must for ever remain undecided.   Considering the exquisite elaboration given to the Pietà of the Vatican, the Madonna at Bruges, the Bacchus and the David, the Moses and parts of the Medicean

[1] Lettere, No. cdlxii.

monuments, I incline to think that, with time enough at his disposal, he would have carried out these rounds in all their details. A criticism he made on Donatello, recorded for us by Condivi, to the effect that this great master's works lost their proper effect on close inspection through a want of finish, confirms my opinion.[1] Still there is no doubt that he must have been pleased, as all true lovers of art are, with the picturesque effect—an effect as of things half seen in dreams or emergent from primeval substances—which the imperfection of the craftsman's labour leaves upon the memory.

At this time Michelangelo's mind seems to have been much occupied with circular compositions. He painted a large Holy Family of this shape for his friend Angelo Doni, which may, I think, be reckoned the only easel-picture attributable with absolute certainty to his hand.[2] Condivi simply says that he received seventy ducats for this fine work. Vasari adds one of his prattling stories to the effect that Doni thought forty sufficient ; whereupon Michelangelo took the picture back, and said he would not

[1] Condivi, p. 22.
[2] If the enigmatical Deposition in the National Gallery be really Michelangelo's work, it might perhaps be assigned to this period. The head of the old man supporting Christ seems to be drawn from the same model as the S. Joseph ; but I regard this as a feeble attempt to reproduce the Doni S. Joseph by a later craftsman. It can be stated here that none of the pictures attributed to Michelangelo, as the Fates of the Pitti and his own portrait in the Capitol, are by his hand. I rely on Heath Wilson for the Doni Madonna being an oil-painting. Heath Wilson, p. 60.

let it go for less than a hundred : Doni then offered
the original sum of seventy, but Michelangelo replied that if he was bent on bargaining he should
not pay less than 140. Be this as it may, one of
the most characteristic products of the master's
genius came now into existence. The Madonna
is seated in a kneeling position on the ground ;
she throws herself vigorously backward, lifting the
little Christ upon her right arm, and presenting
him to a bald-headed old man, S. Joseph, who
seems about to take him in his arms. This group,
which forms a tall pyramid, is balanced on both
sides by naked figures of young men reclining
against a wall at some distance, while a remarkably
ugly little S. John can be discerned in one corner.
There is something very powerful and original in
the composition of this sacred picture, which, as in
the case of all Michelangelo's early work, develops
the previous traditions of Tuscan art on lines which
no one but himself could have discovered. The central figure of the Madonna, too, has always seemed
to me a thing of marvellous beauty, and of stupendous
power in the strained attitude and nobly modelled
arms.   It has often been asked what the male nudes
have got to do with the subject. Probably Michelangelo intended in this episode to surpass a Madonna by Luca Signorelli, with whose genius he
obviously was in sympathy, and who felt, like him,
the supreme beauty of the naked adolescent form.
Signorelli had painted a circular Madonna with two

nudes in the landscape distance for Lorenzo de' Medici. The picture is hung now in the gallery of the Uffizi. It is enough perhaps to remark that Michelangelo needed these figures for his scheme, and for filling the space at his disposal. He was either unable or unwilling to compose a background of trees, meadows, and pastoral folk in the manner of his predecessors. Nothing but the infinite variety of human forms upon a barren stage of stone or arid earth would suit his haughty sense of beauty. The nine persons who make up the picture are all carefully studied from the life, and bear a strong Tuscan stamp. S. John is literally ignoble, and Christ is a commonplace child. The Virgin Mother is a magnificent *contadina* in the plenitude of adult womanhood. Those, however, who follow Mr. Ruskin in blaming Michelangelo for carelessness about the human face and head, should not fail to notice what sublime dignity and grace he has communicated to his model here. In technical execution the Doni Madonna is faithful to old Florentine usage, but lifeless and unsympathetic. We are disagreeably reminded by every portion of the surface that Lionardo's subtle play of tones and modulated shades, those *sfumature*, as Italians call them, which transfer the mystic charm of nature to the canvas, were as yet unknown to the great draughtsman. There is more of atmosphere, of colour suggestion, and of chiaroscuro in the marble *tondi* described above. Moreover, in spite of very careful modelling, Michelangelo has failed to make us feel the successive planes of his composition.   The whole seems flat, and each distance, instead of being graduated, starts forward to the eye.   He required, at this period of his career, the relief of sculpture in order to express the roundness of the human form and the relative depth of objects placed in a receding order. If anything were needed to make us believe the story of his saying to Pope Julius II. that sculpture and not painting was his trade, this superb design, so deficient in the essential qualities of painting proper, would suffice.   Men infinitely inferior to himself in genius and sense of form, a Perugino, a Francia, a Fra Bartolommeo, an Albertinelli, possessed more of the magic which evokes pictorial beauty.   Nevertheless, with all its aridity, rigidity, and almost repulsive hardness of colour, the Doni Madonna ranks among the great pictures of the world.   Once seen it will never be forgotten : it tyrannises and dominates the imagination by its titanic power of drawing.   No one, except perhaps Lionardo, could draw like that, and Lionardo would not have allowed his linear scheme to impose itself so remorselessly upon the mind.

VI.

Just at this point of his development, Michelangelo was brought into competition with Lionardo da Vinci, the only living rival worthy of his genius. During the year 1503 Piero Soderini determined to adorn the hall of the Great Council in the Palazzo Vecchio with huge mural frescoes, which should represent scenes in Florentine history. Documents regarding the commencement of these works and the contracts made with the respective artists are unfortunately wanting. But it appears that Da Vinci received a commission for one of the long walls in the autumn of that year.[1] We have items of expenditure on record which show that the Municipality of Florence assigned him the Sala del Papa at S. Maria Novella before February 1504, and were preparing the necessary furniture for the construction of his Cartoon.[2] It seems that he was hard at work upon the 1st of April, receiving fifteen golden florins a month for his labour. The subject which he chose to treat was the battle of Anghiari in 1440, when the Florentine mercenaries entirely routed the troops of Filippo Maria Visconti, led by Niccolò Piccinino, one of the greatest generals of his age.[3]   In August 1504 Soderini commissioned

[1] Crowe and Cavalcaselle, *Life of Raphael*, vol. i. p. 213.
[2] Gaye, vol. ii. p. 88. When Martin V. took up his residence at Florence in 1419, quarters were assigned to him at S. Maria Novella. They came by custom to be regarded as the abode of Popes on a visit to the city. In the days of Eugenius IV., 1439, when the Greek Council was transferred from Ferrara to Florence, a large hall was erected for its sittings. See *L'Osservatore Fiorentino* (Firenze : Ricci, 1821), vol. iii. p. 135, for a description of the locality.
[3] Capponi, *Storia della Rep. di Firenze*, vol. ii. p. 22. This was one of the bloodless battles of Condottiere warfare. Machiavelli says that only one man was killed ; yet it had important political results.

Michelangelo to prepare Cartoons for the opposite wall of the great Sala, and assigned to him a workshop in the Hospital of the Dyers at S. Onofrio. A minute of expenditure, under date October 31, 1504, shows that the paper for the Cartoon had been already provided; and Michelangelo continued to work upon it until his call to Rome at the beginning of 1505. Lionardo's battle-piece consisted of two groups on horseback engaged in a fierce struggle for a standard. Michelangelo determined to select a subject which should enable him to display all his power as the supreme draughtsman of the nude. He chose an episode from the war with Pisa, when, on the 28th of July 1364, a band of 400 Florentine soldiers were surprised bathing by Sir John Hawkwood and his English riders. It goes by the name of the Battle of Pisa, though the event really took place at Cascina on the Arno, some six miles above that city.[1]

We have every reason to regard the composition of this Cartoon as the central point in Michelangelo's life as an artist. It was the watershed, so to speak, which divided his earlier from his later manner; and if we attach any value to the critical judgment of his enthusiastic admirer, Cellini, even the roof of the Sistine fell short of its perfection. Important, however, as it certainly is in the history of his development, I must defer speak-

---

[1] See Moritz Thausing, *Michelangelo's Entwurf zu dem Karton.* Leipzig : Seemann, 1878.

ing of it in detail until the end of the next chapter. For some reason or other, unknown to us, he left his work unfinished early in 1505, and went, at the Pope's invitation, to Rome. When he returned, in the ensuing year, to Florence, he resumed and completed the design. Some notion of its size may be derived from what we know about the materials supplied for Lionardo's Cartoon. This, say Crowe and Cavalcaselle, "was made up of one ream and twenty-nine quires, or about 288 square feet of royal folio paper, the mere pasting of which necessitated a consumption of eighty-eight pounds of flour, the mere lining of which required three pieces of Florentine linen."[1]

Condivi, summing up his notes of this period spent by Michelangelo at Florence, says:[2] "He stayed there some time without working to much purpose in his craft, having taken to the study of poets and rhetoricians in the vulgar tongue, and to the composition of sonnets for his pleasure." It is difficult to imagine how Michelangelo, with all his engagements, found the leisure to pursue these literary amusements. But Condivi's biography is the sole authentic source which we possess for the great master's own recollections of his past life. It is, therefore, not improbable that in the sentence I have quoted we may find some explanation of the want of finish observable in his productions at this point. Michelangelo was, to a

---

[1] *Life of Raphael*, vol. i. p. 213.   [2] Condivi, p. 23.

large extent, a dreamer; and this single phrase throws light upon the expense of time, the barren spaces, in his long laborious life. The poems we now possess by his pen are clearly the wreck of a vast multitude; and most of those accessible in manuscript and print belong to a later stage of his development. Still the fact remains that in early manhood he formed the habit of conversing with writers of Italian and of fashioning his own thoughts into rhyme. His was a nature capable indeed of vehement and fiery activity, but by constitution somewhat saturnine and sluggish, only energetic when powerfully stimulated; a meditative man, glad enough to be inert when not spurred forward on the path of strenuous achievement. And so, it seems, the literary bent took hold upon him as a relief from labour, as an excuse for temporary inaction. In his own art, the art of design, whether this assumed the form of sculpture or of painting or of architecture, he did nothing except at the highest pressure. All his accomplished work shows signs of the intensest cerebration. But he tried at times to slumber, sunk in a wise passiveness. Then he communed with the poets, the prophets, and the prose-writers of his country. We can well imagine, therefore, that, tired with the labours of the chisel or the brush, he gladly gave himself to composition, leaving half finished on his easel things which had for him their adequate accomplishment.

I think it necessary to make these suggestions, because, in my opinion, Michelangelo's inner life and his literary proclivities have been hitherto too much neglected in the scheme of his psychology. Dazzled by the splendour of his work, critics are content to skip spaces of months and years, during which the creative genius of the man smouldered. It is, as I shall try to show, in those intervals, dimly revealed to us by what remains of his poems and his correspondence, that the secret of this man, at once so tardy and so energetic, has to be discovered.

A great master of a different temperament, less solitary, less saturnine, less sluggish, would have formed a school, as Raffaello did. Michelangelo formed no school, and was incapable of confiding the execution of his designs to any subordinates. This is also a point of the highest importance to insist upon. Had he been other than he was—a gregarious man, contented with the *à peu près* in art— he might have sent out all those twelve Apostles for the Duomo from his workshop. Raffaello would have done so ; indeed, the work which bears his name in Rome could not have existed except under these conditions. Now nothing is left to us of the twelve Apostles except a rough-hewn sketch of S. Matthew. Michelangelo was unwilling or unable to organise a band of craftsmen fairly interpretative of his manner. When his own hand failed, or when he lost the passion for his labour, he left the thing unfinished. And much of this incompleteness in his life-work seems to me due to his being what I called a dreamer. He lacked the merely business faculty, the power of utilising hands and brains. He could not bring his genius into open market, and stamp inferior productions with his countersign. Willingly he retired into the solitude of his own self, to commune with great poets and to meditate upon high thoughts, while he indulged the emotions arising from forms of strength and beauty presented to his gaze upon the pathway of experience.

CHAPTER IV.

I.

AMONG the many nephews whom Sixtus IV. had raised to eminence, the most distinguished was

Giuliano della Rovere, Cardinal of S. Pietro in Vincoli, and Bishop of Ostia. This man possessed a fiery temper, indomitable energy, and the combative instinct which takes delight in fighting for its own sake. Nature intended him for a warrior; and, though circumstances made him chief of the Church, he discharged his duties as a Pontiff in the spirit of a general and a conqueror. When Julius II. was elected in November 1503, it became at once apparent that he intended to complete what his hated predecessors, the Borgias, had begun, by reducing to his sway all the provinces over which the See of Rome had any claims, and creating a central power in Italy. Unlike the Borgias, however, he entertained no plan of raising his own family to sovereignty at the expense of the Papal power. The Della Roveres were to be contented with their Duchy of Urbino, which came to them by inheritance from the Montefeltri. Julius dreamed of Italy for the Italians, united under the hegemony of the Supreme Pontiff, who from Rome extended his spiritual authority and political influence over the whole of Western Europe. It does not enter into the scheme of this book to relate the series of wars and alliances in which this belligerent Pope involved his country, and the final failure of his policy, so far as the liberation of Italy from the barbarians was concerned. Suffice it to say, that at the close of his stormy reign he had reduced the States of the Church to more or less complete obedience, bequeathing to his successors an ecclesiastical kingdom which the enfeebled condition of the peninsula at large enabled them to keep intact.

There was nothing petty or mean in Julius II. ; his very faults bore a grandiose and heroic aspect. Turbulent, impatient, inordinate in his ambition, reckless in his choice of means, prolific of immense projects, for which a lifetime would have been too short, he filled the ten years of his pontificate with a din of incoherent deeds and vast schemes half accomplished. Such was the man who called Michelangelo to Rome at the commencement of 1505. Why the sculptor was willing to leave his Cartoon unfinished, and to break his engagement with the Operai del Duomo, remains a mystery. It is said that the illustrious architect, Giuliano da San Gallo, who had worked for Julius while he was cardinal, and was now his principal adviser upon matters of art, suggested to the Pope that Buonarroti could serve him admirably in his ambitious enterprises for the embellishment of the Eternal City. We do not know for certain whether Julius, when he summoned Michelangelo from Florence, had formed the design of engaging him upon a definite piece of work. The first weeks of his residence in Rome are said to have been spent in inactivity, until at last Julius proposed to erect a huge monument of marble for his own tomb.[1]

[1] This is Condivi's statement. Still the Pope may have made some definite proposal before Michelangelo left Florence. Condivi thought

Thus began the second and longest period of Michelangelo's art-industry. Henceforth he was destined to labour for a series of Popes, following their whims with distracted energies and a lamentable waste of time. The incompleteness which marks so much of his performance was due to the rapid succession of these imperious masters, each in turn careless about the schemes of his predecessor, and bent on using the artist's genius for his own profit. It is true that nowhere but in Rome could Michelangelo have received commissions on so vast a scale. Nevertheless we cannot but regret the fate which drove him to consume years of hampered industry upon what Condivi calls "the tragedy of Julius's tomb," upon quarrying and road-making for Leo X., upon the abortive plans at S. Lorenzo, and upon architectural and engineering works, which were not strictly within his province. At first it seemed as though fortune was about to smile on him. In Julius he found a patron who could understand and appreciate his powers. Between the two men there existed a strong bond of sympathy due to community of temperament. Both aimed at colossal achievements in their respective fields of action. The imagination of both was fired by large and simple rather than luxurious and subtle thoughts. Both were *uomini terribili*, to use

he went there immediately after Julius's election (November 1503). He knew that he did not begin to work till 1505 ; so he had a whole year left unaccounted for.

a phrase denoting vigour of character and energy of genius, made formidable by an abrupt, uncompromising spirit. Both worked with what the Italians call fury, with the impetuosity of dæmonic natures; and both left the impress of their individuality stamped indelibly upon their age. Julius, in all things grandiose, resolved to signalise his reign by great buildings, great sculpture, great pictorial schemes. There was nothing of the dilettante and collector about him. He wanted creation at a rapid rate and in enormous quantities. To indulge this craving, he gathered round him a band of demigods and Titans, led by Bramante, Raffaello, Michelangelo, and enjoyed the spectacle of a new world of art arising at his bidding through their industry of brain and hand.

II.

What followed upon Michelangelo's arrival in Rome may be told in Condivi's words:[1] "Having reached Rome, many months elapsed before Julius

[1] Condivi, p. 23. He is wrong about the *many months*, because he thought that Michelangelo came to Rome at the end of 1503. He really came early in 1505, perhaps after February 28, when a payment was made to him for the Cartoon (Gaye, ii. p. 93). He went in April of that year to quarry marbles at Carrara. The delay was, therefore, of at most a few weeks, during which he may have designed the tomb of Julius.

decided on what great work he would employ him.
At last it occurred to him to use his genius in the
construction of his own tomb. The design furnished
by Michelangelo pleased the Pope so much that he
sent him off immediately to Carrara, with commission to quarry as much marble as was needful for
that undertaking. Two thousand ducats were put
to his credit with Alamanni Salviati at Florence for
expenses. He remained more than eight months
among those mountains, with two servants and a
horse, but without any salary except his keep. One
day, while inspecting the locality, the fancy took
him to convert a hill which commands the sea-shore
into a Colossus, visible by mariners afar. The shape
of the huge rock, which lent itself admirably to
such a purpose, attracted him ; and he was further
moved to emulate the ancients, who, sojourning in
the place peradventure with the same object as himself, in order to while away the time, or for some
other motive, have left certain unfinished and rough-
hewn monuments, which give a good specimen of
their craft. And assuredly he would have carried
out this scheme, if time enough had been at his
disposal, or if the special purpose of his visit to
Carrara had permitted. I one day heard him lament
bitterly that he had not done so. Well, then, after
quarrying and selecting the blocks which he deemed
sufficient, he had them brought to the sea, and left
a man of his to ship them off. He returned to
Rome, and having stopped some days in Florence

on the way, when he arrived there, he found that part of the marble had already reached the Ripa.[1] There he had them disembarked, and carried to the Piazza of S. Peter's behind S. Caterina, where he kept his lodging, close to the corridor connecting the Palace with the Castle of S. Angelo. The quantity of stone was enormous, so that, when it was all spread out upon the square, it stirred amazement in the minds of most folk, but joy in the Pope's. Julius indeed began to heap favours upon Michelangelo; for when he had begun to work, the Pope used frequently to betake himself to his house, conversing there with him about the tomb, and about other works which he proposed to carry out in concert with one of his brothers.[2] In order to arrive more conveniently at Michelangelo's lodgings, he had a drawbridge thrown across from the corridor, by which he might gain privy access."

The date of Michelangelo's return to Rome is fixed approximately by a contract signed at Carrara between him and two shipowners of Lavagna. This deed is dated November 12, 1505. It shows that thirty-four cartloads of marble were then ready for shipment, together with two figures weighing fifteen cartloads more. We have a right to assume that Michelangelo left Carrara soon after completing

---

[1] That is, the Tiber shore below the Aventine. The right bank is still called Porto di Ripa, and the left Marmorata.

[2] Probably Giovanni, Prefect of Rome, and founder of the Della Rovere dynasty at Urbino.

this transaction. Allowing, then, for the journey and the halt at Florence, he probably reached Rome in the last week of that month.[1]

III.

The first act in the tragedy of the sepulchre had now begun, and Michelangelo was embarked upon one of the mightiest undertakings which a sovereign of the stamp of Julius ever intrusted to a sculptor of his titanic energy. In order to form a conception of the magnitude of the enterprise, I am forced to enter into a discussion regarding the real nature of the monument. This offers innumerable difficulties, for we only possess imperfect notices regarding the original design, and two doubtful drawings belonging to an uncertain period. Still it is impossible to understand those changes in the Basilica of S. Peter's which were occasioned by the project of Julius, or to comprehend the immense annoyances to which the tomb exposed Michelangelo, without grappling with its details. Condivi's text must serve for guide. This, in fact, is the sole source of any positive value. He describes the tomb, as he believed it to have been first planned, in the following paragraph :[2]—

"To give some notion of the monument, I will

say that it was intended to have four faces: two of
eighteen cubits, serving for the sides, and two of
twelve for the ends, so that the whole formed one
great square and a half.[1] Surrounding it externally
were niches to be filled with statues, and between
each pair of niches stood terminal figures, to the
front of which were attached on certain consoles projecting from the wall another set of statues bound
like prisoners. These represented the Liberal Arts,
and likewise Painting, Sculpture, Architecture, each
with characteristic emblems, rendering their identi-
fication easy. The intention was to show that all
the talents had been taken captive by death, together
with Pope Julius, since never would they find
another patron to cherish and encourage them as
he had done. Above these figures ran a cornice,
giving unity to the whole work. Upon the flat
surface formed by this cornice were to be four large
statues, one of which, that is, the Moses, now exists
at S. Pietro ad Vincula. And so, arriving at the
summit, the tomb ended in a level space, whereon
were two angels who supported a sarcophagus.
One of them appeared to smile, rejoicing that the
soul of the Pope had been received among the
blessed spirits; the other seemed to weep, as sorrow-
ing that the world had been robbed of such a man.[2]
From one of the ends, that is, by the one which was

[1] According to Heath Wilson, 34½ feet English by 23 (p. 74).
.[2] Vasari speaks of Heaven rejoicing, and Cybele, the goddess of earth,
lamenting.   Vol. xii. p. 181.

at the head of the monument, access was given to a little chamber like a chapel, enclosed within the monument, in the midst of which was a marble chest, wherein the corpse of the Pope was meant to be deposited. The whole would have been executed with stupendous finish. In short, the sepulchre included more than forty statues, not counting the histories in half-reliefs, made of bronze, all of them pertinent to the general scheme and representative of the mighty Pontiff's actions."

Vasari's account differs in some minor details from Condivi's, but it is of no authoritative value. Not having appeared in the edition of 1550, we may regard it as a *rechauffée* of Condivi, with the usual sauce provided by the Aretine's imagination. The only addition I can discover which throws light upon Condivi's narrative is that the statues in the niches were meant to represent provinces conquered by Julius. This is important, because it leads us to conjecture that Vasari knew a drawing now preserved in the Uffizi, and sought, by its means, to add something to his predecessor's description. The drawing will occupy our attention shortly; but it may here be remarked that in 1505, the date of the first project, Julius was only entering upon his conquests. It would have been a gross act of flattery on the part of the sculptor, a flying in the face of Nemesis on the part of his patron, to design a sepulchre anticipating length of life and luck sufficient for these triumphs.

What then Condivi tells us about the first scheme is, that it was intended to stand isolated in the tribune of S. Peter's ; that it formed a rectangle of a square and half a square ; that the podium was adorned with statues in niches flanked by projecting dadoes supporting captive arts, ten in number ; that at each corner of the platform above the podium a seated statue was placed, one of which we may safely identify with the Moses ; and that above this, surmounting the whole monument by tiers, arose a second mass, culminating in a sarcophagus supported by two angels. He further adds that the tomb was entered at its extreme end by a door, which led to a little chamber where lay the body of the Pope, and that bronze bas-reliefs formed a prominent feature of the total scheme. He reckons that more than forty statues would have been required to complete the whole design, although he has only mentioned twenty-two of the most prominent.[1]

More than this we do not know about the first project. We have no contracts and no sketches that can be referred to the date 1505. Much confusion has been introduced into the matter under consideration by the attempt to reconcile Condivi's description with the drawing I have just alluded to. Heath Wilson even used that drawing to impugn Condivi's accuracy with regard to the number of the captives and the seated figures on the plat-

[1] On the calculation of ten captives on consoles, six in niches, four seated figures on the platform, and two angels.

form. The drawing in question, as we shall presently see, is of great importance for the subsequent history of the monument; and I believe that it to some extent preserves the general aspect which the tomb, as first designed, was intended to present. Two points about it, however, prevent our taking it as a true guide to Michelangelo's original conception. One is that it is clearly only part of a larger scheme of composition. The other is that it shows a sarcophagus, not supported by angels, but posed upon the platform. Moreover, it corresponds to the declaration appended in 1513 by Michelangelo to the first extant document we possess about the tomb.

Julius died in February 1513, leaving, it is said, to his executors directions that his sepulchre should not be carried out upon the first colossal plan.[1] If he did so, they seem at the beginning of their trust to have disregarded his intentions. Michelangelo expressly states in one of his letters that the Cardinal of Agen wished to proceed with the tomb, but on a larger scale.[2] A deed dated May 6, 1513, was signed, at the end of which Michelangelo specified the details of the new design. It differed from the former in many important respects, but most of all in the fact that now the structure was to be

---

[1] Two of the executors—Lorenzo Pucci, afterwards Cardinal of Santiquattro, and Cardinal Leonardo Grosso della Rovere, Bishop of Agen, commonly called Aginensis—were specially commissioned to see the tomb finished.

[2] Lettere, No. ccclxxxiii., to Fattucci.

attached to the wall of the church. I cannot do better than translate Michelangelo's specifications.[1] They run as follows: "Let it be known to all men that I, Michelangelo, sculptor of Florence, undertake to execute the sepulchre of Pope Julius in marble, on the commission of the Cardinal of Agens and the Datary (Pucci), who, after his death, have been appointed to complete this work, for the sum of 16,500 golden ducats of the Camera; and the composition of the said sepulchre is to be in the form ensuing: A rectangle visible from three of its sides, the fourth of which is attached to the wall and cannot be seen. The front face, that is, the head of this rectangle, shall be twenty palms in breadth and fourteen in height, the other two, running up against the wall, shall be thirty-five palms long and likewise fourteen palms in height.[2] Each of these three sides shall contain two tabernacles, resting on a basement which shall run round the said space, and shall be adorned with pilasters, architrave, frieze, and cornice, as appears in the little wooden model. In each of the said six tabernacles will be placed two figures about one palm taller than life (*i.e.* 6¾ feet), twelve in all; and in front of each pilaster which flanks a tabernacle shall stand a figure of similar size, twelve in all. On the

[1] Lettere, Contratto xi. p. 636.
[2] The Italian *palmo* is said to be 9 inches. This makes the dimensions work out as follows: 15 feet by 26 feet 3 inches, height 10 feet 6 inches.

platform above the said rectangular structure stands a sarcophagus with four feet, as may be seen in the model, upon which will be Pope Julius sustained by two angels at his head, with two at his feet; making five figures on the sarcophagus, all larger than life, that is, about twice the size.[1] Round about the said sarcophagus will be placed six dadoes or pedestals, on which six figures of the same dimensions will sit. Furthermore, from the platform, where it joins the wall, springs a little chapel about thirty-five palms high (26 feet 3 inches), which shall contain five figures larger than all the rest, as being farther from the eye. Moreover, there shall be three histories, either of bronze or of marble, as may please the said executors, introduced on each face of the tomb between one tabernacle and another." All this Michelangelo undertook to execute in seven years for the stipulated sum.

The new project involved thirty-eight colossal statues ; and, fortunately for our understanding of it, we may be said with almost absolute certainty to possess a drawing intended to represent it. Part of this is a pen-and-ink sketch at the Uffizi, which has frequently been published, and part is a sketch in the Berlin Collection. These have been put together by Professor Middleton of Cambridge, who

---

[1] The dimensions here specified seem quite extraordinary. The podium is only 10 feet 6 inches high ; but the figures on its faces are to be 6 feet 9 inches ; those upon its surface to be about 11 feet 8 inches high ; and those upon the chapel still larger.

has also made out a key-plan of the tomb. With regard to its proportions and dimensions as compared with Michelangelo's specification, there remain some difficulties, with which I cannot see that Professor Middleton has grappled.[1] It is perhaps not improbable, as Heath Wilson suggested, that the drawing had been thrown off as a picturesque forecast of the monument without attention to scale. Anyhow, there is no doubt that in this sketch, so happily restored by Professor Middleton's sagacity and tact, we are brought close to Michelangelo's conception of the colossal work he never was allowed to execute. It not only answers to the description translated above from the sculptor's own appendix to the contract, but it also throws light upon the original plan of the tomb designed for the tribune of S. Peter's. The basement of the podium has been preserved, we may assume, in its more salient features. There are the niches spoken of by Condivi, with Vasari's conquered provinces prostrate at the feet of winged Victories. These are flanked by the terminal figures, against which, upon projecting consoles, stand the bound captives. At the right hand facing us, upon the upper platform, is seated Moses, with a different action of the hands, it is true, from that which Michelangelo finally

---

[1] See Heath Wilson, pp. 196, 197, for a statement of these discrepancies and a criticism of the specification. Professor Middleton regards the drawings he has so ably brought together as only forming one of many sketches furnished by Michelangelo "after the death of Pope Julius."

adopted. Near him is a female figure, and the two figures grouped upon the left angle seem to be both female. To some extent these statues bear out Vasari's tradition that the platform in the first design was meant to sustain figures of the contemplative and active life of the soul—Dante's Leah and Rachel.

This great scheme was never carried out. The fragments which may be safely assigned to it are the Moses at S. Pietro in Vincoli and the two bound captives of the Louvre ; the Madonna and Child, Leah and Rachel, and two seated statues also at S. Pietro in Vincoli, belong to the plan, though these have undergone considerable alterations. Some other scattered fragments of the sculptor's work may possibly be connected with its execution. Four male figures roughly hewn, which are now wrought into the rock-work of a grotto in the Boboli Gardens, together with the young athlete trampling on a prostrate old man (called the Victory) and the Adonis of the Museo Nazionale at Florence, have all been ascribed to the sepulchre of Julius in one or other of its stages. But these attributes are doubtful, and will be criticised in their proper place and time.[1] Suffice it now to say that Vasari reports, beside the Moses, Victory, and two Captives at the Louvre, eight figures for the tomb blocked out by Michelangelo at Rome, and five blocked out at Florence.

[1] Discrepancies in the scale and dimensions of these several statues render the whole question very puzzling.

Continuing the history of this tragic undertaking, we come to the year 1516. On the 8th of July in that year, Michelangelo signed a new contract, whereby the previous deed of 1513 was annulled.[1] Both of the executors were alive and parties to this second agreement.[2] " A model was made, the width of which is stated at twenty-one feet, after the monument had been already sculptured of a width of almost twenty-three feet. The architectural design was adhered to with the same pedestals and niches and the same crowning cornice of the first story. There were to be six statues in front, but the conquered provinces were now dispensed with. There was also to be one niche only on each flank, so that the projection of the monument from the wall was reduced more than half, and there were to be only twelve statues beneath the cornice and one relief, instead of twenty-four statues and three reliefs. On the summit of this basement a shrine was to be erected, within which was placed the effigy of the Pontiff on his sarcophagus, with two heavenly guardians. The whole of the statues described in this third contract amount to nineteen." Heath Wilson observes, with much propriety, that the most singular fact about these successive contracts is the departure from certain fixed proportions both of the architectural parts and the statues, involving a serious loss of outlay and of work. Thus the two

[1] Lettere, Contratto xvi. pp. 644–651.
[2] I quote part of Heath Wilson's description, pp. 222, 223.

Captives of the Louvre became useless, and, as we know, they were given away to Ruberto Strozzi in a moment of generosity by the sculptor.[1] The sitting figures detailed in the deed of 1516 are shorter than the Moses by one foot. The standing figures, now at S. Pietro in Vincoli, correspond to the specifications. What makes the matter still more singular is, that after signing the contract under date July 8, 1516, Michelangelo in November of the same year ordered blocks of marble from Carrara with measurements corresponding to the specifications of the deed of 1513.[2]

The miserable tragedy of the sepulchre dragged on for another sixteen years. During this period the executors of Julius passed away, and the Duke Francesco Maria della Rovere replaced them. He complained that Michelangelo neglected the tomb, which was true, although the fault lay not with the sculptor, but with the Popes, his task-masters. Legal proceedings were instituted to recover a large sum of money, which, it was alleged, had been disbursed without due work delivered by the master. Michelangelo had recourse to Clement VII., who, being anxious to monopolise his labour, undertook to arrange matters with the Duke. On the 29th of April 1532 a third and solemn con-

[1] In a petition addressed to Paul III. Michelangelo gives the reason why these statues had to be abandoned, owing to a change of scale in the tomb. Lettere, No. cdxxxiii.

[2] Contract with Francesco Pelliccia, November 1, 1516; Vasari, xii. p. 352.

tract was signed at Rome in presence of the Pope, witnessed by a number of illustrious personages.[1] This third contract involved a fourth design for the tomb, which Michelangelo undertook to furnish, and at the same time to execute six statues with his own hand. On this occasion the notion of erecting it in S. Peter's was finally abandoned. The choice lay between two other Roman churches, that of S. Maria del Popolo, where monuments to several members of the Della Rovere family existed, and that of S. Pietro in Vincoli, from which Julius II. had taken his cardinal's title. Michelangelo decided for the latter, on account of its better lighting. The six statues promised by Michelangelo are stated in the contract to be "begun and not completed, extant at the present date in Rome or in Florence." Which of the several statues blocked out for the monument were to be chosen is not stated; and as there are no specifications in the document, we cannot identify them with exactness. At any rate, the Moses must have been one; and it is possible that the Leah and Rachel, Madonna, and two seated statues, now at S. Pietro, were the other five.

It might have been thought that at last the tragedy had dragged on to its conclusion. But no; there was a fifth act, a fourth contract, a fifth design. Paul III. succeeded to Clement VII., and, having seen the Moses in Michelangelo's workshop,

[1] Lettere, Contratto lv. pp. 702–706.

declared that this one statue was enough for the deceased Pope's tomb. The Duke Francesco Maria della Rovere died in 1538, and was succeeded by his son, Guidobaldo II. The new Duke's wife was a granddaughter of Paul III., and this may have made him amenable to the Pope's influence. At all events, upon the 20th of August 1542 a final contract was signed, stating that Michelangelo had been prevented "by just and legitimate impediments from carrying out" his engagement under date April 29, 1532, releasing him from the terms of the third deed, and establishing new conditions.[1] The Moses, finished by the hand of Michelangelo, takes the central place in this new monument. Five other statues are specified : " to wit, a Madonna with the child in her arms, which is already finished ; a Sibyl, a Prophet, an Active Life and a Contemplative Life, blocked out and nearly completed by the said Michelangelo." These four were given to Raffaello da Montelupo to finish. The reclining portrait-statue of Julius, which was carved by Maso del Bosco, is not even mentioned in this contract. But a deed between the Duke's representative and the craftsmen Montelupo and Urbino exists, in which the latter undertakes to see that Michelangelo shall retouch the Pope's face.[2]

---

[1] Lettere, Contratto lxiii. p. 715. See also the contracts with Raffaello da Montelupo, Giovanni de' Marchesi, and Francesco l'Urbino, Nos. lix., lx., lxi., lxiv., all of which relate to the tomb.

[2] Lettere, Contratto lxiv. p. 718.

Thus ended the tragedy of the tomb of Pope Julius II. It is supposed to have been finally completed in 1545, and was set up where it still remains uninjured at S. Pietro in Vincoli.[1]

IV.

I judged it needful to anticipate the course of events by giving this brief history of a work begun in 1505, and carried on with so many hindrances and alterations through forty years of Michelangelo's life. We shall often have to return to it, since the matter cannot be lightly dismissed. The tomb of Julius empoisoned Michelangelo's manhood, hampered his energy, and brought but small if any profit to his purse. In one way or another it is always cropping up, and may be said to vex his biographers and the students of his life as much as it annoyed himself. We may now return to those early days in Rome, when the project had still a fascination both for the sculptor and his patron.

The old Basilica of S. Peter on the Vatican is said to have been built during the reign of Constantine, and to have been consecrated in 324 A.D. It

---

[1] See Lettere, No. cdxliii., to the bankers Salvestro da Montauto and Co., on January 25, 1545, ordering them to make the last payment to Raffaello da Montelupo. It is indorsed by the Duke of Urbino's envoy, Hieronimo Tiranno. Another letter of the same year to the same bankers, No. cdlii., shows that Montelupo's work was finished.

was one of the largest of those Roman buildings, measuring 435 feet in length from the great door to the end of the tribune. A spacious open square or atrium, surrounded by a cloister-portico, gave access to the church. This, in the Middle Ages, gained the name of the Paradiso. A kind of tabernacle, in the centre of the square, protected the great bronze fir-cone, which was formerly supposed to have crowned the summit of Hadrian's Mausoleum, the Castle of S. Angelo.[1] Dante, who saw it in the courtyard of S. Peter's, used it as a standard for his giant Nimrod. He says—

> La faccia sua mi parea lunga e grossa,
> Come la pina di San Pietro a Roma.
> —(*Inf.* xxxi. 58.)

This mother-church of Western Christendom was adorned inside and out with mosaics in the style of those which may still be seen at Ravenna. Above the lofty row of columns which flanked the central aisle ran processions of saints and sacred histories. They led the eye onward to what was called the Arch of Triumph, separating this portion of the building from the transept and the tribune. The concave roof of the tribune itself was decorated with a colossal Christ, enthroned between S. Peter and S. Paul, surveying the vast spaces of his house : the lord and master, before whom pilgrims from all parts of Europe came to pay tribute and to perform acts of homage. The columns were of precious

---

[1] It was really in antique, as in medieval, times a fountain.

marbles, stripped from Pagan palaces and temples; and the roof was tiled with plates of gilded bronze, torn in the age of Heraclius from the shrine of Venus and of Roma on the Sacred Way.

During the eleven centuries which elapsed between its consecration and the decree for its destruction, S. Peter's had been gradually enriched with a series of monuments, inscriptions, statues, frescoes, upon which were written the annals of successive ages of the Church. Giotto worked there under Benedict II. in 1340. Pope after Pope was buried there. In the early period of Renaissance sculpture, Mino da Fiesole, Pollaiuolo, and Filarete added works in bronze and marble, which blent the grace of Florentine religious tradition with quaint neo-pagan mythologies. These treasures, priceless for the historian, the antiquary, and the artist, were now going to be ruthlessly swept away at a pontiff's bidding, in order to make room for his haughty and self-laudatory monument. Whatever may have been the artistic merits of Michelangelo's original conception for the tomb, the spirit was in no sense Christian. Those rows of captive Arts and Sciences, those Victories exulting over prostrate cities, those allegorical colossi symbolising the mundane virtues of a mighty ruler's character, crowned by the portrait of the Pope, over whom Heaven rejoiced while Cybele deplored his loss—all this pomp of power and parade of ingenuity harmonised but little with the humility of a contrite soul returning to its

Maker and its Judge. The new temple, destined to supersede the old basilica, embodied an aspect of Latin Christianity which had very little indeed in common with the piety of the primitive Church. S. Peter's, as we see it now, represents the majesty of Papal Rome, the spirit of a secular monarchy in the hands of priests ; it is the visible symbol of that schism between the Teutonic and the Latin portions of the Western Church which broke out soon after its foundation, and became irreconcilable before the cross was placed upon its cupola. It seemed as though in sweeping away the venerable traditions of eleven hundred years, and replacing Rome's time-honoured Mother-Church with an edifice bearing the brand-new stamp of hybrid neo-pagan architecture, the Popes had wished to signalise that rupture with the past and that atrophy of real religious life which marked the counter-reformation.

Julius II. has been severely blamed for planning the entire reconstruction of his cathedral. It must, however, be urged in his defence that the structure had already, in 1447, been pronounced insecure. Nicholas V. ordered his architects, Bernardo Rossellini and Leo Battista Alberti, to prepare plans for its restoration. It is, of course, impossible for us to say for certain whether the ancient fabric could have been preserved, or whether its dilapidations had gone so far as to involve destruction. Bearing in mind the recklessness of the Renaissance and the passion which the Popes had for engaging in colossal undertakings, one is inclined to suspect that the unsound state of the building was made a pretext for beginning a work which flattered the architectural tastes of Nicholas, but was not absolutely necessary. However this may have been, foundations for a new tribune were laid outside the old apse, and the wall rose some feet above the ground before the Pope's death. Paul II. carried on the building; but during the pontificates of Sixtus, Innocent, and Alexander it seems to have been neglected. Meanwhile nothing had been done to injure the original basilica; and when Julius announced his intention of levelling it to the ground, his cardinals and bishops entreated him to refrain from an act so sacrilegious. The Pope was not a man to take advice or make concessions. Accordingly, turning a deaf ear to these entreaties, he had plans prepared by Giuliano da San Gallo and Bramante. Those eventually chosen were furnished by Bramante; and San Gallo, who had hitherto enjoyed the fullest confidence of Julius, is said to have left Rome in disgust. For reasons which will afterwards appear, he could not have done so before the summer months of 1506.[1]

It is not yet the proper time to discuss the building of S. Peter's. Still, with regard to Bramante's plan, this much may here be said. It was designed in the form of a Greek cross, surmounted with a

---

[1] From a letter of Pietro Rosselli, quoted by Gotti, i. 46, we gather that San Gallo may have left Rome as early as May 10.

huge circular dome and flanked by two towers.
Bramante used to boast that he meant to raise the
Pantheon in the air; and the plan, as preserved
for us by Serlio, shows that the cupola would have
been constructed after that type. Competent judges,
however, declare that insuperable difficulties must
have arisen in carrying out this design, while the
piers constructed by Bramante were found in
effect to be wholly insufficient for their purpose.
For the æsthetic beauty and the commodiousness
of his building we have the strongest evidence in
a letter written by Michelangelo, who was by no
means a partial witness.[1] "It cannot be denied,"
he says, "that Bramante's talent as an architect
was equal to that of any one from the times of the
ancients until now. He laid the first plan of S.
Peter's, not confused, but clear and simple, full of
light and detached from surrounding buildings,
so that it interfered with no part of the palace.
It was considered a very fine design, and indeed
any one can see with his own eyes now that it is
so. All the architects who departed from Bramante's scheme, as did Antonio da San Gallo, have
departed from the truth." Though Michelangelo
gave this unstinted praise to Bramante's genius as
a builder, he blamed him severely both for his want
of honesty as a man, and also for his vandalism in
dealing with the venerable church he had to replace.
"Bramante," says Condivi, "was addicted, as every-

[1] Lettere, No. cdlxxiv.

body knows, to every kind of pleasure. He spent
enormously, and, though the pension granted him
by the Pope was large, he found it insufficient for
his needs. Accordingly he made profit out of the
works committed to his charge, erecting the walls
of poor material, and without regard for the substantial and enduring qualities which fabrics on so
huge a scale demanded. This is apparent in the
buildings at S. Peter's, the Corridore of the Belvedere, the Convent of San Pietro ad Vincula, and
other of his edifices, which have had to be
strengthened and propped up with buttresses and
similar supports in order to prevent them tumbling
down." Bramante, during his residence in Lombardy, developed a method of erecting piers with
rubble enclosed by hewn stone or plaster-covered
brickwork. This enabled an unconscientious builder
to furnish bulky architectural masses, which presented a specious aspect of solidity and looked
more costly than they really were. It had the
additional merit of being easy and rapid in execution. Bramante was thus able to gratify the
whims and caprices of his impatient patron, who
desired to see the works of art he ordered rise like
the fabric of Aladdin's lamp before his very eyes.
Michelangelo is said to have exposed the architect's
trickeries to the Pope ; what is more, he complained
with just and bitter indignation of the wanton ruth-
lessness with which Bramante set about his work
of destruction. I will again quote Condivi here,

for the passage seems to have been inspired by the great sculptor's verbal reminiscences : " The worst was, that while he was pulling down the old S. Peter's, he dashed those marvellous antique columns to the ground, without paying the least attention, or caring at all when they were broken into fragments, although he might have lowered them gently and preserved their shafts intact. Michelangelo pointed out that it was an easy thing enough to erect piers by placing brick on brick, but that to fashion a column like one of these taxed all the resources of art."

On the 18th of April 1506, Julius performed the ceremony of laying the foundation-stone of the new S. Peter's.[1] The place chosen was the great sustaining pier of the dome, near which the altar of S. Veronica now stands. A deep pit had been excavated, into which the aged Pope descended fearlessly, only shouting to the crowd above that they should stand back and not endanger the falling in of the earth above him. Coins and medals were duly deposited in a vase, over which a ponderous block of marble was lowered, while Julius, bareheaded, sprinkled the stone with holy water and gave the pontifical benediction. On the same day he wrote a letter to Henry VII. of England, informing the King that " by the guidance of our Lord and Saviour Jesus Christ he had undertaken to restore the old basilica, which was perishing through age."

[1] See Crowe and Cavalcaselle, *Life of Raphael*, vol. i. p. 381.

V.

The terms of cordial intimacy which subsisted between Julius and Michelangelo at the close of 1505 were destined to be disturbed. The Pope intermitted his visits to the sculptor's workshop, and began to take but little interest in the monument. Condivi directly ascribes this coldness to the intrigues of Bramante, who whispered into the Pontiff's ear that it was ill-omened for a man to construct his own tomb in his lifetime. It is not at all improbable that he said something of the sort, and Bramante was certainly no good friend to Michelangelo. A manœuvring and managing individual, entirely unscrupulous in his choice of means, condescending to flattery and lies, he strove to stand as patron between the Pope and subordinate craftsmen. Michelangelo had come to Rome under San Gallo's influence, and Bramante had just succeeded in winning the commission to rebuild S. Peter's over his rival's head. It was important for him to break up San Gallo's party, among whom the sincere and uncompromising Michelangelo threatened to be very formidable. The jealousy which he felt for the man was envenomed by a fear lest he should speak the truth about his own dishonesty. To discredit Michelangelo with the Pope, and, if possible, to drive him out of Rome, was therefore Bramante's interest :

more particularly as his own nephew, Raffaello da Urbino, had now made up his mind to join him there. We shall see that he succeeded in expelling both San Gallo and Buonarroti during the course of 1506, and that in their absence he reigned, together with Raffaello, almost alone in the art-circles of the Eternal City.

I see no reason, therefore, to discredit the story told by Condivi and Vasari regarding the Pope's growing want of interest in his tomb. Michelangelo himself, writing from Rome in 1542, thirty-six years after these events, says that "all the dissensions between Pope Julius and me arose from the envy of Bramante and Raffaello da Urbino, and this was the cause of my not finishing the tomb in his lifetime. They wanted to ruin me. Raffaello indeed had good reason; for all he had of art he owed to me." [1] But, while we are justified in attributing much to Bramante's intrigues, it must be remembered that the Pope at this time was absorbed in his plans for conquering Bologna. Overwhelmed with business and anxious about money, he could not have had much leisure to converse with sculptors.

Michelangelo was still in Rome at the end of January. On the 31st of that month he wrote to his father, complaining that the marbles did not arrive quickly enough, and that he had to keep Julius in good humour with promises.[2] At the same time he begged Lodovico to pack up all his drawings,

[1] Lettere, No. cdxxxv.   [2] Lettere, No. iii.

and to send them, well secured against bad weather, by the hand of a carrier. It is obvious that he had no thoughts of leaving Rome, and that the Pope was still eager about the monument. Early in the spring he assisted at the discovery of the Laocoon. Francesco, the son of Giuliano da San Gallo, describes how Michelangelo was almost always at his father's house; and coming there one day, he went, at the architect's invitation, down to the ruins of the Palace of Titus.[1] "We set off, all three together; I on my father's shoulders. When we descended into the place where the statue lay, my father exclaimed at once, 'That is the Laocoon, of which Pliny speaks.' The opening was enlarged, so that it could be taken out; and after we had sufficiently admired it, we went home to breakfast." Julius bought the marble for 500 crowns, and had it placed in the Belvedere of the Vatican. Scholars praised it in Latin lines of greater or lesser merit, Sadoleto writing even a fine poem;[2] and Michelangelo is said, but without trustworthy authority, to have assisted in its restoration.

This is the last glimpse we have of Michelangelo before his flight from Rome. Under what circumstances he suddenly departed may be related in the words of a letter addressed by him to Giuliano da

---

[1] Grimm, vol. i. p. 276. The place where this antique marble was discovered was really the Thermæ of Titus.

[2] Printed in *Poemata Selecta Italorum*, Oxonii, 1808; also in a note to Lessing's *Laokoon*.

San Gallo in Rome upon the 2nd of May 1506, after his return to Florence.[1]

" GIULIANO,—Your letter informs me that the Pope was angry at my departure, as also that his Holiness is inclined to proceed with the works agreed upon between us, and that I may return and not be anxious about anything.

"About my leaving Rome, it is a fact that on Holy Saturday I heard the Pope, in conversation with a jeweller at table and with the Master of Ceremonies, say that he did not mean to spend a farthing more on stones, small or great. This caused me no little astonishment. However, before I left his presence, I asked for part of the money needed to carry on the work. His Holiness told me to return on Monday. I did so, and on Tuesday, and on Wednesday, and on Thursday, as the Pope saw. At last, on Friday morning, I was sent away, or plainly turned out of doors. The man who did this said he knew me, but that such were his orders. I, who had heard the Pope's words on Saturday, and now perceived their result in deeds, was utterly cast down. This was not, however, quite the only reason of my departure; there was something else, which I do not wish to communicate; enough that it made me think that, if I stayed in Rome, that city would be my tomb before it was the Pope's. And this was the cause of my sudden departure.

[1] Lettere, No. cccxliii.

" Now you write to me at the Pope's instance. So I beg you to read him this letter, and inform his Holiness that I am even more than ever disposed to carry out the work."

Further details may be added from subsequent letters of Michelangelo. Writing in January 1524 to his friend Giovanni Francesco Fattucci, he says : [1] " When I had finished paying for the transport of these marbles, and all the money was spent, I furnished the house I had upon the Piazza di S. Pietro with beds and utensils at my own expense, trusting to the commission of the tomb, and sent for workmen from Florence, who are still alive, and paid them in advance out of my own purse. Meanwhile Pope Julius changed his mind about the tomb, and would not have it made. Not knowing this, I applied to him for money, and was expelled from the chamber. Enraged at such an insult, I left Rome on the moment. The things with which my house was stocked went to the dogs. The marbles I had brought to Rome lay till the date of Leo's creation on the Piazza, and both lots were injured and pillaged." [2]

Again, a letter of October 1542, addressed to some prelate, contains further particulars.[3] We

[1] Lettere, No. ccclxxxiii.

[2] In the *abbozzo* (ccclxxxiv): " Finding myself engaged in great expenses, and seeing his Holiness indisposed to pay, I complained to him ; this annoyed him so much that he had me turned out of the antechamber. Upon which I became angry and left home suddenly."

[3] Lettere, No. cdxxxv.

learn he was so short of money that he had to
borrow about 200 ducats from his friend Baldassare
Balducci at the bank of Jacopo Gallo. The episode
at the Vatican and the flight to Poggibonsi are
related thus :—

"To continue my history of the tomb of Julius:
I say that when he changed his mind about building it in his lifetime, some ship-loads of marble
came to the Ripa, which I had ordered a short
while before from Carrara; and as I could not get
money from the Pope to pay the freightage, I had
to borrow 150 or 200 ducats from Baldassare
Balducci, that is, from the bank of Jacopo Gallo.
At the same time workmen came from Florence,
some of whom are still alive ; and I furnished the
house which Julius gave me behind S. Caterina
with beds and other furniture for the men, and
what was wanted for the work of the tomb. All
this being done without money, I was greatly
embarrassed. Accordingly, I urged the Pope with
all my power to go forward with the business,
and he had me turned away by a groom one morning when I came to speak upon the matter. A
Lucchese bishop, seeing this, said to the groom :
'Do you not know who that man is?' The groom
replied to me : 'Excuse me, gentleman ; I have
orders to do this.' I went home, and wrote as
follows to the Pope : 'Most blessed Father, I
ɳave been turned out of the palace to-day by your
orders ; wherefore I give you notice that from this

time forward, if you want me, you must look for me elsewhere than at Rome.' I sent this letter to Messer Agostino, the steward, to give it to the Pope. Then I sent for Cosimo, a carpenter, who lived with me and looked after household matters, and a stone-heaver, who is still alive, and said to them: 'Go for a Jew, and sell everything in the house, and come to Florence.' I went, took the post, and travelled towards Florence. The Pope, when he had read my letter, sent five horsemen after me, who reached me at Poggibonsi about three hours after nightfall, and gave me a letter from the Pope to this effect: 'When you have seen these present, come back at once to Rome, under penalty of our displeasure.' The horsemen were anxious I should answer, in order to prove that they had overtaken me. I replied then to the Pope, that if he would perform the conditions he was under with regard to me, I would return; but otherwise he must not expect to have me again. Later on, while I was at Florence, Julius sent three briefs to the Signory. At last the latter sent for me and said: 'We do not want to go to war with Pope Julius because of you. You must return; and if you do so, we will write you letters of such authority that, should he do you harm, he will be doing it to this Signory.' Accordingly I took the letters, and went back to the Pope, and what followed would be long to tell."

These passages from Michelangelo's correspondence

confirm Condivi's narrative of the flight from Rome, showing that he had gathered his information from the sculptor's lips. Condivi differs only in making Michelangelo send a verbal message, and not a written letter, to the Pope.[1] "Enraged by this repulse, he exclaimed to the groom: 'Tell the Pope that if henceforth he wants me, he must look for me elsewhere.'"

It is worth observing that only the first of these letters, written shortly after the event, and intended for the Pope's ear, contains a hint of Michelangelo's dread of personal violence if he remained in Rome. His words seem to point at poison or the dagger. Cellini's autobiography yields sufficient proof that such fears were not unjustified by practical experience; and Bramante, though he preferred to work by treachery of tongue, may have commanded the services of assassins, *uomini arditi e facinorosi*, as they were somewhat euphemistically called. At any rate, it is clear that Michelangelo's precipitate departure and vehement refusal to return were occasioned by more pungent motives than the Pope's frigidity. This has to be noticed, because we learn from several incidents of the same kind in the master's life that he was constitutionally subject to sudden fancies and fears of imminent danger to his person from an enemy. He had already quitted Bologna in haste (p. 48 above) from dread of assassination or maltreatment at the hands of native sculptors.

---

[1] Condivi, p. 29.

VI.

The negotiations which passed between the Pope and the Signory of Florence about what may be called the extradition of Michelangelo form a curious episode in his biography, throwing into powerful relief the importance he had already acquired among the princes of Italy. I propose to leave these for the commencement of my next chapter, and to conclude the present with an account of his occupations during the summer months at Florence.

Signor Gotti says that he passed three months away from Julius in his native city.[1] Considering that he arrived before the end of April, and reached Bologna at the end of November 1506, we have the right to estimate this residence at about seven months.[2] A letter written to him from Rome on the 4th of August shows that he had not then left Florence upon any intermediate journey of importance.[3] Therefore there is every reason to suppose

[1] Gotti, i. 47. He follows Vasari.

[2] In a draft for his famous letter to Fattucci (No. ccclxxxiv.), Michelangelo himself declares that he "remained about seven or eight months in hiding, as it were, because of his fear of the Pope."

[3] Gotti, ii. 51. Curiously enough, he seems to have gone a second time to Carrara, about May 20, to purchase marbles for the tomb of Julius. See Vasari, xii. p. 347. I am not sure that he may not have gone there at Soderini's orders to order the famous block of marble for the Cacus.

that he enjoyed a period of half a year of leisure, which he devoted to finishing his Cartoon for the Battle of Pisa.

It had been commenced, as we have seen, in a workshop at the Spedale dei Tintori. When he went to Bologna in the autumn, it was left, exposed presumably to public view, in the Sala del Papa at S. Maria Novella.[1] It had therefore been completed; but it does not appear that Michelangelo had commenced his fresco in the Sala del Gran Consiglio.

Lionardo began to paint his Battle of the Standard in March 1505. The work advanced rapidly; but the method he adopted, which consisted in applying oil colours to a fat composition laid thickly on the wall, caused the ruin of his picture. He is said to have wished to reproduce the encaustic process of the ancients, and lighted fires to harden the surface of the fresco.[2] This melted the wax in the lower portions of the paste, and made the colours run. At any rate, no traces of the painting now remain in the Sala del Gran Consiglio, the walls of which are covered by the mechanical and frigid brush-work of Vasari. It has even been suggested that Vasari

[1] Condivi is our authority for these facts.

[2] The whole could not have been completed. Vasari says that Lionardo left off in disgust; and a letter from Soderini to his agent at Milan, October 9, 1506, complains that "Lionardo acted ill toward the Republic, since he took a large sum of money, *and made but a small beginning of a great work he was engaged to do.*" Gaye, ii. 87. Professor Middleton reminds me that in his experiment at encaustic painting Lionardo followed the directions given by Vitruvius (vii. 9. 3).

knew more about the disappearance of his predecessor's masterpiece than he has chosen to relate.[1]
Lionardo's Cartoon has also disappeared, and we
know the Battle of Anghiari only by Edelinck's engraving from a drawing of Rubens, and by some
doubtful sketches.[2]

The same fate was in store for Michelangelo's
Cartoon. All that remains to us of that great work
is the chiaroscuro transcript at Holkham, a sketch
for the whole composition in the Albertina Gallery
at Vienna, which differs in some important details
from the Holkham group, several interesting pen-and-
chalk drawings by Michelangelo's own hand, also in
the Albertina Collection, and a line-engraving by
Marcantonio Raimondi, commonly known as "Les
Grimpeurs."[3]

We do not know at what exact time Michelangelo
finished his Cartoon in 1506.[4] He left it, says

[1] Heath Wilson, p. 70.

[2] Crowe and Cavalcaselle attribute some pieces in Raphael's sketch-
book to transcripts made at Florence from Lionardo's fresco. *Life
of Raphael*, i. 274.

[3] The whole subject is well treated by M. Thausing, *Michelangelo's
Entwurf.* Leipzig : Seemann, 1878.

[4] Nearly all the critics who have entered into the details of this
question, Milanesi (in Vasari), Gotti, Crowe and Cavalcaselle (in *Life of
Raphael*), Münz (*L'Œuvre et la Vie*), give the date August 1505. They
do this on the strength of two entries in Gaye, vol. ii. p. 93. These are
minutes of payments, one on February 28, 1505, to Michelangelo for
work done ; the other, on August 30, 1505, to a ropemaker for setting up
the Cartoon. Something is wrong here. Even supposing that Michelangelo did not leave Florence for Rome as early as January 1505,
he was almost certainly at Carrara in August 1505. The only way
to reconcile these dates is to suppose that Michelangelo was paid in

Condivi, in the Sala del Papa.   Afterwards it must have been transferred to the Sala del Gran Consiglio ; for Albertini, in his *Memoriale*, or Guide-Book to Florence, printed in 1510, speaks of both "the works of Lionardo da Vinci and the designs of Michelangelo" as then existing in that hall.   Vasari asserts that it was taken to the house of the Medici, and placed in the great upper hall, but gives no date.   This may have taken place on the return of the princely family in 1512.   Cellini confirms this view, since he declares that when he was copying the Cartoon, which could hardly have happened before 1513, the Battle of Pisa was at the Palace of the Medici, and the Battle of Anghiari at the Sala del Papa.[1]   The way in which it finally disappeared is involved in some obscurity, owing to Vasari's spite and mendacity.   In the first, or 1550, edition of the "Lives

February 1505 for work done before he went to Rome, and that the Cartoon in its unfinished state was framed and hung during his absence in August 1505.   It is quite clear, from Condivi, Vasari, and Soderini's letter of November 27 (Gaye, ii. 92), that he was working on the Cartoon in 1506.   In the letter to Fattucci (No. ccclxxxiii.) Michelangelo himself says that when he went to Rome the Cartoon was in progress : he expected to be paid 3000 ducats, and thought the money was already half gained.   Like so much of his work, he probably left it in a stage bordering upon completion.   His subsequent labour in 1506 may have brought it to that unexampled finish which Vasari praises.

[1] Albertini, quoted by Milanesi, Vas. vii. 33, note ; Vasari, xii. 179 ; Cellini, *Vita*, i. cap. 12.   Albertini, I may observe, does not use the word *cartone*, but *disegni*.   Yet I think it probable that he meant the former, and that in 1510 the Cartoon was in the Sala del Gran Consiglio.   It appears from Michelangelo's correspondence (Lettere, pp. 84, 92, 95) that in the year 1508 it must have still been in the Sala del Papa.

of the Painters," he wrote as follows:[1] "Having
become a regular object of study to artists, the Cartoon
was carried to the house of the Medici, into the great
upper hall; and this was the reason that it came
with too little safeguard into the hands of those said
artists: inasmuch as, during the illness of the Duke
Giuliano, when no one attended to such matters, it
was torn in pieces by them and scattered abroad, so
that fragments may be found in many places, as is
proved by those existing now in the house of Uberto
Strozzi, a gentleman of Mantua, who holds them in
great respect." When Vasari published his second
edition, in 1568, he repeated this story of the destruction of the Cartoon, but with a very significant
alteration.[2] Instead of saying "it was torn in pieces
by them," he now printed "it was torn in pieces, *as
hath been told elsewhere*." Now Bandinelli, Vasari's
mortal enemy, and the scapegoat for all the sins of
his generation among artists, died in 1559, and
Vasari felt that he might safely defame his memory.
Accordingly he introduced a Life of Bandinelli into
the second edition of his work, containing the
following passage:[3] "Baccio was in the habit of
frequenting the place where the Cartoon stood more
than any other artists, and had in his possession a
false key; what follows happened at the time when

[1] I quote from a manuscript copy of this edition, and cannot therefore
give the page. The illness of Giuliano, Duke of Nemours, is probably
the one which preceded his death in 1516.

[2] Vasari, xii. p. 179.   [3] Vasari, x. p. 296.

Piero Soderini was deposed in 1512, and the Medici returned. Well, then, while the palace was in tumult and confusion through this revolution, Baccio went alone, and tore the Cartoon into a thousand fragments. Why he did so was not known; but some surmised that he wanted to keep certain pieces of it by him for his own use; some, that he wished to deprive young men of its advantages in study; some, that he was moved by affection for Lionardo da Vinci, who suffered much in reputation by this design ; some, perhaps with sharper intuition, believed that the hatred he bore to Michelangelo inspired him to commit the act. The loss of the Cartoon to the city was no slight one, and Baccio deserved the blame he got, for everybody called him envious and spiteful." This second version stands in glaring contradiction to the first, both as regards the date and the place where the Cartoon was destroyed. It does not, I think, deserve credence, for Cellini, who was a boy of twelve in 1512, could hardly have drawn from it before that date ; and if Bandinelli was so notorious for his malignant vandalism as Vasari asserts, it is most improbable that Cellini, while speaking of the Cartoon in connection with Torrigiano, should not have taken the opportunity to cast a stone at the man whom he detested more than any one in Florence. Moreover, if Bandinelli had wanted to destroy the Cartoon for any of the reasons above assigned to him, he would not have dispersed fragments to be treasured up with reverence. At the close of this tedious summary I ought to add that Condivi expressly states : [1] " I do not know by what ill-fortune it subsequently came to ruin." He adds, however, that many of the pieces were found about in various places, and that all of them were preserved like sacred objects. We have, then, every reason to believe that the story told in Vasari's first edition is the literal truth. Copyists and engravers used their opportunity, when the palace of the Medici was thrown into disorder by the severe illness of the Duke of Nemours, to take away portions of Michelangelo's Cartoon for their own use in 1516.

Of the Cartoon and its great reputation Cellini gives us this account : [2] " Michelangelo portrayed a number of foot-soldiers, who, the season being summer, had gone to bathe in the Arno. He drew them at the very moment the alarm is sounded, and the men all naked run to arms ; so splendid is their action, that nothing survives of ancient or of modern art which touches the same lofty point of excellence ; and, as I have already said, the design of the great Lionardo was itself most admirably beautiful. These two Cartoons stood, one in the palace of the Medici, the other in the hall of the Pope. So long as they remained intact, they were the school of the world. Though the divine Michelangelo in later

---

[1] Condivi, p. 31.

[2] *Vita*, lib. i. cap. 12, Englished by J. A. Symonds.

life finished that great chapel of Pope Julius (the Sistine), he never rose halfway to the same pitch of power; his genius never afterwards attained to the force of those first studies." Allowing for some exaggeration due to enthusiasm for things enjoyed in early youth, this is a very remarkable statement. Cellini knew the frescoes of the Sistine well, yet he maintains that they were inferior in power and beauty to the Battle of Pisa. It seems hardly credible; but, if we believe it, the legend of Michelangelo's being unable to execute his own designs for the vault of that chapel falls to the ground.

VII.

The great Cartoon has become less even than a memory, and so, perhaps, we ought to leave it in the limbo of things inchoate and unaccomplished. But this it was not, most emphatically. Decidedly it had its day, lived and sowed seeds for good or evil through its period of brief existence: so many painters of the grand style took their note from it; it did so much to introduce the last phase of Italian art, the phase of efflorescence, the phase deplored by critics steeped in mediæval feeling. To recapture something of its potency from the description of contemporaries is therefore our plain duty, and for this we must have recourse to Vasari's text.

He says:[1] "Michelangelo filled his canvas with nude men, who, bathing at the time of summer heat in Arno, were suddenly called to arms, the enemy assailing them. The soldiers swarmed up from the river to resume their clothes ; and here you could behold depicted by the master's godlike hands one hurrying to clasp his limbs in steel and give assistance to his comrades, another buckling on the cuirass, and many seizing this or that weapon, with cavalry in squadrons giving the attack. Among the multitude of figures, there was an old man, who wore upon his head an ivy wreath for shade. Seated on the ground, in act to draw his hose up, he was hampered by the wetness of his legs ; and while he heard the clamour of the soldiers, the cries, the rumbling of the drums, he pulled with all his might; all the muscles and sinews of his body were seen in strain ; and what was more, the contortion of his mouth showed what agony of haste he suffered, and how his whole frame laboured to the toe-tips. Then there were drummers and men with flying garments, who ran stark naked toward the fray. Strange postures too : this fellow upright, that man kneeling, or bent down, or on the point of rising ; all in the air foreshortened with full conquest over every difficulty. In addition, you discovered groups of figures sketched in various methods, some outlined with charcoal, some etched with strokes, some shadowed with the stump,

---

[1] Vasari, xii. 177 et seq. Condivi, a more faithful describer than Vasari, is silent here.

some relieved in white-lead ; the master having sought to prove his empire over all materials of draughtsmanship. The craftsmen of design remained therewith astonied and dumbfounded, recognising the furthest reaches of their art revealed to them by this unrivalled masterpiece. Those who examined the forms I have described, painters who inspected and compared them with works hardly less divine, affirm that never in the history of human achievement was any product of a man's brain seen like to them in mere supremacy. And certainly we have the right to believe this ; for when the Cartoon was finished, and carried to the Hall of the Pope, amid the acclamation of all artists, and to the exceeding fame of Michelangelo, the students who made drawings from it, as happened with foreigners and natives through many years in Florence, became men of mark in several branches. This is obvious, for Aristotele da San Gallo worked there, as did Ridolfo Ghirlandajo, Raffaello Sanzio da Urbino, Francesco Granaccio, Baccio Bandinelli, and Alonso Berugetta, the Spaniard ; they were followed by Andrea del Sarto, Franciabigio, Jacopo Sansovino, Rosso, Maturino, Lorenzetto, Tribolo, then a boy, Jacopo da Pontormo, and Pierin del Vaga : all of them first-rate masters of the Florentine school."

It does not appear from this that Vasari pretended to have seen the great Cartoon. Born in 1512, he could not indeed have done so ; but there breathes through his description a gust of enthusiasm, an afflatus of concurrent witnesses to its surpassing grandeur. Some of the details raise a suspicion that Vasari had before his eyes the transcript *en grisaille* which he says was made by Aristotele da San Gallo, and also the engraving by Marcantonio Raimondi. The prominence given to the ivy-crowned old soldier troubled by his hose confirms the accuracy of the Holkham picture and the Albertina drawing.[1] But none of these partial transcripts left to us convey that sense of multitude, space, and varied action which Vasari's words impress on the imagination. The fullest, that at Holkham, contains nineteen figures, and these are schematically arranged in three planes, with outlying subjects in foreground and background. Reduced in scale, and treated with the arid touch of a feeble craftsman, the linear composition suggests no large æsthetic charm. It is simply a bas-relief of carefully selected attitudes and vigorously studied movements—nineteen men, more or less unclothed, put together with the scientific view of illustrating possibilities and conquering difficulties in postures of the adult male body. The extraordinary effect, as of something superhuman, produced by the Cartoon upon contemporaries, and preserved for us in Cellini's and Vasari's narratives, must then have been due to unexampled qualities

---

[1] Pages 12 and 13 of Thausing's essay. The fine early sketch by Michelangelo's own hand at Vienna, opposite page 8 of the same essay, shows the old man in the foreground. He must have been a main feature in the composition.

of strength in conception, draughtsmanship, and execution. It stung to the quick an age of artists who had abandoned the representation of religious sentiment and poetical feeling for technical triumphs and masterly solutions of mechanical problems in the treatment of the nude figure. We all know how much more than this Michelangelo had in him to give, and how unjust it would be to judge a masterpiece from his hand by the miserable relics now at our disposal. Still I cannot refrain from thinking that the Cartoon for the Battle of Pisa, taken up by him as a field for the display of his ability, must, by its very brilliancy, have accelerated the ruin of Italian art. Cellini, we saw, placed it above the frescoes of the Sistine. In force, veracity, and realism it may possibly have been superior to those sublime productions. Everything we know about the growth of Michelangelo's genius leads us to suppose that he departed gradually but surely from the path of Nature. He came, however, to use what he had learned from Nature as means for the expression of soul-stimulating thoughts. This, the finest feature of his genius, no artist of the age was capable of adequately comprehending. Accordingly, they agreed in extolling a cartoon which displayed his faculty of dealing with *un bel corpo ignudo* as the climax of his powers.

As might be expected, there was no landscape in the Cartoon. Michelangelo handled his subject wholly from the point of view of sculpture. A broken

bank and a retreating platform, a few rocks in the
distance and a few waved lines in the foreground,
showed that the naked men were by a river.   Michelangelo's unrelenting contempt for the many-formed
and many-coloured stage on which we live and
move—his steady determination to treat men and
women as nudities posed in the void, with just
enough of solid substance beneath their feet to make
their attitudes intelligible—is a point which must
over and over again be insisted on.   In the psychology of the master, regarded from any side one likes
to take, this constitutes his leading characteristic.
It gives the key, not only to his talent as an artist,
but also to his temperament as a man.

Marcantonio seems to have felt and resented the
aridity of composition, the isolation of plastic form,
the tyranny of anatomical science, which even the
most sympathetic of us feel in Michelangelo.   This
master's engraving of three lovely nudes, the most
charming memento preserved to us from the Cartoon, introduces a landscape of grove and farm, field
and distant hill, lending suavity to the muscular
male body and restoring it to its proper place among
the sinuous lines and broken curves of Nature.
That the landscape was adapted from a copper-plate
of Lucas van Leyden signifies nothing.   It serves
the soothing purpose which sensitive nerves, irritated by Michelangelo's aloofness from all else but
thought and naked flesh and posture, gratefully
acknowledge.

While Michelangelo was finishing his Cartoon, Lionardo da Vinci was painting his fresco. Circumstances may have brought the two chiefs of Italian art frequently together in the streets of Florence. There exists an anecdote of one encounter, which, though it rests upon the credit of an anonymous writer, and does not reflect a pleasing light upon the hero of this biography, cannot be neglected.[1] "Lionardo," writes our authority, "was a man of fair presence, well-proportioned, gracefully endowed, and of fine aspect. He wore a tunic of rose-colour, falling to his knees; for at that time it was the fashion to carry garments of some length; and down to the middle of his breast there flowed a beard beautifully curled and well arranged.[2] Walking with a friend near S. Trinità, where a company of honest folk were gathered, and talk was going on about some passage from Dante, they called to Lionardo, and begged him to explain its meaning. It so happened that just at this moment Michelangelo went by, and, being hailed by one of them, Lionardo answered: 'There goes Michelangelo; he will interpret the verses you require.' Whereupon Michelangelo, who thought he spoke in this way to make fun of him, replied in anger: 'Explain them yourself, you who made the model of a horse to cast in bronze, and could not cast it, and to your

[1] Gotti, vol. i. p. 48.

[2] This recalls Lionardo's chalk-drawings of his own head in old age, and the oil-picture at the Uffizi.

shame left it in the lurch.'[1] With these words, he turned his back to the group, and went his way. Lionardo remained standing there, red in the face for the reproach cast at him; and Michelangelo, not satisfied, but wanting to sting him to the quick, added : 'And those Milanese capons believed in your ability to do it!'"

We can only take anecdotes for what they are worth, and that may perhaps be considered slight when they are anonymous. This anecdote, however, in the original Florentine diction, although it betrays a partiality for Lionardo, bears the aspect of truth to fact. Moreover, even Michelangelo's admirers are bound to acknowledge that he had a rasping tongue, and was not incapable of showing his bad temper by rudeness. From the period of his boyhood, when Torrigiano smashed his nose, down to the last years of his life in Rome, when he abused his nephew Lionardo and hurt the feelings of his best and oldest friends, he discovered signs of a highly nervous and fretful temperament. It must be admitted that the dominant qualities of nobility and generosity in his nature were alloyed by suspicion bordering on littleness, and by petulant yieldings to the irritation of the moment which are incompatible with the calm of an Olympian genius.

[1] The equestrian statue of Francesco Sforza.

CHAPTER V.

I.

WHILE Michelangelo was living and working at Florence, Bramante had full opportunity to poison the Pope's mind in Rome. It is commonly believed, on the faith of a sentence in Condivi, that Bramante, when he dissuaded Julius from building the tomb in his own lifetime, suggested the painting of the Sistine Chapel. We are told that he proposed Michelangelo for this work, hoping his genius would be hampered by a task for which he was not fitted. There are many improbabilities in this story; not the least being our certainty that the fame of the Cartoon must have reached Bramante before Michelangelo's arrival in the first months of 1505. But the Cartoon did not prove that Buonarroti was a practical wall-painter or colourist; and we have reason to believe that Julius had himself conceived the notion of intrusting the Sistine to his sculptor. A good friend of Michelangelo, Pietro Rosselli, wrote this letter on the subject, May 6, 1506:[1] "Last Saturday evening, when the Pope was at supper, I showed him some designs which Bramante and I had to test; so, after supper, when I had displayed them, he called for Bramante, and said: 'San Gallo is going to Florence to-morrow, and will bring Michelangelo back with him.' Bramante answered: 'Holy Father, he will not be able to do anything of the kind. I

[1] Gotti, i. p. 46.

have conversed much with Michelangelo, and he has often told me that he would not undertake the chapel, which you wanted to put upon him; and that, you notwithstanding, he meant only to apply himself to sculpture, and would have nothing to do with painting.' To this he added: 'Holy Father, I do not think he has the courage to attempt the work, because he has small experience in painting figures, and these will be raised high above the line of vision, and in foreshortening (*i.e.*, because of the vault). That is something different from painting on the ground.' The Pope replied: 'If he does not come, he will do me wrong; and so I think that he is sure to return.' Upon this I up, and gave the man a sound rating in the Pope's presence, and spoke as I believe you would have spoken for me; and for the time he was struck dumb, as though he felt that he had made a mistake in talking as he did. I proceeded as follows: 'Holy Father, that man never exchanged a word with Michelangelo, and if what he has just said is the truth, I beg you to cut my head off, for he never spoke to Michelangelo; also I feel sure that he is certain to return, if your Holiness requires it.' "

This altercation throws doubt on the statement that Bramante originally suggested Michelangelo as painter of the Sistine. He could hardly have turned round against his own recommendation; and, more-over, it is likely that he would have wished to keep so great a work in the hands of his own set, Raffaello, Peruzzi, Sodoma, and others.[1]

Meanwhile, Michelangelo's friends in Rome wrote encouraging him to come back. They clearly thought that he was hazarding both profit and honour if he stayed away.[2] But Michelangelo, whether the constitutional timidity of which I have spoken, or other reasons damped his courage, felt that he could not trust to the Pope's mercies. What effect San Gallo may have had upon him, supposing this architect arrived in Florence at the middle of May, can only be conjectured. The fact remains that he continued stubborn for a time. In the lengthy autobiographical letter written to some prelate in 1542, Michelangelo relates what followed:[3] "Later on, while I was at Florence, Julius sent three briefs to the Signory. At last the latter sent for me and said : ' We do not want to go to war with Pope Julius because of you. You must return ; and if you do so, we will write you letters of such authority that, should he do you harm, he will be doing it to this Signory. Accordingly I took the letters, and went back to the Pope."

Condivi gives a graphic account of the transactions which ensued.[4] "During the months he stayed in Florence three papal briefs were sent to

[1] For the social gatherings of painters at Bramante's house in Rome, see Vasari, xiii. 73.

[2] See Giovanni Balducci's letter, May 8, 1506, in Gotti, vol. ii. p. 52.

[3] Lettere, No. cdxxxv.   [4] Condivi, p. 30.

the Signory, full of threats, commanding that he should be sent back by fair means or by force. Piero Soderini, who was Gonfalonier for life at that time, had sent him against his own inclination to Rome when Julius first asked for him.   Accordingly, when the first of these briefs arrived, he did not compel Michelangelo to go, trusting that the Pope's anger would calm down.   But when the second and the third were sent, he called Michelangelo and said : 'You have tried a bout with the Pope on which the King of France would not have ventured ; therefore you must not go on letting yourself be prayed for.   We do not wish to go to war on your account with him, and put our state in peril.   Make your mind up to return.'   Michelangelo, seeing himself brought to this pass, and still fearing the anger of the Pope, bethought him of taking refuge in the East.   The Sultan indeed besought him with most liberal promises, through the means of certain Franciscan friars, to come and construct a bridge from Constantinople to Pera, and to execute other great works.   When the Gonfalonier got wind of this intention he sent for Michelangelo and used these arguments to dissuade him : ' It were better to choose death with the Pope than to keep in life by going to the Turk.   Nevertheless, there is no fear of such an ending ; for the Pope is well disposed, and sends for you because he loves you, not to do you harm.   If you are afraid, the Signory will send you with the title of ambassador; forasmuch as public personages are never treated with violence, since this would be done to those who send them.' "

We only possess one brief from Julius to the Signory of Florence. It is dated Rome, July 8, 1506, and contains this passage:[1] " Michelangelo the sculptor, who left us without reason, and in mere caprice, is afraid, as we are informed, of returning, though we for our part are not angry with him, knowing the humours of such men of genius. In order, then, that he may lay aside all anxiety, we. rely on your loyalty to convince him in our name, that if he returns to us, he shall be uninjured and unhurt, retaining our apostolic favour in the same measure as he formerly enjoyed it." The date, July 8, is important in this episode of Michelangelo's life. Soderini sent back an answer to the Pope's brief within a few days, affirming that " Michelangelo the sculptor is so terrified[2] that, notwithstanding the promise of his Holiness, it will be necessary for the Cardinal of Pavia to write a letter signed by his own hand to us, guaranteeing his safety and immunity. We have done, and are doing, all we can to make him go back; assuring your Lordship that, unless he is gently handled, he will quit Florence, as he has already twice wanted to

[1] Bottari, *Lett. Pitt.*, iii. p. 472.
[2] Michelangelo, in one draft of his letter to Fattucci (Lettere, No. ccclxxxiv.), writes: "Dipoi circa sette o otto mesi che io stetti *quasi ascoso per paura*, sendo crucciato meco el Papa."

do." This letter is followed by another addressed
to the Cardinal of Volterra ·under date July 28.[1]
Soderini repeats that Michelangelo will not budge,
because he has as yet received no definite safe-conduct. It appears that in the course of August the
negotiations had advanced to a point at which
Michelangelo was willing to return. On the last
day of the month the Signory drafted a letter to the
Cardinal of Pavia in which they say that " Michelangelo Buonarroti, sculptor, citizen of Florence, and
greatly loved by us, will exhibit these letters present,
having at last been persuaded to repose confidence
in his Holiness." They add that he is coming in
good spirits and with good-will. Something may
have happened to renew his terror, for this despatch
was not delivered, and nothing more is heard of the
transaction till toward the close of November. It
is probable, however, that Soderini suddenly discovered how little Michelangelo was likely to be
wanted ; Julius, on the 27th of August, having
started on what appeared to be his mad campaign
against Perugia and Bologna. On the 21st of
November following the Cardinal of Pavia sent an
autograph letter from Bologna to the Signory,
urgently requesting that they would despatch
Michelangelo immediately to that town, inasmuch
as the Pope was impatient for his arrival, and
wanted to employ him on important works. Six

[1] See Gaye, vol. ii. pp. 83, 84, 85, 91, 93, for the whole correspondence.

days later, November 27, Soderini writes two letters, one to the Cardinal of Pavia and one to the Cardinal of Volterra, which finally conclude the whole business. The epistle to Volterra begins thus : "The bearer of these present will be Michelangelo, the sculptor, whom we send to please and satisfy his Holiness. We certify that he is an excellent young man, and in his own art without peer in Italy, perhaps also in the universe. We cannot recommend him more emphatically. His nature is such, that with good words and kindness, if these are given him, he will do everything ; one has to show him love and treat him kindly, and he will perform things which will make the whole world wonder." The letter to Pavia is written more familiarly, reading like a private introduction. In both of them Soderini enhances the service he is rendering the Pope by alluding to the magnificent design for the Battle of Pisa which Michelangelo must leave unfinished.[1]

Before describing his reception at Bologna, it may be well to quote two sonnets here which throw an interesting light upon Michelangelo's personal feeling for Julius and his sense of the corruption of the Roman Curia.[2] The first may well have been written during this residence at Florence ;[3] and the autograph of the second has these curious

[1] He says that Michelangelo has *principiato una storia per il pubblico che sarà cosa admiranda.*

[2] *Rime:* Sonnets, Nos. iii. and iv.

[3] A drawing at Oxford for the battle of Pisa has this sonnet written on the back. See Robinson, p. 21.

words added at the foot of the page : "*Vostro Michel-angniolo, in Turchia.*"   Rome itself, the Sacred City, has become a land of infidels, and Michelangelo, whose thoughts are turned to the Levant, implies that he would find himself no worse off with the Sultan than the Pope.

> My Lord ! if ever ancient saw spake sooth,
>   Hear this which saith : Who can doth never will.
>   Lo, thou hast lent thine ear to fables still,
>   Rewarding those who hate the name of truth.
> I am thy drudge, and have been from my youth—
>   Thine, like the rays which the sun's circle fill ;
>   Yet of my dear time's waste thou think'st no ill :
>   The more I toil, the less I move thy ruth.
> Once 'twas my hope to raise me by thy height ;
>   But 'tis the balance and the powerful sword
>   Of Justice, not false Echo, that we need.
> Heaven, as it seems, plants virtue in despite
>   Here on the earth, if this be our reward—
>   To seek for fruit on trees too dry to breed.

> Here helms and swords are made of chalices :
>   The blood of Christ is sold so much the quart :
>   His cross and thorns are spears and shields ; and short
>   Must be the time ere even His patience cease.
> Nay, let Him come no more to raise the fees
>   Of this foul sacrilege beyond report :
>   For Rome still flays and sells Him at the court,
>   Where paths are closed to virtue's fair increase.
> Now were fit time for me to scrape a treasure,
>   Seeing that work and gain are gone ; while he
>   Who wears the robe, is my Medusa still.
> God welcomes poverty perchance with pleasure :
>   But of that better life what hope have we,
>   When the blessed banner leads to nought but ill ?

While Michelangelo was planning frescoes and venting his bile in sonnets, the fiery Pope had started on his perilous career of conquest. He called the Cardinals together, and informed them that he meant to free the cities of Perugia and Bologna from their tyrants. God, he said, would protect His Church; he could rely on the support of France and Florence. Other Popes had stirred up wars and used the services of generals; he meant to take the field in person. Louis XII. is reported to have jeered among his courtiers at the notion of a high-priest riding to the wars. A few days afterwards, on the 27th of August, the Pope left Rome attended by twenty-four cardinals and 500 men-at-arms. He had previously secured the neutrality of Venice and a promise of troops from the French court. When Julius reached Orvieto, he was met by Gian-paolo Baglioni, the bloody and licentious despot of Perugia. Notwithstanding Baglioni knew that Julius was coming to assert his supremacy, and notwithstanding the Pope knew that this might drive to desperation a man so violent and stained with crime as Baglioni, they rode together to Perugia, where Gianpaolo paid homage and supplied his haughty guest with soldiers. The rashness of this act of Julius sent a thrill of admiration throughout Italy, stirring that sense of *terribilità* which fascinated the imagination of the Renaissance. Machiavelli, commenting upon the action of the Baglioni, remarks that the event proved how difficult it is for a man to be perfectly and scientifically wicked. Gianpaolo, he says, murdered his relations, oppressed his subjects, and boasted of being a father by his sister; yet, when he got his worst enemy into his clutches, he had not the spirit to be magnificently criminal, and murder or imprison Julius. From Perugia the Pope crossed the Apennines, and found himself at Imola upon the 20th of October. There he received news that the French governor of Milan, at the order of his king, was about to send him a reinforcement of 600 lances and 3000 foot-soldiers. This announcement, while it cheered the heart of Julius, struck terror into the Bentivogli, masters of Bologna. They left their city and took refuge in Milan, while the people of Bologna sent envoys to the Pope's camp, surrendering their town and themselves to his apostolic clemency. On the 11th of November, S. Martin's day, Giuliano della Rovere made his triumphal entry into Bologna, having restored two wealthy provinces to the states of the Church by a stroke of sheer audacity, unparalleled in the history of any previous pontiff. Ten days afterwards we find him again renewing negotiations with the Signory for the extradition of Michelangelo.

II.

"Arriving then one morning at Bologna, and going to hear Mass at S. Petronio, there met him the Pope's grooms of the stable, who immediately recognised him, and brought him into the presence of his Holiness, then at table in the Palace of the Sixteen.[1] When the Pope beheld him, his face clouded with anger, and he cried : 'It was your duty to come to seek us, and you have waited till we came to seek you ;' meaning thereby that his Holiness having travelled to Bologna, which is much nearer to Florence than Rome, he had come to find him out. Michelangelo knelt, and prayed for pardon in a loud voice, pleading in his excuse that he had not erred through frowardness, but through great distress of mind, having been unable to endure the expulsion he received. The Pope remained holding his head low and answering nothing, evidently much agitated ; when a certain prelate, sent by Cardinal Soderini to put in a good word for Michelangelo, came forward and said : 'Your Holiness might overlook his fault ; he did wrong through ignorance : these painters, outside their art, are all like this.' Thereupon the Pope answered in a fury : 'It is you, not I, who are insulting him. It is you, not he, who are the ignoramus and the rascal. Get hence out of my sight, and bad luck to you !' When

---

[1] Condivi, p. 31.

the fellow did not move, he was cast forth by the servants, as Michelangelo used to relate, with good round kicks and thumpings. So the Pope, having spent the surplus of his bile upon the bishop, took Michelangelo apart and pardoned him. Not long afterwards he sent for him and said : 'I wish you to make my statue on a large scale in bronze. I mean to place it on the façade of San Petronio.' When he went to Rome in course of time, he left 1000 ducats at the bank of Messer Antonmaria da Lignano for this purpose. But before he did so Michelangelo had made the clay model. Being in some doubt how to manage the left hand, after making the Pope give the benediction with the right, he asked Julius, who had come to see the statue, if he would like it to hold a book. 'What book?' replied he : 'a sword ! I know nothing about letters, not I.' Jesting then about the right hand, which was vehement in action, he said with a smile to Michelangelo : 'That statue of yours, is it blessing or cursing?' To which the sculptor : 'Holy Father, it is threatening this people of Bologna if they are not prudent.' "

Michelangelo's letter to Fattucci confirms Condivi's narrative.[1] "When Pope Julius went to Bologna the first time, I was forced to go there with a rope round my neck to beg his pardon. He ordered me to make his portrait in bronze, sitting, about seven cubits (14 feet) in height. When he

[1] Lettere, No. ccclxxxiii.

asked what it would cost, I answered that I thought
I could cast it for 1000 ducats; but that this was
not my trade, and that I did not wish to undertake
it.   He answered: 'Go to work ; you shall cast it
over and over again till it succeeds ; and I will give
you enough to satisfy your wishes.'   To put it
briefly, I cast the statue twice ; and at the end of
two years, at Bologna, I found that I had four and
a half ducats left.   I never received anything more
for this job ; and all the moneys I paid out during
the said two years were the 1000 ducats with which
I promised to cast it.   These were disbursed to me
in instalments by Messer Antonio Maria da Legnano,
a Bolognese."

The statue must have been more than thrice life-
size, if it rose fourteen feet in a sitting posture.
Michelangelo worked at the model in a hall called
the Stanza del Pavaglione behind the Cathedral.
Three experienced workmen were sent, at his request, from Florence, and he began at once upon
the arduous labour.   His domestic correspondence,
which at this period becomes more copious and interesting, contains a good deal of information concerning his residence at Bologna.   His mode of life,
as usual, was miserable and penurious in the extreme.
This man, about whom popes and cardinals and gon-
faloniers had been corresponding, now hired a single
room with one bed in it, where, as we have seen,
he slept together with his three assistants.   There
can be no doubt that such eccentric habits prevented

Michelangelo from inspiring his subordinates with
due respect.   The want of control over servants and
workmen, which is a noticeable feature of his
private life, may in part be attributed to this cause.
And now, at Bologna, he soon got into trouble with
the three craftsmen he had engaged to help him.
They were Lapo d'Antonio di Lapo, a sculptor at
the Opera del Duomo ; Lodovico del Buono, surnamed Lotti, a metal-caster and founder of cannon ;
and Pietro Urbano, a craftsman who continued long
in his service.   Lapo boasted that he was executing
the statue in partnership with Michelangelo and
upon equal terms, which did not seem incredible
considering their association in a single bedroom.
Beside this, he intrigued and cheated in money
matters.   The master felt that he must get rid of
him, and send the fellow back to Florence.   Lapo,
not choosing to go alone, lest the truth of the affair
should be apparent, persuaded Lodovico to join
him; and when they reached home, both began
to calumniate their master.   Michelangelo, knowing
that they were likely to do so, wrote to his brother
Buonarroto on the 1st of February 1507 :[1] "I inform you further how on Friday morning I sent
away Lapo and Lodovico, who were in my service.
Lapo, because he is good for nothing and a rogue,
and could not serve me.   Lodovico is better, and I
should have been willing to keep him another two
months, but Lapo, in order to prevent blame falling

___

[1] Lettere, No. 1.

on himself alone, worked upon the other so that both went away together.   I write you this, not that I regard them, for they are not worth three farthings, the pair of them, but because if they come to talk to Lodovico (Buonarroti) he must not be surprised at what they say.   Tell him by no means to lend them his ears; and if you want to be informed about them, go to Messer Angelo, the herald of the Signory;[1] for I have written the whole story to him, and he will, out of his kindly feeling, tell you just what happened."

In spite of these precautions, Lapo seems to have gained the ear of Michelangelo's father, who wrote a scolding letter in his usual puzzle-headed way. Michelangelo replied in a tone of real and ironical humility, which is exceedingly characteristic:[2] "Most revered father, I have received a letter from you to-day, from which I learn that you have been informed by Lapo and Lodovico.   I am glad that you should rebuke me, because I deserve to be rebuked as a ne'er-do-well and sinner as much as any one, or perhaps more.   But you must know that I have not been guilty in the affair for which you take me to task now, neither as regards them nor any one else, except it be in doing more than was my duty." After this exordium he proceeds to give an elabo-

---

[1] His surname was Manfidi. As second herald of the Signory, he took part in the debate upon the placing of the David. See above, p. 94. He was a good friend of Michelangelo's, and one of his letters is preserved in the Archiv. Buon., Cod. ix. No. 506.

[2] Lettere, No. iv., date February 8, 1507.

rate explanation of his dealings with Lapo, and the man's roguery.

The correspondence with Buonarroto turns to a considerable extent upon a sword-hilt which Michelangelo designed for the Florentine, Pietro Aldobrandini.[1] It was the custom then for gentlemen to carry swords and daggers with hilt and scabbard wonderfully wrought by first-rate artists. Some of these, still extant, are among the most exquisite specimens of sixteenth-century craft.[2] This little affair gave Michelangelo considerable trouble. First of all, the man who had to make the blade was long about it. From the day when the Pope came to Bologna, he had more custom than all the smiths in the city were used in ordinary times to deal with. Then, when the weapon reached Florence, it turned out to be too short. Michelangelo affirmed that he had ordered it exactly to the measure sent, adding that Aldobrandini was " probably not born to wear a dagger at his belt." He bade his brother present it to Filippo Strozzi, as a compliment from the Buonarroti family; but the matter was bungled. Probably Buonarroto tried to get some valuable equivalent; for Michelangelo writes to say that he is sorry " he behaved so scurvily toward Filippo in so trifling an affair."

Nothing at all transpires in these letters regard-

---

[1] Lettere, Nos. xlviii., xlix., liv., lv., lvii., lviii.

[2] See, for example, the illustrations to Yriarte's *Autour des Borgia* Paris : Rothschild, 1891. Troisième Partie.

ing the company kept by Michelangelo at Bologna.
The few stories related by tradition which refer to
this period are not much to the sculptor's credit for
courtesy.[1]   The painter Francia, for instance, came
to see the statue, and made the commonplace remark
that he thought it very well cast and of excellent
bronze.   Michelangelo took this as an insult to his
design, and replied : " I owe the same thanks to
Pope Julius who supplied the metal, as you do to
the colourmen who sell you paints."   Then, turning
to some gentlemen present there, he added that
Francia was " a blockhead."   Francia had a son remarkable for youthful beauty.   When Michelangelo
first saw him he asked whose son he was, and, on
being informed, uttered this caustic compliment :[2]
" Your father makes handsomer living figures than
he paints them."   On some other occasion, a stupid
Bolognese gentleman asked whether he thought
his statue or a pair of oxen were the bigger.
Michelangelo replied :[3] " That is according to the
oxen.   If Bolognese, oh! then without a doubt
ours of Florence are smaller."   Possibly Albrecht
Dürer may have met him in the artistic circles of
Bologna, since he came from Venice on a visit

[1] Vasari, xii. p. 186.

[2] Compare this with Benv. da Imola's story about Giotto.   " When
Dante saw some of Giotto's children, very ugly and like their father,
he asked how it was that he painted such fair figures and begat such
foul ones.   Giotto smiled and answered : ' It is because I paint by day,
and make models of living men by night.' "

[3] The point seems to depend upon the fact that *bue* in Italy is the name
for a dullard or a cuckold.

during these years;[1] but nothing is known about their intercourse.

III.

Julius left Bologna on the 22nd of February 1507. Michelangelo remained working diligently at his model. In less than three months it was nearly ready to be cast. Accordingly, the sculptor, who had no practical knowledge of bronze-founding, sent to Florence for a man distinguished in that craft, Maestro dal Ponte of Milan. During the last three years he had been engaged as Master of the Ordnance under the Republic. His leave of absence was signed upon the 15th of May 1507.

Meanwhile the people of Bologna were already planning revolution. The Bentivogli retained a firm hereditary hold on their affections, and the government of priests is never popular, especially among the nobles of a state. Michelangelo writes to his brother Giovan Simone (May 2) describing the bands of exiles who hovered round the city and kept its burghers in alarm:[2] "The folk are stifling in their coats of mail; for during four days past the whole county is under arms, in great confusion and peril, especially the party of the Church." The Papal Legate, Francesco Alidosi, Cardinal of Pavia,

[1] Grimm, vol. i. p. 319.   [2] Lettere, No. cxxvi.

took such prompt measures that the attacking troops were driven back.[1]   He also executed some of the citizens who had intrigued with the exiled family. The summer was exceptionally hot, and plague hung about; all articles of food were dear and bad.[2] Michelangelo felt miserable, and fretted to be free; but the statue kept him hard at work.

When the time drew nigh for the great operation, he wrote in touching terms to Buonarroto:[3] "Tell Lodovico (their father) that in the middle of next month I hope to cast my figure without fail.   Therefore, if he wishes to offer prayers or aught else for its good success, let him do so betimes, and say that I beg this of him."   Nearly the whole of June elapsed, and the business still dragged on. At last, upon the 1st of July, he advised his brother thus:[4] "We have cast my figure, and it has come out so badly that I verily believe I shall have to do it all over again.   I reserve details, for I have other things to think of.   Enough that it has gone wrong.   Still I thank God, because I take every-

---

[1] This man, of considerable ability but bad character, abused the confidence of Julius.   When Bologna broke loose from the Papal rule in 1511, the calamity was ascribed, apparently with justice, to his treason and incompetence.   The Duke Francesco Maria della Rovere, acting as general for his uncle Julius, stabbed the Cardinal with his own hands to death upon the open street of Ravenna.   This happened on the 24th of May—one of the most memorable acts of violence in Italian Renaissance annals.   A good account of the whole matter is given in Dennistoun's "Dukes of Urbino," vol. ii. p. 314 et seq.

[2] Lettere, Nos. lv., lxviii., lxxiv.

[3] Lettere, No. lx., date May 26.

[4] Lettere, Nos. lxii., lxiii.

thing for the best." From the next letter we learn that only the lower half of the statue, up to the girdle, was properly cast. The metal for the rest remained in the furnace, probably in the state of what Cellini called a cake.[1] The furnace had to be pulled down and rebuilt, so as to cast the upper half. Michelangelo adds that he does not know whether Master Bernardino mismanaged the matter from ignorance or bad luck. " I had such faith in him that I thought he could have cast the statue without fire. Nevertheless, there is no denying that he is an able craftsman, and that he worked with good-will. Well, he has failed, to my loss and also to his own, seeing he gets so much blame that he dares not lift his head up in Bologna." The second casting must have taken place about the 8th of July; for on the 10th Michelangelo writes that it is done, but the clay is too hot for the result to be reported, and Bernardino left yesterday.[2] When the statue was uncovered, he was able to reassure his brother:[3] " My affair might have turned out much better, and also much worse. At all events, the whole is there, so far as I can see ; for it is not yet quite disengaged. I shall want, I think, some months to work it up with file and hammer, because it has come out rough. Well, well, there is much to thank God for ; as I said, it might have been worse." On

---

[1] *Vita*, lib. ii. 76.   [2] Lettere, No. lxiv.
[3] Lettere, Nos. lxv., lxvi.

making further discoveries, he finds that the cast is
far less bad than he expected ; but the labour of
cleaning it with the polishing tools proved longer
and more irksome than he expected :[1] " I am
exceedingly anxious to get away home, for here I
pass my life in huge discomfort and with extreme
fatigue.   I work night and day, do nothing else ;
and the labour I am forced to undergo is such, that
if I had to begin the whole thing over again, I do
not think I could survive it.   Indeed, the undertaking has been one of enormous difficulty ; and
if it had been in the hand of another man, we
should have fared but ill with it.   However, I believe that the prayers of some one have sustained
and kept me in health, because all Bologna thought
I should never bring it to a proper end."   We can
see that Michelangelo was not unpleased with the
result ; and the statue must have been finished soon
after the New Year.   However, he could not leave
Bologna.   On the 18th of February 1508 he writes
to Buonarroto that he is kicking his heels, having
received orders from the Pope to stay until the
bronze was placed.[2]   Three days later—that is, upon
the 21st of February—the Pope's portrait was
hoisted to its pedestal above the great central door
of S. Petronio.

It remained there rather less than three years.
When the Papal Legate fled from Bologna in 1511,

[1] Lettere, No. lxxii., date November 10, 1507.
[2] Lettere, No. lxxv.

and the party of the Bentivogli gained the upper hand, they threw the mighty mass of sculptured bronze, which had cost its maker so much trouble, to the ground. That happened on the 30th of December. The Bentivogli sent it to the Duke Alfonso d'Este of Ferrara, who was a famous engineer and gunsmith. He kept the head intact, but cast a huge cannon out of part of the material, which took the name of La Giulia. What became of the head is unknown. It is said to have weighed 600 pounds.[1]

So perished another of Michelangelo's masterpieces; and all we know for certain about the statue is that Julius was seated, in full pontificals, with the triple tiara on his head, raising the right hand to bless, and holding the keys of S. Peter in the left.[2]

Michelangelo reached Florence early in March. On the 18th of that month he began again to occupy his house at Borgo Pinti, taking it this time on hire from the Operai del Duomo.[3] We may suppose, therefore, that he intended to recommence work on the Twelve Apostles. A new project seems also to have been started by his friend Soderini—that of making him erect a colossal statue of Hercules subduing Cacus opposite the David. The Gonfalonier was in correspondence with the Marquis of Carrara

---

[1] See the notices collected by Gotti, vol. i. p. 66.
[2] *Cronaca Bolognese*, MS., quoted by Milanesi ; Vasari, xii. 348.
[3] Gaye, vol. ii. p. 477.

on the 10th of May about a block of marble for
this giant;[1] but Michelangelo at that time had returned to Rome, and of the Cacus we shall hear
more hereafter.

IV.

When Julius received news that his statue had
been duly cast and set up in its place above the
great door of S. Petronio, he began to be anxious
to have Michelangelo once more near his person.
The date at which the sculptor left Florence again
for Rome is fixed approximately by the fact that
Lodovico Buonarroti emancipated his son from
parental control upon the 13th of March 1508.
According to Florentine law, Michelangelo was not
of age, nor master over his property and person,
until this deed had been executed.[2]

In the often-quoted letter to Fattucci he says:[3]
"The Pope was still unwilling that I should complete the tomb, and ordered me to paint the vault
of the Sistine. We agreed for 3000 ducats. The
first design I made for this work had twelve apostles
in the lunettes, the remainder being a certain space
filled in with ornamental details, according to the

[1] Gaye, vol. ii. p. 97.
[2] It was registered in the State Archive on the 28th of March.
Gotti, vol. i. p. 70.
[3] Lettere, No. ccclxxxiii.

usual manner. After I had begun, it seemed to me that this would turn out rather meanly; and I told the Pope that the Apostles alone would yield a poor effect, in my opinion. He asked me why. I answered, 'Because they too were poor.' Then he gave me commission to do what I liked best, and promised to satisfy my claims for the work, and told me to paint down to the pictured histories upon the lower row." [1]

There is little doubt that Michelangelo disliked beginning this new work, and that he would have greatly preferred to continue the sepulchral monument, for which he had made such vast and costly preparations. He did not feel certain how he should succeed in fresco on a large scale, not having had any practice in that style of painting since he was a prentice under Ghirlandajo. It is true that the Cartoon for the Battle of Pisa had been a splendid success; still this, as we have seen, was not coloured, but executed in various methods of outline and chiaroscuro. Later on, while seriously engaged upon the Sistine, he complains to his father: [2] "I am still in great distress of mind, because it is now a year since I had a farthing from the Pope; and I do not ask, because my work is not going forward in a way that seems to me to deserve it. That comes from its difficulty, and

[1] Had this been done, he would have obliterated the double row of Botticelli's Popes.

[2] Lettere, No. x., date January 27, 1509.

also *from this not being my trade.*"[1] And so I waste my time without results. God help me."

We may therefore believe Condivi when he asserts that "Michelangelo, who had not yet practised colouring, and knew that the painting of a vault is very difficult, endeavoured by all means to get himself excused, putting Raffaello forward as the proper man, and pleading that this was not his trade, and that he should not succeed."[2] Condivi states in the same chapter that Julius had been prompted to intrust him with the Sistine by Bramante, who was jealous of his great abilities, and hoped he might fail conspicuously when he left the field of sculpture. I have given my reasons above for doubting the accuracy of this tradition; and what we have just read of Michelangelo's own hesitation confirms the statements made by Bramante in the Pope's presence, as recorded by Rosselli.[3] In fact, although we may assume the truth of Bramante's hostility, it is difficult to form an exact conception of the intrigues he carried on against Buonarroti.

Julius would not listen to any arguments. Accordingly, Michelangelo made up his mind to obey the patron whom he nicknamed his Medusa. Bramante was commissioned to erect the scaffolding, which he did so clumsily, with beams suspended

---

[1] Also in the Sonnet to Giovanni da Pistoja (*Rime*, v.) he says : "Nè io pittore."

[2] Condivi, p. 34.　　　　[3] See above, p. 176.

from the vault by huge cables, that Michelangelo asked how the holes in the roof would be stopped up when his painting was finished. The Pope allowed him to take down Bramante's machinery, and to raise a scaffold after his own design. The rope alone which had been used, and now was wasted, enabled a poor carpenter to dower his daughter.[1] Michelangelo built his own scaffold free from the walls, inventing a method which was afterwards adopted by all architects for vault-building. Perhaps he remembered the elaborate drawing he once made of Ghirlandajo's assistants at work upon the ladders and wooden platforms at S. Maria Novella.

Knowing that he should need helpers in so great an undertaking, and also mistrusting his own ability to work in fresco, he now engaged several excellent Florentine painters. Among these, says Vasari, were his friends Francesco Granacci and Giuliano Bugiardini, Bastiano da San Gallo surnamed Aristotele, Angelo di Donnino, Jacopo di Sandro, and Jacopo surnamed l'Indaco. Vasari is probably accurate in his statement here ; for we shall see that Michelangelo, in his *Ricordi*, makes mention of five assistants, two of whom are proved by other documents to have been Granacci and Indaco. We also

---

[1] The above facts about the scaffold are related by Vasari, xii. 189. A payment for rope under date October 13, 1508, has been recently edited (*Arch. Stor.*, Ser. terza, vi. 187) ; but its amount does not seem to confirm the story of the dowry.

possess two letters from Granacci which show that Bugiardini, San Gallo, Angelo di Donnino, and Jacopo l'Indaco were engaged in July.[1] The second of Granacci's letters refers to certain disputes and hagglings with the artists. This may have brought Michelangelo to Florence, for he was there upon the 11th of August 1508, as appears from the following deed of renunciation : " In the year of our Lord 1508, on the 11th day of August, Michelangelo, son of Lodovico di Lionardo di Buonarrota, repudiated the inheritance of his uncle Francesco by an instrument drawn up by the hand of Ser Giovanni di Guasparre da Montevarchi, notary of Florence, on the 27th of July 1508."[2] When the assistants arrived at Rome is not certain. It must, however, have been after the end of July.[3] The extracts from Michelangelo's notebooks show that he had already sketched an agreement as to wages several weeks before.[4] " I record how on this day, the 10th of May 1508, I, Michelangelo, sculptor, have received from the Holiness of our Lord Pope Julius II. 500 ducats of the Camera, the which were paid me by Messer Carlino, chamberlain, and Messer Carlo degli Albizzi, on account of the painting of

[1] These letters, dated July 22 and 24, at Florence, are in the Arch. Buon., and are translated by Heath Wilson, p. 125.

[2] Gotti, i. 70, note. Heath Wilson, 127, note, says that he took legal opinion as to whether Michelangelo must have been at Florence for this protocol, and was informed that he must.

[3] See Letters from Granacci, quoted above.

[4] Lettere, *Ricordi*, p. 563.

the vault of the Sistine Chapel, on which I begin to
work to-day, under the conditions and contracts set
forth in a document written by his Most Reverend
Lordship of Pavia, and signed by my hand.

" For the painter-assistants who are to come from
Florence, who will be five in number, twenty gold
ducats of the Camera apiece, on this condition ; that
is to say, that when they are here and are working
in harmony with me, the twenty ducats shall be
reckoned to each man's salary ; the said salary to
begin upon the day they leave Florence. And if
they do not agree with me, half of the said money
shall be paid them for their travelling expenses, and
for their time."

On the strength of this *Ricordo*, it has been
assumed that Michelangelo actually began to paint
the Sistine on the 10th of May 1508. That would
have been physically and literally impossible. He
was still at Florence, agreeing to rent his house in
Borgo Pinti, upon the 18th of March. Therefore he
had no idea of going to Rome at that time. When
he arrived there, negotiations went on, as we have
seen, between him and Pope Julius. One plan for
the decoration of the roof was abandoned, and
another on a grander scale had to be designed. To
produce working Cartoons for that immense scheme
in less than two months would have been beyond
the capacities of any human brain and hands. But
there are many indications that the vault was not
prepared for painting, and the materials for fresco

not accumulated, till a much later date. For instance, we possess a series of receipts by Piero Rosselli, acknowledging several disbursements for the plastering of the roof between May 11 and July 27.[1] We learn from one of these that Granacci was in Rome before June 3 ; and Michelangelo writes for fine blue colours to a certain Fra Jacopo Gesuato at Florence upon the 13th of May.[2] All is clearly in the air as yet, and on the point of preparation. Michelangelo's phrase, " on which I begin to work to-day," will have to be interpreted, therefore, in the widest sense, as implying that he was engaging assistants, getting the architectural foundation ready, and procuring a stock of necessary articles. The whole summer and autumn must have been spent in taking measurements and expanding the elaborate design to the proper scale of working drawings ; and if Michelangelo had toiled alone without his Florentine helpers, it would have been impossible for him to have got through with these preliminary labours in so short a space of time.

Michelangelo's method in preparing his Cartoons seems to have been the following. He first made a small-scale sketch of the composition, sometimes including a large variety of figures. Then he went to the living models, and studied portions of the whole design in careful transcripts from Nature, using black and red chalk, pen, and sometimes bistre. Among the most admirable of his drawings left to

[1] Lettere, p. 563.   [2] Lettere, No. cccxliv.

us are several which were clearly executed with a view to one or other of these great Cartoons. Finally, returning to the first composition, he repeated that, or so much of it as could be transferred to a single sheet, on the exact scale of the intended fresco. These enlarged drawings were applied to the wet surface of the plaster, and their outlines pricked in with dots to guide the painter in his brush-work. When we reflect upon the extent of the Sistine vault (it is estimated at more than 10,000 square feet of surface), and the difficulties presented by its curves, lunettes, spandrels, and pendentives ; when we remember that this enormous space is alive with 343 figures in every conceivable attitude, some of them twelve feet in height, those seated as prophets and sibyls measuring nearly eighteen feet when upright, all animated with extraordinary vigour, presenting types of the utmost variety and vivid beauty, imagination quails before the intellectual energy which could first conceive a scheme so complex, and then carry it out with mathematical precision in its minutest details.[1]

The date on which Michelangelo actually began

[1] A very full account of the measurements of the Sistine and of Michelangelo's method is given by Heath Wilson, chap. vi. In some respects it forms the most valuable part of that excellent and hitherto by far too much neglected work. Heath Wilson enjoyed the singular privilege of making a close examination of the roof ; and what he says about the execution of the frescoes and their present state deserves to be most attentively studied. He has dispelled many illusions ; as, for instance, the old tradition that Michelangelo worked in absolute isolation.

to paint the fresco is not certain. Supposing he
worked hard all the summer, he might have done
so when his Florentine assistants arrived in August;
and, assuming that the letter to his father above
quoted (*Lettere*, x.) bears a right date, he must
have been in full swing before the end of January
1509.　In that letter he mentions that Jacopo,
probably l'Indaco, "the painter whom I brought
from Florence, returned a few days ago; and as he
complained about me here in Rome, it is likely
that he will do so there. Turn a deaf ear to him;
he is a thousandfold in the wrong, and I could say
much about his bad behaviour toward me." Vasari
informs us that these assistants proved of no use;
whereupon, he destroyed all they had begun to do,
refused to see them, locked himself up in the chapel,
and determined to complete the work in solitude.[1]
It seems certain that the painters were sent back
to Florence. Michelangelo had already provided for
the possibility of their not being able to co-operate
with him;[2] but what the cause of their failure was
we can only conjecture. Trained in the methods
of the old Florentine school of fresco-painting, incapable of entering into the spirit of a style so
supereminently noble and so astoundingly original
as Michelangelo's, it is probable that they spoiled
his designs in their attempts to colour them. Harford pithily remarks:[3] "As none of the suitors of

---

[1] Vasari, xii. 190.　　[2] See *Ricordo* quoted above, p. 203.
[3] Harford, vol. i. p. 259.

Penelope could bend the bow of Ulysses, so one hand alone was capable of wielding the pencil of Buonarroti." Still it must not be imagined that Michelangelo ground his own colours, prepared his daily measure of wet plaster, and executed the whole series of frescoes with his own hand. Condivi and Vasari imply, indeed, that this was the case ; but, beside the physical impossibility, the fact remains that certain portions are obviously executed by inferior masters.[1] Vasari's anecdotes, moreover, contradict his own assertion regarding Michelangelo's single-handed labour. He speaks about the caution which the master exercised to guard himself against any treason of his workmen in the chapel.[2] Nevertheless, far the larger part, including all the most important figures, and especially the nudes, belongs to Michelangelo.

These troubles with his assistants illustrate a point upon which I shall have to offer some considerations at a future time. I allude to Michelangelo's inaptitude for forming a school of intelligent fellow-workers, for fashioning inferior natures into at least a sympathy with his aims and methods, and finally for living long on good terms with hired subordinates. All those qualities which the facile and genial Raffaello possessed in such abundance, and which made it possible for that young favourite of heaven and fortune to fill Rome with so much work of mixed merit, were wanting to the stern, exacting, and sensitive Buonarroti.

[1] See Heath Wilson, p. 155.   [2] Vasari, xii. 185.

But the assistants were not the only hindrance to Michelangelo at the outset. Condivi says that[1] "he had hardly begun painting, and had finished the picture of the Deluge, when the work began to throw out mould to such an extent that the figures could hardly be seen through it. Michelangelo thought that this excuse might be sufficient to get him relieved of the whole job. So he went to the Pope and said: 'I already told your Holiness that painting is not my trade ; what I have done is spoiled ; if you do not believe it, send to see.' The Pope sent San Gallo, who, after inspecting the fresco, pronounced that the lime-basis had been put on too wet, and that water oozing out produced this mouldy surface.[2] He told Michelangelo what the cause was, and bade him proceed with the work. So the excuse helped him nothing." About the fresco of the Deluge Vasari relates that, having begun to paint this compartment first, he noticed that the figures were too crowded, and consequently changed his scale in all the other portions of the ceiling. This is a plausible explanation of what is striking—namely, that the story of the Deluge is quite differently planned from the other episodes upon the vaulting. Yet I think it must be rejected, because it implies a total change in all the working cartoons, as well as a remarkable want of foresight.

[1] Condivi, p. 39.
[2] Heath Wilson (p. 141) says the plaster was made of Roman lime and marble dust.

Condivi continues: "While he was painting, Pope Julius used oftentimes to go and see the work, climbing by a ladder, while Michelangelo gave him a hand to help him on to the platform. His nature being eager and impatient of delay, he decided to have the roof uncovered, although Michelangelo had not given the last touches, and had only completed the first half—that is, from the door to the middle of the vault." Michelangelo's letters show that the first part of his work was executed in October. He writes thus to his brother Buonarroto:[1] "I am remaining here as usual, and shall have finished my painting by the end of the week after next—that is, the portion of it which I began; and when it is uncovered, I expect to be paid, and shall also try to get a month's leave to visit Florence."

V.

The uncovering took place upon November 1, 1509. All Rome flocked to the chapel, feeling that something stupendous was to be expected after the long months of solitude and seclusion during which the silent master had been working. Nor were they disappointed. The effect produced by only half of the enormous scheme was overwhelming.

[1] Lettere, No. lxxxi.

As Vasari says,[1] "This chapel lighted up a lamp
for our art which casts abroad lustre enough to
illuminate the world, drowned for so many centuries
in darkness." Painters saw at a glance that the
genius which had revolutionised sculpture was now
destined to introduce a new style and spirit into
their art. This was the case even with Raffaello,
who, in the frescoes he executed at S. Maria della
Pace, showed his immediate willingness to learn
from Michelangelo, and his determination to compete
with him. Condivi and Vasari are agreed upon
this point, and Michelangelo himself, in a moment
of hasty indignation, asserted many years afterwards
that what Raffaello knew of art was derived from
him.[2] That is, of course, an over-statement; for,
beside his own exquisite originality, Raffaello
formed a composite style successively upon Perugino,
Fra Bartolommeo, and Lionardo. He was capable
not merely of imitating, but of absorbing and assimi-
lating to his lucid genius the excellent qualities of
all in whom he recognised superior talent. At the
same time, Michelangelo's influence was undeniable,
and we cannot ignore the testimony of those who
conversed with both great artists—of Julius himself,
for instance, when he said to Sebastian del Piombo :[3]
"Look at the work of Raffaello, who, after seeing
the masterpieces of Michelangelo, immediately aban-

[1] Vasari, xii. 193.   [2] Lettere, No. cdxxxv.
[3] See Sebastiano del Piombo's letter of October 15, 1512, printed in
Gaye, vol. ii. p. 487.

MOTHER AND CHILDREN, DETAIL OF THE FLOOD, fresco, Sistine
Chapel, Vatican, 1509. Collection of Creighton E. Gilbert.

doned Perugino's manner, and did his utmost to approach that of Buonarroti."

Condivi's assertion that the part uncovered in November 1509 was the first half of the whole vault, beginning from the door and ending in the middle, misled Vasari, and Vasari misled subsequent biographers. We now know for certain that what Michelangelo meant by "the portion I began" was the whole central space of the ceiling—that is to say, the nine compositions from Genesis, with their accompanying genii and architectural surroundings. That is rendered clear by a statement in Albertini's Roman Handbook, to the effect that the "upper portion of the whole vaulted roof" had been uncovered when he saw it in 1509.[1] Having established this error in Condivi's narrative, what he proceeds to relate may obtain some credence. " Raffaello, when he beheld the new and marvellous style of Michelangelo's work, being extraordinarily apt at imitation, sought, by Bramante's means, to obtain a commission for the rest." Had Michelangelo ended at a line drawn halfway across the breadth of the vault, leaving the Prophets and Sibyls, the lunettes and pendentives, all finished so far, it would have been a piece of monstrous impudence even in Bramante, and an impossible discourtesy in gentle Raffaello, to have begged for leave to carry on a scheme so marvellously planned. But the history

[1] Albertini, *Mirabilia Urbis*, quoted by Grimm, vol. i. p. 523. Albertini's own words are *pars testudinea superior*.

of the Creation, Fall, and Deluge, when first exposed, looked like a work complete in itself. Michelangelo, who was notoriously secretive, had almost certainly not explained his whole design to painters of Bramante's following; and it is also improbable that he had as yet prepared his working Cartoons for the lower and larger portion of the vault.[1] Accordingly, there remained a large vacant space to cover between the older frescoes by Signorelli, Perugino, Botticelli, and other painters, round the walls below the windows, and that new miracle suspended in the air. There was no flagrant impropriety in Bramante's thinking that his nephew might be allowed to carry the work downward from that altitude. The suggestion may have been that the Sistine Chapel should become a Museum of Italian art, where all painters of eminence could deposit proofs of their ability, until each square foot of wall was covered with competing masterpieces. But when Michelangelo heard of Bramante's intrigues, he was greatly disturbed in spirit. Having begun his task unwillingly, he now felt an equal or greater unwillingness to leave the stupendous conception of his brain unfinished. Against all expectation of himself and others, he had achieved a decisive victory, and was placed at one stroke, as Condivi says, "above the reach of envy." His hand had found its cunning

---

[1] It may be inferred, I think, from a passage in Lettere, No. ccclxxxiii. that Michelangelo only began the Cartoons for the second portion of the Sistine in 1510.

for fresco as for marble. Why should he be interrupted in the full swing of triumphant energy?
"Accordingly, he sought an audience with the
Pope, and openly laid bare all the persecutions he
had suffered from Bramante, and discovered the
numerous misdoings of the man." It was on this
occasion, according to Condivi, that Michelangelo
exposed Bramante's scamped work and vandalism
at S. Peter's. Julius, who was perhaps the only
man in Rome acquainted with his sculptor's scheme
for the Sistine vault, brushed the cobwebs of these
petty intrigues aside, and left the execution of the
whole to Michelangelo.

There is something ignoble in the task of recording rivalries and jealousies between artists and men
of letters. Genius, however, like all things that
are merely ours and mortal, shuffles along the path
of life, half flying on the wings of inspiration, half
hobbling on the feet of interest, the crutches of commissions. Michelangelo, although he made the David
and the Sistine, had also to make money. He was
entangled with shrewd men of business, and crafty
spendthrifts, ambitious intriguers, folk who used
undoubted talents, each in its kind excellent and
pure, for baser purposes of gain or getting on. The
art-life of Rome seethed with such blood-poison;
and it would be sentimental to neglect what entered
so deeply and so painfully into the daily experience
of our hero. Raffaello, kneaded of softer and more
facile clay than Michelangelo, throve in this environ-

ment, and was somehow able—so it seems—to turn its venom to sweet uses. I like to think of the two peers, moving like stars on widely separated orbits, with radically diverse temperaments, proclivities, and habits, through the turbid atmosphere enveloping but not obscuring their lucidity. Each, in his own way, as it seems to me, contrived to keep himself unspotted by the world ; and if they did not understand one another and make friends, this was due to the different conceptions they were framed to take of life, the one being the exact antipodes to the other.[1]

VI.

Postponing descriptive or æsthetic criticism of the Sistine frescoes, I shall proceed with the narration of their gradual completion.

We have few documents to guide us through the period of time which elapsed between the first

---

[1] Raffaello ardently loved women. Michelangelo, so far as we know, was insensible to their attraction. Raffaello enjoyed society, and took innocent pleasure in personal magnificence. Michelangelo preferred solitude, and lived sordidly. Raffaello burned out in a few brilliant years, dying at the age of Byron and Mozart. Michelangelo grew to be a tough old man of nearly ninety, preserving the fire of his temperament to the end. Raffaello sunned himself in the gladness of existence. Michelangelo walked in the shade. The one was genial and *Lebens lustig ;* the other, melancholic and surcharged with *Innigkeit.* Raffaello revelled in the facile and sensuous externalisation of ideas. Michelangelo grappled with intensest problems both of thought and plastic presentation.

uncovering of Michelangelo's work on the roof of the
Sistine (November 1, 1509) and its ultimate accomplishment (October 1512). His domestic correspondence is abundant, and will be used in its proper
place ; but nothing transpires from those pages of
affection, anger, and financial negotiation to throw
light upon the working of the master's mind while
he was busied in creating the sibyls and prophets,
the episodes and idyls, which carried his great Bible
of the Fate of Man downwards through the vaulting
to a point at which the Last Judgment had to be
presented as a crowning climax. For the anxious
student of his mind and life-work, nothing is more
desolating than the impassive silence he maintains
about his doings as an artist. He might have told
us all we want to know, and never shall know here
about them. But while he revealed his personal
temperament and his passions with singular frank-
ness, he locked up the secret of his art, and said
nothing.

Eventually we must endeavour to grasp Michelangelo's work in the Sistine as a whole, although it
was carried out at distant epochs of his life. For
this reason I have thrown these sentences forward,
in order to embrace a wide span of his artistic
energy (from May 10, 1508, to perhaps December
1541). There is, to my mind, a unity of conception between the history depicted on the vault, the
prophets and forecomers on the pendentives, the
types selected for the spandrels, and the final spec-

tacle of the day of doom. Living, as he needs must
do, under the category of time, Michelangelo was
unable to execute his stupendous picture-book of
human destiny in one sustained manner. Years
passed over him of thwarted endeavour and distracted energies—years of quarrying and sculptur-
ing, of engineering and obeying the vagaries of
successive Popes. Therefore, when he came at last
to paint the Last Judgment, he was a worn man,
exhausted in services of many divers sorts. And,
what is most perplexing to the reconstructive critic,
nothing in his correspondence remains to indicate
the stages of his labour. The letters tell plenty
about domestic anxieties, annoyances in his poor
craftsman's household, purchases of farms, indignant
remonstrances with stupid brethren ; but we find in
them, as I have said, no clue to guide us through
that mental labyrinth in which the supreme artist
was continually walking, and at the end of which
he left to us the Sistine as it now is.

VII.

The old reckoning of the time consumed by
Michelangelo in painting the roof of the Sistine,
and the traditions concerning his mode of work
there, are clearly fabulous. Condivi says : " He
finished the whole in twenty months, without hav-

ing any assistance whatsoever, not even of a man to grind his colours." From a letter of September 7, 1510, we learn that the scaffolding was going to be put up again, and that he was preparing to work upon the lower portion of the vaulting.[1] Nearly two years elapse before we hear of it again. He writes to Buonarroto on the 24th of July 1512 :[2] "I am suffering greater hardships than ever man endured, ill, and with overwhelming labour; still I put up with all in order to reach the desired end." Another letter on the 21st of August shows that he expects to complete his work at the end of September; and at last, in October, he writes to his father:[3] "I have finished the chapel I was painting. The Pope is very well satisfied." On the calculation that he began the first part on May 10, 1508, and finished the whole in October 1512, four years and a half were employed upon the work. A considerable part of this time was of course taken up with the preparation of Cartoons ; and the nature of fresco-painting rendered the winter months not always fit for active labour. The climate of Rome is not so mild but that wet plaster might often freeze and crack during December, January, and February. Besides, with all his superhuman energy, Michelangelo could not have painted straight on daily without rest or stop. It seems, too, that the

---

[1] Lettere, No. xxi.   [2] Lettere, No. lxxxvii.
[3] Lettere, Nos. lxxxix., xv. Milanesi dates the second in 1509, but he is wrong, I think.

master was often in need of money, and that he
made two journeys to the Pope to beg for supplies.
In the letter to Fattucci he says:[1] "When the
vault was nearly finished, the Pope was again at
Bologna;[2] whereupon, I went twice to get the
necessary funds, and obtained nothing, and lost all
that time until I came back to Rome. When I
reached Rome, I began to make Cartoons—that
is, for the ends and sides of the said chapel,
hoping to get money at last and to complete the
work. I never could extract a farthing; and when I
complained one day to Messer Bernardo da Bibbiena
and to Atalante,[3] representing that I could not stop
longer in Rome, and that I should be forced to
go away with God's grace, Messer Bernardo told
Atalante he must bear this in mind, for that he
wished me to have money, whatever happened."
When we consider, then, the magnitude of the
undertaking, the arduous nature of the preparatory

[1] Lettere, No. ccclxxxiii.

[2] The date of one of these visits, which may have taken Michelangelo
as far as the Pope's camp before Mirandola, is fixed by a letter of
January 11, 1511, to Buonarroto (Lettere, No. lxxxiv.). The date of
the other is uncertain. See Grimm, vol. i. p. 389. Among the few
documents which throw light upon Michelangelo's movements at this
period is an inedited letter from Agnolo Manfido, State-herald in
Florence, to the sculptor in Rome, dated November 2, 1510, and expressing pleasure at hearing the news of his safe arrival. Arch. Buon.,
Cod. ix. No. 506.

[3] Bibbiena is the Cardinal Dovizi, and famous author of the
Calandra. Atalante was a natural son of Manetto Migliorotti, a
Florentine, who learned to play on the lute from Lionardo da Vinci.
He occupied a post in the Fabric of S. Peter's between 1513 and 1516.
See Milanesi, Lettere, p. 428, note.

studies, and the waste of time in journeys and through other hindrances, four and a half years are not too long a period for a man working so much alone as Michelangelo was wont to do.

We have reason to believe that, after all, the frescoes of the Sistine were not finished in their details. "It is true," continues Condivi, "that I have heard him say he was not suffered to complete the work according to his wish. The Pope, in his impatience, asked him one day when he would be ready with the Chapel, and he answered: 'When I shall be able.' To which his Holiness replied in a rage: 'You want to make me hurl you from that scaffold!' Michelangelo heard and remembered, muttering: 'That you shall not do to me.' So he went straightway, and had the scaffolding taken down. The frescoes were exposed to view on All Saints' day,[1] to the great satisfaction of the Pope, who went that day to service there, while all Rome flocked together to admire them. What Michelangelo felt forced to leave undone was the retouching of certain parts with ultramarine upon dry ground, and also some gilding, to give the whole a richer effect. Giulio, when his heat cooled down, wanted Michelangelo to make these last additions; but he, considering the trouble it would be to build up all that scaffolding afresh, observed that what was missing mattered little.

[1] Condivi is here, as elsewhere, mixing up the first with the second portion of the work.

'You ought at least to touch it up with gold,' replied the Pope; and Michelangelo, with that familiarity he used toward his Holiness, said carelessly: 'I have not observed that men wore gold.' The Pope rejoined: 'It will look poor.' Buonarroti added: 'Those who are painted there were poor men.'[1] So the matter turned into pleasantry, and the frescoes have remained in their present state." Condivi goes on to state that Michelangelo received 3000 ducats for all his expenses, and that he spent as much as twenty or twenty-five ducats on colours alone. Upon the difficult question of the moneys earned by the great artist in his life-work, I shall have to speak hereafter, though I doubt whether any really satisfactory account can now be given of them.

VIII.

Michelangelo's letters to his family in Florence throw a light at once vivid and painful over the circumstances of his life during these years of sustained creative energy. He was uncomfortable in his bachelor's home, and always in difficulties

---

[1] Michelangelo, in the letter to Fattucci (see Appendix), refers this repartee to the first period of his work upon the Sistine. It was characteristic of the man to leave the frescoes without ornament, and perhaps without the final finish he had planned.

with his servants. " I am living here in discontent, not thoroughly well, and undergoing great fatigue, without money, and with no one to look after me." [1] Again, when one of his brothers proposed to visit him in Rome, he writes: [2] " I hear that Gismondo means to come hither on his affairs. Tell him not to count on me for anything; not because I do not love him as a brother, but because I am not in the position to assist him. I am bound to care for myself first, and I cannot provide myself with necessaries. I live here in great distress and the utmost bodily fatigue, have no friends, and seek none. I have not even time enough to eat what I require. Therefore let no additional burdens be put upon me, for I could not bear another ounce." In the autumn of 1509 he corresponded with his father about the severe illness of an assistant work-man whom he kept, and also about a boy he wanted sent from Florence. [3] " I should be glad if you could hear of some lad at Florence, the son of good parents and poor, used to hardships, who would be willing to come and live with me here, to do the work of the house, buy what I want, and go around on messages; in his leisure time he could learn. Should such a boy be found, please let me know; because there are only rogues here, and I am

---

[1] Lettere, No. v., date June 1508.

[2] Lettere, No. lxxx., October 17, 1509.

[3] Lettere, Nos. ix., xviii., xix. Milanesi dates No. ix. November 5, 1508; but it is clearly in connection with the other two, dated January 1510.

in great need of some one." All through his life, Michelangelo adopted the plan of keeping a young fellow to act as general servant, and at the same time to help in art-work. Three of these servants are interwoven with the chief events of his later years, Pietro Urbano, Antonio Mini, and Francesco d'Amadore, called Urbino, the last of whom became his faithful and attached friend till death parted them. Women about the house he could not bear. Of the serving-maids at Rome he says:[1] "They are all strumpets and swine." Well, it seems that Lodovico found a boy, and sent him off to Rome. What followed is related in the next letter. "As regards the boy you sent me, that rascal of a mule-teer cheated me out of a ducat for his journey. He swore that the bargain had been made for two broad golden ducats, whereas all the lads who come here with the muleteers pay only ten carlins. I was more angry at this than if I had lost twenty-five ducats, because I saw that his father had re-solved to send him on mule-back like a gentleman. Oh, I had never such good luck, not I! Then both the father and the lad promised that he would do everything, attend to the mule, and sleep upon the ground, if it was wanted. And now I am obliged to look after him. As if I needed more worries than the one I have had ever since I arrived here! My apprentice, whom I left in Rome, has been ill from the day on which I returned until now. It

[1] Lettere, No. ccxxxv.

is true that he is getting better; but he lay for about a month in peril of his life, despaired of by the doctors, and I never went to bed. There are other annoyances of my own; and now I have the nuisance of this lad, who says that he does not want to waste time, that he wants to study, and so on. At Florence he said he would be satisfied with two or three hours a day. Now the whole day is not enough for him, but he must needs be drawing all the night. It is all the fault of what his father tells him. If I complained, he would say that I did not want him to learn. I really require some one to take care of the house; and if the boy had no mind for this sort of work, they ought not to have put me to expense. But they are good-for-nothing, and are working toward a certain end of their own. Enough, I beg you to relieve me of the boy; he has bored me so that I cannot bear it any longer. The muleteer has been so well paid that he can very well take him back to Florence. Besides, he is a friend of the father. Tell the father to send for him home. I shall not pay another farthing. I have no money. I will have patience till he sends; and if he does not send, I will turn the boy out of doors. I did so already on the second day of his arrival, and other times also, and the father does not believe it.

"*P.S.*—If you talk to the father of the lad, put the matter to him nicely: as that he is a good boy, but too refined, and not fit for my service, and say that he had better send for him home."

The repentant postscript is eminently character-istic of Michelangelo. He used to write in haste, apparently just as the thoughts came. Afterwards he read his letter over, and softened its contents down, if he did not, as sometimes happened, feel that his meaning required enforcement; in that case he added a stinging tail to the epigram. How little he could manage the people in his employ is clear from the last notice we possess about the unlucky lad from Florence. "I wrote about the. boy, to say that his father ought to send for him, and that I would not disburse more money. This I now confirm. The driver is paid to take him back. At Florence he will do well enough, learning his trade and dwelling with his parents. Here he is not worth a farthing, and makes me toil like a beast of burden; and my other apprentice has not left his bed. It is true that I have not got him in the house; for when I was so tired out that I could not bear it, I sent him to the room of a brother of his. I have no money."

These household difficulties were a trifle, how-ever, compared with the annoyances caused by the stupidity of his father and the greediness of his brothers. While living like a poor man in Rome, he kept continually thinking of their welfare. The letters of this period are full of references to the purchase of land, the transmission of cash when it was to be had, and the establishment of Buonarroto in a draper's business. They, on their part, were never satisfied, and repaid his kindness with ingratitude. The following letter to Giovan Simone shows how terrible Michelangelo could be when he detected baseness in a brother : [1]—

"GIOVAN SIMONE,—It is said that when one does good to a good man, he makes him become better, but that a bad man becomes worse. It is now many years that I have been endeavouring with words and deeds of kindness to bring you to live honestly and in peace with your father and the rest of us. You grow continually worse. I do not say that you are a scoundrel; but you are of such sort that you have ceased to give satisfaction to me or anybody. I could read you a long lesson on your ways of living ; but they would be idle words, like all the rest that I have wasted. To cut the matter short, I will tell you as a fact beyond all question that you have nothing in the world : what you spend and your house-room, I give you, and have given you these many years, for the love of God, believing you to be my brother like the rest. Now, I am sure that you are not my brother, else you would not threaten my father. Nay, you are a beast; and as a beast I mean to treat you. Know that he who sees his father threatened or roughly handled is bound to risk his

[1] Lettere, No. cxxvii., date July 1508.

own life in this cause. Let that suffice. I repeat that you have nothing in the world; and if I hear the least thing about your ways of going on, I will come to Florence by the post, and show you how far wrong you are, and teach you to waste your substance, and set fire to houses and farms you have not earned. Indeed you are not where you think yourself to be. If I come, I will open your eyes to what will make you weep hot tears, and recognise on what false grounds you base your arrogance.

"I have something else to say to you, which I have said before. If you will endeavour to live rightly, and to honour and revere your father, I am willing to help you like the rest, and will put it shortly within your power to open a good shop. If you act otherwise, I shall come and settle your affairs in such a way that you will recognise what you are better than you ever did, and will know what you have to call your own, and will have it shown to you in every place where you may go. No more. What I lack in words I will supply with deeds.

"MICHELANGELO *in Rome.*

"I cannot refrain from adding a couple of lines. It is as follows. I have gone these twelve years past drudging about through Italy, borne every shame, suffered every hardship, worn my body out in every toil, put my life to a thousand hazards, and all with the sole purpose of helping the fortunes of my family. Now that I have begun to raise it up a little, you only, you alone, choose to destroy and bring to ruin in one hour what it has cost me so many years and such labour to build up. By Christ's body this shall not be; for I am the man to put to the rout ten thousand of your sort, whenever it be needed. Be wise in time, then, and do not try the patience of one who has other things to vex him." [1]

Even Buonarroto, who was the best of the brothers and dearest to his heart, hurt him by his grasping-ness and want of truth. He had been staying at Rome on a visit, and when he returned to Florence it appears that he bragged about his wealth, as if the sums expended on the Buonarroti farms were not part of Michelangelo's earnings. The conse-quence was that he received a stinging rebuke from his elder brother.[2] "The said Michele told me you mentioned to him having spent about sixty ducats at Settignano. I remember your saying here too at table that you had disbursed a large sum out of your own pocket. I pretended not to under-stand, and did not feel the least surprise, because I know you. I should like to hear from your in-gratitude out of what money you gained them. If

---

[1] Passerini (in Gotti, ii. 19) thinks that this letter drove Giovan Simone abroad. He went, it seems, to Lisbon, intending to take ship for the Indies. However, he was back again in 1512, and set up busi-ness with Buonarroto.

[2] Lettere, No. xcii., date July 30, 1513. It must be said, in a spirit of equity to Michelangelo's family, that suspiciousness formed a strong element in his character. The letter quoted above seems to be an instance of this failing. As usual there were faults upon both sides, in these domestic rubs.

you had enough sense to know the truth, you would not say : ' I spent so and so much of my own ; ' also you would not have come here to push your affairs with me, seeing how I have always acted toward you in the past, but would have rather said : ' Michelangelo remembers what he wrote to us, and if he does not now do what he promised, he must be prevented by something of which we are ignorant,' and then have kept your peace ; because it is not well to spur the horse that runs as fast as he is able, and more than he is able. But you have never known me, and do not know me. God pardon you ; for it is He who granted me the grace to bear what I do bear and have borne, in order that you might be helped. Well, you will know me when you have lost me."

Michelangelo's angry moods rapidly cooled down. At the bottom of his heart lay a deep and abiding love for his family. There is something caressing in the tone with which he replies to grumbling letters from his father.[1] "Do not vex yourself. God did not make us to abandon us." "If you want me, I will take the post, and be with you in two days. Men are worth more than money." His warm affection transpires even more clearly in the two following documents :[2] "I should like you to be thoroughly convinced that all the

---

[1] Lettere, Nos. xx., xxi., date September 1510.

[2] Lettere, Nos. vii., xxii., dates August 1508, September 15, 1510, both addressed to Lodovico.

labours I have ever undergone have not been
more for myself than for your sake. What I have
bought, I bought to be yours so long as you live.
If you had not been here, I should have bought
nothing. Therefore, if you wish to let the house
and farm, do so at your pleasure. This income,
together with what I shall give you, will enable
you to live like a lord." At a time when Lodovico
was much exercised in his mind and spirits by a
lawsuit, his son writes to comfort the old man.
" Do not be discomfited, nor give yourself an ounce
of sadness. Remember that losing money is not
losing one's life. I will more than make up to
you what you must lose. Yet do not attach too
much value to worldly goods, for they are by nature
untrustworthy. Thank God that this trial, if it
was bound to come, came at a time when you have
more resources than you had in years past. Look
to preserving your life and health, but let your
fortunes go to ruin rather than suffer hardships ; for
I would sooner have you alive and poor; if you
were dead, I should not care for all the gold in
the world. If those chatterboxes or any one else
reprove you, let them talk, for they are men without
intelligence and without affection."

References to public events are singularly scanty
in this correspondence. Much as Michelangelo felt
the woes of Italy—and we know he did so by his
poems—he talked but little, doing his work daily
like a wise man all through the dust and din stirred

up by Julius and the League of Cambrai. The
lights and shadows of Italian experience at that
time are intensely dramatic. We must not altogether forget the vicissitudes of war, plague, and
foreign invasion, which exhausted the country,
while its greatest men continued to produce immortal masterpieces. Aldo Manuzio was quietly
printing his complete edition of Plato, and Michelangelo was transferring the noble figure of a prophet or a sibyl to the plaster of the Sistine, while
young Gaston de Foix was dying at the point of
victory upon the bloody shores of the Ronco. Sometimes, however, the disasters of his country touched
Michelangelo so nearly that he had to write or speak
about them. After the battle of Ravenna, on the
11th of April 1512, Raimondo de Cardona and his
Spanish troops brought back the Medici to Florence.
On their way, the little town of Prato was sacked with
a barbarity which sent a shudder through the whole
peninsula. The Cardinal Giovanni de' Medici, who
entered Florence on the 14th of September, established his nephews as despots in the city, and inti-
midated the burghers by what looked likely to be
a reign of terror. These facts account for the uneasy tone of a letter written by Michelangelo to
Buonarroto.[1] Prato had been taken by assault upon
the 30th of August, and was now prostrate after
those hideous days of torment, massacre, and outrage indescribable which followed. In these circum-

[1] Lettere, No. xc., date September 5, 1512.

stances Michelangelo advises his family to "escape into a place of safety, abandoning their household gear and property ; for life is far more worth than money." If they are in need of cash, they may draw upon his credit with the Spedalingo of S. Maria Novella.[1] The constitutional liability to panic which must be recognised in Michelangelo emerges at the close of the letter. "As to public events, do not meddle with them either by deed or word. Act as though the plague were raging. Be the first to fly." The Buonarroti did not take his advice, but remained at Florence, enduring agonies of terror. It was a time when disaffection toward the Medicean princes exposed men to risking life and limb. Rumours reached Lodovico that his son had talked imprudently at Rome. He wrote to inquire what truth there was in the report, and Michelangelo replied :[2] "With regard to the Medici, I have never spoken a single word against them, except in the way that everybody talks—as, for instance, about the sack of Prato ; for if the stones could have cried out, I think they would have spoken. There have been many other things said since then, to which, when I heard them, I have answered : 'If they are really acting in this way, they are doing wrong;' not that I believed the reports ; and God grant they are not true. About a month ago, some one who makes a

---

[1] This functionary acted as Michelangelo's banker, and helped him with advice in the purchase of land.

[2] Lettere, No. xxxvi., date October 1512.

show of friendship for me spoke very evilly about their deeds. I rebuked him, told him that it was not well to talk so, and begged him not to do so again to me. However, I should like Buonarroto quietly to find out how the rumour arose of my having calumniated the Medici ; for if it is some one who pretends to be my friend, I ought to be upon my guard."

The Buonarroti family, though well affected toward Savonarola, were connected by many ties of interest and old association with the Medici, and were not powerful enough to be the mark of violent political persecution. Nevertheless, a fine was laid upon them by the newly restored Government. This drew forth the following epistle from Michelangelo :[1]—

" DEAREST FATHER,—Your last informs me how things are going on at Florence, though I already knew something. We must have patience, commit ourselves to God, and repent of our sins ; for these trials are solely due to them, and more particularly to pride and ingratitude. I never conversed with a people more ungrateful and puffed up than the Florentines. Therefore, if judgment comes, it is but right and reasonable. As for the sixty ducats you tell me you are fined, I think this a scurvy trick, and am exceedingly annoyed. However, we must have patience as long as it pleases God. I

[1] Lettere, No. xxxvii., date October 1512.

will write and enclose two lines to Giuliano de' Medici. Read them, and if you like to present them to him, do so ; you will see whether they are likely to be of any use. If not, consider whether we can sell our property and go to live elsewhere. . . . Look to your life and health ; and if you cannot share the honours of the land like other burghers, be contented that bread does not fail you, and live well with Christ, and poorly, as I do here ; for I live in a sordid way, regarding neither life nor honours—that is, the world—and suffer the greatest hardships and innumerable anxieties and dreads. It is now about fifteen years since I had a single hour of well-being, and all that I have done has been to help you, and you have never recognised this nor believed it. God pardon us all ! I am ready to go on doing the same so long as I live, if only I am able."

We have reason to believe that the petition to Giuliano proved effectual, for in his next letter he congratulates his father upon their being restored to favour.[1] In the same communication he mentions a young Spanish painter whom he knew in Rome, and whom he believes to be ill at Florence. This was probably the Alonso Berughetta who made a copy of the Cartoon for the Battle of Pisa. In July 1508 Michelangelo wrote twice about a Spaniard who wanted leave to study the Cartoon ; first begging Buonarroto to procure the keys for him, and

---

[1] Lettere, No. xxxviii. The phrase is *ribenedetti*.

afterwards saying that he is glad to hear that the permission was refused.[1] It does not appear certain whether this was the same Alonso; but it is interesting to find that Michelangelo disliked his Cartoon being copied. We also learn from these letters that the Battle of Pisa then remained in the Sala del Papa.[2]

IX.

I will conclude this chapter by translating a sonnet addressed to Giovanni da Pistoja, in which Michelangelo humorously describes the discomforts he endured while engaged upon the Sistine.[3] Condivi tells us that from painting so long in a strained attitude, gazing up at the vault, he lost for some time the power of reading except when he lifted the paper above his head and raised his eyes. Vasari corroborates the narrative from his own experience in the vast halls of the Medicean palace.[4]

> I've grown a goitre by dwelling in this den—
>   As cats from stagnant streams in Lombardy,
>   Or in what other land they hap to be—
>   Which drives the belly close beneath the chin:

---

[1] Lettere, Nos. lxxvi., lxxviii.

[2] At least that is the inference of Milanesi. Lettere, p. 95, note.

[3] *Rime;* Sonnet, No. v. The autograph has a funny little caricature upon the margin, showing a man, with protruded stomach and head bent back, using his brush upon a surface high above him.

[4] Condivi, p. 41 ; Vasari, xii. 193.

My beard turns up to heaven; my nape falls in,
  Fixed on my spine: my breast-bone visibly
  Grows like a harp: a rich embroidery
Bedews my face from brush-drops thick and thin.
My loins into my paunch like levers grind:
  My buttock like a crupper bears my weight;
  My feet unguided wander to and fro;
In front my skin grows loose and long; behind,
  By bending it becomes more taut and strait;
  Crosswise I strain me like a Syrian bow:
    Whence false and quaint, I know,
Must be the fruit of squinting brain and eye;
For ill can aim the gun that bends awry.
    Come then, Giovanni, try
To succour my dead pictures and my fame,
Since foul I fare and painting is my shame.

CHAPTER VI.

I.

THE Sistine Chapel was built in 1473 by Baccio Pontelli, a Florentine architect, for Pope Sixtus IV. It is a simple barn-like chamber, 132 feet in length, 44 in breadth, and 68 in height from the pavement. The ceiling consists of one expansive flattened vault, the central portion of which offers a large plane surface, well adapted to fresco decoration. The building is lighted by twelve windows, six upon each side of its length. These are placed high up, their rounded arches running parallel with the first spring of the vaulting. The ends of the chapel are closed by flat walls, against the western of which is raised the altar.

When Michelangelo was called to paint here, he found both sides of the building, just below the windows, decorated in fresco by Perugino, Cosimo Rosselli, Sandro Botticelli, Luca Signorelli, and Domenico Ghirlandajo. These masters had depicted, in a series of twelve subjects, the history of Moses and the life of Jesus. Above the lines of fresco, in the spaces between the windows and along the eastern end at the same height, Botticelli painted a row of twenty-eight Popes. The spaces below the frescoed histories, down to the seats which ran along the pavement, were blank, waiting for the tapestries which Raffaello afterwards supplied from cartoons now in possession of the English Crown.

At the west end, above the altar, shone three decorative frescoes by Perugino, representing the Assumption of the Virgin, between the finding of Moses and the Nativity. The two last of these pictures opened respectively the history of Moses and the life of Christ, so that the Old and New Testaments were equally illustrated upon the Chapel walls. At the opposite, or eastern end, Ghirlandajo painted the Resurrection, and there was a corresponding picture of Michael contending with Satan for the body of Moses.

Such was the aspect of the Sistine Chapel when Michelangelo began his great work. Perugino's three frescoes on the west wall were afterwards demolished to make room for his Last Judgment. The two frescoes on the east wall are now poor pictures by very inferior masters; but the twelve Scripture histories and Botticelli's twenty-eight Popes remain from the last years of the fifteenth century.[1]

Taken in their aggregate, the wall-paintings I have described afforded a fair sample of Umbrian and Tuscan art in its middle or *quattrocento* age of evolution. It remained for Buonarroti to cover the vault and the whole western end with masterpieces displaying what Vasari called the "modern" style in its most sublime and imposing manifestation. At the same time he closed the cycle of the figurative

---

[1] This *quattrocento* work was carried out before 1484, immediately after the building of the chapel. Vasari ascribes these Popes to Botticelli.

arts, and rendered any further progress on the same lines impossible. The growth which began with Niccolò of Pisa and with Cimabue, which advanced through Giotto and his school, Perugino and Pinturicchio, Piero della Francesca and Signorelli, Fra Angelico and Benozzo Gozzoli, the Ghirlandajo brothers, the Lippi and Botticelli, effloresced in Michelangelo, leaving nothing for after-comers but manneristic imitation.

II.

Michelangelo, instinctively and on principle, re-acted against the decorative methods of the fifteenth century. If he had to paint a biblical or mytho-logical subject, he avoided landscapes, trees, flowers, birds, beasts, and subordinate groups of figures. He eschewed the arabesques, the labyrinths of foliage and fruit enclosing pictured panels, the candelabra and gay bands of variegated patterns, which enabled a *quattrocento* painter, like Gozzoli or Pinturicchio, to produce brilliant and harmonious general effects at a small expenditure of intellectual energy. Where the human body struck the keynote of the music in a work of art, he judged that such simple adjuncts and naïve concessions to the pleasure of the eye should be avoided.[1] An architectural foundation for

[1] See Vasari, xii. p. 234.

the plastic forms to rest on, as plain in structure and as grandiose in line as could be fashioned, must suffice. These principles he put immediately to the test in his first decorative undertaking. For the vault of the Sistine he designed a mighty architectural framework in the form of a hypæthral temple, suspended in the air on jutting pilasters, with bold cornices, projecting brackets, and ribbed arches flung across the void of heaven. Since the whole of this ideal building was painted upon plaster, its inconsequence, want of support, and disconnection from the ground-plan of the chapel do not strike the mind. It is felt to be a mere basis for the display of pictorial art, the theatre for a thousand shapes of dignity and beauty.

I have called this imaginary temple hypæthral, because the master left nine openings in the flattened surface of the central vault. They are unequal in size, five being short parallelograms, and four being spaces of the same shape but twice their length. Through these the eye is supposed to pierce the roof and discover the unfettered region of the heavens. But here again Michelangelo betrayed the inconsequence of his invention. He filled the spaces in question with nine dominant paintings, representing the history of the Creation, the Fall, and the Deluge. Taking our position at the west end of the chapel and looking upwards, we see in the first compartment God dividing light from darkness; in the second, creating the sun and the moon and the solid earth;

CUMAEAN SIBYL, fresco, Sistine Chapel, Vatican, about 1511.
Collection of Creighton E. Gilbert.

in the third, animating the ocean with His brooding influence; in the fourth, creating Adam; in the fifth, creating Eve. The sixth represents the temptation of our first parents and their expulsion from Paradise. The seventh shows Noah's sacrifice before entering the ark; the eighth depicts the Deluge, and the ninth the drunkenness of Noah. It is clear that, between the architectural conception of a roof opening on the skies and these pictures of events which happened upon earth, there is no logical connection. Indeed, Michelangelo's new system of decoration bordered dangerously upon the barocco style, and contained within itself the germs of a vicious mannerism.

It would be captious and unjust to push this criticism home. The architectural setting provided for the figures and the pictures of the Sistine vault is so obviously conventional, every point of vantage has been so skilfully appropriated to plastic uses, every square inch of the ideal building becomes so naturally, and without confusion, a pedestal for the human form, that we are lost in wonder at the synthetic imagination which here for the first time combined the arts of architecture, sculpture, and painting in a single organism. Each part of the immense composition, down to the smallest detail, is necessary to the total effect. We are in the presence of a most complicated yet mathematically ordered scheme, which owes life and animation to one master-thought. In spite of its complexity and scientific precision, the vault of the Sistine does not strike the mind as being artificial or worked out by calculation, but as being predestined to existence, inevitable, a cosmos instinct with vitality.

On the pendentives between the spaces of the windows, running up to the ends of each of the five lesser pictures, Michelangelo placed alternate prophets and sibyls upon firm projecting consoles. Five sibyls and five prophets run along the side-walls of the chapel. The end-walls sustain each of them a prophet. These twelve figures are intro-duced as heralds and pioneers of Christ the Saviour, whose presence on the earth is demanded by the fall of man and the renewal of sin after the Deluge. In the lunettes above the windows and the arched recesses or spandrels over them are depicted scenes setting forth the genealogy of Christ and of his Mother. At each of the four corner-spandrels of the ceiling, Michelangelo painted, in spaces of a very peculiar shape and on a surface of embarrassing inequality, one magnificent subject symbolical of man's redemption. The first is the raising of the Brazen Serpent in the wilderness; the second, the punishment of Haman; the third, the victory of David over Goliath; the fourth, Judith with the head of Holofernes.

Thus, with a profound knowledge of the Bible, and with an intense feeling for religious symbolism, Michelangelo unrolled the history of the creation of the world and man, the entrance of sin into the human heart, the punishment of sin by water, and the reappearance of sin in Noah's family. Having done this, he intimated, by means of four special mercies granted to the Jewish people—types and symbols of God's indulgence—that a Saviour would arise to redeem the erring human race. In confirmation of this promise, he called twelve potent witnesses, seven of the Hebrew prophets and five of the Pagan sibyls. He made appeal to history, and set around the thrones on which these witnesses are seated scenes detached from the actual lives of our Lord's human ancestors.

The intellectual power of this conception is at least equal to the majesty and sublime strength of its artistic presentation. An awful sense of coming doom and merited damnation hangs in the thunderous canopy of the Sistine vault, tempered by a solemn and sober expectation of the Saviour. It is much to be regretted that Christ, the Desired of all Nations, the Redeemer and Atoner, appears nowhere adequately represented in the Chapel. When Michelangelo resumed his work there, it was to portray him as an angered Hercules, hurling curses upon helpless victims. The august rhetoric of the ceiling loses its effective value when we can nowhere point to Christ's life and work on earth; when there is no picture of the Nativity, none of the Crucifixion, none of the Resurrection; and when the feeble panels of a Perugino and a Cosimo Rosselli are crushed into insignificance by the terrible Last

Judgment. In spite of Buonarroti's great creative strength, and injuriously to his real feeling as a Christian, the piecemeal production which governs all large art undertakings results here in a maimed and one-sided rendering of what theologians call the Scheme of Salvation.

III.

So much has been written about the pictorial beauty, the sublime imagination, the dramatic energy, the profound significance, the exact science, the shy graces, the terrible force, and finally the vivid powers of characterisation displayed in these frescoes, that I feel it would be impertinent to attempt a new discourse upon a theme so time-worn. I must content myself with referring to what I have already published, which will, I hope, be sufficient to demonstrate that I do not avoid the task for want of enthusiasm.[1] The study of much rhetorical criticism makes me feel strongly that, in front of certain masterpieces, silence is best, or, in lieu of silence, some simple pregnant sayings, capable of rousing folk to independent observation.

These convictions need not prevent me, however, from fixing attention upon a subordinate matter, but one which has the most important bearing upon

[1] *Renaissance in Italy*, "The Fine Arts," pp. 342–346, 407–412.

Michelangelo's genius. After designing the architectural theatre which I have attempted to describe, and filling its main spaces with the vast religious drama he unrolled symbolically in a series of primeval scenes, statuesque figures, and countless minor groups contributing to one intellectual conception ; he proceeded to charge the interspaces—all that is usually left for facile decorative details—with an army of passionately felt and wonderfully executed nudes, forms of youths and children, naked or half draped, in every conceivable posture and with every possible variety of facial type and expression. On pedestals, cornices, medallions, tympanums, in the angles made by arches, wherever a vacant plane or unused curve was found, he set these vivid transcripts from humanity in action. We need not stop to inquire what he intended by that host of plastic shapes evoked from his imagination. The triumphant leaders of the crew, the twenty lads who sit upon their consoles, sustaining medallions by ribands which they lift, have been variously and inconclusively interpreted. In the long row of Michelangelo's creations, those young men are perhaps the most significant—athletic adolescents, with faces of feminine delicacy and poignant fascination. But it serves no purpose to inquire what they symbolise. If we did so, we should have to go further, and ask, What do the bronze figures below them, twisted into the boldest attitudes the human frame can take, or the twinned children on the pedestals, signify? In this region, the region of pure plastic play, when art drops the wand of the interpreter and allows physical beauty to be a law unto itself, Michelangelo demonstrated that no decorative element in the hand of a really supreme master is equal to the nude.

Previous artists, with a strong instinct for plastic as opposed to merely picturesque effect, had worked upon the same line.   Donatello revelled in the rhythmic dance and stationary grace of children. Luca Signorelli initiated the plan of treating complex ornament by means of the mere human body; and for this reason, in order to define the position of Michelangelo in Italian art-history, I shall devote the next section of this chapter to Luca's work at Orvieto.   But Buonarroti in the Sistine carried their suggestions to completion.   The result is a mapped-out chart of living figures—a vast pattern, each detail of which is a masterpiece of modelling. After we have grasped the intellectual content of the whole, the message it was meant to inculcate, the spiritual meaning present to the maker's mind, we discover that, in the sphere of artistic accomplishment, as distinct from intellectual suggestion, one rhythm of purely figurative beauty has been carried throughout—from God creating Adam to the boy who waves his torch above the censer of the Erythrean sibyl.

IV.

Of all previous painters, only Luca Signorelli deserves to be called the forerunner of Michelangelo, and his Chapel of S. Brizio in the Cathedral at Orvieto in some remarkable respects anticipates the Sistine. This eminent master was commissioned in 1499 to finish its decoration, a small portion of which had been begun by Fra Angelico. He completed the whole Chapel within the space of two years; so that the young Michelangelo, upon one of his journeys to or from Rome, may probably have seen the frescoes in their glory. Although no visit to Orvieto is recorded by his biographers, the fame of these masterpieces by a man whose work at Florence had already influenced his youthful genius must certainly have attracted him to a city which lay on the direct route from Tuscany to the Campagna.

The four walls of the Chapel of S. Brizio are covered with paintings setting forth events immediately preceding and following the day of judgment. A succession of panels, differing in size and shape, represent the preaching of Antichrist, the destruction of the world by fire, the resurrection of the body, the condemnation of the lost, the reception of saved souls into bliss, and the final states of heaven and hell. These main subjects occupy the upper spaces of each wall, while below them are placed portraits of poets, surrounded by

rich and fanciful arabesques, including various episodes from Dante and antique mythology. Obeying
the spirit of the fifteenth century, Signorelli did not
aim at what may be termed an architectural effect in
his decoration of this building. Each panel of the
whole is treated separately, and with very unequal
energy, the artist seeming to exert his strength
chiefly in those details which made demands on his
profound knowledge of the human form and his
enthusiasm for the nude. The men and women of
the Resurrection, the sublime angels of Heaven and
of the Judgment, the discoloured and degraded
fiends of Hell, the magnificently foreshortened
clothed figures of the Fulminati, the portraits in the
preaching of Antichrist, reveal Luca's specific quality
as a painter, at once impressively imaginative and
crudely realistic. There is something in his way of
regarding the world and of reproducing its aspects
which dominates our fancy, does violence to our
sense of harmony and beauty, leaves us broken and
bewildered, resentful and at the same moment en-
thralled. He is a power which has to be reckoned
with; and the reason for speaking about him at
length here is that, in this characteristic blending of
intense vision with impassioned realistic effort after
truth to fact, this fascination mingled with repulsion,
he anticipated Michelangelo. Deep at the root of
all Buonarroti's artistic qualities lie these contra-
dictions. Studying Signorelli, we study a parallel
psychological problem. The chief difference between

the two masters lies in the command of æsthetic synthesis, the constructive sense of harmony, which belonged to the younger, but which might, we feel, have been granted in like measure to the elder, had Luca been born, as Michelangelo was, to complete the evolution of Italian figurative art, instead of marking one of its most important intermediate moments.

The decorative methods and instincts of the two men were closely similar. Both scorned any element of interest or beauty which was not strictly plastic—the human body supported by architecture or by rough indications of the world we live in. Signorelli invented an intricate design for arabesque pilasters, one on each side of the door leading from his chapel into the Cathedral. They are painted *en grisaille,* and are composed exclusively of nudes, mostly male, perched or grouped in a marvellous variety of attitudes upon an ascending series of slender-stemmed vases, which build up gigantic candelabra by their aggregation. The naked form is treated with audacious freedom. It appears to be elastic in the hands of the modeller. Some dead bodies carried on the backs of brawny porters are even awful by the contrast of their wet-clay limpness with the muscular energy of brutal life beneath them. Satyrs giving drink to one another, fauns whispering in the ears of stalwart women, centaurs trotting with corpses flung across their cruppers, combatants trampling in frenzy upon prostrate enemies, men

sunk in self-abandonment to sloth or sorrow—such
are the details of these incomparable columns, where
our sense of the grotesque and vehement is immediately corrected by a perception of rare energy in
the artist who could play thus with his plastic
puppets.

We have here certainly the preludings to Michelangelo's serener, more monumental work in the Sistine Chapel. The leading motive is the same in
both great masterpieces. It consists in the use of
the simple body, if possible the nude body, for the
expression of thought and emotion, the telling of a
tale, the delectation of the eye by ornamental details.
It consists also in the subordination of the female
to the male nude as the symbolic unit of artistic
utterance. Buonarroti is greater than Signorelli
chiefly through that larger and truer perception of
æsthetic unity which seems to be the final outcome
of a long series of artistic efforts. The arabesques,
for instance, with which Luca wreathed his portraits
of the poets, are monstrous, bizarre, in doubtful taste.
Michelangelo, with a finer instinct for harmony, a
deeper grasp on his own dominant ideal, excluded
this element of *quattrocento* decoration from his
scheme. Raffaello, with the graceful tact essential
to the style, developed its crude rudiments into the
choice forms of fanciful delightfulness which charm
us in the Loggie.

Signorelli loved violence. A large proportion of
the circular pictures painted *en grisaille* on these

walls represent scenes of massacre, assassination, torture, ruthless outrage. One of them, extremely spirited in design, shows a group of three executioners hurling men with millstones round their necks into a raging river from the bridge which spans it. The first victim flounders half merged in the flood; a second plunges head foremost through the air; the third stands bent upon the parapet, his shoulders pressed down by the varlets on each side, at the very point of being flung to death by drowning. In another of these pictures a man seated upon the ground is being tortured by the breaking of his teeth, while a furious fellow holds a club suspended over him, in act to shatter his thigh-bones. Naked soldiers wrestle in mad conflict, whirl staves above their heads, fling stones, displaying their coarse muscles with a kind of frenzy. Even the classical subjects suffer from extreme dramatic energy of treatment. Ceres, seeking her daughter through the plains of Sicily, dashes frantically on a car of dragons, her hair dishevelled to the winds, her cheeks gashed by her own crooked fingers. Eurydice struggles in the clutch of bestial devils; Pluto, like a mediæval Satan, frowns above the scene of fiendish riot; the violin of Orpheus thrills faintly through the infernal tumult. Gazing on the spasms and convulsions of these grim subjects, we are inclined to credit a legend preserved at Orvieto to the effect that the painter depicted his own unfaithful mistress in the naked woman who is being borne on a demon's back through the air to hell.

No one who has studied Michelangelo impartially will deny that in this preference for the violent he came near to Signorelli. We feel it in his choice of attitude, the strain he puts upon the lines of plastic composition, the stormy energy of his conception and expression. It is what we call his *terribilità*. But here again that dominating sense of harmony, that instinct for the necessity of subordinating each artistic element to one strain of architectonic music, which I have already indicated as the leading note of difference between him and the painter of Cortona, intervened to elevate his terribleness into the region of sublimity. The violence of Michelangelo, unlike that of Luca, lay not so much in the choice of savage subjects (cruelty, ferocity, extreme physical and mental torment) as in a forceful, passionate, tempestuous way of handling all the themes he treated. The angels of the Judgment, sustaining the symbols of Christ's Passion, wrestle and bend their agitated limbs like athletes. Christ emerges from the sepulchre, not in victorious tranquillity, but with the clash and clangour of an irresistible energy set free. Even in the Crucifixion, one leg has been wrenched away from the nail which pierced its foot, and writhes round the knee of the other still left riven to the cross. The loves of Leda and the Swan, of Ixion and Juno, are spasms of voluptuous pain;

the sleep of the Night is troubled with fantastic
dreams, and the Dawn starts into consciousness
with a shudder of prophetic anguish. There is not a
hand, a torso, a simple nude, sketched by this extraordinary master, which does not vibrate with nervous
tension, as though the fingers that grasped the pen
were clenched and the eyes that viewed the model
glowed beneath knit brows. Michelangelo, in fact,
saw nothing, felt nothing, interpreted nothing, on
exactly the same lines as any one who had preceded
or who followed him. His imperious personality he
stamped upon the smallest trifle of his work.

Luca's frescoes at Orvieto, when compared with
Michelangelo's in the Sistine, mark the transition
from the art of the fourteenth, through the art of
the fifteenth, to that of the sixteenth century, with
broad and trenchant force. They are what Mar-
lowe's dramas were to Shakespeare's. They retain
much of the mediæval tradition both as regards form
and sentiment. We feel this distinctly in the treatment of Dante, whose genius seems to have exerted at
least as strong an influence over Signorelli's imagination as over that of Michelangelo. The episodes
from the Divine Comedy are painted in a rude
Gothic spirit. The spirits of Hell seem borrowed
from grotesque bas-reliefs of the Pisan school. The
draped, winged, and armed angels of Heaven are
posed with a ceremonious research of suavity or grandeur. These and other features of his work carry
us back to the period of Giotto and Niccolò Pisano.

But the true force of the man, what made him a commanding master of the middle period, what distinguished him from all his fellows of the *quattrocento*, is the passionate delight he took in pure humanity—the nude, the body studied under all its aspects and with no repugnance for its coarseness—man in his crudity made the sole sufficient object for figurative art, anatomy regarded as the crowning and supreme end of scientific exploration. It is this in his work which carries us on toward the next age, and justifies our calling Luca " the morning-star of Michelangelo."

It would be wrong to ascribe too much to the immediate influence of the elder over the younger artist—at any rate in so far as the frescoes of the Chapel of S. Brizio may have determined the creation of the Sistine. Yet Vasari left on record that " even Michelangelo followed the manner of Signorelli, as any one may see." Undoubtedly, Buonarroti, while an inmate of Lorenzo de' Medici's palace at Florence, felt the power of Luca's Madonna with the naked figures in the background; the leading motive of which he transcended in his Doni Holy Family.[1] Probably at an early period he had before his eyes the bold nudities, uncompromising designs, and awkward composition of Luca's so-called School of Pan.[2] In like manner, we may be sure that during

---

[1] Both of these pictures will be found in the Uffizi.

[2] Now in the Berlin Museum. The picture can with some reason be identified with a tempera-painting presented to Lorenzo the Magnificent by Signorelli.

his first visit to Rome he was attracted by Signorelli's solemn fresco of Moses in the Sistine. These things were sufficient to establish a link of connection between the painter of Cortona and the Florentine sculptor. And when Michelangelo visited the Chapel of S. Brizio, after he had fixed and formed his style (exhibiting his innate force of genius in the Pietà, the Bacchus, the Cupid, the David, the statue of Julius, the Cartoon for the Battle of Pisa), that early bond of sympathy must have been renewed and enforced. They were men of a like temperament, and governed by kindred æsthetic instincts. Michelangelo brought to its perfection that system of working wholly through the human form which Signorelli initiated. He shared his violence, his *terribilità*, his almost brutal candour. In the fated evolution of Italian art, describing its parabola of vital energy, Michelangelo softened, sublimed, and harmonised his predecessor's qualities. He did this by abandoning Luca's naïvetés and crudities; exchanging his savage transcripts from coarse life for profoundly studied idealisations of form; subordinating his rough and casual design to schemes of balanced composition, based on architectural relations; penetrating the whole accomplished work, as he intended it should be, with a solemn and severe strain of unifying intellectual melody.

Viewed in this light, the vault of the Sistine and the later fresco of the Last Judgment may be taken as the final outcome of all previous Italian art upon a single line of creative energy, and that line the one anticipated by Luca Signorelli. In like manner, the Stanze and Loggie of the Vatican were the final outcome of the same process upon another line, suggested by Perugino and Fra Bartolommeo.

Michelangelo adapted to his own uses and bent to his own genius motives originated by the Pisani, Giotto, Giacopo della Quercia, Donatello, Masaccio, while working in the spirit of Signorelli. He fused and recast the antecedent materials of design in sculpture and painting, producing a quintessence of art beyond which it was impossible to advance without breaking the rhythm, so intensely strung, and without contradicting too violently the parent inspiration. He strained the chord of rhythm to its very utmost, and made incalculable demands upon the religious inspiration of its predecessors. His mighty talent was equal to the task of transfusion and remodelling which the exhibition of the supreme style demanded. But after him there remained nothing for successors left except mechanical imitation, soulless rehandling of themes he had exhausted by reducing them to his imperious imagination in a crucible of fiery intensity.

V.

No critic with a just sense of phraseology would call Michelangelo a colourist in the same way as

Titian and Rubens were colourists. Still it cannot
be denied with justice that the painter of the Sistine
had a keen perception of what his art required in this
region, and of how to attain it. He planned a comprehensive architectural scheme, which served as setting
and support for multitudes of draped and undraped
human figures. The colouring is kept deliberately
low and subordinate to the two main features of the
design—architecture, and the plastic forms of men
and women. Flesh-tints, varying from the strong
red tone of Jonah's athletic manhood, through the
glowing browns of the seated Genii, to the delicate
carnations of Adam and the paler hues of Eve;
orange and bronze in draperies, medallions, decorative nudes; russets like the tints of dead leaves;
lilacs, cold greens, blue used sparingly; all these
colours are dominated and brought into harmony by
the greys of the architectural setting. It may indeed
be said that the different qualities of flesh-tints, the
architectural greys, and a dull bronzed yellow strike
the chord of the composition. Reds are conspicuous
by their absence in any positive hue. There is no
vermilion, no pure scarlet or crimson, but a mixed
tint verging upon lake. The yellows are brought
near to orange, tawny, bronze, except in the hair of
youthful personages, a large majority of whom are
blonde. The only colour which starts out staringly is
ultramarine, owing of course to this mineral material
resisting time and change more perfectly than the
pigments with which it is associated. The whole

scheme leaves a grave harmonious impression on the mind, thoroughly in keeping with the sublimity of the thoughts expressed. No words can describe the beauty of the flesh-painting, especially in the figures of the Genii, or the technical delicacy with which the modelling of limbs, the modulation from one tone to another, have been carried from silvery transparent shades up to the strongest accents.

VI.

Mr. Ruskin has said, and very justly said, that " the highest art can do no more than rightly represent the human form." [1] This is what the Italians of the Renaissance meant when, through the mouths of Ghiberti, Buonarroti, and Cellini, they proclaimed that the perfect drawing of a fine nude, "un bel corpo ignudo," was the final test of mastery in plastic art. Mr. Ruskin develops his text in sentences which have peculiar value from his lips. "This is the simple test, then, of a perfect school—that it has represented the human form so that it is impossible to conceive of its being better done. And that, I repeat, has been accomplished twice only : once in Athens, once in Florence. And so narrow is the excellence even of these two exclusive schools, that it cannot be said of either of them that they repre-

[1] *Aratra Pentelici,* ed. 1872, p. 180 (Section 183 of the Lectures).

sented the entire human form. The Greeks perfectly drew and perfectly moulded the body and
limbs, but there is, so far as I am aware, no instance
of their representing the face as well as any great
Italian. On the other hand, the Italian painted and
carved the face insuperably; but I believe there is
no instance of his having perfectly represented the
body, which, by command of his religion, it became
his pride to despise and his safety to mortify."

We need not pause to consider whether the
Italian's inferiority to the Greek's in the plastic
modelling of human bodies was due to the artist's
own religious sentiment. That seems a far-fetched
explanation for the shortcomings of men so frankly
realistic and so scientifically earnest as the masters
of the Cinque Cento were. Michelangelo's magnificent cartoon of Leda and the Swan, if it falls short
of some similar subject in some *gabinetto segreto* of
antique fresco, does assuredly not do so because
the draughtsman's hand faltered in pious dread or
pious aspiration. Nevertheless, Ruskin is right in
telling us that no Italian modelled a female nude
equal to the Aphrodite of Melos, or a male nude
equal to the Apoxyomenos of the Braccio Nuovo.
He is also right in pointing out that no Greek sculptor approached the beauty of facial form and expression which we recognise in Raffaello's Madonna
di San Sisto, in Sodoma's S. Sebastian, in Guercino's
Christ at the Corsini Palace, in scores of early
Florentine sepulchral monuments and pictures, in

Umbrian saints and sweet strange portrait-fancies by Da Vinci.

The fact seems to be that Greek and Italian plastic art followed different lines of development, owing to the difference of dominant ideas in the races, and to the difference of social custom. Religion naturally played a foremost part in the art-evolution of both epochs. The anthropomorphic Greek mythology encouraged sculptors to concentrate their attention upon what Hegel called "the sensuous manifestation of the idea," while Greek habits rendered them familiar with the body frankly exhibited. Mediæval religion withdrew Italian sculptors and painters from the problems of purely physical form, and obliged them to study the expression of sentiments and aspirations which could only be rendered by emphasising psychical qualities revealed through physiognomy. At the same time, modern habits of life removed the naked body from their ken.

We may go further, and observe that the conditions under which Greek art flourished developed what the Germans call "Allgemeinheit," a tendency to generalise, which was inimical to strongly marked facial expression or characterisation. The conditions of Italian art, on the other hand, favoured an opposite tendency—to particularise, to enforce detail, to emphasise the artist's own ideal or the model's quality. When the type of a Greek deity had been fixed, each successive master varied this within the closest limits possible. For centuries the type remained fundamentally unaltered, undergoing subtle transformations, due partly to the artist's temperament, and partly to changes in the temper of society. Consequently those aspects of the human form which are capable of most successful generalisation, the body and the limbs, exerted a kind of conventional tyranny over Greek art. And Greek artists applied to the face the same rules of generalisation which were applicable to the body.

The Greek god or goddess was a sensuous manifestation of the idea, a particle of universal godhood incarnate in a special fleshly form, corresponding to the particular psychological attributes of the deity whom the sculptor had to represent. No deviation from the generalised type was possible. The Christian God, on the contrary, is a spirit; and all the emanations from this spirit, whether direct, as in the person of Christ, or derived, as in the persons of the saints, owe their sensuous form and substance to the exigencies of mortal existence, which these persons temporarily and phenomenally obeyed. Since, then, the sensuous manifestation has now become merely symbolic, and is no longer an indispensable investiture of the idea, it may be altered at will in Christian art without irreverence. The utmost capacity of the artist is now exerted, not in enforcing or refining a generalised type, but in discovering some new facial expression which shall reveal psychological quality in a particular being. Doing so, he inevitably insists upon the face; and having formed a face expressive of some defined quality, he can hardly give to the body that generalised beauty which belongs to a Greek nymph or athlete.

What we mean by the differences between Classic and Romantic art lies in the distinctions I am drawing. Classicism sacrifices character to breadth. Romanticism sacrifices breadth to character. Classic art deals more triumphantly with the body, because the body gains by being broadly treated. Romantic art deals more triumphantly with the face, because the features lose by being broadly treated.

This brings me back to Mr. Ruskin, who, in another of his treatises, condemns Michelangelo for a want of variety, beauty, feeling, in his heads and faces. Were this the case, Michelangelo would have little claim to rank as one of the world's chief artists. We have admitted that the Italians did not produce such perfectly beautiful bodies and limbs as the Greeks did, and have agreed that the Greeks produced less perfectly beautiful faces than the Italians. Suppose, then, that Michelangelo failed in his heads and faces, he, being an Italian, and therefore confessedly inferior to the Greeks in his bodies and limbs, must, by the force of logic, emerge less meritorious than we thought him.

VII.

To many of my readers the foregoing section will appear superfluous, polemical, sophistic—three bad things. I wrote it, and I let it stand, however, because it serves as preface to what I have to say in general about Michelangelo's ideal of form. He was essentially a Romantic as opposed to a Classic artist. That is to say, he sought invariably for character—character in type, character in attitude, character in every action of each muscle, character in each extravagance of pose. He applied the Romantic principle to the body and the limbs, exactly to that region of the human form which the Greeks had conquered as their province. He did so with consummate science and complete mastery of physiological law. What is more, he compelled the body to become expressive, not, as the Greeks had done, of broad general conceptions, but of the most intimate and poignant personal emotions. This was his main originality. At the same time, being a Romantic, he deliberately renounced the main tradition of that manner. He refused to study portraiture, as Vasari tells us, and as we see so plainly in the statues of the Dukes at Florence. He generalised his faces, composing an ideal cast of features out of several types. In the rendering of the face and head, then, he chose to be a Classic, while in the treatment of the body he was vehemently modern. In all his work which is not meant to be dramatic—that is, excluding the damned souls in the Last Judgment, the bust of Brutus, and some keen psychological designs—character is sacrificed to a studied ideal of form, so far as the face is concerned. That he did this wilfully, on principle, is certain. The proof remains in the twenty heads of those incomparable genii of the Sistine, each one of whom possesses a beauty and a quality peculiar to himself alone. They show that, if he had so chosen, he could have played upon the human countenance with the same facility as on the human body, varying its expressiveness *ad infinitum.*

Why Michelangelo preferred to generalise the face and to particularise the body remains a secret buried in the abysmal deeps of his personality. In his studies from the model, unlike Lionardo, he almost always left the features vague, while working out the trunk and limbs with strenuous passion. He never seems to have been caught and fascinated by the problem offered by the eyes and features of a male or female. He places masks or splendid commonplaces upon frames palpitant and vibrant with vitality in pleasure or in anguish.

In order to guard against an apparent contradiction, I must submit that, when Michelangelo particularised the body and the limbs, he strove to make them the symbols of some definite passion or emotion. He seems to have been more anxious about the suggestions afforded by their pose and muscular employment than he was about the expression of the features. But we shall presently discover that, so far as pure physical type is concerned, he early began to generalise the structure of the body, passing finaliy into what may not unjustly be called a mannerism of form.

These points may be still further illustrated by what a competent critic has recently written upon Michelangelo's treatment of form.[1] " No one," says Professor Brücke, "ever knew so well as Michelangelo Buonarroti how to produce powerful and strangely harmonious effects by means of figures in themselves open to criticism, simply by his mode of placing and ordering them, and of distributing their lines. For him a figure existed only in his particular representation of it; how it would have looked in any other position was a matter of no concern to him." We may even go further, and maintain that Michelangelo was sometimes wilfully indifferent to the physical capacities of the human body in his passionate research of attitudes which present picturesque and novel beauty.[2] The ancients worked on quite a different method. They created standard types which, in every conceivable posture, would

---

[1] *The Human Figure; its Beauties and Defects.* By Ernest Brücke. English translation. London : Grevel, 1891.

[2] I have tested several of the genii of the Sistine by placing an exceptionally supple and intelligent model exactly in their attitudes. It seemed to me clear that, however admirable as arrangements of lines and suggestions of audacious posture they may be, some of these figures strain the possibilities of nature beyond their limits.

exhibit the grace and symmetry belonging to well-proportioned frames. Michelangelo looked to the effect of a particular posture. He may have been seduced by his habit of modelling figures in clay instead of going invariably to the living subject, and so may have handled nature with unwarrantable freedom. Anyhow, we have here another demonstration of his romanticism.

VIII.

The true test of the highest art is that it should rightly represent the human form. Agreed upon this point, it remains for us to consider in what way Michelangelo conceived and represented the human form. If we can discover his ideal, his principles, his leading instincts in this decisive matter, we shall unlock, so far as that is possible, the secret of his personality as man and artist. The psychological quality of every great master must eventually be determined by his mode of dealing with the phenomena of sex.

In Pheidias we find a large impartiality. His men and women are cast in the same mould of grandeur, inspired with equal strength and sweetness, antiphonal notes in dual harmony. Praxiteles leans to the female, Lysippus to the male ; and so, through all the gamut of the figurative craftsmen, we discover more or less affinity for man or woman. One is swayed by woman and her gracefulness, the other by man and his vigour. Few have realised the Pheidian perfection of doing equal justice.

Michelangelo emerges as a mighty master who was dominated by the vision of male beauty, and who saw the female mainly through the fascination of the other sex. The defect of his art is due to a certain constitutional callousness, a want of sensuous or imaginative sensibility for what is specifically feminine.

Not a single woman carved or painted by the hand of Michelangelo has the charm of early youth or the grace of virginity. The Eve of the Sistine, the Madonna of S. Peter's, the Night and Dawn of the Medicean Sacristy, are female in the anatomy of their large and grandly modelled forms, but not feminine in their sentiment. This proposition requires no proof. It is only needful to recall a Madonna by Raphael, a Diana by Correggio, a Leda by Lionardo, a Venus by Titian, a S. Agnes by Tintoretto. We find ourselves immediately in a different region— the region of artists who loved, admired, and comprehended what is feminine in the beauty and the temperament of women. Michelangelo neither loved, nor admired, nor yielded to the female sex. Therefore he could not deal plastically with what is best and loveliest in the female form. His plastic ideal of the woman is masculine. He builds a colossal frame of muscle, bone, and flesh, studied with supreme

anatomical science.   He gives to Eve the full pelvis
and enormous haunches of an adult matron.   It
might here be urged that he chose to symbolise the
fecundity of her who was destined to be the mother
of the human race.   But if this was his meaning,
why did he not make Adam a corresponding symbol
of fatherhood?   Adam is an adolescent man, colossal
in proportions, but beardless, hairless ; the attributes
of sex in him are developed, but not matured by use.
The Night, for whom no symbolism of maternity was
needed, is a woman who has passed through many
pregnancies.   Those deeply delved wrinkles on the
vast and flaccid abdomen sufficiently indicate this.
Yet when we turn to Michelangelo's sonnets on
Night, we find that he habitually thought of her as
a mysterious and shadowy being, whose influence,
though potent for the soul, disappeared before the
frailest of all creatures bearing light.[1] The Dawn,
again, in her deep lassitude, has nothing of vernal
freshness.   Built upon the same type as the Night,
she looks like Messalina dragging herself from
heavy slumber, for once satiated as well as tired,
stricken for once with the conscience of disgust.
When he chose to depict the acts of passion or of
sensual pleasure, a similar want of sympathy with
what is feminine in womanhood leaves an even
more discordant impression on the mind.   I would

[1] Sonnets xlii.-xliv.   It is possible that a line in the first of these
sonnets may throw some light upon the symbolism of La Notte : " Ma
l'ombra sol a piantar l' uomo serve."

base the proof of this remark upon the marble Leda of the Bargello Museum, and an old engraving of Ixion clasping the phantom of Juno under the form of a cloud.[1] In neither case do we possess Michelangelo's own handiwork; he must not, therefore, be credited with the revolting expression, as of a drunken profligate, upon the face of Leda. Yet in both cases he is indubitably responsible for the general design, and for the brawny carnality of the repulsive woman. I find it difficult to resist the conclusion that Michelangelo felt himself compelled to treat women as though they were another and less graceful sort of males. The sentiment of woman, what really distinguishes the sex, whether voluptuously or passionately or poetically apprehended, emerges in no eminent instance of his work. There

[1] The history of the Leda will be found in Chapter IX. of this work. I should have preferred to cite the Cartoon at Burlington House, or the picture in the National Gallery, were they not practically unknown to the public. There are many repetitions of the Leda scattered through Europe, agreeing in the general lines of composition. The print of Ixion shows him in the act of embracing a herculean woman, with fierce passion, in a contorted and suggestive attitude, among the clouds. At the right of the composition above, Juno in her car is seen modelling a cloud-form. Below is a landscape with ruins, a lion couchant on a marble plinth, a stone satyr without arms; also one naked man crossing a torrent on a withered tree-trunk, and another clothed praying to the skies. The engraving is executed in the manner of Jacopo Caraglio, and Perino del Vaga's name has been connected with the design. Mr. Louis Fagan, of the British Museum, to whom I wrote for information, referred me to Bartsch, vol. xx. p. 99, No. 1. It is impossible, I think, that any one but Michelangelo should have been the originator of the conception. We know from Vasari that Perino del Vaga was a diligent student of Michelangelo's works, and that he was an associate of his familiar friend Piloto.

is a Cartoon at Naples for a Bacchante, which
Bronzino transferred to canvas and coloured. This
design illustrates the point on which I am insisting.
An athletic circus-rider of mature years, with abnor-
mally developed muscles, might have posed as model
for this female votary of Dionysus. Before he made
this drawing, Michelangelo had not seen those
frescoes of the dancing Bacchantes from Pompeii ;
nor had he perhaps seen the Mænads on Greek
bas-reliefs tossing wild tresses backwards, swaying
virginal lithe bodies to the music of the tambourine.
We must not, therefore, compare his concept with
those masterpieces of the later classical imagination.
Still, many of his contemporaries, vastly inferior to
him in penetrative insight, a Giovanni da Udine, a
Perino del Vaga, a Primaticcio, not to speak of
Raffaello or of Lionardo, felt what the charm of
youthful womanhood upon the revel might be. He
remained insensible to the melody of purely feminine
lines ; and the only reason why his transcripts from
the female form are not gross like those of Flemish
painters, repulsive like Rembrandt's, fleshly like
Rubens's, disagreeable like the drawings made
by criminals in prisons, is that they have little
womanly about them.

Lest these assertions should appear too dogmatic,
I will indicate the series of works in which I recognise Michelangelo's sympathy with genuine female
quality. All the domestic groups, composed of
women and children, which fill the lunettes and

groinings between the windows in the Sistine Chapel, have a charming twilight sentiment of family life or maternal affection. They are among the loveliest and most tranquil of his conceptions. The Madonna above the tomb of Julius II. cannot be accused of masculinity, nor the ecstatic figure of the Rachel beneath it. Both of these statues represent what Goethe called " das ewig Weibliche " under a truly felt and natural aspect. The Delphian and Erythrean Sibyls are superb in their majesty. Again, in those numerous designs for Crucifixions, Depositions from the Cross, and Pietàs, which occupied so much of Michelangelo's attention during his old age, we find an intense and pathetic sympathy with the sorrows of Mary, expressed with noble dignity and a pious sense of godhead in the human mother. It will be remarked that throughout the cases I have reserved as exceptions, it is not woman in her plastic beauty and her radiant charm that Michelangelo has rendered, but woman in her tranquil or her saddened and sorrow-stricken moods. What he did not comprehend and could not represent was woman in her girlishness, her youthful joy, her physical attractiveness, her magic of seduction.

Michelangelo's women suggest demonic primitive beings, composite and undetermined products of the human race in evolution, before the specific qualities of sex have been eliminated from a general predominating mass of masculinity. At their best, they carry us into the realm of Lucretian imagination. He

could not have incarnated in plastic form Shakespeare's Juliet and Imogen, Dante's Francesca da
Rimini, Tasso's Erminia and Clorinda ; but he
might have supplied a superb illustration to the
opening lines of the Lucretian epic, where Mars
lies in the bed of Venus, and the goddess spreads
her ample limbs above her Roman lover.   He might
have evoked images tallying the vision of primal
passion in the fourth book of that poem.[1] As I have
elsewhere said, writing about Lucretius : " There is
something almost tragic in these sighs and pantings
and pleasure-throes, these incomplete fruitions of
souls pent within their frames of flesh.   We seem
to see a race of men and women such as never lived,
except perhaps in Rome or in the thought of Michelangelo, meeting in leonine embracements that yield
pain, whereof the climax is, at best, relief from
rage and respite for a moment from consuming fire.
There is a life elemental rather than human in those
mighty limbs ; and the passion that twists them on
the marriage-bed has in it the stress of storms, the
rampings and roarings of leopards at play.   Take
this single line :—

> et Venus in silvis jungebat corpora amantum.

What a picture of primeval breadth and vastness !
The forest is the world, and the bodies of the lovers
are things natural and unashamed, and Venus is

---

[1] *De Rerum Natura*, iv. 1037–1208.

the tyrannous instinct that controls the blood in spring." [1]

What makes Michelangelo's crudity in his plastic treatment of the female form the more remarkable is that in his poetry he seems to feel the influence of women mystically. I shall have to discuss this topic in another place. It is enough here to say that, with very few exceptions, we remain in doubt whether he is addressing a woman at all. There are none of those spontaneous utterances by which a man involuntarily expresses the outgoings of his heart to a beloved object, the throb of irresistible emotion, the physical ache, the sense of wanting, the joys and pains, the hopes and fears, the ecstasies and disappointments, which belong to genuine passion. The woman is, for him, an allegory, something he has not approached and handled. Of her personality we learn nothing. Of her bodily presentment, the eyes alone are mentioned ; and the eyes are treated as the path to Paradise for souls which seek emancipation from the flesh. Raffaello's few and far inferior sonnets vibrate with an intense and potent sensibility to this woman or to that. Michelangelo's "donna" might just as well be a man ; and indeed the poems he addressed to men, though they have nothing sensual about them, reveal a finer touch in the emotion of the writer. It is difficult to connect this vaporous incorporeal "donna" of the poems with those brawny colossal adult females

---

[1] *Sketches and Studies in Italy*, Article on Lucretius.

of the statues, unless we suppose that Michelangelo remained callous both to the physical attractions and the emotional distinction of woman as she actually is.

I have tried to demonstrate that, plastically, he did not understand women, and could not reproduce their form in art with sympathetic feeling for its values of grace, suavity, virginity, and frailty. He imported masculine qualities into every female theme he handled. The case is different when we turn to his treatment of the male figure. It would be impossible to adduce a single instance, out of the many hundreds of examples furnished by his work, in which a note of femininity has been added to the masculine type.[1] He did not think enough of women to reverse the process, and create hermaphroditic beings like the Apollino of Praxiteles or the S. Sebastian of Sodoma. His boys and youths and adult men remain, in the truest and the purest sense of the word, virile. Yet with what infinite variety, with what a deep intelligence of its resources, with what inexhaustible riches of enthusiasm and science, he played upon the lyre of the male nude! How far more fit for purposes of art he felt the man to be than the woman is demonstrated, not only by his approaching woman from the masculine side, but also by his close attention to none but male qualities in men. I need not insist or enlarge upon this point. The fact is apparent to every one

[1] Except occasionally in the face ; in the body and the limbs, never.

with eyes to see. It would be futile to expound
Michelangelo's fertility in dealing with the motives
of the male figure as minutely as I judged it necessary to explain the poverty of his inspiration through
the female. But it ought to be repeated that, over the
whole gamut of the scale, from the grace of boyhood,
through the multiform delightfulness of adolescence
into the firm force of early manhood, and the sterner
virtues of adult age, one severe and virile spirit
controls his fashioning of plastic forms. He even
exaggerates what is masculine in the male, as he
caricatures the female by ascribing impossible virility
to her. But the exaggeration follows here a line of
mental and moral rectitude. It is the expression of
his peculiar sensibility to physical structure.

IX.

When we study the evolution of Michelangelo's
ideal of form, we find at the beginning of his life
a very short period in which he followed the traditions of Donatello and imitated Greek work. The
seated Madonna in bas-relief and the Giovannino
belong to this first stage. So does the bas-relief of
the Centaurs. It soon becomes evident, however, that
Michelangelo was not destined to remain a continu-
ator of Donatello's manner or a disciple of the classics.
The next period, which includes the Madonna

della Febbre, the Bruges Madonna, the Bacchus, the
Cupid, and the David, is marked by an intense
search after the truth of Nature. Both Madonnas
might be criticised for unreality, owing to the enormous development of the thorax and something artificial in the type of face. But all the male figures
seem to have been studied from the model. There
is an individuality about the character of each, a
naturalism, an aiming after realistic expression,
which separate this group from previous and subsequent works by Buonarroti. Traces of Donatello's
influence survive in the treatment of the long large
hands of David, the cast of features selected for that
statue, and the working of the feet. Indeed it may
be said that Donatello continued through life to
affect the genius of Michelangelo by a kind of sympathy, although the elder master's naïveté was soon
discarded by the younger.

The second period culminated in the Cartoon
for the Battle of Pisa. This design appears to
have fixed the style now known to us as Michelangelesque, and the loss of it is therefore irreparable. It exercised the consummate science which
he had acquired, his complete mastery over the
male nude. It defined his firm resolve to treat
linear design from the point of view of sculpture
rather than of painting proper. It settled his determination to work exclusively through and by the
human figure, rejecting all subordinate elements of
decoration. Had we possessed this epoch-making

masterpiece, we should probably have known Michelangelo's genius in its flower-period of early ripeness, when anatomical learning was still combined with a sustained dependence upon Nature. The transition from the second to the third stage in this development of form-ideal remains imperfectly explained, because the bathers in the Arno were necessary to account for the difference between the realistic David and the methodically studied genii of the Sistine.

The vault of the Sistine shows Michelangelo's third manner in perfection. He has developed what may be called a scheme of the human form. The apparently small head, the enormous breadth of shoulder, the thorax overweighing the whole figure, the finely modelled legs, the large and powerful extremities, which characterise his style henceforward, culminate in Adam, repeat themselves throughout the genii, govern the prophets. But Nature has not been neglected. Nothing is more remarkable in that vast decorative mass of figures than the variety of types selected, the beauty and animation of the faces, the extraordinary richness, elasticity, and freshness of the attitudes presented to the eye. Every period of life has been treated with impartial justice, and both sexes are adequately handled. The Delphian, Erythrean, and Libyan Sibyls display a sublime sense of facial beauty. The Eve of the Temptation has even something of positively feminine charm. This is probably due to the fact that Michelangelo here studied expression and felt the necessity of dramatic characterisation in this part of his work. He struck each chord of what may be called the poetry of figurative art, from the epic cantos of Creation, Fall, and Deluge, through the tragic odes uttered by prophets and sibyls, down to the lyric notes of the genii, and the sweet idyllic strains of the groups in the lunettes and spandrels.

It cannot be said that even here Michelangelo felt the female nude as sympathetically as he felt the male. The women in the picture of the Deluge are colossal creatures, scarcely distinguishable from the men except by their huge bosoms. His personal sense of beauty finds fullest expression in the genii. The variations on one theme of youthful loveliness and grace are inexhaustible; the changes rung on attitude, and face, and feature are endless. The type, as I have said, has already become schematic. It is adolescent, but the adolescence is neither that of the Greek athlete nor that of the nude model. Indeed, it is hardly natural; nor yet is it ideal in the Greek sense of that term. The physical gracefulness of a slim ephebus was never seized by Michelangelo. His Ganymede displays a massive trunk and brawny thighs. Compare this with the Ganymede of Titian. Compare the Cupid at South Kensington with the Praxitelean Genius of the Vatican — the Adonis and the Bacchus of the Bargello with Hellenic statues. The bulk and force of maturity are combined with the smoothness of boyhood and with a delicacy of face that borders on the feminine.

It is an arid region, the region of this mighty master's spirit. There are no heavens and no earth or sea in it; no living creatures, forests, flowers; no bright colours, brilliant lights, or cavernous darks. In clear grey twilight appear a multitude of naked forms, both male and female, yet neither male nor female of the actual world; rather the brood of an inventive intellect, teeming with pre-occupations of abiding thoughts and moods of feeling, which become for it incarnate in these stupendous figures. It is as though Michelangelo worked from the image in his brain outwards to a physical presentment supplied by his vast knowledge of life, creating forms proper to his own specific concept. Nowhere else in plastic art does the mental world peculiar to the master press in so immediately, without modification and without mitigation, upon our sentient imagination. I sometimes dream that the inhabitants of the moon may be like Michelangelo's men and women, as I feel sure its landscape resembles his conception of the material universe.

What I have called Michelangelo's third manner, the purest manifestation of which is to be found in the vault of the Sistine, sustained itself for a period of many years. The surviving fragments of sculpture for the tomb of Julius, especially the Captives of the Louvre and the statues in the Sacristy at

S. Lorenzo, belong to this stage. A close and intimate *rapport* with Nature can be perceived in all the
work he designed and executed during the pontificates of Leo and Clement. The artist was at his
fullest both of mental energy and physical vigour.
What he wrought now bears witness to his plenitude of manhood. Therefore, although the type
fixed for the Sistine prevailed—I mean that generalisation of the human form in certain wilfully
selected proportions, conceived to be ideally beautiful or necessary for the grand style in vast architectonic schemes of decoration—still it is used with
an exquisite sensitiveness to the pose and structure
of the natural body, a delicate tact in the defini-
tion of muscle and articulation, an acute feeling for
the qualities of flesh and texture. None of the
creations of this period, moreover, are devoid of
intense animating emotions and ideas.

Unluckily, during all the years which intervened
between the Sistine vault and the Last Judgment,
Michelangelo was employed upon architectural problems and engineering projects, which occupied
his genius in regions far removed from that of figurative art. It may, therefore, be asserted, that although he did not retrograde from want of practice,
he had no opportunity of advancing further by the
concentration of his genius on design. This accounts, I think, for the change in his manner which
we notice when he began to paint in Rome under
Pope Paul III. The fourth stage in his development

of form is reached now. He has lost nothing of his vigour, nothing of his science. But he has drifted away from Nature. All the innumerable figures of the Last Judgment, in all their varied attitudes, with divers moods of dramatic expression, are diagrams wrought out imaginatively from the stored-up resources of a lifetime. It may be argued that it was impossible to pose models, in other words, to appeal to living men and women, for the foreshortenings of falling or soaring shapes in that huge drift of human beings. This is true; and the strongest testimony to the colossal powers of observation possessed by Michelangelo is that none of all those attitudes are wrong. We may verify them, if we take particular pains to do so, by training the sense of seeing to play the part of a detective camera.[1] Michelangelo was gifted with a unique faculty for seizing momentary movements, fixing them upon his memory, and transferring them to fresco by means of his supreme acquaintance with the bony structure and the muscular capacities of the human frame. Regarded from this point of view, the Last Judgment was an unparalleled success. As such the contemporaries of Buonarroti hailed it. Still, the breath of life has exhaled from all those bodies, and the tyranny of the schematic ideal of form is felt in each of them. Without meaning to be irreverent,

---

[1] I may refer here to an article I published on "Swiss Athletic Sports" in the *Fortnightly Review* for September 1891, where I have handled this topic more at length.

we might fancy that two elastic lay-figures, one
male, the other female, both singularly similar in
shape, supplied the materials for the total composition.   Of the dramatic intentions and suggestions
underlying these plastic and elastic shapes I am
not now speaking.   It is my present business to
establish the phases through which my master's
sense of form passed from its cradle to its grave.[1]

In the frescoes of the Cappella Paolina, so ruined
at this day that we can hardly value them, the
mechanic manner of the fourth stage seems to reach
its climax.   Ghosts of their former selves, they still
reveal the poverty of creative and spontaneous inspiration which presided over their nativity.

[1] A passage from Vasari's introduction explains Michelangelo's way
of dealing with figures in relief and foreshortenings.   He says that "it
was the divine master's habit to make little models of clay or wax ; and
from these, because they keep their position better than live beings, he
drew the outlines, lights, and shades of his figures" (Vasari, vol. i.
p. 157).   It is probable that he used this method while designing the
Last Judgment ; for many postures there are such as no living creature
could maintain for more than a few seconds.   Thus he brought his
profound knowledge of anatomy and his power as a sculptor into the
service of painting, and forced the art of painting to the very extreme
verge of possibility.   What strikes us as manneristic in his later fresco-
work may be attributed to this habit, implying the great man's wish to
seize and perpetuate movements of the body beyond the scope of a
sincere and thorough transcript from the living nude.   It is said that
Correggio adopted the same method for his bold foreshortenings ; and
we are told that Tintoretto drew from plastic figures suspended
under artificial lighting.   Enthusiastic study of the works produced in
this way by masters of indubitable genius enabled lesser folk to play
with the human form in every kind of hazardous attitude, and led
onward to that decadence with which we connect the names of the
Macchinesti.

Michelangelo's fourth manner might be compared with that of Milton in "Paradise Regained" and "Samson Agonistes." Both of these great artists in old age exaggerate the defects of their qualities. Michelangelo's ideal of line and proportion in the human form becomes stereotyped and strained, as do Milton's rhythms and his Latinisms. The generous wine of the Bacchus and of "Comus," so intoxicating in its newness, the same wine in the Sistine and "Paradise Lost," so overwhelming in its mature strength, has acquired an austere aridity. Yet, strange to say, amid these autumn stubbles of declining genius we light upon oases more sweet, more tenderly suggestive, than aught the prime produced. It is not my business to speak of Milton here. I need not recall his "Knights of Logres and of Lyonesse," or resume his Euripidean garlands showered on Samson's grave. But, for my master Michelangelo, it will suffice to observe that all the grace his genius held, refined, of earthly grossness quit, appeared, under the dominance of this fourth manner, in the mythological subjects he composed for Tommaso Cavalieri, and, far more nobly, in his countless studies for the celebration of Christ's Passion. The designs bequeathed to us from this period are very numerous. They were never employed in the production of any monumental work of sculpture or of painting. For this very reason, because they were occasional improvisations, preludes, dreams of things to be, they preserve the finest bloom, the Indian summer of his fancy. Lovers of Michelangelo must dedicate their latest and most loving studies to this phase of his fourth manner.

X.

If we seek to penetrate the genius of an artist, not merely forming a correct estimate of his technical ability and science, but also probing his personality to the core, as near as this is possible for us to do, we ought to give our undivided study to his drawings. It is there, and there alone, that we come face to face with the real man, in his unguarded moments, in his hours of inspiration, in the laborious effort to solve a problem of composition, or in the happy flow of genial improvisation. Michelangelo was wont to maintain that all the arts are included in the art of design. Sculpture, painting, architecture, he said, are but subordinate branches of draughtsmanship. And he went so far as to assert that the mechanical arts, with engineering and fortification, nay, even the minor arts of decoration and costume, owe their existence to design. The more we reflect upon this apparent paradox, the more shall we feel it to be true. At any rate, there are no products of human thought and feeling capable of being expressed by form which do not find their common denominator in a linear drawing. The simplicity of a sketch, the comparative rapidity with which it is produced, the concentration of meaning demanded by its rigid economy of means, render it more symbolical, more like the hieroglyph of its maker's mind, than any finished work can be. We may discover a greater mass of interesting objects in a painted picture or a carved statue ; but we shall never find exactly the same thing, never the involuntary revelation of the artist's soul, the irrefutable witness to his mental and moral qualities, to the mysteries of his genius and to its limitations.

If this be true of all artists, it is in a peculiar sense true of Michelangelo. Great as he was as sculptor, painter, architect, he was only perfect and impeccable as draughtsman. Inadequate realisation, unequal execution, fatigue, satiety, caprice of mood, may sometimes be detected in his frescoes and his statues ; but in design we never find him faulty, hasty, less than absolute master over the selected realm of thought. His most interesting and instructive work remains what he performed with pen and chalk in hand. Deeply, therefore, must we regret the false modesty which made him destroy masses of his drawings, while we have reason to be thankful for those marvellous photographic processes which nowadays have placed the choicest of his masterpieces within the reach of every one.

The following passages from Vasari's and Condivi's Lives deserve attention by those who approach the

study of Buonarroti's drawings.[1] Vasari says : " His
powers of imagination were such, that he was frequently compelled to abandon his purpose, because
he could not express by the hand those grand
and sublime ideas which he had conceived in his
mind ; nay, he has spoiled and destroyed many works
for this cause; and I know, too, that some short
time before his death he burnt a large number of his
designs, sketches, and cartoons, that none might see
the labours he had endured, and the trials to which
he had subjected his spirit, in his resolve not to fall
short of perfection.[2] I have myself secured some
drawings by his hand, which were found in Florence,
and are now in my book of designs, and these,
although they give evidence of his great genius, yet
prove also that the hammer of Vulcan was necessary
to bring Minerva from the head of Jupiter. He
would construct an ideal shape out of nine, ten, and
even twelve different heads, for no other purpose
than to obtain a certain grace of harmony and composition which is not to be found in the natural
form, and would say that the artist must have his
measuring tools, not in the hand, but in the eye,
because the hands do but operate, it is the eye that
judges ; he pursued the same idea in architecture
also." Condivi adds some information regarding his
extraordinary fecundity and variety of invention :

[1] Vasari, xii. p. 271 ; Condivi, p. 83.
[2] This is confirmed by the statement of the ambassador Averardo
Serristori, *op. cit.*, p. 415.

" He was gifted with a most tenacious memory, the power of which was such that, though he painted so many thousands of figures, as any one can see, he never made one exactly like another or posed in the same attitude. Indeed, I have heard him say that he never draws a line without remembering whether he has drawn it before ; erasing any repetition, when the design was meant to be exposed to public view. His force of imagination is also most extraordinary. This has been the chief reason why he was never quite satisfied with his own work, and always depreciated its quality, esteeming that his hand failed to attain the idea which he had formed within his brain."

XI.

The four greatest draughtsmen of this epoch were Lionardo da Vinci, Michelangelo, Raffaello, and Andrea del Sarto. They are not to be reckoned as equals; for Lionardo and Michelangelo outstrip the other two almost as much as these surpass all lesser craftsmen. Each of the four men expressed his own peculiar vision of the world with pen, or chalk, or metal point, finding the unique inevitable line, the exact touch and quality of stroke, which should present at once a lively transcript from real Nature, and a revelation of the artist's particular way of feeling Nature. In Lionardo it is a line of subtlety and infinite suggestiveness; in Michelangelo it compels attention, and forcibly defines the essence of the object; in Raffaello it carries melody, the charm of an unerring rhythm; in Andrea it seems to call for tone, colour, atmosphere, and makes their presence felt. Raffaello was often faulty: even in the wonderful pen-drawing of two nudes he sent to Albrecht Dürer as a sample of his skill, we blame the knees and ankles of his models. Lionardo was sometimes wilful, whimsical, seduced by dreamland, like a godborn amateur. Andrea allowed his facility to lead him into languor, and lacked passion. Michelangelo's work shows none of these shortcomings; it is always technically faultless, instinct with passion, supereminent in force. But we crave more of grace, of sensuous delight, of sweetness, than he chose, or perhaps was able, to communicate. We should welcome a little more of human weakness if he gave a little more of divine suavity.

Michelangelo's style of design is that of a sculptor, Andrea's of a colourist, Lionardo's of a curious student, Raffaello's of a musician and improvisatore. These distinctions are not merely fanciful, nor based on what we know about the men in their careers. We feel similar distinctions in the case of all great draughtsmen. Titian's chalk-studies, Fra Bartolommeo's, so singularly akin to Andrea del Sarto's, Giorgione's pen-and-ink sketch for a Lucretia, are seen at once by their richness and blurred outlines to be the work of colourists.[1] Signorelli's transcripts from the nude, remarkably similar to those of Michelangelo, reveal a sculptor rather than a painter.[2] Botticelli, with all his Florentine precision, shows that, like Lionardo, he was a seeker and a visionary in his anxious feeling after curve and attitude. Mantegna seems to be graving steel or cutting into marble. It is easy to apply this analysis in succession to any draughtsman who has style. To do so would, however, be superfluous : we should only be enforcing what is a truism to all intelligent students of art—namely, that each individual stamps his own specific quality upon his handiwork ; reveals even in the neutral region of design his innate preference for colour or pure form as a channel of expression ; betrays the predominance of mental energy or sensuous charm, of scientific curiosity or plastic force, of passion or of tenderness, which controls his nature. This inevitable and unconscious revelation of the man in art-work strikes us as being singularly modern. We do not apprehend it to at all the same extent in the sculpture of the ancients, whether it be that our sympathies are too remote from Greek and Roman ways of feeling, or whether the ancients really conceived art more collectively in masses, less individually as persons.

---

[1] Two heads of old men by Titian in the Louvre ; Fra Bartolommeo's cartoons in the Accademia, and his red-chalk drawings in the Uffizi at Florence ; Giorgione's Lucretia in the Uffizi.
[2] Two studies of men in black chalk in the Louvre.

No master exhibits this peculiarly modern quality more decisively than Michelangelo, and nowhere is the personality of his genius, what marks him off and separates him from all fellow-men, displayed with fuller emphasis than in his drawings. To use the words of a penetrative critic,[1] from whom it is a pleasure to quote : " The thing about Michelangelo is this ; he is not, so to say, at the head of a class, but he stands apart by himself : he is not possessed of a skill which renders him unapproached or unapproachable ; but rather, he is of so unique an order, that no other artist whatever seems to suggest comparison with him." Mr. Selwyn Image goes on to define in what a true sense the words " creator " and " creative " may be applied to him : how the shows and appearances of the world were for him but hieroglyphs of underlying ideas, with which his soul was familiar, and from which he worked again outward ; "his learning and skill in the arts supplying to his hand such large and adequate symbols of them as are otherwise beyond attainment." This, in a very difficult and impalpable region of æsthetic criticism, is finely said, and accords with Michelangelo's own utterances upon art and beauty in his poems. Dwelling like a star apart, communing with the eternal ideas, the permanent relations of the universe, uttering his inmost thoughts about these mysteries through the vehicles of science and

[1] Mr. Selwyn Image, "On the Distinctive Genius of J. F. Millet," *Century Guild Hobby Horse*, October 1891.

of art, for which he was so singularly gifted, Michelangelo, in no loose or trivial sense of that phrase, proved himself to be a creator. He introduces us to a world seen by no eyes except his own, compels us to become familiar with forms unapprehended by our senses, accustoms us to breathe a rarer and more fiery atmosphere than we were born into.

The vehicles used by Michelangelo in his designs were mostly pen and chalk. He employed both a sharp-nibbed pen of some kind, and a broad flexible reed, according to the exigencies of his subject or the temper of his mood. The chalk was either red or black, the former being softer than the latter. I cannot remember any instances of those chiaroscuro washes which Raffaello handled in so masterly a manner, although Michelangelo frequently combined bistre shading with pen outlines. In like manner he does not seem to have favoured the metal point upon prepared paper, with which Lionardo produced unrivalled masterpieces. Some drawings, where the yellow outline bites into a parchment paper, blistering at the edges, suggest a rusty metal in the instrument. We must remember, however, that the inks of that period were frequently corrosive, as is proved by the state of many documents now made illegible through the gradual attrition of the paper by mineral acids. It is also not impossible that artists may have already invented what we call steel pens. Sarpi, in the seventeenth century, thanks a correspondent for the gift of one of these mechanical devices. Speaking broadly, the reed and the quill, red and black chalk, or *matita*, were the vehicles of Michelangelo's expression as a draughtsman. I have seen very few examples of studies heightened with white chalk, and none produced in the fine Florentine style of Ghirlandajo by white chalk alone upon a dead-brown surface. In this matter it is needful to speak with diffidence ; for the sketches of our master are so widely scattered that few students can have examined the whole of them ; and photographic reproductions, however admirable in their fidelity to outline, do not always give decisive evidence regarding the materials employed.[1]

One thing seems manifest. Michelangelo avoided those mixed methods with which Lionardo, the

[1] It is interesting to relate here what Vasari, in his introduction (vol. i. p. 154), says about the materials used by draughtsmen in his lifetime. They are as follows : 1, charcoal ; 2, a red stone, brought from German quarries ; 3, a black stone, of the same description, brought from France ; 4, a pen or metal point upon prepared ground of different colours ; 5, washes of white lead, with a gummy medium applied to dark paper, the modelling being produced by simple high lights ; 6, pen and ink. He does not mention matita in this place by name—that is an iron ore of red or brown hue, and is probably the stone alluded to above under numbers 2 and 3. Our prepared chalks do not appear to have been invented, and only faint approaches toward the *pastille* polychrome of modern art can be found in some of Lionardo's experiments. We cannot affirm that black-lead was a vehicle in use under its present form of pencil. Yet, if we may include it in the general description of matita, this was perhaps known to draughtsmen of the sixteenth century. Some written memoranda and rough jottings of design by Michelangelo indicate it to the eye. In order to be fully informed upon the subject, it would be necessary to submit portions of original drawings to chemical analysis. So far as I know, this has not yet been attempted.

magician, wrought wonders. He preferred an instrument which could be freely, broadly handled, inscribing form in strong plain strokes upon the candid paper. The result attained, whether wrought by bold lines, or subtly hatched, or finished with the utmost delicacy of modulated shading, has always been traced out conscientiously and firmly, with one pointed stylus (pen, chalk, or matita), chosen for the purpose. As I have said, it is the work of a sculptor, accustomed to wield chisel and mallet upon marble, rather than that of a painter, trained to secure effects by shadowings and glazings.

It is possible, I think, to define, at least with some approximation to precision, Michelangelo's employment of his favourite vehicles for several purposes and at different periods of his life. A broad-nibbed pen was used almost invariably in making architectural designs of cornices, pilasters, windows, also in plans for military engineering. Sketches of tombs and edifices, intended to be shown to patrons, were partly finished with the pen; and here we find a subordinate and very limited use of the brush in shading. Such performances may be regarded as products of the workshop rather than as examples of the artist's mastery. The style of them is often conventional, suggesting the intrusion of a pupil or the deliberate adoption of an office mannerism. The pen plays a foremost part in all the greatest and most genial creations of his fancy when it worked energetically in preparation for sculpture or for fresco. The Louvre is rich in masterpieces of this kind—the fiery study of a David; the heroic figures of two male nudes, hatched into stubborn salience like pieces of carved wood; the broad conception of the Madonna at S. Lorenzo in her magnificent repose and passionate cascade of fallen draperies; the repulsive but superabundantly powerful profile of a goat-like faun. These, and the stupendous studies of the Albertina Collection at Vienna, including the supine man with thorax violently raised, are worked with careful hatchings, stroke upon stroke, effecting a suggestion of plastic roundness. But we discover quite a different use of the pen in some large simple outlines of seated female figures at the Louvre; in thick, almost muddy, studies at Vienna, where the form emerges out of oft-repeated sodden blotches; in the grim light and shade, the rapid suggestiveness of the dissection scene at Oxford. The pen in the hand of Michelangelo was the tool by means of which he realised his most trenchant conceptions and his most picturesque impressions. In youth and early manhood, when his genius was still vehement, it seems to have been his favourite vehicle.

The use of chalk grew upon him in later life, possibly because he trusted more to his memory now, and loved the dreamier softer medium for uttering his fancies. Black chalk was employed for rapid notes of composition, and also for the more elaborate productions of his pencil. To this material we owe the head of Horror which he gave to Gherardo Perini (in the Uffizi), the Phaethon, the Tityos, the Ganymede he gave to Tommaso Cavalieri (at Windsor). It is impossible to describe the refinements of modulated shading and the precision of predetermined outlines by means of which these incomparable drawings have been produced. They seem to melt and to escape inspection, yet they remain fixed on the memory as firmly as forms in carven basalt.

The whole series of designs for Christ's Crucifixion and Deposition from the Cross are executed in chalk, sometimes black, but mostly red. It is manifest, upon examination, that they are not studies from the model, but thoughts evoked and shadowed forth on paper. Their perplexing multiplicity and subtle variety—as though a mighty improvisatore were preluding again and yet again upon the clavichord to find his theme, abandoning the search, renewing it, altering the key, changing the accent—prove that this continued seeking with the crayon after form and composition was carried on in solitude and abstract moments. Incomplete as the designs may be, they reveal Michelangelo's loftiest dreams and purest visions. The nervous energy, the passionate grip upon the subject, shown in the pen-drawings, are absent here. These qualities are replaced by meditation and an air of rapt devotion. The drawings for the Passion might be called the prayers and pious thoughts of the stern master.

Red chalk he used for some of his most brilliant

conceptions. It is not necessary to dwell upon the bending woman's head at Oxford, or the torso of the lance-bearer at Vienna. Let us confine our attention to what is perhaps the most pleasing and most perfect of all Michelangelo's designs—the " Bersaglio," or the "Arcieri," in the Queen's collection at Windsor.

It is a group of eleven naked men and one woman, fiercely footing the air, and driving shafts with all their might to pierce a classical terminal figure, whose face, like that of Pallas, and broad breast are guarded by a spreading shield The draughtsman has indicated only one bow, bent with fury by an old man in the background. Yet all the actions proper to archery are suggested by the violent gestures and strained sinews of the crowd. At the foot of the terminal statue, Cupid lies asleep upon his wings, with idle bow and quiver. Two little genii of love, in the background, are lighting up a fire, puffing its flames, as though to drive the archers onward. Energy and ardour, impetuous movement and passionate desire, could not be expressed with greater force, nor the tyranny of some blind impulse be more imaginatively felt. The allegory seems to imply that happiness is not to be attained, as human beings mostly strive to seize it, by the fierce force of the carnal passions. It is the contrast between celestial love asleep in lustful souls, and vulgar love inflaming tyrannous appetites :[1]—

[1] *Rime*, Sonnet No. liii.

The one love soars, the other downward tends ;
  The soul lights this, while that the senses stir,
  And still lust's arrow at base quarry flies.

This magnificent design was engraved during
Buonarroti's lifetime, or shortly afterwards, by Niccolò Beatrizet.   Some follower of Raffaello used the
print for a fresco in the Palazzo Borghese at Rome.
It forms one of the series in which Raffaello's marriage of Alexander and Roxana is painted.   This
has led some critics to ascribe the drawing itself
to the Urbinate.   Indeed, at first sight, one might
almost conjecture that the original chalk study was
a genuine work of Raffaello, aiming at rivalry with
Michelangelo's manner.   The calm beauty of the
statue's classic profile, the refinement of all the faces,
the exquisite delicacy of the adolescent forms, and
the dominant veiling of strength with grace, are not
precisely Michelangelesque.   The technical execution of the design, however, makes its attribution
certain.   Well as Raffaello could draw, he could not
draw like this.   He was incapable of rounding and
modelling the nude with those soft stipplings and
granulated shadings which bring the whole surface out like that of a bas-relief in polished marble.
His own drawing for Alexander and Roxana, in red
chalk, and therefore an excellent subject for comparison with the Arcieri, is hatched all over in
straight lines ; a method adopted by Michelangelo
when working with the pen, but, so far as I am
aware, never, or very rarely, used when he was hand-

ling chalk.   The style of this design and its exquisite workmanship correspond exactly with the finish of the Cavalieri series at Windsor.   The paper, moreover, is indorsed in Michelangelo's handwriting with a memorandum bearing the date April 12, 1530.   We have then in this masterpiece of draughtsmanship an example, not of Raffaello in a Michelangelising mood, but of Michelangelo for once condescending to surpass Raffaello on his own ground of loveliness and rhythmic grace.[1]

[1] Morelli, in his book upon the Borghese and Doria Galleries, suggests that the drawing of Alexander and Roxana in question above was really a work of Sodoma's.   If that be so, it does not invalidate the argument.

CHAPTER VII.

Rome under Pietro Urbano's care in the autumn of 1521.—Urbano mishandles it.—History of the statue.—The generosity of Metello Varj.—Criticism of the work.

I.

JULIUS died upon the 21st of February 1513. "A prince," says Guicciardini, "of inestimable courage and tenacity, but headlong, and so extravagant in the schemes he formed, that his own prudence and moderation had less to do with shielding him from ruin than the discord of sovereigns and the circumstances of the times in Europe : worthy, in all truth, of the highest glory had he been a secular potentate, or if the pains and anxious thought he employed in augmenting the temporal greatness of the Church by war had been devoted to her spiritual welfare in the arts of peace."

Italy rejoiced when Giovanni de' Medici was selected to succeed him, with the title of Leo X. "Venus ruled in Rome with Alexander, Mars with Julius, now Pallas enters on her reign with Leo." Such was the tenor of the epigrams which greeted Leo upon his triumphal progress to the Lateran. It was felt that a Pope of the house of Medici would be a patron of arts and letters, and it was hoped that the son of Lorenzo the Magnificent might restore the equilibrium of power in Italy. Leo X. has enjoyed a greater fame than he deserved. Extolled as an Augustus in his lifetime, he left his name to what is called the golden age of Italian culture.

Yet he cannot be said to have raised any first-rate men of genius, or to have exercised a very wise patronage over those whom Julius brought forward. Michelangelo and Raffaello were in the full swing of work when Leo claimed their services. We shall see how he hampered the rare gifts of the former by employing him on uncongenial labours; and it was no great merit to give a free rein to the inexhaustible energy of Raffaello. The project of a new S. Peter's belonged to Julius. Leo only continued the scheme, using such assistants as the times provided after Bramante's death in 1514. Julius instinctively selected men of soaring and audacious genius, who were capable of planning on a colossal scale. Leo delighted in the society of clever people, poetasters, petty scholars, lutists, and buffoons. Rome owes no monumental work to his inventive brain, and literature no masterpiece to his discrimination. Ariosto, the most brilliant poet of the Renaissance, returned in disappointment from the Vatican. "When I went to Rome and kissed the foot of Leo," writes the ironical satirist, "he bent down from the holy chair, and took my hand and saluted me on both cheeks. Besides, he made me free of half the stamp-dues I was bound to pay; and then, breast full of hope, but smirched with mud, I retired and took my supper at the Ram."

The words which Leo is reported to have spoken to his brother Giuliano when he heard the news of his election, express the character of the man and mark the difference between his ambition and that of Julius. " Let us enjoy the Papacy, since God has given it us." To enjoy life, to squander the treasures of the Church on amusements, to feed a rabble of flatterers, to contract enormous debts, and to disturb the peace of Italy, not for some vast scheme of ecclesiastical aggrandisement, but in order to place the princes of his family on thrones, that was Leo's conception of the Papal privileges and duties. The portraits of the two Popes, both from the hand of Raffaello, are eminently characteristic. Julius, bent, white-haired, and emaciated, has the nervous glance of a passionate and energetic temperament. Leo, heavy-jawed, dull-eyed, with thick lips and a brawny jowl, betrays the coarser fibre of a sensualist.

II.

We have seen already that Julius, before his death, provided for his monument being carried out upon a reduced scale. Michelangelo entered into a new contract with the executors, undertaking to finish the work within the space of seven years from the date of the deed, May 6, 1513.[1] He received in several payments, during that year and the years 1514, 1515, 1516, the total sum of 6100 golden ducats.[2] This proves that he must have pushed the

[1] Lettere, Contratti, No. xi. p. 635.   [2] Lettere, Ricordi, p. 564.

various operations connected with the tomb vigorously forward, employing numerous workpeople,
and ordering supplies of marble.[1] In fact, the
greater part of what remains to us of the unfinished
monument may be ascribed to this period of comparatively uninterrupted labour. Michelangelo had
his workshop in the Macello de' Corvi, but we
know very little about the details of his life there.
His correspondence happens to be singularly scanty
between the years 1513 and 1516. One letter,
however, written in May 1518, to the Capitano of
Cortona throws a ray of light upon this barren tract
of time, and introduces an artist of eminence, whose
intellectual affinity to Michelangelo will always remain a matter of interest.[2] "While I was at Rome,
in the first year of Pope Leo, there came the Master
Luca Signorelli of Cortona, painter. I met him one
day near Monte Giordano, and he told me that he
was come to beg something from the Pope, I forget
what: he had run the risk of losing life and limb
for his devotion to the house of Medici, and now it
seemed they did not recognise him : and so forth,
saying many things I have forgotten.[3] After these
discourses, he asked me for forty giulios [a coin

---

[1] Condivi (p. 43) expressly states that he "engaged many masters
from Florence."

[2] Lettere, No. cccliv.

[3] This incident illustrates what Ariosto writes in the 4th Satire about
the people who persecuted Leo, when he was made Pope, with claims
for service rendered and devotion shown during the exile of the Medici.
Lines 154-168.

equal in value to the more modern paolo, and worth
perhaps eight shillings of present money], and
told me where to send them to, at the house of a
shoemaker, his lodgings. I not having the money
about me, promised to send it, and did so by the
hand of a young man in my service, called Silvio,
who is still alive and in Rome, I believe. After the
lapse of some days, perhaps because his business
with the Pope had failed, Messer Luca came to my
house in the Macello de' Corvi, the same where I
live now, and found me working on a marble statue,
four cubits in height, which has the hands bound
behind the back, and bewailed himself with me,
and begged another forty, saying that he wanted
to leave Rome. I went up to my bedroom, and
brought the money down in the presence of a
Bolognese maid I kept, and I think the Silvio
above mentioned was also there. When Luca got
the cash, he went away, and I have never seen
him since; but I remember complaining to him,
because I was out of health and could not work,
and he said: 'Have no fear, for the angels from
heaven will come to take you in their arms and aid
you.'" This is in several ways an interesting document. It brings vividly before our eyes magnificent
expensive Signorelli and his meanly living comrade, each of them mighty masters of a terrible
and noble style, passionate lovers of the nude, devoted to masculine types of beauty, but widely and
profoundly severed by differences in their personal

tastes and habits.[1] It also gives us a glimpse into Michelangelo's workshop at the moment when he was blocking out one of the bound Captives at the Louvre. It seems from what follows in the letter that Michelangelo had attempted to recover the money through his brother Buonarroto, but that Signorelli refused to acknowledge his debt. The Capitano wrote that he was sure it had been discharged. "That," adds Michelangelo, "is the same as calling me the biggest blackguard ; and so I should be, if I wanted to get back what had been already paid. But let your Lordship think what you like about it, I am bound to get the money, and so I swear." The remainder of the autograph is torn and illegible ; it seems to wind up with a threat.

The records of this period are so scanty that every detail acquires a certain importance for Michelangelo's biographer. By a deed executed on the 14th of June 1514, we find that he contracted to make a figure of Christ in marble, "life-sized, naked, erect, with a cross in his arms, and in such attitude as shall seem best to Michelangelo."[2] The persons who ordered the statue were Bernardo Cencio (a Canon of S. Peter's), Mario Scappucci, and Metello Varj dei Porcari, a Roman of ancient blood. They undertook to pay 200 golden ducats for the work ; and

---

[1] See Vasari's *Life of Signorelli*, who was a relative of his, for the grand train of life he led, and also for Michelangelo's addiction to his manner. Vol. vi. pp. 147, 142.

[2] Lettere, Contratti, No. xiv.

Michelangelo promised to finish it within the space of four years, when it was to be placed in the Church of S. Maria sopra Minerva. Metello Varj, though mentioned last in the contract, seems to have been the man who practically gave the commission, and to whom Michelangelo was finally responsible for its performance. He began to hew it from a block, and discovered black veins in the working. This, then, was thrown aside, and a new marble had to be attacked. The statue, now visible at the Minerva, was not finished until the year 1521, when we shall have to return to it again.

There is a point of some interest in the wording of this contract, on which, as facts to dwell upon are few and far between at present, I may perhaps allow myself to digress. The master is here described as *Michelangelo (di Lodovico) Simoni, Scultore*. Now Michelangelo always signed his own letters Michelangelo Buonarroti, although he addressed the members of his family by the surname of Simoni. This proves that the patronymic usually given to the house at large was still Simoni, and that Michelangelo himself acknowledged that name in a legal document. The adoption of Buonarroti by his brother's children and descendants may therefore be ascribed to usage ensuing from the illustration of their race by so renowned a man. It should also be observed that at this time Michelangelo is always described in deeds as sculptor, and that he frequently signs with *Michelangelo, Scultore*. Later on in life he changed his views. He wrote in 1548 to his nephew Lionardo :[1] " Tell the priest not to write to me again as *Michelangelo the sculptor*, for I am not known here except as Michelangelo Buonarroti. Say, too, that if a citizen of Florence wants to have an altar-piece painted, he must find some painter; for I was never either sculptor or painter in the way of one who keeps a shop. I have always avoided that, for the honour of my father and my brothers. True, I have served three Popes ; but that was a matter of necessity." Earlier, in 1543, he had written to the same effect :[2] " When you correspond with me, do not use the superscription *Michelangelo Simoni*, nor *sculptor;* it is enough to put *Michelangelo Buonarroti*, for that is how I am known here." On another occasion, advising his nephew what surname the latter ought to adopt, he says :[3] " I should certainly use *Simoni*, and if the whole (that is, the whole list of patronymics in use at Florence) is too long, those who cannot read it may leave it alone." These communications prove that, though he had come to be known as Buonarroti, he did not wish the family to drop their old surname of Simoni. The reason was that he believed in their legendary descent from the Counts of Canossa through a Podestà of Florence, traditionally known as Simone da Canossa. This

[1] Lettere, No. cxcix.   [2] Lettere, No. cxlvii.
[3] Lettere, No. clxxxviii., date December 17, 1547. Compare No. clxxii., December 1546, where he insists on Lionardo's using the full name. He wanted him to write *Lionardo di Buonarroto Buonarroti Simoni.*

opinion had been confirmed in 1520, as we have seen above, by a letter he received from the Conte Alessandro da Canossa, addressing him as "Honoured kinsman." In the correspondence with Lionardo, Michelangelo alludes to this act of recognition:[1] "You will find a letter from the Conte Alessandro da Canossa in the book of contracts. He came to visit me at Rome, and treated me like a relative. Take care of it." The dislike expressed by Michelangelo to be called *sculptor*, and addressed upon the same terms as other artists, arose from a keen sense of his nobility. The feeling emerges frequently in his letters between 1540 and 1550. I will give a specimen:[2] "As to the purchase of a house, I repeat that you ought to buy one of honourable condition, at 1500 or 2000 crowns; and it ought to be in our quarter (Santa Croce), if possible. I say this, because an honourable mansion in the city does a family great credit. It makes more impression than farms in the country ; and we are truly burghers, who claim a very noble ancestry. I always strove my utmost to resuscitate our house, but I had not brothers able to assist me. Try then to do what I write you, and make Gismondo come back to live in Florence, so that I may not endure the shame of hearing it said here that I have a brother at Settignano who trudges after oxen. One day, when I find the time, I will tell you all about our origin, and whence we sprang, and when we came to Flo-

[1] Lettere, No. cxc.   [2] Lettere, No. clxxi., date December 4, 1546.

rence. Perhaps you know nothing about it; still
we ought not to rob ourselves of what God gave us."
The same feeling runs through the letters he wrote
Lionardo about the choice of a wife. One example
will suffice :[1] "I believe that in Florence there are
many noble and poor families with whom it would
be a charity to form connections. If there were no
dower, there would also be no arrogance. Pay no
heed should people say you want to ennoble yourself, since it is notorious that we are ancient citizens
of Florence, and as noble as any other house."

Michelangelo, as we know now, was mistaken in
accepting his supposed connection with the illustrious Counts of Canossa, whose castle played so
conspicuous a part in the struggle between Hilde-
brand and the Empire, and who were imperially allied
through the connections of the Countess Matilda.
Still he had tradition to support him, confirmed by
the assurance of the head of the Canossa family.
Nobody could accuse him of being a snob or par-
venu. He lived like a poor man, indifferent to
dress, establishment, and personal appearances. Yet
he prided himself upon his ancient birth ; and since
the Simoni had been indubitably noble for several
generations, there was nothing despicable in his
desire to raise his kinsfolk to their proper station.
Almost culpably careless in all things that concerned
his health and comfort, he spent his earnings for the
welfare of his brothers, in order that an honourable

---

[1] Lettere, No. ccx., date February 1, 1549.

posterity might carry on the name he bore, and which he made illustrious. We may smile at his peevishness in repudiating the title of *sculptor* after bearing it through so many years of glorious labour ; but when he penned the letter I have quoted, he was the supreme artist of Italy, renowned as painter, architect, military engineer ; praised as poet ; befriended with the best and greatest of his contemporaries ; recognised as unique, not only in the art of sculpture. If he felt some pride of race, we cannot blame the plain-liver and high-thinker, who, robbing himself of luxuries and necessaries even, enabled his kinsmen to maintain their rank among folk gently born and nobly nurtured.[1]

III.

In June 1515 Michelangelo was still working at the tomb of Julius. But a letter to Buonarroto shows that he was already afraid of being absorbed for other purposes by Leo :[2] " I am forced to put great strain upon myself this summer in order to complete my undertaking ; for I think that I shall soon be obliged to enter the Pope's service. For this reason, I have bought some twenty migliaia [measure of

[1] A glance at the pedigree shows how the Simoni came to be impoverished after the death of Lodovico's grandfather.

[2] Lettere, No. xcvii., date June 16, 1515.

weight] of brass to cast certain figures." The monument then was so far advanced that, beside having a
good number of the marble statues nearly finished,
he was on the point of executing the bronze reliefs
which filled their interspaces.   We have also reason
to believe that the architectural basis forming the
foundation of the sepulchre had been brought well
forward, since it is mentioned in the next ensuing
contracts.

Just at this point, however, when two or three
years of steady labour would have sufficed to termin-
ate this mount of sculptured marble, Leo diverted
Michelangelo's energies from the work, and wasted
them in schemes that came to nothing.   When
Buonarroti penned that sonnet in which he called
the Pope his Medusa, he might well have been
thinking of Leo, though the poem ought probably
to be referred to the earlier pontificate of Julius.
Certainly the Medici did more than the Della Rovere
to paralyse his power and turn the life within him
into stone.   Writing to Sebastiano del Piombo in
1521, Michelangelo shows how fully he was aware
of this.[1]   He speaks of "the three years I have
lost."

A meeting had been arranged for the late autumn
of 1515 between Leo X. and Francis I. at Bologna.
The Pope left Rome early in November, and reached
Florence on the 30th.   The whole city burst into a
tumult of jubilation, shouting the Medicean cry of

[1] Lettere, No. ccclxxiv.

"*Palle*" as Leo passed slowly through the streets, raised in his pontifical chair upon the shoulders of his running footmen. Buonarroto wrote a long and interesting account of this triumphal entry to his brother in Rome.[1] He describes how a procession was formed by the Pope's court and guard and the gentlemen of Florence. " Among the rest, there went a bevy of young men, the noblest in our commonwealth, all dressed alike with doublets of violet satin, holding gilded staves in their hands. They paced before the Papal chair, a brave sight to see. And first there marched his guard, and then his grooms, who carried him aloft beneath a rich canopy of brocade, which was sustained by members of the College,[2] while round about the chair walked the Signory." The procession moved onward to the Church of S. Maria del Fiore, where the Pope stayed to perform certain ceremonies at the high altar, after which he was carried to his apartments at S. Maria Novella.[3] Buonarroto was one of the Priors during this month, and accordingly he took an official part in all the entertainments and festivities, which continued for three days. On the 3rd of December Leo left Florence for Bologna, where Francis arrived upon

---

[1] Gotti, i. p. 104.

[2] *Collegi.* These were the sixteen banner-bearers of the Companies, and twelve worthies chosen to represent the quarters of the town, who were associated as colleagues with the Signory. See Capponi's *Storia*, vol. i. p. 647. The Signory was formed by the eight Priors of the Arts and the Gonfalonier of Justice.

[3] See above, p. 118, note 2, for a description of the Papal lodgings.

the 11th.   Their conference lasted till the 15th,
when Francis returned to Milan.   On the 18th Leo
began his journey back to Florence, which he re-
entered on the 22nd.   On Christmas day (Buonarroto
writes *Pasqua*) a grand Mass was celebrated at S.
Maria Novella, at which the Signory attended.   The
Pope celebrated in person, and, according to custom
on high state occasions, the water with which he
washed his hands before and during the ceremony
had to be presented by personages of importance.
"This duty," says Buonarroto, "fell first to one of
the Signori, who was Giannozzo Salviati ; and as I
happened that morning to be Proposto,[1] I went
the second time to offer water to his Holiness ; the
third time, this was done by the Duke of Camerino,
and the fourth time by the Gonfalonier of Justice."
Buonarroto remarks that "he feels pretty certain it
will be all the same to Michelangelo whether he
hears or does not hear about these matters.   Yet,
from time to time, when I have leisure, I scribble a
few lines."

Buonarroto himself was interested in this event; for,
having been one of the Priors, he received from Leo
the title of Count Palatine, with reversion to all his
posterity.   Moreover, for honourable addition to his
arms, he was allowed to bear a chief charged with
the Medicean ball and fleur-de-lys, between the capital
letters L. and X.

---

[1] One of the Priors was chosen for three days to be the chairman of
the Signory.   He walked before the rest, and so forth.

Whether Leo conceived the plan of finishing the façade of S. Lorenzo at Florence before he left Rome, or whether it occurred to him during this visit, is not certain. The church had been erected by the Medici and other magnates from Brunelleschi's designs, and was perfect except for the façade. In its sacristy lay the mortal remains of Cosimo, Lorenzo the Magnificent, and many other members of the Medicean family. Here Leo came on the first Sunday in Advent to offer up prayers, and the Pope is said to have wept upon his father's tomb. It may possibly have been on this occasion that he adopted the scheme so fatal to the happiness of the great sculptor. Condivi clearly did not know what led to Michelangelo's employment on the façade of S. Lorenzo, and Vasari's account of the transaction is involved. Both, however, assert that he was wounded, even to tears, at having to abandon the monument of Julius, and that he prayed in vain to be relieved of the new and uncongenial task.

IV.

Leo at first intended to divide the work between several masters, giving Buonarroti the general direction of the whole. He ordered Giuliano da San Gallo, Raffaello da Urbino, Baccio d'Agnolo, Andrea and Jacopo Sansovino to prepare plans. While

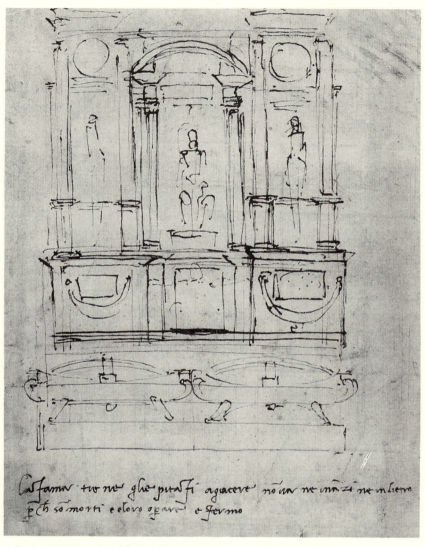

SKETCH FOR TOMBS, Medici Chapel project, pen and ink, about
1524. British Museum, London. Collection of Creighton E. Gilbert.

these were in progress, Michelangelo also thought that he would try his hand at a design. As ill-luck ruled, Leo preferred his sketch to all the rest. Vasari adds that his unwillingness to be associated with any other artist in the undertaking, and his refusal to follow the plans of an architect, prevented the work from being executed, and caused the men selected by Leo to return in desperation to their ordinary pursuits.[1] There may be truth in the report ; for it is certain that, after Michelangelo had been forced to leave the tomb of Julius and to take part in the façade, he must have claimed to be sole master of the business. The one thing we know about his mode of operation is, that he brooked no rival near him, mistrusted collaborators, and found it difficult to co-operate even with the drudges whom he hired at monthly wages.

Light is thrown upon these dissensions between Michelangelo and his proposed assistants by a letter which Jacopo Sansovino wrote to him at Carrara on the 30th of June 1517.[2] He betrays his animus at the commencement by praising Baccio Bandinelli, to mention whom in the same breath with Buonarroti was an insult. Then he proceeds : "The Pope, the Cardinal, and Jacopo Salviati are

---

[1] Vasari, vol. xii. p. 201. A letter written by B. Bandinelli, Dec. 7, 1547, corroborates Vasari. He accuses Michelangelo of having wilfully prevented the execution of the façade out of jealousy toward younger masters, and a grudge against the Medici. See *Lett. Pitt.*, i. 70.

[2] Arch. Buon., Cod. xi. No. 691. Part of it is printed by Gotti, vol. i. p. 136.

men who when they say yes, it is a written contract, inasmuch as they are true to their word, and
not what you pretend them to be. You measure
them with your own rod ; for neither contracts nor
plighted troth avail with you, who are always saying nay and yea, according as you think it profitable.
I must inform you, too, that the Pope promised me
the sculptures, and so did Salviati ; and they are
men who will maintain me in my right to them.
In what concerns you, I have done all I could to
promote your interests and honour, not having
earlier perceived that you never conferred a benefit
on any one, and that, beginning with myself, to
expect kindness from you, would be the same as
wanting water not to wet. I have reason for what I
say, since we have often met together in familiar converse, and may the day be cursed on which you ever
said any good about anybody on earth." How Michelangelo answered this intemperate and unjust invective
is not known to us. In some way or other the quarrel
between the two sculptors must have been made up
—probably through a frank apology on Sansovino's
part. When Michelangelo, in 1524, supplied the
Duke of Sessa with a sketch for the sepulchral
monument to be erected for himself and his wife,
he suggested that Sansovino should execute the work,
proving thus by acts how undeserved the latter's hasty
words had been.[1]

The Church of S. Lorenzo exists now just as it

[1] Gotti, i. p. 177.

was before the scheme for its façade occurred to Leo. Not the smallest part of that scheme was carried into effect, and large masses of the marbles quarried for the edifice lay wasted on the Tyrrhene sea-shore. We do not even know what design Michelangelo adopted. A model may be seen in the Accademia at Florence ascribed to Baccio d'Agnolo, and there is a drawing of a façade in the Uffizi attributed to Michelangelo, both of which have been supposed to have some connection with S. Lorenzo. It is hardly possible, however, that Buonarroti's competitors could have been beaten from the field by things so spiritless and ugly. A pen-and-ink drawing at the Museo Buonarroti possesses greater merit, and may perhaps have been a first rough sketch for the façade. It is not drawn to scale or worked out in the manner of practical architects; but the sketch exhibits features which we know to have existed in Buonarroti's plan—masses of sculpture, with extensive bas-reliefs in bronze. In form the façade would not have corresponded to Brunelleschi's building. That, however, signified nothing to Italian architects, who were satisfied when the frontispiece to a church or palace agreeably masked what lay behind it. As a frame for sculpture, the design might have served its purpose, though there are large spaces difficult to account for ; and spiteful folk were surely justified in remarking to the Pope that no one life sufficed for the performance of the whole.

Nothing testifies more plainly to the ascendancy

which this strange man acquired over the imagination of his contemporaries, while yet comparatively young, than the fact that Michelangelo had to relinquish work for which he was pre-eminently fitted (the tomb of Julius) for work to which his previous studies and his special inclinations in nowise called him. He undertook the façade of S. Lorenzo reluctantly, with tears in his eyes and dolour in his bosom, at the Pope Medusa's bidding. He was compelled to re-commence art at a point which hitherto possessed for him no practical importance. The drawings of the tomb, the sketch of the façade, prove that in architecture he was still a novice. Hitherto, he regarded building as the background to sculpture, or the surface on which frescoes might be limned. To achieve anything great in this new sphere implied for him a severe course of preliminary studies. It depends upon our final estimate of Michelangelo as an architect whether we regard the three years spent in Leo's service for S. Lorenzo as wasted. Being what he was, it is certain that, when the commission had been given, and he determined to attack his task alone, the man set himself down to grasp the principles of construction. There was leisure enough for such studies in the years during which we find him moodily employed among Tuscan quarries. The question is whether this strain upon his richly gifted genius did not come too late. When called to paint the Sistine, he complained that painting was no art of his. He painted, and produced a masterpiece ; but sculpture still remained the major influence in all he wrought there. Now he was bidden to quit both sculpture and painting for another field, and, as Vasari hints, he would not work under the guidance of men trained to architecture. The result was that Michelangelo applied himself to building with the full-formed spirit of a figurative artist. The obvious defects and the salient qualities of all he afterwards performed as architect seem due to the forced diversion of his talent at this period to a type of art he had not properly assimilated. Architecture was not the natural mistress of his spirit. He bent his talents to her service at a Pontiff's word, and, with the honest devotion to work which characterised the man, he produced renowned monuments stamped by his peculiar style. Nevertheless, in building, he remains a sublime amateur, aiming at scenical effect, subordinating construction to decoration, seeking ever back toward opportunities for sculpture or for fresco, and occasionally (as in the cupola of S. Peter's) hitting upon a thought beyond the reach of inferior minds.

The paradox implied in this diversion of our hero from the path it ought to have pursued may be explained in three ways. First, he had already come to be regarded as a man of unique ability, from whom everything could be demanded. Next, it was usual for the masters of the Renaissance, from Leo Battista Alberti down to Raffaello da Urbino and Lionardo da Vinci, to undertake all kinds of technical work intrusted to their care by patrons. Finally, Michelangelo, though he knew that sculpture was his goddess, and never neglected her first claim upon his genius, felt in him that burning ambition for greatness, that desire to wrestle with all forms of beauty and all depths of science, which tempted him to transcend the limits of a single art and try his powers in neighbour regions. He was a man born to aim at all, to dare all, to embrace all, to leave his personality deep-trenched on all the provinces of art he chose to traverse.

V.

The whole of 1516 and 1517 elapsed before Leo's plans regarding S. Lorenzo took a definite shape. Yet we cannot help imagining that when Michelangelo cancelled his first contract with the executors of Julius, and adopted a reduced plan for the monument, he was acting under Papal pressure. This was done at Rome in July, and much against the will of both parties. Still it does not appear that any one contemplated the abandonment of the scheme ; for Buonarroti bound himself to perform his new contract within the space of nine years, and to engage " in no work of great importance which should interfere with its fulfilment." He spent a large part of the year 1516 at Carrara, quarrying marbles, and even hired the house of a certain Francesco Pelliccia in that town. On the 1st of November he signed an agreement with the same Pelliccia involving the purchase of a vast amount of marble, whereby the said Pelliccia undertook to bring down four statues of 4½ cubits each and fifteen of 4¼ cubits from the quarries where they were being rough-hewn.[1] It was the custom to block out columns, statues, &c., on the spot where the stone had been excavated, in order probably to save weight when hauling. Thus the blocks arrived at the sea-shore with rudely adumbrated outlines of the shape they were destined to assume under the artist's chisel. It has generally been assumed that the nineteen figures in question were intended for the tomb. What makes this not quite certain, however, is that the contract of July specifies a greatly reduced quantity and scale of statues. Therefore they may have been intended for the façade. Anyhow, the contract above-mentioned with Francesco Pelliccia was cancelled on the 7th of April following, for reasons which will presently appear.[2]

During the month of November 1516 Michelangelo received notice from the Pope that he was wanted in Rome. About the same time news reached him from Florence of his father's severe illness. On the 23rd he wrote as follows to Buonarroto:[3] "I gathered from your last that Lodovico was on the point of dying, and how the doctor finally pronounced that if nothing new occurred he might be considered out of danger. Since it is so, I shall not prepare to come to Florence, for it would be very inconvenient. Still, if there is danger, I should desire to see him, come what might, before he died, if even I had to die together with him. I have good hope, however, that he will get well, and so I do not come. And if he should have a relapse —from which may God preserve him and us—see that he lacks nothing for his spiritual welfare and the sacraments of the Church, and find out from him if he wishes us to do anything for his soul. Also, for the necessaries of the body, take care that he lacks nothing; for I have laboured only and solely for him, to help him in his needs before he dies. So bid your wife look with loving-kindness to his household affairs. I will make everything good to her and all of you, if it be necessary. Do not have the least hesitation, even if you have to expend all that we possess."

We may assume that the subsequent reports regarding Lodovico's health were satisfactory ; for on the 5th of December Michelangelo set out for Rome. The executors of Julius had assigned him free quarters in a house situated in the Trevi district, opposite the public road which leads to S. Maria del Loreto.[1] Here, then, he probably took up

---

[1] It must have been close to the Forum of Trajan, and not far from his old dwelling at the Macello de' Corvi, which lies below the Capitoline

his abode. We have seen that he had bound himself to finish the monument of Julius within the space of nine years, and to engage " in no work of great moment which should interfere with its performance." How this clause came to be inserted in a deed inspired by Leo is one of the difficulties with which the whole tragedy of the sepulchre bristles. Perhaps we ought to conjecture that the Pope's intentions with regard to the façade of S. Lorenzo only became settled in the late autumn. At any rate, he had now to transact with the executors of Julius, who were obliged to forego the rights over Michelangelo's undivided energies which they had acquired by the clause I have just cited. They did so with extreme reluctance, and to the bitter disappointment of the sculptor, who saw the great scheme of his manhood melting into air, dwindling in proportions, becoming with each change less capable of satisfactory performance.

Having at last definitely entered the service of Pope Leo, Michelangelo travelled to Florence, and intrusted Baccio d'Agnolo with the construction of the model of his façade. It may have been upon the occasion of this visit that one of his father's whimsical fits of temper called out a passionate and sorry letter from his son. It appears that Pietro

Hill, just opposite the Column of Trajan. Letters are addressed to him " close by the Church of Loreto." Condivi's only extant letter is superscribed : " A Roma vicino la piazza di S. Apostolo canto la chiesa di Loreto e casa Zanbeccari." Arch. Buon., Cod. vii. 49.

Urbano, Michelangelo's trusty henchman at this period, said something which angered Lodovico, and made him set off in a rage to Settignano :[1]—

"DEAREST FATHER,—I marvelled much at what had happened to you the other day, when I did not find you at home. And now, hearing that you complain of me, and say that I have turned you out of doors, I marvel much the more, inasmuch as I know for certain that never once from the day that I was born till now had I a single thought of doing anything or small or great which went against you ; and all this time the labours I have undergone have been for the love of you alone. Since I returned from Rome to Florence, you know that I have always cared for you, and you know that all that belongs to me I have bestowed on you. Some days ago, then, when you were ill, I promised solemnly never to fail you in anything within the scope of my whole faculties so long as my life lasts ; and this I again affirm. Now I am amazed that you should have forgotten everything so soon. And yet you have learned to know me by experience these thirty years, you and your sons, and are well aware that I have always thought and acted, so far as I was able, for your good. How can you go about saying I have turned you out of doors ? Do you not see what a reputation you have given me by saying I have turned you out ? Only this was wanting to complete

[1] Lettere, No. xxxix.

my tale of troubles, all of which I suffer for your love. You repay me well, forsooth. But let it be as it must: I am willing to acknowledge that I have always brought shame and loss on you, and on this supposition I beg your pardon. Reckon that you are pardoning a son who has lived a bad life and done you all the harm which it is possible to do. And so I once again implore you to pardon me, scoundrel that I am, and not bring on me the reproach of having turned you out of doors ; for that matters more than you imagine to me. After all, I am your son."

From Florence Michelangelo proceeded again to Carrara for the quarrying of marble. This was on the last day of December. From his domestic correspondence we find that he stayed there until at least the 13th of March, 1517 ; but he seems to have gone to Florence just about that date, in order to arrange matters with Baccio d'Agnolo about the model. A fragmentary letter to Buonarroto, dated March 13, shows that he had begun a model of his own at Carrara, and that he no longer needed Baccio's assistance.[1] On his arrival at Florence he wrote to Messer Buoninsegni, who acted as intermediary at Rome between himself and the Pope in all things that concerned the façade :[2]

[1] Lettere, No. cxiii.

[2] It seems to have been the custom to employ these go-betweens. Michelangelo sometimes found them very troublesome, and expressed his feelings frankly in a letter to Pope Clement VII. See Lettere, No. ccclxxxi.

"Messer Domenico, I have come to Florence to see the model which Baccio has finished, and find it a mere child's plaything. If you think it best to have it sent, write to me. I leave again to-morrow for Carrara, where I have begun to make a model in clay with Grassa [a stone-hewer from Settignano]." Then he adds that, in the long run, he believes that he shall have to make the model himself, which distresses him on account of the Pope and the Cardinal Giulio. Lastly, he informs his correspondent that he has contracted with two separate companies for two hundred cartloads of Carrara marble.[1]

An important letter to the same Domenico Buoninsegni, dated Carrara, May 2, 1517, proves that Michelangelo had become enthusiastic about his new design.[2] "I have many things to say to you. So I beg you to take some patience when you read my words, because it is a matter of moment. Well, then, I feel it in me to make this façade of S. Lorenzo such that it shall be a mirror of archi-

---

[1] Lettere, No. cccxlvi. The numerous transactions of Michelangelo with stone-masons, owners of quarries, and so forth, at Carrara, between January 3 and August 20, 1517, will be found in Lettere, pp. 655–670. In February he entered into partnership with a certain Lionardo di Cagione. They were to work together, sharing costs and profits. In March this partnership was dissolved "per buon rispetto."

[2] Lettere, No. cccxlviii. One of the inedited letters in the Arch. Buon. from Bernardo Niccolini to Michelangelo in Carrara (Cod. x. No. 578, date May 18, 1517) throws a glimpse of light upon his daily life. It is indorsed with a *menu* for some meal : "Pani dua, un bochal di vino, una aringa, tortegli," &c. Each item is accompanied by a little pen-drawing : two loaves of bread, a glass decanter, a herring, three round tarts or buns, and so forth, in the master's autograph.

tecture and of sculpture to all Italy. But the Pope and the Cardinal must decide at once whether they want to have it done or not. If they desire it, then they must come to some definite arrangement, either intrusting the whole to me on contract, and leaving me a free hand, or adopting some other plan which may occur to them, and about which I can form no idea." He proceeds at some length to inform Buoninsegni of various transactions regarding the purchase of marble, and the difficulties he encounters in procuring perfect blocks. His estimate for the costs of the whole façade is 35,000 golden ducats, and he offers to carry the work through for that sum in six years. Meanwhile he peremptorily demands an immediate settlement of the business, stating that he is anxious to leave Carrara. The vigorous tone of this document is unmistakable. It seems to have impressed his correspondents ; for Buoninsegni replies upon the 8th of May that the Cardinal expressed the highest satisfaction at " the great heart he had for conducting the work of the façade." [1] At the same time the Pope was anxious to inspect the model.

Leo, I fancy, was always more than half-hearted about the façade. He did not personally sympathise with Michelangelo's character ; and, seeing what his tastes were, it is impossible that he can have really appreciated the quality of his genius. Giulio de' Medici, afterwards Pope Clement VII., was more in sympathy with Buonarroti both as artist and as man.

[1] Gotti, i. 112.

To him we may with probability ascribe the impulse
given at this moment to the project. After several
visits to Florence during the summer, and much correspondence with the Medici through their Roman
agent, Michelangelo went finally, upon the 31st of
August, to have the model completed under his own
eyes by a workman in his native city. It was carefully constructed of wood, showing the statuary in
wax-relief. Nearly four months were expended on
this miniature. The labour was lost, for not a ves-
tige of it now remains. Near the end of December
he despatched his servant, Pietro Urbano, with the
finished work to Rome. On the 29th of that month,
Urbano writes that he exposed the model in Messer
Buoninsegni's apartment, and that the Pope and
Cardinal were very well pleased with it.[1] Buoninsegni
wrote to the same effect, adding, however, that folk
said it could never be finished in the sculptor's lifetime, and suggesting that Michelangelo should hire
assistants from Milan, where he, Buoninsegni, had
seen excellent stonework in progress at the Duomo.

Some time in January 1518, Michelangelo travelled
to Rome, conferred with Leo, and took the façade of
S. Lorenzo on contract.[2] In February he returned
by way of Florence to Carrara, where the quarry-
masters were in open rebellion against him, and

[1] Gotti, i. 112.

[2] The most authentic source of information about events between
December 5, 1516, and February 25, 1518, is Michelangelo's own *Ricordi*,
Lettere, p. 568. The contract is dated January 19, 1518. Lettere,
Contr. xxxiii. p. 671.

refused to carry out their contracts. This forced him to go to Genoa, and hire ships there for the transport of his blocks. Then the Carraresi corrupted the captains of these boats, and drove Michelangelo to Pisa (April 7), where he finally made an arrangement with a certain Francesco Peri to ship the marbles lying on the sea-shore at Carrara.[1]

The reason of this revolt against him at Carrara may be briefly stated. The Medici determined to begin working the old marble quarries of Pietra Santa, on the borders of the Florentine domain, and this naturally aroused the commercial jealousy of the folk at Carrara.[2] " Information," says Condivi, " was sent to Pope Leo that marbles could be found in the high-lands above Pietra Santa, fully equal in quality and beauty to those of Carrara. Michelangelo, having been sounded on the subject, chose to go on quarrying at Carrara rather than to take those belonging to the State of Florence. This he did because he was befriended with the Marchese Alberigo, and lived on a good understanding with him. The Pope wrote to Michelangelo, ordering him to repair to Pietra Santa, and see whether the information he had received from Florence was correct. He did so, and ascertained that the marbles were very hard to work, and ill-adapted to their pur-

---

[1] Lettere, Nos. cccxlix., cxiv., cxv.
[2] By a deed executed May 18, 1515, the commune of Seravezza ceded to Florence all its property in quarries between the mountains of Altissimo and Ceresola. Lettere, Contr. xv. p. 643.

pose ; even had they been of the proper kind, it would
be difficult and costly to convey them to the sea.
A road of many miles would have to be made
through the mountains with pick and crowbar, and
along the plain on piles, since the ground there was
marshy.[1] Michelangelo wrote all this to the Pope,
who preferred, however, to believe the persons who
had written to him from Florence. So he ordered
him to construct the road." The road, it may paren-
thetically be observed, was paid for by the wealthy
Wool Corporation of Florence, who wished to revive
this branch of Florentine industry. " Michelangelo,
carrying out the Pope's commands, had the road laid
down, and transported large quantities of marbles to
the sea-shore. Among these were five columns of
the proper dimensions, one of which may be seen
upon the Piazza di S. Lorenzo. The other four,
forasmuch as the Pope changed his mind and turned
his thoughts elsewhere, are still lying on the sea-
beach. Now the Marquis of Carrara, deeming that
Michelangelo had developed the quarries at Pietra
Santa out of Florentine patriotism, became his enemy,
and would not suffer him to return to Carrara for certain blocks which had been excavated there: all which
proved the source of great loss to Michelangelo."[2]

---

[1] The Arch. Buon. contains an inedited letter from Fra Massimiliano,
Abbot of Camaiore, about the construction of roads on the sea-coast
between that place and the sea (date April 17, 1518, Cod. viii. No. 373).
It has some biographical interest, since the exordium hails Michelangelo as the equal of Apelles, Praxiteles, and Lysippus.

[2] Condivi, p. 44.

When the contract with Francesco Pelliccia was cancelled, April 7, 1517, the project for developing the Florentine stone-quarries does not seem to have taken shape.[1] We must assume, therefore, that the motive for this step was the abandonment of the tomb. The *Ricordi* show that Michelangelo was still buying marbles and visiting Carrara down to the end of February 1518.[2] His correspondence from Pietra Santa and Serravezza, where he lived when he was opening the Florentine quarries of Monte Altissimo, does not begin, with any certainty, until March 1518. We have indeed one letter written to Girolamo del Bardella of Porto Venere upon the 6th of August, without date of year. This was sent from Serravezza, and Milanesi, when he first made use of it, assigned it to 1517.[3] Gotti, following that indication, asserts that Michelangelo began his operations at Monte Altissimo in July 1517; but Milanesi afterwards changed his opinion, and assigned it to the year 1519.[4] I believe he was right, because the first letter, bearing a certain date from Pietra Santa, was written in March 1518 to Pietro Urbano. It contains the account of Michelangelo's difficulties with the Carraresi, and his journey to Genoa and Pisa.[5] We have, therefore, every reason to believe

---

[1] We must bear in mind, however, that the Arte della Lana had acquired property in them so far back as the year 1515. See above, p. 329, note 2. [2] Lettere, p. 568.
[3] Vasari, vol. xii. p. 354. [4] Lettere, No. ccclxvii.
[5] Lettere, No. cccxlix. Notice that Michelangelo's *Ricordo* (Lettere, p. 589) gives no account of a visit to Pietra Santa, and winds up at Carrara

that he finally abandoned Carrara for Pietra Santa at the end of February 1518.

Pietra Santa is a little city on the Tuscan seaboard; Serravezza is a still smaller fortress-town at the foot of the Carrara mountains. Monte Altissimo rises above it; and on the flanks of that great hill lie the quarries Della Finocchiaja, which Michelangelo opened at the command of Pope Leo. It was not without reluctance that Michelangelo departed from Carrara, offending the Marquis Malaspina, breaking his contracts, and disappointing the folk with whom he had lived on friendly terms ever since his first visit in 1505. A letter from the Cardinal Giulio de' Medici shows that great pressure was put upon him.[1] It runs thus: "We have received yours, and shown it to our Lord the Pope. Considering that all your doings are in favour of Carrara, you have caused his Holiness and us no small astonishment. What we heard from Jacopo Salviati contradicts your opinion. He went to examine the marble-quarries at Pietra Santa, and informed us that there are enormous quantities of stone, excellent

on the date February 25, 1518. There is a letter from Donato Benti to Michelangelo in Florence, dated *from* Pietra Santa, February 9, 1518 (Arch. Buon., Cod. vi., No. 53). Another from Domenico Boninsegni to Michelangelo *in* Pietra Santa, dated March 1518 (*ibid.*, Cod. vi., No. 103). In the Archive I found no letter addressed to Michelangelo at Pietra Santa earlier than this. I may here observe that careful examination of the business letters written to Michelangelo by Salviati, Baccio d'Agnolo, Benti, Buoninsegni, Fattucci, Topolino, Niccolini, Urbano, and others, may still throw fresh light on his movements.

[1] Gotti, vol. i. p. 109.

in quality, and easy to bring down. This being the case, some suspicion has arisen in our minds that you, for your own interests, are too partial to the quarries of Carrara, and want to depreciate those of Pietra Santa. This, of a truth, would be wrong in you, considering the trust we have always reposed in your honesty. Wherefore we inform you that, regardless of any other consideration, his Holiness wills that all the work to be done at S. Peter's or S. Reparata, or on the façade of S. Lorenzo, shall be carried out with marbles supplied from Pietra Santa, and no others, for the reasons above written. Moreover, we hear that they will cost less than those of Carrara; but, even should they cost more, his Holiness is firmly resolved to act as I have said, furthering the business of Pietra Santa for the public benefit of the city. Look to it, then, that you carry out in detail all that we have ordered without fail; for if you do otherwise, it will be against the expressed wishes of his Holiness and ourselves, and we shall have good reason to be seriously wroth with you. Our agent Domenico (Buoninsegni) is bidden to write to the same effect. Reply to him how much money you want, and quickly, banishing from your mind every kind of obstinacy."

Michelangelo began to work with his usual energy at roadmaking and quarrying. What he learned of practical business as engineer, architect, master of works, and paymaster during these years among the Carrara mountains must have been of vast importance for his future work. He was preparing himself to organise the fortifications of Florence and the Leonine City, and to crown S. Peter's with the cupola. Quarrying, as I have said, implied cutting out and rough-hewing blocks exactly of the right dimensions for certain portions of a building or a piece of statuary. The master was therefore obliged to have his whole plan perfect in his head before he could venture to order marble. Models, drawings made to scale, careful measurements, were necessary at each successive step. Day and night Buonarroti was at work ; in the saddle early in the morning, among stone-cutters and road-makers ; in the evening, studying, projecting, calculating, settling up accounts by lamplight.

VI.

The narrative of Michelangelo's personal life and movements must here be interrupted in order to notice an event in which he took no common interest. The members of the Florentine Academy addressed a memorial to Leo X., requesting him to authorise the translation of Dante Alighieri's bones from Ravenna to his native city. The document was drawn up in Latin, and dated October 20, 1518.[1]

[1] See Condivi, p. 139, or Gotti, ii. p. 82. The original is shown in the rooms of the State Archives at the Uffizi.

Among the names and signatures appended, Michel-angelo's alone is written in Italian : " I, Michel-angelo, the sculptor, pray the like of your Holiness, offering my services to the divine poet for the erec-tion of a befitting sepulchre to him in some honour-able place in this city." Nothing resulted from this petition, and the supreme poet's remains still rest beneath " the little cupola, more neat than solemn," guarded by Pietro Lombardi's half-length portrait.

Of Michelangelo's special devotion to Dante and the " Divine Comedy " we have plenty of proof. In the first place, there exist the two fine sonnets to his memory, which were celebrated in their author's lifetime, and still remain among the best of his performances in verse.[1] It does not appear when they were composed. The first is probably earlier than the second; for below the autograph of the latter is written, " Messer Donato, you ask of me what I do not possess." The Donato is undoubtedly Donato Giannotti, with whom Michelangelo lived on very familiar terms at Rome about 1545. I will here insert my English translation of these sonnets :—

> From heaven his spirit came, and, robed in clay,
>   The realms of justice and of mercy trod :
>   Then rose a living man to gaze on God,
>   That he might make the truth as clear as day.
> For that pure star, that brightened with his ray
>   The undeserving nest where I was born,
>   The whole wide world would be a prize to scorn ;
>   None but his Maker can due guerdon pay.

---

[1] *Rime :* Sonnets, Nos. i. and ii.

I speak of Dante, whose high work remains
   Unknown, unhonoured by that thankless brood,
   Who only to just men deny their wage.
Were I but he ! Born for like lingering pains,
   Against his exile coupled with his good
   I 'd gladly change the world's best heritage !

No tongue can tell of him what should be told,
   For on blind eyes his splendour shines too strong ;
   'T were easier to blame those who wrought him wrong,
   Than sound his least praise with a mouth of gold.
He to explore the place of pain was bold,
   Then soared to God, to teach our souls by song ;
   The gates heaven oped to bear his feet along,
   Against his just desire his country rolled.
Thankless I call her, and to her own pain
   The nurse of fell mischance ; for sign take this,
   That ever to the best she deals more scorn ;
Among a thousand proofs let one remain ;
   Though ne'er was fortune more unjust than his,
   His equal or his better ne'er was born.

The influence of Dante over Buonarroti's style of composition impressed his contemporaries. Benedetto Varchi, in the proemium to a lecture upon one of Michelangelo's poems, speaks of it as " a most sublime sonnet, full of that antique purity and Dantesque gravity." [1] Dante's influence over the great artist's pictorial imagination is strongly marked in the fresco of the Last Judgment, where Charon's boat, and Minos with his twisted tail, are borrowed direct from the *Inferno*. Condivi, moreover, informs us that the statues of the Lives Contemplative and Active upon the tomb of Julius were suggested by

---

[1] *Rime*, p. lxxxvii.

the Rachel and Leah of the *Purgatorio*. We also know that he filled a book with drawings illustrative of the "Divine Comedy." By a miserable accident this most precious volume, while in the possession of Antonio Montauti, the sculptor, perished at sea on a journey from Livorno to Rome.

But the strongest proof of Michelangelo's reputation as a learned student of Dante is given in Donato Giannotti's Dialogue upon the number of days spent by the poet during his journey through Hell and Purgatory.[1] Luigi del Riccio, who was a great friend of the sculptor's, is supposed to have been walking one day toward the Lateran with Antonio Petreo. Their conversation fell upon Cristoforo Landino's theory that the time consumed by Dante in this transit was the whole of the night of Good Friday, together with the following day. While engaged in this discussion, they met Donato Giannotti taking the air with Michelangelo. The four friends joined company, and Petreo observed that it was a singular good fortune to have fallen that morning upon two such eminent Dante scholars. Donato replied : " With regard to Messer Michelangelo, you have abundant reason to say that he is an eminent *Dantista*, since I am acquainted with no one who understands him better and has a fuller mastery over his works." It is not needful to give a detailed account of Buonarroti's Dantesque criticism, re-

[1] *De' giorni che Dante consumò*, &c. Firenze : Tip. Galileiana, 1589. Sufficient excerpts will be found in Guasti's *Rime*, pp. xxvi.-xxxiv.

ported in these dialogues, although there are good grounds for supposing them in part to represent exactly what Giannotti heard him say. This applies particularly to his able interpretation of the reason why Dante placed Brutus and Cassius in hell—not as being the murderers of a tyrant, but as having laid violent hands upon the sacred majesty of the Empire in the person of Cæsar. The narrative of Dante's journey through Hell and Purgatory, which is put into Michelangelo's mouth, if we are to believe that he really made it extempore and without book, shows a most minute knowledge of the *Inferno*.

VII.

Michelangelo's doings at Serravezza can be traced with some accuracy during the summers of 1518 and 1519. An important letter to Buonarroto, dated April 2, 1518, proves that the execution of the road had not yet been decided on.[1] He is impatient to hear whether the Wool Corporation has voted the necessary funds and appointed him to engineer it. "With regard to the construction of the road here, please tell Jacopo Salviati that I shall carry out his wishes, and he will not be betrayed by me. I do not look after any interests of my own in this matter, but seek to serve my patrons and my country. If I

[1] Lettere, No. cxiv.

begged the Pope and Cardinal to give me full control over the business, it was that I might be able to conduct it to those places where the best marbles are. Nobody here knows anything about them. I did not ask for the commission in order to make money; nothing of the sort is in my head." This proves conclusively that much which has been written about the waste of Michelangelo's abilities on things a lesser man might have accomplished is merely sentimental. On the contrary, he was even accused of begging for the contract from a desire to profit by it. In another letter, of April 18, the decision of the Wool Corporation was still anxiously expected.[1] Michelangelo gets impatient. " I shall mount my horse, and go to find the Pope and Cardinal, tell them how it is with me, leave the business here, and return to Carrara. The folk there pray for my return as one is wont to pray to Christ." Then he complains of the worthlessness and dis- loyalty of the stone-hewers he brought from Florence, and winds up with an angry postscript: " Oh, cursed a thousand times the day and hour when I left Carrara! This is the cause of my utter ruin. But I shall go back there soon. Nowadays it is a sin to do one's duty." On the 22nd of April the Wool Cor- poration assigned to Michelangelo a contract for the quarries, leaving him free to act as he thought best.[2]

[1] Lettere, No. cxvi.
[2] Lettere, p. 137, note. The text of this charter is given, ibid., Contr. xxxvii. p. 679. It appointed Michelangelo to life-management and a monopoly.

Complaints follow about his workmen.[1] One passage is curious : " Sandro, he too has gone away from here. He stopped several months with a mule and a little mule in grand style, doing nothing but fish and make love. He cost me a hundred ducats to no purpose ; has left a certain quantity of marble, giving me the right to take the blocks that suit my purpose. However, I cannot find among them what is worth twenty-five ducats, the whole being a jumble of rascally work. Either maliciously or through ignorance, he has treated me very ill."

Upon the 17th April 1517, Michelangelo had bought a piece of ground in Via Mozza, now Via S. Zanobi, at Florence, from the Chapter of S. Maria del Fiore, in order to build a workshop there. He wished, about the time of the last letter quoted, to get an additional lot of land, in order to have larger space at his command for the finishing of marbles. The negotiations went on through the summer of 1518, and on the 24th of November he records that the purchase was completed. Premises adapted to the sculptor's purpose were erected, which remained

---

[1] Lettere, Nos. cxviii., cxix. Sandro was a stone-hewer of Settignano, the brother of Michelangelo's friend Topolino. By a deed, dated March 15, 1518, it seems that he brought eight stone-cutters from Settignano and its neighbourhood, ibid., Contr. xxxiv. p. 673. Compare Nos. xxxix., xl., xlii. On April 27, 1518, he executed a power of attorney, constituting Donato di Battista Benti, a Florentine, his agent-in-chief at Pietra Santa, ibid., No. xxxviii. p. 681. The Arch. Buon., Cod. vi. Nos. 53–81, contains twenty-nine business letters from this Benti, between February 19, 1518, and July 7, 1521.

in Michelangelo's possession until the close of his life.[1]

In August 1518 he writes to a friend at Florence that the road is now as good as finished, and that he is bringing down his columns.[2] The work is more difficult than he expected. One man's life had been already thrown away, and Michelangelo himself was in great danger. "The place where we have to quarry is exceedingly rough, and the workmen are very stupid at their business. For some months I must make demands upon my powers of patience until the mountains are tamed and the men instructed. Afterwards we shall proceed more quickly. Enough, that I mean to do what I promised, and shall produce the finest thing that Italy has ever seen, if God assists me."

There is no want of heart and spirit in these letters. Irritable at moments, Michelangelo was at bottom enthusiastic, and, like Napoleon Buonaparte, felt capable of conquering the world with his sole arm.

In September we find him back again at Florence, where he seems to have spent the winter. His friends wanted him to go to Rome; they thought that his presence there was needed to restore the confidence of the Medici and to overpower calumniating rivals. In reply to a letter of admonition written in this sense by his friend Lionardo di Compagno,

---

[1] Lettere, p. 141, note 1 ; p. 575. A letter from Daniele da Volterra, dated May 8, 1557, mentions a visit to "la bottega in Via Mozza." Arch. Buon., Cod. x. No. 646.

[2] Lettere, No. ccclvi.

the saddle-maker, he writes :[1] " Your urgent solici-
tations are to me so many stabs of the knife. I am
dying of annoyance at not being able to do what I
should like to do, through my ill-luck." At the
same time he adds that he has now arranged an
excellent workshop, where twenty statues can be set
up together. The drawback is that there are no
means of covering the whole space in and protecting
it against the weather. This yard, encumbered with
the marbles for S. Lorenzo, must have been in the
Via Mozza.

Early in the spring he removed to Serravezza, and
resumed the work of bringing down his blocked-out
columns from the quarries. One of these pillars, six
of which he says were finished, was of huge size,
intended probably for the flanks to the main door
at S. Lorenzo. It tumbled into the river, and was
smashed to pieces. Michelangelo attributed the
accident solely to the bad quality of iron which a
rascally fellow had put into the lewis-ring by means
of which the block was being raised.[2] On this occasion
he again ran considerable risk of injury, and suffered
great annoyance. The following letter of condolence,
written by Jacopo Salviati, proves how much he was
grieved, and also shows that he lived on excellent
terms with the Pope's right-hand man and coun-
sellor :[3] " Keep up your spirits and proceed gallantly

---

[1] Lettere, No. ccclix., date Dec. 21, 1518.
[2] Lettere, No. ccclxiv., to Pietro Urbano, April 20, 1519.
[3] Gotti, i. 126.

with your great enterprise, for your honour requires this, seeing you have commenced the work. Confide in me; nothing will be amiss with you, and our Lord is certain to compensate you for far greater losses than this. Have no doubt upon this point, and if you want one thing more than another, let me know, and you shall be served immediately. Remember that your undertaking a work of such magnitude will lay our city under the deepest obligation, not only to yourself, but also to your family for ever. Great men, and of courageous spirit, take heart under adversities, and become more energetic."

A pleasant thread runs through Michelangelo's correspondence during these years. It is the affection he felt for his workman Pietro Urbano.[1] When he leaves the young man behind him at Florence, he writes frequently, giving him advice, bidding him mind his studies, and also telling him to confess. It happened that Urbano fell ill at Carrara toward the end of August. Michelangelo, on hearing the news, left Florence and travelled by post to Carrara. Thence he had his friend transported on the backs of men to Serravezza, and after his recovery sent him to pick up strength in his native city of Pistoja. In one of the *Ricordi* he reckons the cost of all this at $33\frac{1}{2}$ ducats.[2]

[1] Pietro, in a letter written from Rome, calls him " charissimo quanto padre."

[2] Lettere, p. 579. During his convalescence at Pistoja, Urbano wrote an affectionate letter to his master, which I shall use in Chapter XV.

While Michelangelo was residing at Pietra Santa in 1518, his old friend and fellow-worker, Pietro Rosselli, wrote to him from Rome, asking his advice about a tabernacle of marble which Pietro Soderini had ordered. It was to contain the head of S. John the Baptist, and to be placed in the Church of the Convent of S. Silvestro.[1] On the 7th of June Soderini wrote upon the same topic, requesting a design. This Michelangelo sent in October, the execution of the shrine being intrusted to Federigo Frizzi. The incident would hardly be worth mentioning, except for the fact that it brings to mind one of Michelangelo's earliest patrons, the good-hearted Gonfalonier of Justice, and anticipates the coming of the only woman he is known to have cared for, Vittoria Colonna. It was at S. Silvestro that she dwelt, retired in widowhood, and here occurred those Sunday morning conversations of which Francesco d'Olanda has left us so interesting a record.

During the next year, 1519, a certain Tommaso di Dolfo invited him to visit Adrianople.[2] He reminded him how, coming together in Florence, when Michelangelo lay there in hiding from Pope Julius, they had talked about the East, and he had expressed a wish to travel into Turkey. Tommaso di Dolfo dissuaded him on that occasion, because the

[1] It does not seem to have been completed.

[2] Arch. Buon., Cod. xi. No. 724. I have followed Gotti's version of this man's name. In the manuscript it seemed to me more like Tommaso di Tolpo.

ruler of the province was a man of no taste and careless about the arts. Things had altered since, and he thought there was a good opening for an able sculptor. Things, however, had altered in Italy also, and Buonarroti felt no need to quit the country where his fame was growing daily.

Considerable animation is introduced into the annals of Michelangelo's life at this point by his correspondence with jovial Sebastiano del Piombo. We possess one of this painter's letters, dating as early as 1510, when he thanks Buonarroti for consenting to be godfather to his boy Luciano; a second, of 1512, which contains the interesting account of his conversation with Pope Julius about Michelangelo and Raffaello; and a third, of 1518, turning upon the rivalry between the two great artists.[1] But the bulk of Sebastiano's gossipy and racy communications belongs to the period of thirteen years between 1520 and 1533;[2] then it suddenly breaks off, owing to Michelangelo's having taken up his residence at Rome during the autumn of 1533. A definite rupture at some subsequent period separated the old friends. These letters are a mine of curious information respecting artistic life at Rome. They prove, beyond the possibility of doubt, that, whatever Buonarroti and

[1] Published respectively by Bottari, vol. viii. p. 42 ; Gaye, vol. ii. p. 487 ; and Gotti, vol. ii. p. 56.

[2] Published in one volume by Milanesi and Le Pileur, *Les Correspondants de Michel-Ange, I. Seb. del Piombo.* Paris: Librairie de l'Art, 1890.

Sanzio may have felt, their flatterers, dependants, and creatures cherished the liveliest hostility and lived in continual rivalry. It is somewhat painful to think that Michelangelo could have lent a willing ear to the malignant babble of a man so much inferior to himself in nobleness of nature— have listened when Sebastiano taunted Raffaello as " Prince of the Synagogue," or boasted that a picture of his own was superior to " the tapestries just come from Flanders."[1]   Yet Sebastiano was not the only friend to whose idle gossip the great sculptor indulgently stooped.   Lionardo, the saddle-maker, was even more offensive.   He writes, for instance, upon New Year's Day, 1519, to say that the Resurrection of Lazarus, for which Michelangelo had contributed some portion of the design, was nearly finished,[2] and adds : " Those who understand art rank it far above Raffaello.   The vault, too, of Agostino Chigi has been exposed to view, and is a thing truly disgraceful to a great artist, far worse than the last hall of the Palace.   Sebastiano has nothing to fear."[3]

We gladly turn from these quarrels to what Sebastiano teaches us about Michelangelo's personal character.   The general impression in the world was that he was very difficult to live with.   Julius, for instance, after remarking that Raffaello changed his

[1] Raffaello designed his famous Cartoons for these tapestries.

[2] Gotti, vol. i. p. 127.

[3] The vault is the story of Cupid and Psyche at the Villa Farnesina, executed by Raffaello's pupils.   The last hall of the Vatican is that containing the Incendio del Borgo.

style in imitation of Buonarroti, continued :[1] "'But he
is terrible, as you see ; one cannot get on with him.'
I answered to his Holiness that your terribleness
hurt nobody, and that you only seem to be terrible
because of your passionate devotion to the great
works you have on hand." Again, he relates Leo's
estimate of his friend's character :[2] " I know in what
esteem the Pope holds you, and when he speaks of
you, it would seem that he were talking about a
brother, almost with tears in his eyes ; for he has
told me you were brought up together as boys "
(Giovanni de' Medici and the sculptor were exactly
of the same age), "and shows that he knows and
loves you. But you frighten everybody, even
Popes !" Michelangelo must have complained of
this last remark, for Sebastiano, in a letter dated a
few days later, reverts to the subject :[3] "Touching
what you reply to me about your terribleness, I, for
my part, do not esteem you terrible ; and if I have
not written on this subject, do not be surprised,
seeing you do not strike me as terrible, except only
in art—that is to say, in being the greatest master
who ever lived : that is my opinion ; if I am in error,
the loss is mine." Later on, he tells us what
Clement VII. thought :[4] " One letter to your friend
(the Pope) would be enough ; you would soon see

[1] Gaye, vol. ii. p. 489.
[2] *Les Correspondants, op. cit.*, p. 20, date October 27, 1520.
[3] Ibid., p. 24, November 9, 1520.
[4] Ibid., p. 40, date April 29, 1531.

what fruit it bore; because I know how he values you. He loves you, knows your nature, adores your work, and tastes its quality as much as it is possible for man to do. Indeed, his appreciation is miraculous, and such as ought to give great satisfaction to an artist. He speaks of you so honourably, and with such loving affection, that a father could not say of a son what he does of you. It is true that he has been grieved at times by buzzings in his ear about you at the time of the siege of Florence. He shrugged his shoulders and cried, 'Michelangelo is in the wrong; I never did him any injury.'" It is interesting to find Sebastiano, in the same letter, complaining of Michelangelo's sensitiveness. "One favour I would request of you, that is, that you should come to learn your worth, and not stoop as you do to every little thing, and remember that eagles do not prey on flies. Enough! I know that you will laugh at my prattle; but I do not care; Nature has made me so, and I am not Zuan da Rezzo." [1]

VIII.

The year 1520 was one of much importance for Michelangelo. A *Ricordo* dated March 10 gives a

[1] Giovanni da Reggio, the man who went with a letter of introduction from Michelangelo to the Count of Canossa. Sebastiano writes his name in Venetian.

brief account of the last four years, winding up with the notice that[1] " Pope Leo, perhaps because he wants to get the façade at S. Lorenzo finished quicker than according to the contract made with me, and I also consenting thereto, sets me free . . . and so he leaves me at liberty, under no obligation of accounting to any one for anything which I have had to do with him or others upon his account." It appears from the draft of a letter without date that some altercation between Michelangelo and the Medici preceded this rupture.[2]   He had been withdrawn from Serravezza to Florence in order that he might plan the new buildings at S. Lorenzo ; and the workmen of the Opera del Duomo continued the quarrying business in his absence.   Marbles which he had excavated for S. Lorenzo were granted by the Cardinal de' Medici to the custodians of the cathedral, and no attempt was made to settle accounts.   Michelangelo's indignation was roused by this indifference to his interests, and he complains in terms of extreme bitterness.   Then he sums up all that he has lost, in addition to expected profits.   " I do not reckon the wooden model for the said façade, which I made and sent to Rome ; I do not reckon the period of three years wasted in this work ; I do not reckon that I have been ruined (in health and strength perhaps) by the undertaking ; I do not reckon the enormous insult put on me by being brought here to do the work, and then seeing it

[1] Lettere, p. 581.   [2] Lettere, No. ccclxxiv.

taken away from me, and for what reason I have not
yet learned ; I do not reckon my house in Rome,
which I left, and where marbles, furniture, and
blocked-out statues have suffered to upwards of 500
ducats. Omitting all these matters, out of the 2300
ducats I received, only 500 remain in my hands."

When he was an old man, Michelangelo told
Condivi that Pope Leo changed his mind about S.
Lorenzo. In the often-quoted letter to the prelate
he said :[1] "Leo, not wishing me to work at the tomb
of Julius, *pretended that he wanted to complete* the
façade of S. Lorenzo at Florence." What was the
real state of the case can only be conjectured. It
does not seem that the Pope took very kindly to the
façade ; so the project may merely have been dropped
through carelessness. Michelangelo neglected his
own interests by not going to Rome, where his enemies kept pouring calumnies into the Pope's ears.
The Marquis of Carrara, as reported by Lionardo,
wrote to Leo that "he had sought to do you honour,
and had done so to his best ability. It was your
fault if he had not done more—the fault of your
sordidness, your quarrelsomeness, your eccentric conduct."[2] When, then, a dispute arose between the
Cardinal and the sculptor about the marbles, Leo
may have felt that it was time to break off from
an artist so impetuous and irritable. Still, whatever
faults of temper Michelangelo may have had, and
however difficult he was to deal with, nothing can

---

[1] Lettere, No. cdxxxv., October 1542.   [2] Gotti, vol. i. p. 135.

excuse the Medici for their wanton waste of his physical and mental energies at the height of their development.

On the 6th of April 1520 Raffaello died, worn out with labour and with love, in the flower of his wonderful young manhood. It would be rash to assert that he had already given the world the best he had to offer, because nothing is so incalculable as the evolution of genius. Still we perceive now that his latest manner, both as regards style and feeling, and also as regards the method of execution by assistants, shows him to have been upon the verge of intellectual decline. While deploring Michelangelo's impracticability—that solitary, self-reliant, and exacting temperament which made him reject collaboration, and which doomed so much of his best work to incompleteness—we must remember that to the very end of his long life he produced nothing (except perhaps in architecture) which does not bear the seal and superscription of his fervent self. Raffaello, on the contrary, just before his death, seemed to be exhaling into a nebulous mist of brilliant but unsatisfactory performances. Diffusing the rich and facile treasures of his genius through a host of lesser men, he had almost ceased to be a personality. Even his own work, as proved by the Transfiguration, was deteriorating. The blossom was overblown, the bubble on the point of bursting ; and all those pupils who had gathered round him, drawing like planets from the sun their lustre, sank

at his death into frigidity and insignificance.   Only
Giulio Romano burned with a torrid sensual splendour all his own.   Fortunately for the history of the
Renaissance, Giulio lived to evoke the wonder of
the Mantuan villa, that climax of associated crafts of
decoration, which remains for us the symbol of the
dream of art indulged by Raffaello in his Roman
period.

These pupils of the Urbinate claimed now, on
their master's death, and claimed with good reason,
the right to carry on his great work in the Borgian
apartments of the Vatican.   The Sala de' Pontefici,
or the Hall of Constantine, as it is sometimes called,
remained to be painted.   They possessed designs
bequeathed by Raffaello for its decoration, and Leo,
very rightly, decided to leave it in their hands.
Sebastiano del Piombo, however, made a vigorous
effort to obtain the work for himself.   His Raising
of Lazarus, executed in avowed competition with
the Transfiguration, had brought him into the first
rank of Roman painters.   It was seen what the
man, with Michelangelo to back him up, could do.
We cannot properly appreciate this picture in its
present state.   The glory of the colouring has
passed away ; and it was precisely here that Sebastiano may have surpassed Raffaello, as he was
certainly superior to the school.   Sebastiano wrote
letter after letter to Michelangelo in Florence.[1]   He

---

[1] *Les Correspondants*, *op. cit.*, p. 6, April 20, 1520.   It appears from the
general tenour of the letters I shall quote that Sebastiano would have

first mentions Raffaello's death, " whom may God forgive ; " then says that the "*garzoni*" of the Urbinate are beginning to paint in oil upon the walls of the Sala dei Pontefici.[1] " I pray you to remember me, and to recommend me to the Cardinal, and if I am the man to undertake the job, I should like you to set me to work at it ; for I shall not disgrace you, as indeed I think I have not done already. I took my picture (the Lazarus) once more to the Vatican, and placed it beside Raffaello's (the Transfiguration), and I came without shame out of the comparison." In answer, apparently, to this first letter on the subject, Michelangelo wrote a humorous recommendation of his friend and gossip to the Cardinal Bernardo Dovizi da Bibbiena. It runs thus :[2] " I beg your most reverend Lordship, not as a friend or servant, for I am not worthy to be either, but as a low fellow, poor and brainless, that you will cause Sebastian, the Venetian painter, now that Rafael is dead, to have some share in the works at the Palace. If it should seem to your Lordship that kind offices are thrown away upon a man like me, I might suggest that on some rare occasions a certain sweetness may be found in being kind even to fools, as onions taste well, for a change

liked Michelangelo to obtain the commission for the Sala on his own account, and to intrust himself (Sebastiano) with the execution.

[1] There are two female figures painted in oil there, *Comitas* and *Justitia*. The effect is charming, making one dissatisfied with the chalky dryness of the fresco.

[2] Lettere, No. ccclxxiii.

of food, to one who is tired of capons. You oblige men of mark every day. I beg your Lordship to try what obliging me is like. The obligation will be a very great one, and Sebastian is a worthy man. If, then, your kind offers are thrown away on me, they will not be so on Sebastian, for I am certain he will prove a credit to your Lordship."

In his following missives Sebastiano flatters Michelangelo upon the excellent effect produced by the letter.[1] " The Cardinal informed me that the Pope had given the Hall of the Pontiffs to Raffaello's 'prentices, and they have begun with a figure in oils upon the wall, a marvellous production, which eclipses all the rooms painted by their master, and proves that, when it is finished, this hall will beat the record, and be the finest thing done in painting since the ancients.[2] Then he asked if I had read your letter. I said, No. He laughed loudly, as though at a good joke, and I quitted him with compliments. Bandinelli, who is copying the Laocoon, tells me that the Cardinal showed him your letter, and also showed it to the Pope; in fact, nothing is talked about at the Vatican except your letter, and it makes everybody laugh." He adds that he does not think the hall ought to be committed to young men. Having discovered what sort of things they meant to paint there, battle-pieces and vast

---

[1] *Les Correspondants*, pp. 6–16.

[2] The figure is a Caryatid, at the extreme end of the stanze. Fresco was afterwards adopted by Giulio Romano and Il Fattore.

compositions, he judges the scheme beyond their scope. Michelangelo alone is equal to the task. Meanwhile, Leo, wishing to compromise matters, offered Sebastiano the great hall in the lower apartments of the Borgias, where Alexander VI. used to live, and where Pinturicchio painted— rooms shut up in pious horror by Julius when he came to occupy the palace of his hated and abominable predecessor.[1] Sebastiano's reliance upon Michelangelo, and his calculation that the way to get possession of the coveted commission would depend on the latter's consenting to supply him with designs, emerge in the following passage : " The Cardinal told me that he was ordered by the Pope to offer me the lower hall. I replied that I could accept nothing without your permission, or until your answer came, which is not to hand at the date of writing. I added that, unless I were engaged to Michelangelo, even if the Pope commanded me to paint that hall, I would not do so, because I do not think myself inferior to Raffaello's 'prentices, especially after the Pope, with his own mouth, had offered me half of the upper hall ; and anyhow, I do not regard it as creditable to myself

[1] See Yriarte, *Autour des Borgias*, for an account of these apartments, with plans and illustrations. Cesare Borgia inhabited the upper set of rooms. The lower hall was severely damaged on June 20, 1500, when lightning struck the Vatican, and nearly killed Pope Alexander, who was throned upon the dais. The roof and great chimney crashed in. Since that accident it remained unrepaired. The decoration was eventually assigned to Perino del Vaga.

to paint the cellars, and they to have the gilded chambers. I said they had better be allowed to go on painting. He answered that the Pope had only done this to avoid rivalries. The men possessed designs ready for that hall, and I ought to remember that the lower one was also a hall of the Pontiffs. My reply was that I would have nothing to do with it; so that now they are laughing at me, and I am so worried that I am well-nigh mad." Later on he adds: "It has been my object, through you and your authority, to execute vengeance for myself and you too, letting malignant fellows know that there are other demigods alive beside Raffael da Urbino and his 'prentices." The vacillation of Leo in this business, and his desire to make things pleasant, are characteristic of the man, who acted just in the same way while negotiating with princes.

IX.

When Michelangelo complained that he was "rovinato per detta opera di San Lorenzo," he probably did not mean that he was ruined in purse, but in health and energy.[1] For some while after Leo gave him his liberty, he seems to have remained comparatively inactive. During this period the sacristy at S. Lorenzo and the Medicean tombs were

[1] Lettere, ccclxxiv. p. 416.

probably in contemplation.[1] Giovanni Cambi says
that they were begun at the end of March 1520.[2]
But we first hear something definite about them in
a *Ricordo* which extends from April 9 to August
19, 1521.[3] Michelangelo says that on the former
of these dates he received money from the Cardinal
de' Medici for a journey to Carrara, whither he went
and stayed about three weeks, ordering marbles for
" the tombs which are to be placed in the new sacristy
at S. Lorenzo. And there I made out drawings to
scale, and measured models in clay for the said
tombs." He left his assistant Scipione of Settignano at Carrara as overseer of the work, and returned
to Florence. On the 20th of July following he went
again to Carrara, and stayed nine days. On the
16th of August the contractors for the blocks, all of
which were excavated from the old Roman quarry
of Polvaccio, came to Florence, and were paid for on
account. Scipione returned on the 19th of August.
It may be added that the name of Stefano, the
miniaturist, who acted as Michelangelo's factotum

[1] An obscure phrase in the document quoted above (No. ccclxxiv.) has
been taken to indicate that the project had been conceived as early as
the spring of 1519. "At that same time the Cardinal, by orders from
the Pope, removed me from my work of quarrying, because they said
they did not wish me to be bothered with excavating marbles, and they
would have them forwarded to me in Florence, and *made a new convention.*" The new convention, however, may have been a new arrangement as to the manner of carrying on and paying the façade.

[2] Vasari, xii. 358. If Cambi reckoned in Florentine style, his reference would be to March 1521, which agrees with the *Ricordo* to be quoted
next above.

[3] Lettere, p. 582.

through several years, is mentioned for the first time in this minute and interesting record.

That the commission for the sacristy came from the Cardinal Giulio, and not from the Pope, appears in the document I have just cited. The fact is confirmed by a letter written to Fattucci in 1523 :[1] "About two years have elapsed since I returned from Carrara, whither I had gone to purchase marbles for the tombs of the Cardinal." The letter is curious in several respects, because it shows how changeable through many months Giulio remained about the scheme; at one time bidding Michelangelo prepare plans and models, at another refusing to listen to any proposals; then warming up again, and saying that, if he lived long enough, he meant to erect the façade as well. The final issue of the affair was, that after Giulio became Pope Clement VII., the sacristy went forward, and Michelangelo had to put the sepulchre of Julius aside. During the pontificate of Adrian, we must believe that he worked upon his statues for that monument, since a Cardinal was hardly powerful enough to command his services; but when the Cardinal became Pope, and threatened to bring an actionagainst him for moneys received, the case was altered. The letter to Fattucci, when carefully studied, leads to these conclusions.

Very little is known to us regarding his private life in the year 1521. We only possess one letter,

---

[1] Lettere, No. ccclxxix.

relating to the purchase of a house.[1]   In October he stood godfather to the infant son of Niccolò Soderini, nephew of his old patron, the Gonfalonier.[2]

This barren period is marked by only one considerable event — that is, the termination of the Cristo Risorto, or Christ Triumphant, which had been ordered by Metello Varj dei Porcari in 1514. The statue seems to have been rough-hewn at the quarries, packed up, and sent to Pisa on its way to Florence as early as December 1518,[3] but it was not until March 1521 that Michelangelo began to occupy himself about it seriously.   He then despatched Pietro Urbano to Rome with orders to complete it there,[4] and to arrange with the purchaser for placing

[1] Lettere, No. ccclxxv., addressed to Giusto di Matteo in Pisa. The house was in Via Mozza. Pietro Urbano refers to the transaction in a letter written from Rome, which proves that he was then at work on the Cristo Risorto. The month was March.

[2] Gotti, vol. i. p. 145.

[3] See Lettere, No. cclxix., addressed to Lionardo, the saddler, in Rome. Milanesi gives the date, December 21, 1518. It shows that Michelangelo was then waiting for the marble, and hoping to begin work upon it.

[4] This appears from one of Michelangelo's letters, Lettere, No. ccclxxv. Gotti (vol. i. p. 140) says that the month was August, but gives no reason. Since Sebastiano began to write about Urbano's doings on the 6th of September, the young man must already have been some time in Rome. We possess a *Ricordo* by Michelangelo (*Carte Michelangiolesche*, No. 2) which proves that on the 2nd of May 1521 Michelangelo paid Lionardo in Rome four ducats on account of Pietro ; also a letter from Pietro to Michelangelo, without date, written from Rome. In it Pietro says he has heard that his master had been to Carrara, and is about to buy the house " della Masina." Now Michelangelo went to Carrara in April, and in March he wrote a letter about this house (No. ccclxxv.). Pietro informs him that the statue has not yet arrived, but he hopes for it about the 19th. He also promises to avoid the company of dissolute

it upon a pedestal. Sebastiano's letters contain some references to this work, which enable us to understand how wrong it would be to accept it as a representative piece of Buonarroti's own handicraft. On the 9th of November 1520 he writes that his gossip, Giovanni da Reggio, "goes about saying that you did not execute the figure, but that it is the work of Pietro Urbano. Take good care that it should be seen to be from your hand, so that poltroons and babblers may burst." [1]   On the 6th of September 1521 he returns to the subject. [2] Urbano was at this time resident in Rome, and behaving himself so badly, in Sebastiano's opinion, that he feels bound to make a severe report.   "In the first place, you sent him to Rome with the statue to finish and erect it. What he did and left undone you know already. But I must inform you that he has spoiled the marble wherever he touched it. In particular, he shortened the right foot and cut the toes off; the hands too, especially the right hand, which holds the cross, have been mutilated in the fingers. Frizzi says they seem to have been worked by a biscuit-maker, not wrought in marble, but kneaded by some one used to dough. I am no judge, not being familiar with

Florentines more than he had previously done. This throws light on what followed. Florentine society in Rome was notorious for vicious conduct. His letter must have been written early in April. It is published by Daelli, *Carte Michelangiolesche Inedite*, No. 7.

[1] *Les Correspondants*, p. 24. Urbano was then at Florence, working on the statue under Michelangelo's directions.

[2] Ibid., p. 28.

the method of stone-cutting; but I can tell you
that the fingers look to me very stiff and dumpy.[1]
It is clear also that he has been peddling at the
beard; and I believe my little boy would have done so
with more sense, for it looks as though he had used
a knife without a point to chisel the hair. This can
easily be remedied, however. He has also spoiled
one of the nostrils. A little more, and the whole
nose would have been ruined, and only God could
have restored it." Michelangelo apparently had
already taken measures to transfer the Christ from
Urbano's hands to those of the sculptor Federigo
Frizzi. This irritated his former friend and work-
man. "Pietro shows a very ugly and malignant
spirit after finding himself cast off by you. He
does not seem to care for you or any one alive, but
thinks he is a great master. He will soon find out
his mistake, for the poor young man will never be
able to make statues. He has forgotten all he knew
of art, and the knees of your Christ are worth more
than all Rome together." It was Sebastiano's wont
to run babbling on in this way. Once again he
returns to Pietro Urbano. "I am informed that he
has left Rome; he has not been seen for several
days, has shunned the Court, and I certainly believe
that he will come to a bad end. He gambles, wants
all the women of the town, struts like a Ganymede
in velvet shoes through Rome, and flings his cash

[1] There is no sign of this in the statue. A little stiff, perhaps, but
not cut down in length.

about. Poor fellow ! I am sorry for him, since, after all, he is but young."

Such was the end of Pietro Urbano. Michelangelo was certainly unfortunate with his apprentices. One cannot help fancying he may have spoiled them by indulgence. Vasari, mentioning Pietro, calls him " a person of talent, but one who never took the pains to work." [1]

Frizzi brought the Christ Triumphant into its present state, patching up what " the lither lad " from Pistoja had boggled.[2] Buonarroti, who was sincerely attached to Varj, and felt his artistic reputation now at stake, offered to make a new statue. But the magnanimous Roman gentleman replied that he was entirely satisfied with the one he had received. He regarded and esteemed it " as a thing of gold," and, in refusing Michelangelo's offer, added that " this proved his noble soul and generosity, inasmuch as, when he had already made what could not be surpassed and was incomparable, he still wanted to serve his friend better." [3] The price originally stipulated was paid, and Varj added an autograph testimonial, strongly affirming his contentment with the whole transaction.

These details prove that the Christ of the Minerva must be regarded as a mutilated masterpiece. Michel-

[1] Vol. xii. p. 274.

[2] Hardly anything is known about this sculptor. See above, p. 344, for a mention of his name.

[3] Gotti, i. 143. There are twenty-three letters from Varj, chiefly about these affairs, in the Arch. Buon., Cod. xi., Nos. 740-761.

angelo is certainly responsible for the general conception, the pose, and a large portion of the finished
surface, details of which, especially in the knees,
so much admired by Sebastiano, and in the robust
arms, are magnificent. He designed the figure
wholly nude, so that the heavy bronze drapery
which now surrounds the loins, and bulges drooping
from the left hip, breaks the intended harmony of
lines. Yet, could this brawny man have ever suggested any distinctly religious idea?[1] Christ, victor
over Death and Hell, did not triumph by ponderosity
and sinews. The spiritual nature of his conquest,
the ideality of a divine soul disencumbered from
the flesh, to which it once had stooped in love for
sinful man, ought certainly to have been empha-
sised, if anywhere through art, in the statue of a
Risen Christ. Substitute a scaling-ladder for the
cross, and here we have a fine life-guardsman,
stripped and posing for some classic battle-piece.
We cannot quarrel with Michelangelo about the
face and head. Those vulgarly handsome features,
that beard, pomaded and curled by a barber's
'prentice, betray no signs of his inspiration. Only
in the arrangement of the hair, hyacinthine locks
descending to the shoulders, do we recognise the
touch of the divine sculptor.

The Christ became very famous. Francis I. had

---

[1] Heath Wilson says : " This statue, considered as a work of expression and religious art, is in both respects without a parallel in its
irreverence " (p. 266).

it cast and sent to Paris, to be repeated in bronze. What is more strange, it has long been the object of a religious cult. The right foot, so mangled by poor Pietro, wears a fine brass shoe, in order to prevent its being kissed away. This almost makes one think of Goethe's hexameter: "Wunderthätige Bilder sind meist nur schlechte Gemälde." Still it must be remembered that excellent critics have found the whole work admirable. Gsell-Fels says:[1] "It is his second Moses; in movement and physique one of the greatest masterpieces; as a Christ-ideal, the heroic conception of a humanist." That last observation is just. We may remember that Vida was composing his *Christiad* while Frizzi was curling the beard of the Cristo Risorto. Vida always speaks of Jesus as *Heros,* and of God the Father as *Superum Pater Nimbipotens* or *Regnator Olympi.*[2]

---

[1] *Rom und Mittel-Italien,* vol. ii. p. 370. Burckhardt (*Cicerone, Sculptur,* Leipzig, Seeman, 1869, p. 672) says: "It is one of his most amiable works. The upper part of the body is one of the finest motives of later modern art. The sweet expression and formation of the face may be as little suitable to the Highest as any Christ is; and yet," &c. Even Heath Wilson, who had a proper sense of the impropriety, artistic and religious, of this Christ, remarks that "the hair of the beard, which must be assumed to be Frizzi's work, does him great credit." This beard consists of patches, like tigers' claws or foliage, carved out to hide anatomical structure. None of the favourable critics notice the indecent and unnatural bulk of the abdomen.

[2] See my *Renaissance in Italy,* vol. ii. p. 399. I ought to add that, since I wrote the above critique, working mainly by the help of Alinari's photographs, I have studied the statue again in the church of the Minerva. Under that dim light, it diffuses a grace and sweetness which no reproduction renders. Without retracting my opinion, I recognise a kind of fascination in the figure.

CHAPTER VIII.

I.

LEO X. expired upon the 1st day of December
1521. The vacillating game he played in European
politics had just been crowned with momentary success. Some folk believed that the Pope died of joy
after hearing that his Imperial allies had entered
the town of Milan ; others thought that he succumbed

365

to poison.   We do not know what caused his death.
But the unsoundness of his constitution, overtaxed
by dissipation and generous living, in the midst of
public cares for which the man had hardly nerve
enough, may suffice to account for a decease certainly sudden and premature.   Michelangelo, born
in the same year, was destined to survive him
through more than eight lustres of the life of man.

Leo was a personality whom it is impossible to
praise without reserve.   The Pope at that time in
Italy had to perform three separate functions.   His
first duty was to the Church.   Leo left the See of
Rome worse off than he found it: financially bankrupt,
compromised by vague schemes set on foot for the
aggrandisement of his family, discredited by many
shameless means for raising money upon spiritual
securities.   His second duty was to Italy.   Leo left
the peninsula so involved in a mesh of meaningless
entanglements, diplomatic and aimless wars, that
anarchy and violence proved to be the only exit from
the situation.   His third duty was to that higher culture which Italy dispensed to Europe, and of which
the Papacy had made itself the leading propagator.
Here Leo failed almost as conspicuously as in all
else he attempted.   He debased the standard of art
and literature by his ill-placed liberalities, seeking
quick returns for careless expenditure, not selecting
the finest spirits of his age for timely patronage,
diffusing no lofty enthusiasm, but breeding round
him mushrooms of mediocrity.

Nothing casts stronger light upon the low tone of Roman society created by Leo than the outburst of frenzy and execration which exploded when a Fleming was elected as his successor. Adrian Florent, belonging to a family surnamed Dedel, emerged from the scrutiny of the Conclave into the pontifical chair. He had been the tutor of Charles V., and this may suffice to account for his nomination. Cynical wits ascribed that circumstance to the direct and unexpected action of the Holy Ghost. He was the one foreigner who occupied the seat of S. Peter after the period when the metropolis of Western Christendom became an Italian principality. Adrian, by his virtues and his failings, proved that modern Rome, in her social corruption and religious indifference, demanded an Italian Pontiff. Single-minded and simple, raised unexpectedly by circumstances into his supreme position, he shut his eyes resolutely to art and culture, abandoned diplomacy, and determined to act only as the chief of the Catholic Church. In ecclesiastical matters Adrian was undoubtedly a worthy man. He returned to the original conception of his duty as the Primate of Occidental Christendom ; and what might have happened had he lived to impress his spirit upon Rome, remains beyond the reach of calculation. Dare we conjecture that the sack of 1527 would have been averted ?

Adrian reigned only a year and eight months. He had no time to do anything of permanent value, and was hardly powerful enough to do it, even if time and opportunity had been afforded. In the thunderstorm gathering over Rome and the Papacy, he represents that momentary lull during which men hold their breath and murmur. All the place-seekers, parasites, flatterers, second-rate artificers, folk of facile talents, whom Leo gathered round him, vented their rage against a Pope who lived sparely, shut up the Belvedere, called statues "idols of the Pagans," and spent no farthing upon twangling lutes and frescoed chambers. Truly Adrian is one of the most grotesque and significant figures upon the page of modern history. His personal worth, his inadequacy to the needs of the age, and his incompetence to control the tempest loosed by Della Roveres, Borgias, and Medici around him, give the man a tragic irony.

After his death, upon the 23rd of September 1523, the Cardinal Giulio dei Medici was made Pope. He assumed the title of Clement VII. upon the 9th of November. The wits who saluted Adrian's doctor with the title of "Saviour of the Fatherland," now rejoiced at the election of an Italian and a Medici. The golden years of Leo's reign would certainly return, they thought; having no foreknowledge of the tragedy which was so soon to be enacted, first at Rome, and afterwards at Florence. Michelangelo wrote to his friend Topolino at Carrara :[1] "You will have heard that Medici is made Pope ; all the world

_____
[1] Lettere, No. ccclxxx.

seems to me to be delighted, and I think that here at Florence great things will soon be set on foot in our art. Therefore, serve well and faithfully."

II.

Our records are very scanty, both as regards personal details and art-work, for the life of Michelangelo during the pontificate of Adrian VI. The high esteem in which he was held throughout Italy is proved by three incidents which may shortly be related. In 1522, the Board of Works for the cathedral church of S. Petronio at Bologna decided to complete the façade. Various architects sent in designs ; among them Peruzzi competed with one in the Gothic style, and another in that of the Classical revival. Great differences of opinion arose in the city as to the merits of the rival plans, and the Board in July invited Michelangelo, through their secretary, to come and act as umpire. They promised to reward him magnificently.[1] It does not appear that Michelangelo accepted the offer. In 1523, Cardinal Grimani, who was a famous collector of art-objects, wrote begging for some specimen of his craft. Grimani left it open to him " to choose material and subject ; painting, bronze, or marble, according to his fancy." Michelangelo must have

[1] See the letter of Ascanio de Novi, reported by Gotti, vol. i. p. 176.

promised to fulfil the commission, for we have a
letter from Grimani thanking him effusively.[1] He
offers to pay fifty ducats at the commencement of the
work, and what Michelangelo thinks fit to demand
at its conclusion: "for such is the excellence of
your ability, that we shall take no thought of money-
value." Grimani was Patriarch of Aquileja. In the
same year, 1523, the Genoese entered into negotiations for a colossal statue of Andrea Doria, which
they desired to obtain from the hand of Michelangelo. Its execution must have been seriously
contemplated, for the Senate of Genoa banked 300
ducats for the purpose.[2] We regret that Michelangelo could not carry out a work so congenial to
his talent as this ideal portrait of the mighty Signor
Capitano would have been; but we may console ourselves by reflecting that even his energies were not
equal to all tasks imposed upon him. The real matter
for lamentation is that they suffered so much waste in
the service of vacillating Popes.

To the year 1523 belongs, in all probability, the last
extant letter which Michelangelo wrote to his father.
Lodovico was dissatisfied with a contract which had
been drawn up on the 16th of June in that year, and
by which a certain sum of money, belonging to the
dowry of his late wife, was settled in reversion upon
his eldest son.[3] Michelangelo explains the tenor

[1] Gotti, vol. ii. p. 61, date July 11, 1523.
[2] Gotti, i. 177.
[3] Lettere, No. xliv. See Milanesi's note.

of the deed, and then breaks forth into the following bitter and ironical invective: "If my life is a nuisance to you, you have found the means of protecting yourself, and will inherit the key of that treasure which you say that I possess. And you will be acting rightly; for all Florence knows how mighty rich you were, and how I always robbed you, and deserve to be chastised. Highly will men think of you for this. Cry out and tell folk all you choose about me, but do not write again, for you prevent my working. What I have now to do is to make good all you have had from me during the past five-and-twenty years. I would rather not tell you this, but I cannot help it. Take care, and be on your guard against those whom it concerns you. A man dies but once, and does not come back again to patch up things ill done. You have put off till the death to do this. May God assist you!"

In another draft of this letter Lodovico is accused of going about the town complaining that he was once a rich man, and that Michelangelo had robbed him. Still, we must not take this for proved; one of the great artist's main defects was an irritable suspiciousness, which caused him often to exaggerate slights and to fancy insults. He may have attached too much weight to the grumblings of an old man, whom at the bottom of his heart he loved dearly.

III.

Clement, immediately after his election, resolved on setting Michelangelo at work in earnest on the Sacristy. At the very beginning of January he also projected the building of the Laurentian Library, and wrote, through his Roman agent, Giovanni Francesco Fattucci, requesting to have two plans furnished, one in the Greek, the other in the Latin style.[1] Michelangelo replied as follows:[2] "I gather from your last that his Holiness our Lord wishes that I should furnish the design for the library. I have received no information, and do not know where it is to be erected. It is true that Stefano talked to me about the scheme, but I paid no heed. When he returns from Carrara I will inquire, and will do all that is in my power, *albeit architecture is not my profession*." There is something pathetic in this reiterated assertion that his real art was sculpture. At the same time Clement wished to provide for him for life. He first proposed that Buonarroti should promise not to marry, and should enter into minor orders. This would have enabled him to enjoy some ecclesiastical benefice, but it would also have handed him over firmly bound to the service of the Pope. Circumstances already hampered him enough, and Michelangelo, who chose to remain

[1] Correspondence in Gotti, vol. i. pp. 165, 166.
[2] Lettere, No. ccclxxxv.

his own master, refused. As Berni wrote : " Voleva far da se, non comandato." As an alternative, a pension was suggested. It appears that he only asked for fifteen ducats a month, and that his friend Pietro Gondi had proposed twenty-five ducats. Fattucci, on the 13th of January 1524, rebuked him in affectionate terms for his want of pluck, informing him that " Jacopo Salviati has given orders that Spina should be instructed to pay you a monthly provision of fifty ducats." Moreover, all the disbursements made for the work at S. Lorenzo were to be provided by the same agent in Florence, and to pass through Michelangelo's hands.[1] A house was assigned him, free of rent, at S. Lorenzo, in order that he might be near his work. Henceforth he was in almost weekly correspondence with Giovanni Spina on affairs of business, sending in accounts and drawing money by means of his then trusted servant, Stefano, the miniaturist.[2]

That Stefano did not always behave himself according to his master's wishes appears from the following characteristic letter addressed by Michelangelo to his friend Pietro Gondi:[3] "The poor man, who is ungrateful, has a nature of this sort, that if you help him in his needs, he says that what

[1] See Gotti, i. 157.

[2] Giovanni Spina, the Pope's Florentine agent, seems to have been in the bank of the Salviati (Lettere, No. cccxcii.) Stefano di Tommaso started in life as a *miniatore*. Michelangelo made him clerk of the works at S. Lorenzo, overseer at Carrara, &c., in the way he adopted for the employment of his principal *garzone*.

[3] Lettere, No. ccclxxxvii., date January 26, 1524.

you gave him came out of superfluities; if you put him in the way of doing work for his own good, he says you were obliged, and set him to do it because you were incapable; and all the benefits which he received he ascribes to the necessities of the benefactor. But when everybody can see that you acted out of pure benevolence, the ingrate waits until you make some public mistake, which gives him the opportunity of maligning his benefactor and winning credence, in order to free himself from the obligation under which he lies. This has invariably happened in my case. No one ever entered into relations with me—I speak of workmen—to whom I did not do good with all my heart. Afterwards, some trick of temper, or some madness, which they say is in my nature, which hurts nobody except myself, gives them an excuse for speaking evil of me and calumniating my character. Such is the reward of all honest men."

These general remarks, he adds, apply to Stefano, whom he placed in a position of trust and responsibility, in order to assist him. "What I do is done for his good, because I have undertaken to benefit the man, and cannot abandon him; but let him not imagine or say that I am doing it because of my necessities, for, God be praised, I do not stand in need of men." He then begs Gondi to discover what Stefano's real mind is. This is a matter of great importance to him for several reasons, and especially for this: " If I omitted to justify myself, and were to put another in his place, I should be published among the Piagnoni for the biggest traitor who ever lived, even though I were in the right."

We conclude, then, that Michelangelo thought of dismissing Stefano, but feared lest he should get into trouble with the powerful political party, followers of Savonarola, who bore the name of Piagnoni at Florence. Gondi must have patched the quarrel up, for we still find Stefano's name in the *Ricordi* down to April 4, 1524. Shortly after that date, Antonio Mini seems to have taken his place as Michelangelo's right-hand man of business.[1] These details are not so insignificant as they appear. They enable us to infer that the Sacristy of S. Lorenzo may have been walled and roofed in before the end of April 1524; for, in an undated letter to Pope Clement, Michelangelo says that Stefano has finished the lantern, and that it is universally admired.[2] With regard to this lantern, folk told him that he would make it better than Brunelleschi's. " Different perhaps, but better, no ! " he answered.

[1] Lettere, pp. 592, 593. On an original drawing in the British Museum is written in Michelangelo's autograph, "Disegna Antonio, disegna Antonio, disegna e non perder tempo." A pleasant record of his interest in his pupils. See Fagan, *op. cit.*, p. 99.

[2] Lettere, No. ccclxxxi. The date of the roofing in of the Sacristy is generally given as 1525 ; but, if Stefano constructed the cupola, we ought to suppose that he did it before the date of his disappearance from the *Ricordi*. Also we have a note of November 9, 1524, recording a payment made for glazing the windows of the lantern with oiled paper. See Lettere, p. 596. Indeed the *Ricordi* prove that the building was going briskly forward during the early months of 1524. Consult Springer, vol. ii. p. 214.

The letter to Clement just quoted is interesting in several respects. The boldness of the beginning makes one comprehend how Michelangelo was terrible to even Popes :—

"MOST BLESSED FATHER,—Inasmuch as intermediates are often the cause of grave misunderstandings, I have summoned up courage to write without their aid to your Holiness about the tombs at S. Lorenzo. I repeat, I know not which is preferable, the evil that does good, or the good that hurts. I am certain, mad and wicked as I may be, that if I had been allowed to go on as I had begun, all the marbles needed for the work would have been in Florence to-day, and properly blocked out, with less cost than has been expended on them up to this date; and they would have been superb, as are the others I have brought here."

After this he entreats Clement to give him full authority in carrying out the work, and not to put superiors over him. Michelangelo, we know, was extremely impatient of control and interference; and we shall see, within a short time, how excessively the watching and spying of busybodies worried and disturbed his spirits.[1]

But these were not his only sources of annoyance. The heirs of Pope Julius, perceiving that Michelangelo's time and energy were wholly absorbed at S. Lorenzo, began to threaten him with a lawsuit. Clement, wanting apparently to mediate between

[1] Especially Lettere, No. cd.

the litigants, ordered Fattucci to obtain a report from the sculptor, with a full account of how matters stood.   This evoked the long and interesting document which has been so often cited.[1]   There is no doubt whatever that Michelangelo acutely felt the justice of the Duke of Urbino's grievances against him.   He was broken-hearted at seeing to be wanting in his sense of honour and duty.   People, he says, accused him of putting the money which had been paid for the tomb out at usury, " living meanwhile at Florence and amusing himself."   It also hurt him deeply to be distracted from the cherished project of his early manhood in order to superintend works for which he had no enthusiasm, and which lay outside his sphere of operation.

It may, indeed, be said that during these years Michelangelo lived in a perpetual state of uneasiness and anxiety about the tomb of Julius.   As far back as 1518 the Cardinal Leonardo Grosso, Bishop of Agen, and one of Julius's executors, found it necessary to hearten him with frequent letters of encouragement.   In one of these, after commending his zeal in extracting marbles and carrying on the monument, the Cardinal proceeds: [2]   " Be then of good

---

[1] Lettere, No. ccclxxxiii.   I will place a translation of it in the Appendix.

[2] Arch. Buon., Cod. vii. No. 136.   The letter is dated October 24, 1518.   " State de bono animo el non prenderti passione alcuna che più crediamo a una minima vostra parola che a tutto el resto ne dicesse el contrario.   Cognoscemo la fede vostra et tanto li credemo devotissimo a noi proprii, et se bisognerà cosa alcuna de quanto noi possemo volemo com altre volte ve havemo ditto ne piagliati ogni ampla siguretà perchè

courage, and do not yield to any perturbations of the
spirit, for we put more faith in your smallest word
than if all the world should say the contrary. We
know your loyalty, and believe you to be wholly
devoted to our person ; and if there shall be need of
aught which we can supply, we are willing, as we
have told you on other occasions, to do so ; rest then
in all security of mind, because we love you from
the heart, and desire to do all that may be agreeable
to you." This good friend was dead at the time we
have now reached, and the violent Duke Francesco
Maria della Rovere acted as the principal heir of
Pope Julius.[1]

In a passion of disgust he refused to draw his
pension, and abandoned the house at S. Lorenzo.
This must have happened in March 1524, for his
friend Leonardo writes to him from Rome upon the
24th :[2] " I am also told that you have declined
your pension, which seems to me mere madness,
and that you have thrown the house up, and do not
work. Friend and gossip, let me tell you that
you have plenty of enemies, who speak their

---

ve amamo ex corde et desideramo farvi ogni piacere." I doubt whether
I have got the words right of this passage. The two following letters,
Nos. 136 and 137, dated December 29, 1518, and May 19, 1519 (?), are
to the same effect, breathing a spirit of thorough confidence and warm
attachment.

[1] The Cardinal Aginensis died in the autumn of 1520. Sebastiano
del Piombo, writing to Michelangelo, says that poison was suspected.
"A dirti el vero si bisbiglia che 'l cardinale è stato avvelenato." *Les
Correspondants*, p. 20.

[2] Gotti, i. 157.

worst; also that the Pope and Pucci and Jacopo
Salviati are your friends, and have plighted their
troth to you. It is unworthy of you to break your
word to them, especially in an affair of honour.
Leave the matter of the tomb to those who wish
you well, and who are able to set you free without
the least encumbrance, and take care you do not
come short in the Pope's work. Die first. And
take the pension, for they give it with a willing
heart." How long he remained in contumacy is
not quite certain; apparently until the 29th of
August. We have a letter written on that day to
Giovanni Spina:[1] "After I left you yesterday, I
went back thinking over my affairs; and, seeing
that the Pope has set his heart on S. Lorenzo, and
how he urgently requires my service, and has appointed me a good provision in order that I may
serve him with more convenience and speed; seeing
also that not to accept it keeps me back, and that I
have no good excuse for not serving his Holiness;
I have changed my mind, and whereas I hitherto
refused, I now demand it (*i.e.*, the salary), considering this far wiser, and for more reasons than I care
to write; and, more especially, I mean to return to
the house you took for me at S. Lorenzo, and settle
down there like an honest man : inasmuch as it sets
gossip going, and does me great damage not to go

---

[1] Lettere, No. cccxci. There is, however, a letter (No. cccxc.) which
Milanesi dates August 8, 1524. In it Michelangelo writes to Spina for
money for the library, and signs " at S. Lorenzo."

back there." From a *Ricordo* dated October 19, 1524, we learn in fact that he then drew his full pay for eight months.[1]

IV.

Since Michelangelo was now engaged upon the Medicean tombs at S. Lorenzo, it will be well to give some account of the several plans he made before deciding on the final scheme, which he partially executed. We may assume, I think, that the sacristy, as regards its general form and dimensions, faithfully represents the first plan approved by Clement. This follows from the rapidity and regularity with which the structure was completed. But then came the question of filling it with sarcophagi and statues. As early as November 28, 1520, Giulio de' Medici, at that time Cardinal, wrote from the Villa Magliana to Buonarroti, addressing him thus: "*Spectabilis vir, amice noster charissime.*"[2] He says that he is pleased with the design for the chapel, and with the notion of placing the four tombs in the middle. Then he proceeds to make some sensible remarks upon the difficulty of getting these huge masses of statuary into the space provided for them. Michelangelo, as Heath Wilson has pointed out, very slowly acquired the sense of

Lettere, p. 596. See too p. 440.   [2] Gotti, i. 150.

MEDICI CHAPEL, San Lorenzo, Florence, begun 1520. Alinari/Art Resource, NY.

proportion on which technical architecture depends. His early sketches only show a feeling for mass and picturesque effect, and a strong inclination to subordinate the building to sculpture.

It may be questioned who were the four Medici for whom these tombs were intended. Cambi, in a passage quoted above, writing at the end of March 1520 (?), says that two were raised for Giuliano, Duke of Nemours, and Lorenzo, Duke of Urbino, and that the Cardinal meant one to be for himself. The fourth he does not speak about. It has been conjectured that Lorenzo the Magnificent and his brother Giuliano, fathers respectively of Leo and of Clement, were to occupy two of the sarcophagi ; and also, with greater probability, that the two Popes, Leo and Clement, were associated with the Dukes.

Before 1524 the scheme expanded, and settled into a more definite shape. The sarcophagi were to support statue-portraits of the Dukes and Popes, with Lorenzo the Magnificent and his brother Giuliano. At their base, upon the ground, were to repose six rivers, two for each tomb, showing that each sepulchre would have held two figures. The rivers were perhaps Arno, Tiber, Metauro, Po, Taro, and Ticino. This we gather from a letter written to Michelangelo on the 23rd of May in that year.[1] Michelangelo made designs to meet this plan, but whether the tombs were still detached from the wall does not appear. Standing inside the sacristy, it

[1] Gotti, i. 158.

seems impossible that six statue-portraits and six
river gods on anything like a grand scale could
have been crowded into the space, especially when
we remember that there was to be an altar, with
other objects described as ornaments—"gli altri
ornamenti." Probably the Madonna and Child,
with SS. Cosimo and Damiano, now extant in the
chapel, formed an integral part of the successive
schemes.

One thing is certain, that the notion of placing
the tombs in the middle of the sacristy was soon
abandoned. All the marble panelling, pilasters,
niches, and so forth, which at present clothe the
walls and dominate the architectural effect, are
clearly planned for mural monuments. A rude
sketch preserved in the Uffizi throws some light
upon the intermediate stages of the scheme.[1] It is
incomplete, and was not finally adopted; but we
see in it one of the four sides of the chapel, divided
vertically above into three compartments, the middle
being occupied by a Madonna, the two at the sides
filled in with bas-reliefs. At the base, on sarcophagi
or *cassoni*, recline two nude male figures. The space
between these and the upper compartments seems
to have been reserved for allegorical figures, since
a colossal naked boy, ludicrously out of scale with
the architecture and the recumbent figures, has been
hastily sketched in. In architectural proportion
and sculpturesque conception this design is very

[1] Published in *L'Œuvre et la Vie*, p. 269.

poor. It has the merit, however, of indicating a moment in the evolution of the project when the mural scheme had been adopted. The decorative details which surmount the composition confirm the feeling every one must have, that, in their present state, the architecture of the Medicean monuments remains imperfect.

In this process of endeavouring to trace the development of Michelangelo's ideas for the sacristy, seven original drawings at the British Museum are of the greatest importance.[1] They may be divided into three groups. One sketch seems to belong to the period when the tombs were meant to be placed in the centre of the chapel. It shows a single facet of the monument, with two sarcophagi placed side by side and seated figures at the angles. Five are variations upon the mural scheme, which was eventually adopted. They differ considerably in details, proving what trouble the designer took to combine a large number of figures in a single plan. He clearly intended at some time to range the Medicean statues in pairs, and studied several types of curve for their sepulchral urns. The feature common to all of them is a niche, of door or window shape, with a powerfully indented architrave. Reminiscences of the design for the tomb of Julius are not infrequent; and it may be remarked, as throwing a

---

[1] Four are in chalk, two in pen and ink. The seventh, which shows a different conception, but may be assigned with probability to the same series, is in chalk, worked over with the pen.

side-light upon that irrecoverable project of his earlier manhood, that the figures posed upon the various spaces of architecture differ in their scale. Two belonging to this series are of especial interest, since we learn from them how he thought of introducing the rivers at the basement of the composition. It seems that he hesitated long about the employment of circular spaces in the framework of the marble panelling. These were finally rejected. One of the finest and most comprehensive of the drawings I am now describing contains a rough draft of a curved sarcophagus, with an allegorical figure reclining upon it, indicating the first conception of the Dawn. Another, blurred and indistinct, with clumsy architectural environment, exhibits two of these allegories, arranged much as we now see them at S. Lorenzo. A river-god, recumbent beneath the feet of a female statue, carries the eye down to the ground, and enables us to comprehend how these subordinate figures were wrought into the complex harmony of flowing lines he had imagined. The seventh study differs in conception from the rest; it stands alone. There are four handlings of what begins like a huge portal, and is gradually elaborated into an architectural scheme containing three great niches for statuary. It is powerful and simple in design, governed by semicircular arches—a feature which is absent from the rest.

All these drawings are indubitably by the hand of Michelangelo, and must be reckoned among his first free efforts to construct a working plan. The Albertina Collection at Vienna yields us an elaborate design for the sacristy, which appears to have been worked up from some of the rougher sketches. It is executed in pen, shaded with bistre, and belongs to what I have ventured to describe as office work.[1] It may have been prepared for the inspection of Leo and the Cardinal. Here we have the sarcophagi in pairs, recumbent figures stretched upon a shallow curve inverted, colossal orders of a bastard Ionic type, a great central niche framing a seated Madonna, two male figures in side niches, suggestive of Giuliano and Lorenzo as they were at last conceived, four allegorical statues, and, to crown the whole structure, candelabra of a peculiar shape, with a central round, supported by two naked genii. It is difficult, as I have before observed, to be sure how much of the drawings executed in this way can be ascribed with safety to Michelangelo himself. They are carefully outlined, with the precision of a working architect; but the sculptural details bear the aspect of what may be termed a generic Florentine style of draughtsmanship.

Two important letters from Michelangelo to Fattucci, written in October 1525 and April 1526, show that he had then abandoned the original scheme, and adopted one which was all but carried into effect.[2] " I am working as hard as I can, and in fifteen days I shall begin the other captain. After-

---

[1] See above, Chapter VI. Section 11.   [2] Lettere, Nos. cd. and cdii.

wards the only important things left will be the four rivers. The four statues on the sarcophagi, the four figures on the ground which are the rivers, the two captains, and Our Lady, who is to be placed upon the tomb at the head of the chapel ; these are what I mean to do with my own hand. Of these I have begun six ; and I have good hope of finishing them in due time, and carrying the others forward in part, which do not signify so much." The six he had begun are clearly the Dukes and their attendant figures of Day, Night, Dawn, Evening. The Madonna, one of his noblest works, came within a short distance of completion. SS. Cosimo and Damiano passed into the hands of Montelupo and Montorsoli. Of the four rivers we have only fragments in the shape of some exquisite little models. Where they could have been conveniently placed is difficult to imagine ; possibly they were abandoned from a feeling that the chapel would be overcrowded.

V.

According to the plan adopted in this book, I shall postpone such observations as I have to make upon the Medicean monuments until the date when Michelangelo laid down his chisel, and shall now proceed with the events of his life during the years 1525 and 1526.

GIULIANO DE MEDICI, marble, 1520s. Medici Chapel,
San Lorenzo, Florence. Alinari/Art Resource, NY.

He continued to be greatly troubled about the tomb of Julius II. The lawsuit instituted by the Duke of Urbino hung over his head; and though he felt sure of the Pope's powerful support, it was extremely important, both for his character and comfort, that affairs should be placed upon a satisfactory basis. Fattucci in Rome acted not only as Clement's agent in business connected with S. Lorenzo; he also was intrusted with negotiations for the settlement of the Duke's claims. The correspondence which passed between them forms, therefore, our best source of information for this period. On Christmas Eve in 1524 Michelangelo writes from Florence to his friend, begging him not to postpone a journey he had in view, if the only business which detained him was the trouble about the tomb.[1] A pleasant air of manly affection breathes through this document, showing Michelangelo to have been unselfish in a matter which weighed heavily and daily on his spirits. How greatly he was affected can be inferred from a letter written to Giovanni Spina on the 19th of April 1525. While reading this, it must be remembered that the Duke laid his action for the recovery of a considerable balance, which he alleged to be due to him upon disbursements made for the monument. Michelangelo, on the contrary, asserted that he was out of pocket, as we gather from the lengthy report he forwarded in 1524 to Fattucci.[2]

[1] Lettere, No. cccxciii.
[2] Lettere, No. ccclxxxiii. See Appendix.

The difficulty in the accounts seems to have arisen from the fact that payments for the Sistine Chapel and the tomb had been mixed up. The letter to Spina runs as follows:[1] "There is no reason for sending a power of attorney about the tomb of Pope Julius, because I do not want to plead. They cannot bring a suit if I admit that I am in the wrong; so I assume that I have sued and lost, and have to pay; and this I am disposed to do, if I am able. Therefore, if the Pope will help me in the matter—and this would be the greatest satisfaction to me, seeing I am too old and ill to finish the work—he might, as intermediary, express his pleasure that I should repay what I have received for its performance, so as to release me from this burden, and to enable the relatives of Pope Julius to carry out the undertaking by any master whom they may choose to employ. In this way his Holiness could be of very great assistance to me. Of course I desire to reimburse as little as possible, always consistently with justice. His Holiness might employ some of my arguments, as, for instance, the time spent for the Pope at Bologna, and other times wasted without any compensation, according to the statements I have made in full to Ser Giovan Francesco (Fattucci). Directly the terms of restitution have been settled, I will engage my property, sell, and put myself in a position to repay the money. I shall then be able to think of the Pope's orders and to work; as it is, I can hardly be said to live, far less to work. There

[1] Lettere, No. cccxciv.

is no other way of putting an end to the affair more safe for myself, nor more agreeable, nor more certain to ease my mind. It can be done amicably without a lawsuit. I pray to God that the Pope may be willing to accept the mediation, for I cannot see that any one else is fit to do it."

Giorgio Vasari says that he came in the year 1525 for a short time as pupil to Michelangelo.[1] In his own biography he gives the date, more correctly, 1524. At any rate, the period of Vasari's brief apprenticeship was closed by a journey which the master made to Rome, and Buonarroti placed the lad in Andrea del Sarto's workshop. " He left for Rome in haste. Francesco Maria, Duke of Urbino, was again molesting him, asserting that he had received 16,000 ducats to complete the tomb, while he stayed idling at Florence for his own amusement. He threatened that, if he did not attend to the work, he would make him suffer. So, when he arrived there, Pope Clement, who wanted to command his services, advised him to reckon with the Duke's agents, believing that, for what he had already done, he was rather creditor than debtor. The matter remained thus." We do not know when this journey to Rome took place. From a hint in the letter of December 24, 1524, to Fattucci, where Michelangelo observes that only he in person would be able to arrange matters, it is possible that we may refer it to the beginning of 1525. Probably he was able

---

[1] Vasari, xii. p. 204. See note 2.

to convince, not only the Pope, but also the Duke's agents that he had acted with scrupulous honesty, and that his neglect of the tomb was due to circumstances over which he had no control, and which he regretted as acutely as anybody. There is no shadow of doubt that this was really the case. Every word written by Michelangelo upon the subject shows that he was heart-broken at having to abandon the long-cherished project.

Some sort of arrangement must have been arrived at. Clement took the matter into his own hands, and during the summer of 1525 amicable negotiations were in progress. On the 4th of September Michelangelo writes again to Fattucci, saying that he is quite willing to complete the tomb upon the same plan as that of the Pope Pius (now in the Church of S. Andrea della Valle)—that is, to adopt a mural system instead of the vast detached monument.[1] This would take less time. He again urges his friend not to stay at Rome for the sake of these affairs. He hears that the plague is breaking out there. " And I would rather have you alive than my business settled. If I die before the Pope, I shall not have to settle any troublesome affairs. If I live, I am sure the Pope will settle them, if not now, at some other time. So come back. I was with your mother yesterday, and advised her, in the presence of Granacci and John the turner, to send for you home."

[1] Lettere, No. cccxcviii.

While in Rome Michelangelo conferred with Clement about the sacristy and library at S. Lorenzo. For a year after his return to Florence he worked steadily at the Medicean monuments, but not without severe annoyances, as appears from the following to Fattucci :[1] "The four statues I have in hand are not yet finished, and much has still to be done upon them. The four rivers are not begun, because the marble is wanting, and yet it is here. I do not think it opportune to tell you why. With regard to the affairs of Julius, I am well disposed to make the tomb like that of Pius in S. Peter's, and will do so little by little, now one piece and now another, and will pay for it out of my own pocket, if I keep my pension and my house, as you promised me. I mean, of course, the house at Rome, and the marbles and other things I have there.[2] So that, in fine, I should not have to restore to the heirs of Julius, in order to be quit of the contract, anything which I have hitherto received ; the tomb itself, completed after the pattern of that of Pius, sufficing for my full discharge. Moreover, I undertake to perform the work within a reasonable time, and to finish the statues with my own hand." He then turns to his present troubles at Florence. The pension was in arrears, and busybodies annoyed him with interferences of all sorts. " If my pension were paid, as was arranged, I would never stop

---

[1] Lettere, No. cd., date October 24, 1525.
[2] Near the Forum of Trajan. See above

working for Pope Clement with all the strength I have, small though that be, since I am old. At the same time I must not be slighted and affronted as I am now, for such treatment weighs greatly on my spirits. The petty spites I speak of have prevented me from doing what I want to do these many months; one cannot work at one thing with the hands, another with the brain, especially in marble. 'Tis said here that these annoyances are meant to spur me on; but I maintain that those are scurvy spurs which make a good steed jib. I have not touched my pension during the past year, and struggle with poverty. I am left in solitude to bear my troubles, and have so many that they occupy me more than does my art; I cannot keep a man to manage my house through lack of means."

Michelangelo's dejection caused serious anxiety to his friends. Jacopo Salviati, writing on the 30th October from Rome, endeavoured to restore his courage.[1] " I am greatly distressed to hear of the fancies you have got into your head. What hurts me most is that they should prevent your working, for that rejoices your ill-wishers, and confirms them in what they have always gone on preaching about your habits." He proceeds to tell him how absurd it is to suppose that Baccio Bandinelli is preferred before him. " I cannot perceive how Baccio could in any way whatever be compared to you, or his work be set on the same level as your

[1] Gotti, i. 173.

own." The letter winds up with exhortations to work. " Brush these cobwebs of melancholy away ; have confidence in his Holiness ; do not give occasion to your enemies to blaspheme, and be sure that your pension will be paid; I pledge my word for it." Buonarroti, it is clear, wasted his time, not through indolence, but through allowing the gloom of a suspicious and downcast temperament—what the Italians call *accidia*—to settle on his spirits.

Skipping a year, we find that these troublesome negotiations about the tomb were still pending. He still hung suspended between the devil and the deep sea, the importunate Duke of Urbino and the vacillating Pope. Spina, it seems, had been writing with too much heat to Rome, probably urging Clement to bring the difficulties about the tomb to a conclusion. Michelangelo takes the correspondence up again with Fattucci on November 6, 1526.[1] What he says at the beginning of the letter is significant. He knows that the political difficulties in which Clement had become involved were sufficient to distract his mind, as Julius once said, from any interest in "stones small or big." Well, the letter starts thus : "I know that Spina wrote in these days past to Rome very hotly about my affairs with regard to the tomb of Julius. If he blundered, seeing the times in which we live, I am to blame, for I prayed him urgently to write. It is possible that the trouble of my soul made me say more than I ought. Infor-

[1] Lettere, No. cdiii.

mation reached me lately about that affair which alarmed me greatly. It seems that the relatives of Julius are very ill-disposed towards me. And not without reason.[1]—The suit is going on, and they are demanding capital and interest to such an amount that a hundred of my sort could not meet the claims. This has thrown me into terrible agitation, and makes me reflect where I should be if the Pope failed me. I could not live a moment. It is that which made me send the letter alluded to above. Now, I do not want anything but what the Pope thinks right. I know that he does not desire my ruin and my disgrace."

He proceeds to notice that the building work at S. Lorenzo is being carried forward very slowly, and money spent upon it with increasing parsimony. Still he has his pension and his house ; and these imply no small disbursements. He cannot make out what the Pope's real wishes are. If he did but know Clement's mind, he would sacrifice everything to please him. " Only if I could obtain permission to begin something, either here or in Rome, for the tomb of Julius, I should be extremely glad ; for, indeed, I desire to free myself from that obligation more than to live." The letter closes on a note of sadness : "If I am unable to write what you will understand, do not be surprised, for I have lost my wits entirely."

---

[1] I think he means that his fright is not unreasonable. Or the "not without reason" may be ironical.

After this we hear nothing more about the tomb in Michelangelo's correspondence till the year 1531. During the intervening years Italy was convulsed by the sack of Rome, the siege of Florence, and the French campaigns in Lombardy and Naples. Matters only began to mend when Charles V. met Clement at Bologna in 1530, and established the affairs of the peninsula upon a basis which proved durable. That fatal lustre (1526–1530) divided the Italy of the Renaissance from the Italy of modern times with the abruptness of an Alpine watershed. Yet Michelangelo, aged fifty-one in 1526, was destined to live on another thirty-eight years, and, after the death of Clement, to witness the election of five successive Popes. The span of his life was not only extraordinary in its length, but also in the events it comprehended. Born in the mediæval pontificate of Sixtus IV., brought up in the golden days of Lorenzo de' Medici, he survived the Franco-Spanish struggle for supremacy, watched the progress of the Reformation, and only died when a new Church and a new Papacy had been established by the Tridentine Council amid states sinking into the repose of decrepitude.

VI.

We must return from this digression, and resume the events of Michelangelo's life in 1525.

The first letter to Sebastiano del Piombo is referred to April of that year.[1] He says that a picture, probably the portrait of Anton Francesco degli Albizzi, is eagerly expected at Florence. When it arrived in May, he wrote again under the influence of generous admiration for his friend's performance:[2] "Last evening our friend the Captain Cuio and certain other gentlemen were so kind as to invite me to sup with them. This gave me exceeding great pleasure, since it drew me forth a little from my melancholy, or shall we call it my mad mood. Not only did I enjoy the supper, which was most agreeable, but far more the conversation. Among the topics discussed, what gave me most delight was to hear your name mentioned by the Captain; nor was this all, for he still added to my pleasure, nay, to a superlative degree, by saying that, in the art of painting he held you to be sole and without peer in the whole world, and that so you were esteemed at Rome. I could not have been better pleased. You see that my judgment is confirmed; and so you must not deny that you are peerless, when I write it, since I have a crowd of witnesses to my opinion. There is

[1] Lettere, No. cccxcvi.
[2] Lettere, No. cccxcvii. Cuio Dini died in the sack of Rome.

a picture too of yours here, God be praised, which wins credence for me with every one who has eyes." Correspondence was carried on during this year regarding the library at S. Lorenzo; and though I do not mean to treat at length about that building in this chapter, I cannot omit an autograph post-script added by Clement to one of his secretary's missives:[1] " Thou knowest that Popes have no long lives; and we cannot yearn more than we do to behold the chapel with the tombs of our kinsmen, or at any rate to hear that it is finished. Likewise, as regards the library. Wherefore we recommend both to thy diligence. Meantime we will betake us (as thou saidst erewhile) to a wholesome patience, praying God that He may put it into thy heart to push the whole forward together. Fear not that either work to do or rewards shall fail thee while we live. Farewell, with the blessing of God and ours.—JULIUS."

Michelangelo began the library in 1526, as appears from his *Ricordi*. Still the work went on slowly, not through his negligence, but, as we have seen, from the Pope's preoccupation with graver matters. He had a great many workmen in his service at this period,[2] and employed celebrated masters in their crafts, as Tasso and Carota for wood-carving, Battista del Cinque and Ciapino for carpentry, upon the various fittings of the library. All these details

---

[1] Gotti, i. 166. The Pope signs with his baptismal name.
[2] See a list of stone-hewers in *Ricordo*, August 31, 1524, p. 584.

he is said to have designed ; and it is certain that he
was considered responsible for their solidity and handsome appearance. Sebastiano, for instance, wrote
to him about the benches : [1] " Our Lord wishes that
the whole work should be of carved walnut. He
does not mind spending three florins more ; for that
is a trifle, if they are Cosimesque in style, I mean
resemble the work done for the magnificent Cosimo."
Michelangelo could not have been the solitary worker
of legend and tradition. The nature of his present
occupations rendered this impossible. For the completion of his architectural works he needed a band
of able coadjutors. Thus in 1526 Giovanni da
Udine came from Rome to decorate the vault of the
sacristy with frescoed arabesques.[2] His work was

<hr />

[1] *Les Correspondants*, p. 104.

[2] This painter was one of Raffaello's pupils who enjoyed Michelangelo's intimacy. There is a letter addressed by Giovanni to him as early
as the year 1522, "L'otava di Pasqua di Risurecione," Arch. Buon., Cod.
ix. No. 729. The supposition that he came to Florence in 1526 is founded
on a letter by Fattucci in that year (Gotti, i. 170) ; but I believe, from
one of his own letters which I shall proceed to quote, that he did
not begin to paint until 1531. We find him writing on the 25th of
December 1531 to Michelangelo (ibid., No. 730) saying that the Pope
wants him to execute the *stucchi* of his "Cappella hover Tribuna."
He adds, what is interesting, that all his workpeople have perished in
the sack of Rome, and that he is obliged to educate a new set : "in
queste frangenti di Roma, e bisogna farne de novi." Then he begs
Buonarroti to send him particulars regarding the shape and dimensions
of the chapel, which shows that when Clement thought of sending him
in 1526, he had been prevented by the troubles of the times. He
worked entirely under Michelangelo's orders, and designed the beautiful windows for the library. An inedited letter from Giovan Francesco
Bini in Rome to Michelangelo in Florence, dated August 3, 1533
(Arch. Buon., Cod. vi. No. 92), indicates that he was still at work. Bini

nearly terminated in 1533, when some question arose about painting the inside of the lantern. Sebastiano, apparently in good faith, made the following burlesque suggestion:[1] "For myself, I think that the Ganymede would go there very well; one could put an aureole about him, and turn him into a S. John of the Apocalypse when he is being caught up into the heavens." The whole of one side of the Italian Renaissance, its so-called neo-paganism, is contained in this remark.

While still occupied with thoughts about S. Lorenzo, Clement ordered Michelangelo to make a receptacle for the precious vessels and reliques collected by Lorenzo the Magnificent. It was first intended to place this chest, in the form of a ciborium, above the high altar, and to sustain it on four columns. Eventually, the Pope resolved that it should be a sacrarium, or cabinet for holy things, and that this should stand above the middle entrance door to the church. The chest was finished, and its contents remained there until the reign of the Grand-Duke Pietro Leopoldo, when they were removed to the chapel next the old sacristy.

Another very singular idea occurred to his Holiness in the autumn of 1525. He made Fattucci write

---

says the Pope is willing to give Giovanni leave of absence, but that he must return: "che M. Giov. da Udine vadia ove desidera sua Sta è contenta ma che torni," &c. Michelangelo left Florence himself in the autumn of that year.

[1] *Les Correspondants*, p. 104. Sebastiano probably alludes to some design for a Ganymede made by Michelangelo.

that he wished to erect a colossal statue on the piazza of S. Lorenzo, opposite the Stufa Palace. The giant was to surmount the roof of the Medicean Palace, with its face turned in that direction and its back to the house of Luigi della Stufa. Being so huge, it would have to be composed of separate pieces fitted together.[1] Michelangelo speedily knocked this absurd plan on the head in a letter which gives a good conception of his dry and somewhat ponderous humour.[2]

"About the Colossus of forty cubits, which you tell me is to go or to be placed at the corner of the loggia in the Medicean garden, opposite the corner of Messer Luigi della Stufa, I have meditated not a little, as you bade me. In my opinion that is not the proper place for it, since it would take up too much room on the roadway. I should prefer to put it at the other, where the barber's shop is. This would be far better in my judgment, since it has the square in front, and would not encumber the street. There might be some difficulty about pulling down the shop, because of the rent. So it has occurred to me that the statue might be carved in a sitting position; the Colossus would be so lofty that if we made it hollow inside, as indeed is the proper method for a thing which has to be put together from pieces, the shop might be enclosed within it, and the rent be saved. And inasmuch as the shop has a chimney in its present state, I thought of placing

[1] Gotti, i. 168.   [2] Lettere, No. cccxcix.

a cornucopia in the statue's hand, hollowed out for the smoke to pass through. The head too would be hollow, like all the other members of the figure. This might be turned to a useful purpose, according to the suggestion made me by a huckster on the square, who is my good friend. He privily confided to me that it would make an excellent dovecote. Then another fancy came into my head, which is still better, though the statue would have to be considerably heightened. That, however, is quite feasible, since towers are built up of blocks; and then the head might serve as bell-tower to San Lorenzo, which is much in need of one. Setting up the bells inside, and the sound booming through the mouth, it would seem as though the Colossus were crying mercy, and mostly upon feast-days, when peals are rung most often and with bigger bells."

Nothing more is heard of this fantastic project; whence we may conclude that the irony of Michelangelo's epistle drove it out of the Pope's head.

CHAPTER IX.

1. Michelangelo was at Florence during the sack of Rome.—Meagre documents relating to 1528.—Death of Buonarroto.—Cellini and Michelangelo.—Valerio Belli.—2. Florence expects a siege and prepares to arm.—Michelangelo elected a member of the Nove della Milizia in April 1529.—He begins to fortify S. Miniato.— Inspects the fortress of Pisa.—Difficulties with the Gonfalonier Capponi.—Sent to Ferrara in July.—3. He was certainly in Florence after the middle of September.—Sudden flight to Venice at the end of this month. — Letter to Giovanni Battista della Palla.—Various notices regarding the reason of this flight.—Question whether he had already been in Venice during the summer of this year.—The *Ricordo*, September 10.—4. Residence on the Giudecca in Venice.—A sentence of outlawry issued against him at Florence.—The Signory grant him a safe-conduct home, if he will return.—Palla's letters.—Michelangelo in Florence again at the end of November 1529.—Progress of the siege.—Malatesta Baglioni betrays the city.—Capitulation, August 1530.—5. Baccio Valori and the return of the Medici.—Persecution of the Florentine patriots.—Michelangelo goes into hiding, but is pardoned by Clement, and set to work again at S. Lorenzo.—The Cacus and Hercules.—The tempera picture of a Leda, and its history.— Michelangelo's attitude toward subjects for art-work.—The Apollo begun for Baccio Valori.—6. Lodovico at Pisa during the siege.— Young Lionardo Buonarroti.—Michelangelo works steadily at the Medicean monuments.—Invitations to Rome.—Negotiations about the tomb of Julius.—Michelangelo's health suffers from overwork and worry.—Clement issues a brief enjoining him to spare his strength.—Sebastiano's efforts with the Pope and Duke of Urbino end in a new contract for the tomb, April 29, 1532.—Further troubles connected with this contract.—Condivi's general history of the affair.—7. Michelangelo in disfavour with Duke Alessandro de' Medici.—His attitude toward the reigning family.—Clement, on his way to France, meets him at S. Miniato al Tedesco.—

Lodovico Buonarroti dies about this time.—Michelangelo leaves
Florence in the late autumn of 1534.—His poem on Lodovico's
death.

I.

It lies outside the scope of this work to describe
the series of events which led up to the sack of
Rome in 1527. Clement, by his tortuous policy,
and by the avarice of his administration, had alien-
ated every friend and exasperated all his foes. The
Eternal City was in a state of chronic discontent
and anarchy. The Colonna princes drove the Pope
to take refuge in the Castle of S. Angelo ; and when
the Lutheran rabble raised by Frundsberg poured
into Lombardy, the Duke of Ferrara assisted them
to cross the Po, and the Duke of Urbino made no
effort to bar the passes of the Apennines. Losing
one leader after the other, these ruffians, calling
themselves an Imperial army, but being in reality
the scum and offscourings of all nations, without
any aim but plunder and ignorant of policy, reached
Rome upon the 6th of May. They took the city by
assault, and for nine months Clement, leaning from
the battlements of Hadrian's Mausoleum, watched
smoke ascend from desolated palaces and desecrated
temples, heard the wailing of women and the groans
of tortured men, mingling with the ribald jests
of German drunkards and the curses of Castilian
bandits. Roaming those galleries and gazing from
those windows, he is said to have exclaimed in the

words of Job: "Why died I not from the womb? why did I not give up the ghost when I came out of the belly?"

The immediate effect of this disaster was that the Medici lost their hold on Florence. The Cardinal of Cortona, with the young princes Ippolito and Alessandro de' Medici, fled from the city on the 17th of May, and a popular government was set up under the presidency of Niccolò Capponi.

During this year and the next, Michelangelo was at Florence; but we know very little respecting the incidents of his life. A *Ricordo* bearing the date April 29 shows the disturbed state of the town.[1] "I record how, some days ago, Piero di Filippo Gondi asked for permission to enter the new sacristy at S. Lorenzo, in order to hide there certain goods belonging to his family, by reason of the perils in which we are now. To-day, upon the 29th of April 1527, he has begun to carry in some bundles, which he says are linen of his sisters; and I, not wishing to witness what he does or to know where he hides the gear away, have given him the key of the sacristy this evening."

There are only two letters belonging to the year 1527. Both refer to a small office which had been awarded to Michelangelo with the right to dispose of the patronage. He offered it to his favourite brother, Buonarroto, who does not seem to have thought it worth accepting.[2]

[1] Lettere, p. 598.   [2] Lettere, Nos. cxxii., cxxiii., August.

The documents for 1528 are almost as meagre. We do not possess a single letter, and the most important *Ricordi* relate to Buonarroto's death and the administration of his property. He died of the plague upon the 2nd of July, to the very sincere sorrow of his brother. It is said that Michelangelo held him in his arms while he was dying, without counting the risk to his own life.[1] Among the minutes of disbursements made for Buonarroto's widow and children after his burial, we find that their clothes had been destroyed because of the infection. All the cares of the family now fell on Michelangelo's shoulders. He placed his niece Francesca in a convent till the time that she should marry, repaid her dowry to the widow Bartolommea, and provided for the expenses of his nephew Lionardo.[2]

For the rest, there is little to relate which has any bearing on the way in which he passed his time before the siege of Florence began. One glimpse, however, is afforded of his daily life and conversation by Benvenuto Cellini, who had settled in Florence after the sack of Rome, and was working in a shop he opened at the Mercato Nuovo.[3] The episode is sufficiently interesting to be quoted. A Sienese gentleman had commissioned Cellini to make him a golden medal, to be worn in the hat.

[1] The Senator Filippo Buonarroti, quoted by Gotti, i. 207.
[2] Ricordi for 1528, in Lettere, pp. 599–601.
[3] Memorie, lib. i. cap. 41.

"The subject was to be Hercules wrenching the lion's mouth. While I was working at this piece, Michel Agnolo Buonarroti came oftentimes to see it. I had spent infinite pains upon the design, so that the attitude of the figure and the fierce passion of the beast were executed in quite a different style from that of any craftsman who had hitherto attempted such groups. This, together with the fact that the special branch of art was totally unknown to Michel Agnolo, made the divine master give such praises to my work that I felt incredibly inspired for further effort.

"Just then I met with Federigo Ginori, a young man of very lofty spirit. He had lived some years in Naples, and being endowed with great charms of person and presence, had been the lover of a Neapolitan princess. He wanted to have a medal made with Atlas bearing the world upon his shoulders, and applied to Michel Agnolo for a design. Michel Agnolo made this answer: ' Go and find out a young goldsmith named Benvenuto ; he will serve you admirably, and certainly he does not stand in need of sketches by me. However, to prevent your thinking that I want to save myself the trouble of so slight a matter, I will gladly sketch you something; but meanwhile speak to Benvenuto, and let him also make a model; he can then execute the better of the two designs.' Federigo Ginori came to me and told me what he wanted, adding thereto how Michel Agnolo had praised me, and how he had suggested I should make a waxen model while he undertook to supply a sketch. The words of that great man so heartened me, that I set myself to work at once with eagerness upon the model; and when I had finished it, a painter who was intimate with Michel Agnolo, called Giuliano Bugiardini, brought me the drawing of Atlas. On the same occasion I showed Giuliano my little model in wax, which was very different from Michel Agnolo's drawing; and Federigo, in concert with Bugiardini, agreed that I should work upon my model. So I took it in hand, and when Michel Agnolo saw it, he praised me to the skies."

The courtesy shown by Michelangelo on this occasion to Cellini may be illustrated by an inedited letter addressed to him from Vicenza.[1] The writer was Valerio Belli, who describes himself as a cornelian-cutter. He reminds the sculptor of a promise once made to him in Florence of a design for an engraved gem. A remarkably fine stone has just come into his hands, and he should much like to begin to work upon it. These proofs of Buonarroti's liberality to brother artists are not unimportant, since he was unjustly accused during his lifetime of stinginess and churlishness.

[1] Date April 21, 1521. "Valerio Belli che taglia le Corniole." Arch. Buon., Cod. vi. No. 52.

II.

At the end of the year 1528 it became clear to the Florentines that they would have to reckon with Clement VII. As early as August 18, 1527, France and England leagued together, and brought pressure upon Charles V., in whose name Rome had been sacked. Negotiations were proceeding, which eventually ended in the peace of Barcelona (June 20, 1529), whereby the Emperor engaged to sacrifice the Republic to the Pope's vengeance. It was expected that the remnant of the Prince of Orange's army would be marched up to besiege the town. Under the anxiety caused by these events, the citizens raised a strong body of militia, enlisted Malatesta Baglioni and Stefano Colonna as generals, and began to take measures for strengthening the defences. What may be called the War Office of the Florentine Republic bore the title of Dieci della Guerra, or the Ten. It was their duty to watch over and provide for all the interests of the commonwealth in military matters, and now at this juncture serious measures had to be taken for putting the city in a state of defence. Already in the year 1527, after the expulsion of the Medici, a subordinate board had been created, to whom very considerable executive and administrative faculties were delegated.[1] This board,

---

[1] The Republic, in fact, adopted Machiavelli's scheme for a national militia, as set forth in his treatise on the Art of War.

called the Nove della Milizia, or the Nine, were em-
powered to enrol all the burghers under arms, and to
take charge of the walls, towers, bastions, and other
fortifications. It was also within their competence
to cause the destruction of buildings, and to compensate the evicted proprietors at a valuation which
they fixed themselves.[1] In the spring of 1529 the
War Office decided to gain the services of Michelangelo, not only because he was the most eminent
architect of his age in Florence, but also because
the Buonarroti family had always been adherents
of the Medicean party, and the Ten judged that
his appointment to a place on the Nove di Milizia
would be popular with the democracy.[2] The patent
conferring this office upon him, together with full
authority over the work of fortification, was issued
on the 6th of April.[3] Its terms were highly com-
plimentary. " Considering the genius and practical
attainments of Michelangelo di Lodovico Buonarroti,
our citizen, and knowing how excellent he is in
architecture, beside his other most singular talents
in the liberal arts, by virtue whereof the common
consent of men regards him as unsurpassed by any
masters of our times ; and, moreover, being assured
that in love and affection toward the country he
is the equal of any other good and loyal burgher ;
bearing in mind, too, the labour he has undergone

[1] Varchi, *Stor. Fior.*, vol. i. p. 184.
[2] See document, quoted by Milanesi, Vasari, xii. 365.
[3] The original is given in Gotti, vol. ii. p. 62.

and the diligence he has displayed, gratis and of
his free will, in the said work (of fortification) up to
this day; and wishing to employ his industry and
energies to the like effect in future ; we, of our
motion and initiative, do appoint him to be governor
and procurator-general over the construction and
fortification of the city walls, as well as every other
sort of defensive operation and munition for the
town of Florence, for one year certain, beginning
with the present date; adding thereto full authority over all persons in respect to the said work
of reparation or pertaining to it." From this pre-
amble it appears that Michelangelo had been already
engaged in volunteer service connected with the defence of Florence. A stipend of one golden florin
per diem was fixed by the same deed ; and upon the
22nd of April following a payment of thirty florins
was decreed, for one month's salary, dating from the
6th of April.[1]

If the Government thought to gain popular sympathy by Michelangelo's appointment, they made
the mistake of alienating the aristocracy. It was
the weakness of Florence, at this momentous crisis
in her fate, to be divided into parties, political,
religious, social; whose internal jealousies deprived
her of the strength which comes alone from unity.
When Giambattista Busini wrote that interesting
series of letters to Benedetto Varchi from which the
latter drew important materials for his annals of the

[1] Vasari, xii. 365.

siege, he noted this fact.[1] "Envy must always be reckoned as of some account in republics, especially when the nobles form a considerable element, as in ours : for they were angry, among other matters, to see a Carducci made Gonfalonier, Michelangelo a member of the Nine, a Cei or a Giugni elected to the Ten."

Michelangelo had scarcely been chosen to control the general scheme for fortifying Florence, when the Signory began to consider the advisability of strengthening the citadels of Pisa and Livorno, and erecting lines along the Arno.[2] Their commissary at Pisa wrote urging the necessity of Buonarroti's presence on the spot. In addition to other pressing needs, the Arno, when in flood, threatened the ancient fortress of the city. Accordingly we find that Michelangelo went to Pisa on the 5th of June, and that he stayed there over the 13th, returning to Florence perhaps upon the 17th of the month.[3] The commissary, who spent several days in conferring with him and in visiting the banks of the Arno, was perturbed in mind because Michelangelo refused to exchange the inn where he alighted for an apartment in the official residence. This is very characteristic of the artist. We shall soon find him, at Ferrara, refusing to quit his hostelry for the Duke's palace, and, at Venice, hiring a remote

[1] Lettere del Busini al Varchi. Firenze : Le Monnier, 1861, p. 133.
[2] Correspondence between the Signory and their commissary, C Tosinghi, at Pisa, between April 28 and May 6. Gaye, ii. 184–185.
[3] Documents in Gaye, ii. 194 ; Vasari, xii. 367.

lodging on the Giudecca in order to avoid the hospitality of S. Mark.

An important part of Michelangelo's plan for the fortification of Florence was to erect bastions covering the hill of S. Miniato. Any one who stands upon the ruined tower of the church there will see at a glance that S. Miniato is the key to the position for a beleaguering force; and "if the enemy once obtained possession of the hill, he would become immediately master of the town."[1] It must, I think, have been at this spot that Buonarroti was working before he received the appointment of controller-general of the works. Yet he found some difficulty in persuading the rulers of the state that his plan was the right one. Busini, using information supplied by Michelangelo himself at Rome in 1549, speaks as follows:[2] "Whatever the reason may have been, Niccolò Capponi, while he was Gonfalonier, would not allow the hill of S. Miniato to be fortified, and Michelangelo, who is a man of absolute veracity, tells me that he had great trouble in convincing the other members of the Government, but that he could never convince Niccolò. However, he began the work, in the way you know, with those fascines of tow. But Niccolò made him abandon it, and sent him to another post; and when he was elected to the Nine, they despatched him twice or thrice outside the city. Each time, on his return, he found

[1] Condivi, p. 47. Probably the words are Michelangelo's.
[2] Busini, p. 103.

the hill neglected, whereupon he complained, feeling this a blot upon his reputation and an insult
to his magistracy.   Eventually, the works went on,
until, when the besieging army arrived, they were
tenable."

Michelangelo had hitherto acquired no practical
acquaintance with the art of fortification.   That the
system of defence by bastions was an Italian invention (although Albert Dürer first reduced it to
written theory in his book of 1527, suggesting im-
provements which led up to Vauban's method) is a
fact acknowledged by military historians.   But it does
not appear that Michelangelo did more than carry out
defensive operations in the manner familiar to his
predecessors.   Indeed, we shall see that some critics
found reason to blame him for want of science in
the construction of his outworks.   When, therefore,
a difference arose between the controller-general of
defences and the Gonfalonier upon this question of
strengthening S. Miniato, it was natural that the
War Office should have thought it prudent to send
their , chief officer to the greatest authority upon
fortification then alive in Italy.[1]   This was the Duke
of Ferrara.   Busini must serve as our text in the
first instance upon this point.[2]   "Michelangelo says
that, when neither Niccolò Capponi nor Baldas-

---

[1] That the Florentine Government was seriously anxious to get the
Duke's advice appears from a letter of Giugni to the Ten, August 9,
1529, recommending them to send the Duke a ground-plan of the city
and its environs for his opinion. See Gaye, ii. 200.

[2] Busini, p. 115.

sare Carducci would agree to the outworks at S. Miniato, he convinced all the leading men except Niccolò of their necessity, showing that Florence could not hold out a single day without them. Accordingly he began to throw up bastions with fascines of tow ; but the result was far from perfect, as he himself confessed. Upon this, the Ten resolved to send him to Ferrara to inspect that renowned work of defence. Thither accordingly he went ; nevertheless, he believes that Niccolò did this in order to get him out of the way, and to prevent the construction of the bastion. In proof thereof he adduces the fact that, upon his return, he found the whole work interrupted."

Furnished with letters to the Duke, and with special missives from the Signory and the Ten to their envoy, Galeotto Giugni, Michelangelo left Florence for Ferrara after the 28th of July, and reached it on the 2nd of August.[1] He refused, as Giugni writes with some regret, to abandon his inn, but was personally conducted with great honour by the Duke all round the walls and fortresses of Ferrara. On what day he quitted that city, and whither he went immediately after his departure, is uncertain. The Ten wrote to Giugni on the 8th of August, saying that his presence was urgently required at Florence, since the work of fortification was going on apace, " a multitude of men being employed, and no respect being paid to

---

[1] Gaye, ii. 197–200.

feast-days and holidays." It would also seem that, toward the close of the month, he was expected at Arezzo, in order to survey and make suggestions on the defences of the city.[1]

These points are not insignificant, since we possess a *Ricordo* by Michelangelo, written upon an unfinished letter bearing the date "Venice, September 10," which has been taken to imply that he had been resident in Venice fourteen days—that is, from the 28th of August. None of his contemporaries or biographers mention a visit to Venice at the end of August 1529. It has, therefore, been conjectured that he went there after leaving Ferrara, but that his mission was one of a very secret nature. This seems inconsistent with the impatient desire expressed by the War Office for his return to Florence after the 8th of August. Allowing for exchange of letters and rate of travelling, Michelangelo could not have reached home much before the 15th. It is also inconsistent with the fact that he was expected in Arezzo at the beginning of September. I shall have to return later on to the *Ricordo* in question, which has an important bearing on the next and most dramatic episode in his biography.

[1] Letter from Ant. Fr. degli Albizzi to the Ten, September 8, 1529. Gaye, ii. 206.

III.

Michelangelo must certainly have been at Florence soon after the middle of September. One of those strange panics to which he was constitutionally subject, and which impelled him to act upon a suddenly aroused instinct, came now to interrupt his work at S. Miniato, and sent him forth into outlawry. It was upon the 21st of September that he fled from Florence, under circumstances which have given considerable difficulty to his biographers. I am obliged to disentangle the motives and to set forth the details of this escapade, so far as it is possible for criticism to connect them into a coherent narrative. With this object in view, I will begin by translating what Condivi says upon the subject.[1]

"Michelangelo's sagacity with regard to the importance of S. Miniato guaranteed the safety of the town, and proved a source of great damage to the enemy. Although he had taken care to secure the position, he still remained at his post there, in case of accidents; and after passing some six months, rumours began to circulate among the soldiers about expected treason. Buonarroti, then, noticing these reports, and being also warned by certain officers who were his friends, approached the Signory, and laid before them what he had heard and seen. He

[1] Condivi, p. 47.

explained the danger hanging over the city, and told them there was still time to provide against it, if they would. Instead of receiving thanks for this service, he was abused, and rebuked as being timorous and too suspicious. The man who made him this answer would have done better had he opened his ears to good advice ; for when the Medici returned, he was beheaded, whereas he might have kept himself alive. When Michelangelo perceived how little his words were worth, and in what certain peril the city stood, he caused one of the gates to be opened, by the authority which he possessed, and went forth with two of his comrades, and took the road for Venice."

As usual with Condivi, this paragraph gives a general and yet substantially accurate account of what really took place. The decisive document, however, which throws light upon Michelangelo's mind in the transaction, is a letter written by him from Venice to his friend Battista della Palla on the 25th of September. Palla, who was an agent for Francis I. in works of Italian art, antiques, and bric-à-brac, had long purposed a journey into France ; and Michelangelo, considering the miserable state of Italian politics, agreed to join him. These explanations will suffice to make the import of Michelangelo's letter clear.[1]

" Battista, dearest friend, I left Florence, as I think you know, meaning to go to France. When

[1] Lettere, No. cdvi.

I reached Venice, I inquired about the road, and they told me I should have to pass through German territory, and that the journey is both perilous and difficult. Therefore I thought it well to ask you, at your pleasure, whether you are still inclined to go, and to beg you ; and so I entreat you, let me know, and say where you want me to wait for you, and we will travel together. I left home without speaking to any of my friends, and in great confusion. You know that I wanted in any case to go to France, and often asked for leave, but did not get it. Nevertheless I was quite resolved, and without any sort of fear, to see the end of the war out first. But on Tuesday morning, September 21, a certain person came out by the gate at S. Nicolò, where I was attending to the bastions, and whispered in my ear that, if I meant to save my life, I must not stay at Florence. He accompanied me home, dined there, brought me horses, and never left my side till he got me outside the city, declaring that this was my salvation. Whether God or the devil was the man, I do not know.

"Pray answer the questions in this letter as soon as possible, because I am burning with impatience to set out. If you have changed your mind, and do not care to go, still let me know, so that I may provide as best I can for my own journey."

What appears manifest from this document is that Michelangelo was decoyed away from Florence by some one, who, acting on his sensitive nervous temperament, persuaded him that his life was in danger. Who the man was we do not know, but he must have been a person delegated by those who had a direct interest in removing Buonarroti from the place. If the controller-general of the defences already scented treason in the air, and was communicating his suspicions to the Signory, Malatesta Baglioni, the arch-traitor, who afterwards delivered Florence over for a price to Clement, could not but have wished to frighten him away.

From another of Michelangelo's letters we learn that he carried 3000 ducats in specie with him on the journey.[1] It is unlikely that he could have disposed so much cash upon his person. He must have had companions.

Talking with Michelangelo in 1549—that is, twenty years after the event—Busini heard from his lips this account of the flight.[2] " I asked Michelangelo what was the reason of his departure from Florence. He spoke as follows: 'I was one of the Nine when the Florentine troops mustered within our lines under Malatesta Baglioni and Mario Orsini and the other generals: whereupon the Ten distributed the men along the walls and bastions, assigning to each captain his own post, with victuals and provisions; and among the rest, they gave eight pieces of artillery to Malatesta for the defence of part of the bastions at S. Miniato. He did not, however, mount these guns within the bastions, but below

---

[1] Lettere, No. cdvii.　　　　[2] Busini, p. 104.

them, and set no guard.' Michelangelo, as architect and magistrate, having to inspect the lines at
S. Miniato, asked Mario Orsini how it was that
Malatesta treated his artillery so carelessly. The
latter answered : ' You must know that the men of
his house are all traitors, and in time he too will
betray this town.' These words inspired him with
such terror that he was obliged to fly, impelled by
dread lest the city should come to misfortune, and
he together with it. Having thus resolved, he
found Rinaldo Corsini, to whom he communicated
his thoughts, and Corsini replied lightly : ' I will go
with you.' So they mounted horse with a sum of
money, and rode to the Gate of Justice, where the
guards would not let them pass. While waiting
there, some one sung out: ' Let him by, for he is
of the Nine, and it is Michelangelo.' So they went
forth, three on horseback, he, Rinaldo, and that
man of his who never left him.[1] They came to
Castelnuovo (in the Garfagnana), and heard that
Tommaso Soderini and Niccolò Capponi were staying there.[2] Michelangelo refused to go and see
them, but Rinaldo went, and when he came back
to Florence, as I shall relate, he reported how
Niccolò had said to him : ' O Rinaldo, I dreamed
to-night that Lorenzo Zampalochi had been made
Gonfalonier ; ' alluding to Lorenzo Giacomini, who
had a swollen leg, and had been his adversary in

[1] Probably Antonio Mini is meant.
[2] They had recently left Florence as exiles.

the Ten. Well, they took the road for Venice; but when they came to Polesella, Rinaldo proposed to push on to Ferrara and have an interview with Galeotto Giugni.[1] This he did, and Michelangelo awaited him, for so he promised. Messer Galeotto, who was spirited and sound of heart, wrought so with Rinaldo that he persuaded him to turn back to Florence. But Michelangelo pursued his journey to Venice, where he took a house, intending in due season to travel into France."

Varchi follows this report pretty closely, except that he represents Rinaldo Corsini as having strongly urged him to take flight, " affirming that the city in a few hours, not to say days, would be in the hands of the Medici." [2] Varchi adds that Antonio Mini rode in company with Michelangelo, and, according to his account of the matter, the three men came together to Ferrara. There the Duke offered hospitality to Michelangelo, who refused to exchange his inn for the palace, but laid all the cash he carried with him at the disposition of his Excellency.

Segni, alluding briefly to this flight of Michelangelo from Florence, says that he arrived at Castelnuovo with Rinaldo Corsini, and that what they communicated to Niccolò Capponi concerning the treachery of Malatesta and the state of the city, so affected the ex-Gonfalonier that he died of a fever after seven days.[3] Nardi, an excellent authority on

---

[1] The Florentine envoy there.   [2] Varchi, *Stor. Fior.*, vol. ii. p. 133.
[3] *Istorie Fiorentini.* Firenze : Barbèra, 1857, p. 137.

all that concerns Florence during the siege, confirms the account that Michelangelo left his post
together with Corsini under a panic ; "by common
agreement, or through fear of war, as man's fragility
is often wont to do."[1] Vasari, who in his account
of this episode seems to have had Varchi's narrative
under his eyes, adds a trifle of information, to the
effect that Michelangelo was accompanied upon his
flight, not only by Antonio Mini, but also by his
old friend Piloto.[2] It may be worth adding that
while reading in the Archivio Buonarroti, I discovered two letters from a friend named Piero
Paesano addressed to Michelangelo on January 1,
1530, and April 21, 1532, both of which speak of
his having "fled from Florence." The earlier plainly
says : "I heard from Santi Quattro (the Cardinal,
probably) that you have left Florence in order to
escape from the annoyance and also from the evil
fortune of the war in which the country is engaged."
These letters, which have not been edited, and the
first of which is important, since it was sent to
Michelangelo in Florence, help to prove that Michelangelo's friends believed he had run away from
Florence.[3]

[1] *Istorie della Città di Firenze.* Firenze : Le Monnier, vol. ii. p. 159.

[2] Vasari, xii. 209. He says the sum of money carried was 12,000
crowns. Varchi calls them 12,000 florins. Michelangelo himself mentions 3000 ducats.

[3] Arch. Buon., Cod. x. 587–588. Paesano writes his first letter from
Regentia, January 1, 1530. He addresses Michelangelo as "Caro Compare," and after some preliminaries, in which he says that his affairs
have taken him to Bologna, he proceeds : "Ho inteso da Santi Quattro

It was necessary to enter into these particulars, partly in order that the reader may form his own judgment of the motives which prompted Michelangelo to desert his official post at Florence, and partly because we have now to consider the *Ricordo* above mentioned, with the puzzling date, September 10.[1] This document is a note of expenses incurred during a residence of fourteen days at Venice. It runs as follows :—

"Honoured Sir. In Venice, this tenth day of September. . . . Ten ducats to Rinaldo Corsini. Five ducats to Messer Loredan for the rent of the house. Seventeen lire for the stockings of Antonio (Mini, perhaps). For two stools, a table to eat on, and a coffer, half a ducat. Eight soldi for straw. Forty soldi for the hire of the bed. Ten lire to the man (*fante*) who came from Florence. Three ducats to Bondino for the journey to Venice with boats. Twenty soldi to Piloto for a pair of shoes. Fourteen days' board in Venice, twenty lire."

It has been argued from the date of the unfinished

che voi vi siete partito da Fiorenza per fugire al fastido et ancora la mala fortuna della guerra del paese." He then offers him free quarters in his own house, wherever that was, so long as Michelangelo chose to stay with him. It appears that this letter was not answered, for on the 21st of April 1532 Paesano writes again, this time from Argento, to his "Compare Carissimo," saying that he wishes to remind him that his old friend is still alive. He then refers to the former letter: "Essendo io a Bologna per visitare Santi Quattro, et lui mi disse che voi eravate fugito di fiorenza et andato a Venezia et io scrissi una lettera a Venezia."

[1] *Lettere*, p. 601.

letter below which these items are jotted down,
that Michelangelo must have been in Venice early
in September, before his flight from Florence at the
end of that month. But whatever weight we may
attach to this single date, there is no corroborative
proof that he travelled twice to Venice, and everything in the *Ricordo* indicates that it refers to the
period of his flight from Florence. The sum paid to
Corsini comes first, because it must have been disbursed when that man broke the journey at Ferrara.
Antonio Mini and Piloto are both mentioned : a
house has been engaged, and furnished with Michelangelo's usual frugality, as though he contemplated
a residence of ' some duration. All this confirms
Busini, Varchi, Segni, Nardi, and Vasari in the
general outlines of their reports. I am of opinion
that, unassisted by further evidence, the *Ricordo*, in
spite of its date, will not bear out Gotti's view that
Michelangelo sought Venice on a privy mission at
the end of August 1529.[1] He was not likely to

---

[1] See Gotti, vol. i. p. 189. I have examined the original document
in the Archivio Buonarroti. The date is certainly correctly given by
Gotti. The unfinished letter runs thus : "Ho^{do} mio maggiore in
Vinegia oggi questo di dieci di secte." Michelangelo sometimes spelt
the month September thus—*Sectembre.* I found an instance of it
in the Codex Vaticanus of the *Rime.* The date may possibly have
contained the error of September, when Michelangelo wished to write
October, and for this reason the word *Secte* may not have been finished.
That the letter was begun and flung aside for some reason seems certain.
Perhaps he preferred to re-write the proper date, October 10, and kept
the discarded rough copy by him. His *Ricordi* are frequently jotted
upon backs of drawings, and any pieces of paper which came to hand.
I ought to add that Signor Gotti has somewhat confused the evidence

have been employed as ambassador extraordinary; the Signory required his services at home; and after Ferrara, Venice had little of importance to show the controller-general of defences in the way of earthworks and bastions.

IV.

Varchi says that Michelangelo, when he reached Venice, "wishing to avoid visits and ceremonies, of which he was the greatest enemy, and in order to live alone, according to his custom, far away from company, retired quietly to the Giudecca; but the Signory, unable to ignore the advent of so eminent a man, sent two of their first noblemen to visit him

of the *Ricordo* by inserting after the words "Dieci lire al fante che venne da Firenze" the following in brackets: "(Bastiano Scarpellino)." Now there is nothing about *Bastiano Scarpellino* in the autograph.

The main argument against the view I have expressed above is Michelangelo's own statement in his letter to Palla, "Io parti' senza far motto a messuno degli amici mia." Gotti and others think this incompatible with Corsini's and Piloto's participation in the flight from Venice. But, in the troubled state of the city, it may have been prudent to mention no names. Besides, Corsini's and Piloto's presence in Venice, supposing Michelangelo went there on a secret mission in August, would have been, to say the least, superfluous. Michelangelo's circumstantial account of his flight was certainly given to Busini in 1549—that is, twenty years after the event. But he is not likely to have forgotten the secret mission of August, if that really took place, or to have confused this with the flight in September. It must furthermore be remembered that Corsini and Piloto were prominent personages in Florentine society. Things recorded of them by contemporaries—Varchi, Segni, Nardi, Vasari—cannot have rested upon wholly false evidence.

in the name of the Republic, and to offer kindly all things which either he or any persons of his train might stand in need of. This public compliment set forth the greatness of his fame as artist, and showed in what esteem the arts are held by their magnificent and most illustrious lordships."[1] Vasari adds that the Doge, whom he calls Gritti, gave him commission to design a bridge for the Rialto, marvellous alike in its construction and its ornament.[2]

Meanwhile the Signory of Florence issued a decree of outlawry against thirteen citizens who had quitted the territory without leave. It was promulgated on the 30th of September, and threatened them with extreme penalties if they failed to appear before the 8th of October.[3] On the 7th of October a second decree was published, confiscating the property of numerous exiles. But this document does not contain the name of Michelangelo; and by a third decree, dated November 16, it appears that the Government were satisfied with depriving him of his office and stopping his pay.[4] We gather indeed, from what Condivi and Varchi relate, that they displayed great eagerness to get him back, and corresponded to this intent with their envoy at Ferrara. Michelangelo's flight from Florence seemed a matter of sufficient importance to be included in the des-

[1] Varchi, ii. 133.
[2] Vasari, xii. 211.   Andrea Gritti died in 1528, and was succeeded by Pietro Lando.
[3] Gotti, ii. 63.   [4] Gotti, vol. i. p. 193.

patches of the French ambassador resident at Venice. Lazare de Baïf, knowing his master's desire to engage the services of the great sculptor, and being probably informed of Buonarroti's own wish to retire to France, wrote several letters in the month of October, telling Francis that Michelangelo might be easily persuaded to join his court.[1] We do not know, however, whether the King acted on this hint.

His friends at home took the precaution of securing his effects, fearing that a decree for their confiscation might be issued. We possess a schedule of wine, wheat, and furniture found in his house, and handed over by the servant Caterina to his old friend Francesco Granacci for safe keeping.[2] They also did their best to persuade Michelangelo that he ought to take measures for returning under a safe-conduct. Galeotto Giugni wrote upon this subject to the War Office, under date October 13, from Ferrara.[3] He says that Michelangelo has begged him to intercede in his favour, and that he is willing to return and lay himself at the feet of their lordships. In answer to this despatch, news was sent to Giugni on the 20th that the Signory had signed a safe-conduct for Buonarroti.[4] On the 22nd Granacci paid Sebastiano di Francesco, a stonecutter, to whom Michelangelo was much attached,

[1] *L'Œuvre et la Vie*, p. 275.
[2] Gotti, ii. 73. It bears date October 12.
[3] Gaye, ii. 209.   [4] Ibid., p. 210.

money for his journey to Venice.[1] It appears that this man set out upon the 23rd, carrying letters from Giovan Battista della Palla, who had now renounced all intention of retiring to France, and was enthusiastically engaged in the defence of Florence. On the return of the Medici, Palla was imprisoned in the castle of Pisa, and paid the penalty of his patriotism by death.[2] A second letter which he wrote to Michelangelo on this occasion deserves to be translated, since it proves the high spirit with which the citizens of Florence were now awaiting the approach of the Prince of Orange and his veteran army.[3] " Yesterday I sent you a letter, together with ten from other friends, and the safe-conduct granted by the Signory for the whole month of November, and though I feel sure that it will reach you safely, I take the precaution of enclosing a copy under this cover. I need hardly repeat what I wrote at great length in my last, nor shall I have recourse to friends for the same purpose. They all of them, I know, with one voice, without the least disagreement or hesitation, have exhorted you, immediately upon the receipt of their letters and the safe-conduct, to return home, in order to preserve your life, your country, your friends, your

---

[1] Ricordo quoted above in Gotti, ii. 73.

[2] Varchi, ii. 397. "Trovossi anch' egli una mattina morto nella prigione, dubitandosi che non dovesse esser chiesto di francia."

[3] Gotti, i. 195. The letter is in the Archivio Buonarroti, Cod. vii. No. 199. It is not quite accurately given by Gotti, the word *fixa* having been misread into *pigra*, and so forth.

honour, and your property, and also to enjoy those times so earnestly desired and hoped for by you.[1] If any one had foretold that I could listen without the least affright to news of an invading army marching on our walls, this would have seemed to me impossible. And yet I now assure you that I am not only quite fearless, but also full of confidence in a glorious victory. For many days past my soul has been filled with such gladness, that if God, either for our sins or for some other reason, according to the mysteries of His just judgment, does not permit that army to be broken in our hands, my sorrow will be the same as when one loses, not a good thing hoped for, but one gained and captured. To such an extent am I convinced in my fixed imagination of our success, and have put it to my capital account. I already foresee our militia system, established on a permanent basis, and combined with that of the territory, carrying our city to the skies.[2] I contemplate a fortification of Florence, not temporary, as it now is, but with walls and bastions to be built hereafter. The principal and most difficult step has been already taken ; the whole space round the town swept clean, without regard for churches or for monasteries, in accordance with the public need. I contemplate in these our fellow-citizens a noble spirit of disdain for all their losses and the bygone

[1] Probably the freedom of the Republic.
[2] This *milizia* had been established on the lines suggested by Machiavelli.

luxuries of villa-life; an admirable unity and fervour for the preservation of liberty; fear of God alone; confidence in Him and in the justice of our cause; innumerable other good things, certain to bring again the age of gold, and which I hope sincerely you will enjoy in company with all of us who are your friends. For all these reasons, I most earnestly entreat you, from the depth of my heart, to come at once and travel through Lucca, where I will meet you, and attend you with due form and ceremony until here: such is my intense desire that our country should not lose you, nor you her. If, after your arrival at Lucca, you should by some accident fail to find me, and you should not care to come to Florence without my company, write a word, I beg. I will set out at once, for I feel sure that I shall get permission. . . . God, by His goodness, keep you in good health, and bring you back to us safe and happy."

Michelangelo set forth upon his journey soon after the receipt of this letter. He was in Ferrara on the 9th of November, as appears from a despatch written by Galeotto Giugni, recommending him to the Government of Florence.[1] Letters patent under the seal of the Duke secured him free passage through the city of Modena and the province of Garfagnana.[2] In spite of these accommodations, he

[1] Gaye, ii. 212.
[2] Under date November 10. The safe-conduct lasted fifteen days. See Gotti, ii. 74.

seems to have met with difficulties on the way, owing to the disturbed state of the country. His friend Giovan Battista Palla was waiting for him at Lucca, without information of his movements, up to the 18th of the month. He had left Florence on the 11th, and spent the week at Pisa and Lucca, expecting news in vain. Then, "with one foot in the stirrup," as he says, "the license granted by the Signory" having expired, he sends another missive to Venice, urging Michelangelo not to delay a day longer.[1] "As I cannot persuade myself that you do not intend to come, I urgently request you to reflect, if you have not already started, that the property of those who incurred outlawry with you is being sold, and if you do not arrive within the term conceded by your safe-conduct—that is, during this month—the same will happen to yourself, without the possibility of any mitigation. If you do come, as I still hope and firmly believe, speak with my honoured friend Messer Filippo Calandrini here, to whom I have given directions for your attendance from this town without trouble to yourself. God keep you safe from harm, and grant we see you shortly in our country, by His aid, victorious."

With this letter, Palla, who was certainly a good friend to the wayward artist, and an amiable man to boot, disappears out of this history. At some time about the 20th of November, Michelangelo returned

[1] Gotti, ii. 72 ; Arch. Buon., Cod. vii. 200.   I shall print the original in the Appendix.

to Florence. We do not know how he finished the journey, and how he was received; but the sentence of outlawry was commuted, on the 23rd, into exclusion from the Grand Council for three years.[1] He set to work immediately at S. Miniato, strengthening the bastions, and turning the church-tower into a station for sharpshooters.[2] Florence by this time had lost all her territory except a few strong places, Pisa, Livorno, Arezzo, Empoli, Volterra.[3] The Emperor Charles V. signed her liberties away to Clement by the peace of Barcelona (June 20, 1529), and the Republic was now destined to be the appanage of his illegitimate daughter in marriage with the bastard Alessandro de' Medici. It only remained for the army of the Prince of Orange to reduce the city. When Michelangelo arrived, the Imperial troops were leaguered on the heights above the town. The inevitable end of the unequal struggle could be plainly foreseen by those who had not Palla's enthusiasm to sustain their faith. In spite of Ferrucci's genius and spirit, in spite of the good-will of the citizens, Florence was bound to fall. While admitting that Michelangelo abandoned his post in a moment of panic, we must do him the justice of remembering that he resumed it when all his darkest prognostications were being slowly but surely

---

[1] Gaye, ii. 214.

[2] This, at any rate, is the tradition of his earlier biographers. We have some reason, however, to doubt whether he was actively employed to any very great extent after his return.

[3] Varchi, ii. 195.

realised. The worst was that his old enemy, Malatesta Baglioni, had now opened a regular system of
intrigue with Clement and the Prince of Orange,
terminating in the treasonable cession of the city.
It was not until August 1530 that Florence finally
capitulated.[1] Still the months which intervened
between that date and Michelangelo's return from
Venice were but a dying close, a slow agony interrupted by spasms of ineffectual heroism.

In describing the works at S. Miniato, Condivi
lays great stress upon Michelangelo's plan for arm-
ing the bell-tower.[2] "The incessant cannonade of
the enemy had broken it in many places, and there
was a serious risk that it might come crashing down,
to the great injury of the troops within the bastion.
He caused a large number of mattresses well stuffed
with wool to be brought, and lowered these by night
from the summit of the tower down to its foundations, protecting those parts which were exposed to
fire. Inasmuch as the cornice projected, the mattresses hung free in air, at the distance of six
cubits from the wall; so that when the missiles of
the enemy arrived, they did little or no damage,
partly owing to the distance they had travelled, and
partly to the resistance offered by this swinging,
yielding panoply." An anonymous writer, quoted
by Milanesi, gives a fairly intelligible account of the
system adopted by Michelangelo.[3] "The outer walls
of the bastion were composed of unbaked bricks,

[1] Varchi, ii. 365.   [2] Condivi, p. 48.   [3] Vasari, xii. 365.

the clay of which was mingled with chopped tow.
Its thickness he filled in with earth; and," adds
this critic, "of all the buildings which remained,
this alone survived the siege."[1] It was objected
that, in designing these bastions, he multiplied the
flanking lines and embrasures beyond what was
either necessary or safe. But, observes the anonymous writer, all that his duty as architect demanded
was that he should lay down a plan consistent with
the nature of the ground, leaving details to practical
engineers and military men.[2] "If, then, he committed any errors in these matters, it was not so
much his fault as that of the Government, who
did not provide him with experienced coadjutors.
But how can mere merchants understand the art of
war, which needs as much science as any other of
the arts, nay more, inasmuch as it is obviously more
noble and more perilous?" The confidence now
reposed in him is further demonstrated by a license
granted on the 22nd of February 1530, empowering
him to ascend the cupola of the Duomo on one
special occasion with two companions, in order to
obtain a general survey of the environs of Florence.[3]

[1] Michelangelo's bastions were afterwards rebuilt upon a permanent
plan. Vauban, when he came to Florence, is said to have surveyed
these works and measured them. I shall print in the Appendix a document supplied me by Cav. Biagi, which refers to the wool used for these
defences.

[2] Compare what Varchi, ii. 147, says upon this point.

[3] Cesare Guasti, *La Cupola di S. M. del Firenze*, quoted by Gotti,
i. 197. The fact that only a single permission for a single day was
granted has induced Springer to believe that, after his return from
Venice, Michelangelo took no prominent part in the defence of Florence.

Michelangelo, in the midst of these serious duties, could not have had much time to bestow upon his art. Still there is no reason to doubt Vasari's emphatic statement that he went on working secretly at the Medicean monuments.[1] To have done so openly while the city was in conflict to the death with Clement, would have been dangerous; and yet every one who understands the artist's temperament must feel that a man like Buonarroti was likely to seek rest and distraction from painful anxieties in the tranquillising labour of the chisel. It is also certain that, during the last months of the siege, he found leisure to paint a picture of Leda for the Duke of Ferrara, which will be mentioned in its proper place.

Florence surrendered in the month of August 1530. The terms were drawn up by Don Ferrante Gonzaga, who commanded the Imperial forces after the death of Filiberto, Prince of Orange, in concert with the Pope's commissary-general, Baccio Valori. Malatesta Baglioni, albeit he went about muttering that Florence " was no stable for mules " (alluding to the fact that all the Medici were bastards), approved of the articles, and showed by his conduct that he had long been plotting treason. The act of capitulation was completed on the 12th, and accepted unwillingly by the Signory. Valori, supported by Baglioni's military force, reigned supreme in the city, and prepared to reinstate the exiled family of

[1] Vasari, xii. 207.

princes.[1]   It is said that Marco Dandolo of Venice, when news reached the Pregadi of the fall of Florence, exclaimed aloud : " Baglioni has put upon his head the cap of the biggest traitor upon record."

V.

The city was saved from wreckage by a lucky quarrel between the Italian and Spanish troops in the Imperial camp. But no sooner was Clement aware that Florence lay at his mercy, than he disregarded the articles of capitulation, and began to act as an autocratic despot. Before confiding the government to his kinsmen, the Cardinal Ippolito and Alessandro Duke of Penna, he made Valori institute a series of criminal prosecutions against the patriots.[2] Battista della Palla and Raffaello Girolami were sent to prison and poisoned. Five citizens were tortured and decapitated in one day of October. Those who had managed to escape from Florence were sentenced to exile, outlawry, and confiscation of goods by hundreds. Charles V. had finally to interfere and put a stop to the fury of the Pope's revenges. How cruel and exasperated the mind of

---

[1] See Capponi, *op. cit.*, lib. vi. cap. 10. Compare Varchi, ii. pp. 373-392.

[2] Varchi, ii. 396-414. Whole pages are occupied by lists of these victims to Papal vengeance.

Clement was, may be gathered from his treatment of Fra Benedetto da Foiano, who sustained the spirit of the burghers by his fiery preaching during the privations of the siege. Foiano fell into the clutches of Malatesta Baglioni, who immediately sent him down to Rome. By the Pope's orders the wretched friar was flung into the worst dungeon in the Castle of S. Angelo, and there slowly starved to death by gradual diminution of his daily dole of bread and water.[1] Readers of Benvenuto Cellini's Memoirs will remember the horror with which he speaks of this dungeon and of its dreadful reminiscences, when it fell to his lot to be imprisoned there.[2]

Such being the mood of Clement, it is not wonderful that Michelangelo should have trembled for his own life or liberty. As Varchi says, "He had been a member of the Nine, had fortified the hill and armed the bell-tower of S. Miniato. What was more annoying, he was accused, though falsely, of proposing to raze the palace of the Medici, where in his boyhood Lorenzo and Piero dei Medici had shown him honour as a guest at their own tables, and to name the space on which it stood the Place of Mules."[3] For this reason he hid himself, as Condivi and Varchi assert, in the house of a trusty friend. The Senator Filippo Buonarroti, who diligently collected traditions about his illustrious ancestor, believed that his real place of retreat was the

---

[1] Varchi, ii. 387.   [2] Cellini, Book I. chap. cxx.
[3] Varchi, ii. 399.

bell-tower of S. Nicolò, beyond the Arno.[1] "When Clement's fury abated," says Condivi, "he wrote to Florence ordering that search should be made for Michelangelo, and adding that when he was found, if he agreed to go on working at the Medicean monuments, he should be left at liberty and treated with due courtesy. On hearing news of this, Michelangelo came forth from his hiding-place, and resumed the statues in the sacristy of S. Lorenzo, moved thereto more by fear of the Pope than by love for the Medici."[2] From correspondence carried on between Rome and Florence during November and December, we learn that his former pension of fifty crowns a month was renewed, and that Giovan Battista Figiovanni, a Prior of S. Lorenzo, was appointed the Pope's agent and paymaster.[3]

An incident of some interest in the art-history of Florence is connected with this return of the Medici, and probably also with Clement's desire to concentrate Michelangelo's energies upon the sacristy. So far back as May 10, 1508, Piero Soderini wrote to the Marquis of Massa-Carrara, begging him to retain a large block of marble until Michelangelo could come in person and superintend its rough-hewing for a colossal statue to be placed on the Piazza.[4] After the death of Leo, the stone was assigned to Baccio Bandinelli; but Michelangelo,

[1] Gotti, i. 199.
[2] Condivi, p. 49. He adds, what is clearly wrong, that it was about fifteen years since Michelangelo had used the sculptor's tools.
[3] Gaye, ii. 221.   [4] Ibid., ii. 97–98.

being in favour with the Government at the time of the expulsion of the Medici, obtained the grant of it. His first intention, in which Bandinelli followed him, was to execute a Hercules trampling upon Cacus, which should stand as pendant to his own David.   By a deliberation of the Signory, under date August 22, 1528, we are informed that the marble had been brought to Florence about three years earlier, and that Michelangelo now received instructions, couched in the highest terms of compliment, to proceed with a group of two figures until its accomplishment.[1] If Vasari can be trusted, Michelangelo made numerous designs and models for the Cacus, but afterwards changed his mind, and thought that he would extract from the block a Samson triumphing over two prostrate Philistines.[2] The evidence for this change of plan is not absolutely conclusive. The deliberation of August 22, 1528, indeed left it open to his discretion whether he should execute a Hercules and Cacus, or any other group of two figures ; and the English nation at South Kensington possesses one of his noble little wax models for a Hercules.[3] We may perhaps, therefore, assume that while Bandinelli adhered to the Hercules and Cacus, Michelangelo finally decided on a Samson. At any rate, the block was restored in

---

[1] Gaye, ii. 97, 98.

[2] See Vasari, *Life of Bandinelli*, vol. x. pp. 305, 306, 311 ; *Life of Pierino da Vinci*, ibid., p. 289.

[3] See J. C. Robinson's *Catalogue to the Italian Sculpture at S. K.*, pp. 141–144.

1530 to Bandinelli, who produced the misbegotten group which still deforms the Florentine Piazza.

Michelangelo had some reason to be jealous of Bandinelli, who exercised considerable influence at the Medicean court, and was an unscrupulous enemy both in word and deed. A man more widely and worse hated than Bandinelli never lived. If any piece of mischief happened which could be fixed upon him with the least plausibility, he bore the blame. Accordingly, when Buonarroti's workshop happened to be broken open, people said that Bandinelli was the culprit. Antonio Mini left the following record of the event:[1] "Three months before the siege, Michelangelo's studio in Via Mozza was burst into with chisels; about fifty drawings of figures were stolen, and among them the designs for the Medicean tombs, with others of great value; also four models in wax and clay. The young men who did it left by accident a chisel marked with the letter M., which led to their discovery. When they knew they were detected, they made off or hid themselves, and sent to say they would return the stolen articles, and begged for pardon." Now the chisel branded with an M. was traced to Michelangelo, the father of Baccio Bandinelli, and no one doubted that he was the burglar.

The history of Michelangelo's Leda, which now survives only in doubtful reproductions, may be introduced by a passage from Condivi's account of his

---

[1] Gotti, i. 203.

master's visit to Ferrara in 1529.[1] " The Duke received him with great demonstrations of joy, no less
by reason of his eminent fame than because Don
Ercole, his son, was Captain of the Signory of
Florence. Riding forth with him in person, there
was nothing appertaining to the business of his
mission which the Duke did not bring beneath his
notice, whether fortifications or artillery. Beside
this, he opened his own private treasure-room, displaying all its contents, and particularly some pictures and portraits of his ancestors, executed by
masters in their time excellent. When the hour
approached for Michelangelo's departure, the Duke
jestingly said to him : ' You are my prisoner now.
If you want me to let you go free, I require that you
shall promise to make me something with your own
hand, according to your will and fancy, be it sculpture or painting.' Michelangelo agreed ; and when
he arrived at Florence, albeit he was overwhelmed
with work for the defences, he began a large piece
for a saloon, representing the congress of the swan
with Leda. The breaking of the egg was also introduced, from which sprang Castor and Pollux, according to the ancient fable. The Duke heard of this ;
and on the return of the Medici, he feared that he
might lose so great a treasure in the popular disturb-
ance which ensued. Accordingly he despatched one
of his gentlemen, who found Michelangelo at home,
and viewed the picture. After inspecting it, the man

---

[1] Condivi, p. 52.

exclaimed : 'Oh! this is a mere trifle.' Michelangelo inquired what his own art was, being aware
that men can only form a proper judgment in the
arts they exercise. The other sneered and answered :
'I am a merchant.' Perhaps he felt affronted at the
question, and at not being recognised in his quality
of nobleman ; he may also have meant to depreciate
the industry of the Florentines, who for the most
part are occupied with trade, as though to say :
'You ask me what my art is ? Is it possible you
think a man like me could be a trader ? ' Michelangelo, perceiving his drift, growled out : 'You are
doing bad business for your lord! Take yourself
away ! ' Having thus dismissed the ducal messenger,
he made a present of the picture, after a short while,
to one of his serving-men, who, having two sisters
to marry, begged for assistance. It was sent to
France, and there bought by King Francis, where it
still exists."

As a matter of fact, we know now that Antonio
Mini, for a long time Michelangelo's man of all
work, became part owner of this Leda, and took it
with him to France.[1] A certain Francesco Tedaldi
acquired pecuniary interest in the picture, of which
one Benedetto Bene made a copy at Lyons in 1532.
The original and the copy were carried by Mini to

---

[1] I do not concur with Heath Wilson's conclusions about the Leda.
Michelangelo probably gave it away to Mini in a fit of pique and generosity. The man raised money on it for his journey with Tedaldi, and
so the latter acquired an interest in it which has thrown some light
upon its fate.

Paris in 1533, and deposited in the house of Giuliano Buonaccorsi, whence they were transferred in
some obscure way to the custody of Luigi Alamanni,
and finally passed into the possession of the King.
Meanwhile, Antonio Mini died, and Tedaldi wrote
a record of his losses and a confused account of
money matters and broker business, which he sent
to Michelangelo in 1540.[1] The Leda remained at
Fontainebleau till the reign of Louis XIII., when
M. Desnoyers, Minister of State, ordered the picture
to be destroyed because of its indecency. Pierre
Mariette says that this order was not carried into
effect; for the canvas, in a sadly mutilated state, re-
appeared some seven or eight years before his date
of writing, and was seen by him. In spite of injuries, he could trace the hand of a great master;
"and I confess that nothing I had seen from the
brush of Michelangelo showed better painting." He
adds that it was restored by a second-rate artist and
sent to England.[2] What became of Mini's copy is
uncertain. We possess a painting in the Dresden
Gallery, a Cartoon in the collection of the Royal
Academy of England, and a large oil picture,
much injured, in the vaults of the National Gallery.[3]

[1] Gotti, i. 201, 202.   [2] Condivi, p. 185.

[3] It is to be regretted that these two great studies of Michelangelo's
Leda are practically hidden from the public eye; one of them may not
improbably be a contemporary replica. The style of the National
Gallery painting, so far as I remember it, is superb in breadth and
grandeur. The pose of the woman and the proportions of her adult
heroic form strongly resemble those of the "Notte," on which marble
Michelangelo was working when he designed her.

In addition to these works, there is a small marble statue in the Museo Nazionale at Florence. All of them represent Michelangelo's design. If mere indecency could justify Desnoyers in his attempt to destroy a masterpiece, this picture deserved its fate. It represented the act of coition between a swan and a woman; and though we cannot hold Michelangelo responsible for the repulsive expression on the face of Leda, which relegates the marble of the Bargello to a place among pornographic works of art, there is no reason to suppose that the general scheme of his conception was abandoned in the copies made of it.

Michelangelo, being a true artist, anxious only for the presentation of his subject, seems to have remained indifferent to its moral quality. Whether it was a crucifixion, or a congress of the swan with Leda, or a rape of Ganymede, or the murder of Holofernes in his tent, or the birth of Eve, he sought to seize the central point in the situation, and to accentuate its significance by the inexhaustible means at his command for giving plastic form to an idea. Those, however, who have paid attention to his work will discover that he always found emotional quality corresponding to the nature of the subject. His ways of handling religious and mythological motives differ in sentiment, and both are distinguished from his treatment of dramatic episodes. The man's mind made itself a mirror to reflect the vision floating over it; he cared not what that vision was, so long as he could render it in lines of plastic harmony, and express the utmost of the feeling which the theme contained.

Among the many statues left unfinished by Michelangelo is one belonging to this period of his life. " In order to ingratiate himself with Baccio Valori," says Vasari, "he began a statue of three cubits in marble. It was an Apollo drawing a shaft from his quiver. This he nearly finished. It stands now in the chamber of the Prince of Florence; a thing of rarest beauty, though not quite completed." [1] This noble piece of sculpture illustrates the certainty and freedom of the master's hand. Though the last touches of the chisel are lacking, every limb palpitates and undulates with life. The marble seems to be growing into flesh beneath the hatched lines left upon its surface. The pose of the young god, full of strength and sinewy, is no less admirable for audacity than for ease and freedom. Whether Vasari was right in his explanation of the action of this figure may be considered more than doubtful. Were we not accustomed to call it an Apollo, we should rather be inclined to class it with the Slaves of the Louvre, to whom in feeling and design it bears a remarkable resemblance. Indeed, it might be conjectured with some probability that, despairing of bringing his great design for the tomb of Julius to a conclusion, he utilised one of the projected captives for his present to the all-powerful vizier of the

[1] Vasari, xii. 212. The Apollo is now in the Bargello. It remained for many years neglected in the theatre of the Boboli Gardens.

Medicean tyrants.   It ought, in conclusion, to be
added, that there was nothing servile in Michelangelo's desire to make Valori his friend.   He had
accepted the political situation; and we have good
reason, from letters written at a later date by Valori
from Rome, to believe that this man took a sincere
interest in the great artist.   Moreover, Varchi, who
is singularly severe in his judgment on the agents
of the Medici, expressly states that Baccio Valori
was "less cruel than the other Palleschi, doing many
and notable services to some persons out of kindly
feeling, and to others for money (since he had little
and spent much); and this he was well able to perform, seeing he was then the lord of Florence, and
the first citizens of the land paid court to him and
swelled his train."[1]

VI.

During the siege Lodovico Buonarroti passed his
time at Pisa.   His little grandson, Lionardo, the
sole male heir of the family, was with him.   Born
September 25, 1519, the boy was now exactly
eleven years old, and by his father's death in 1528
he had been two years an orphan.   Lionardo was
ailing, and the old man wearied to return.   His two
sons, Gismondo and Giansimone, had promised to

[1] Varchi, ii. 397.

fetch him home when the country should be safe for travelling. But they delayed ; and at last, upon the 30th of September, Lodovico wrote as follows to Michelangelo :[1] " Some time since I directed a letter to Gismondo, from whom you have probably learned that I am staying here, and, indeed, too long ; for the flight of Buonarroto's pure soul to heaven, and my own need and earnest desire to come home, and Nardo's state of health, all make me restless. The boy has been for some days out of health and pining, and I am anxious about him." It is probable that some means were found for escorting them both safely to Settignano. We hear no more about Lodovico till the period of his death, the date of which has not been ascertained with certainty.

From the autumn of 1530 on to the end of 1533 Michelangelo worked at the Medicean monuments. His letters are singularly scanty during all this period, but we possess sufficient information from other sources to enable us to reconstruct a portion of his life. What may be called the chronic malady of his existence, that never-ending worry with the tomb of Julius, assumed an acute form again in the spring of 1531. The correspondence with Sebastiano del Piombo, which had been interrupted since 1525, now becomes plentiful, and enables us to follow some of the steps which led to the new and solemn contract of May 1532.

It is possible that Michelangelo thought he ought

[1] Gotti, i. 208.

to go to Rome in the beginning of the year. If we are right in ascribing a letter written by Benvenuto della Volpaia from Rome upon the 18th of January to the year 1531, and not to 1532, he must have already decided on this step. The document is curious in several respects.[1]   " Yours of the 13th informs me that you want a room. I shall be delighted if I can be of service to you in this matter; indeed, it is nothing in respect to what I should like to do for you. I can offer you a chamber or two without the least inconvenience; and you could not confer on me a greater pleasure than by taking up your abode with me in either of the two places which I will now describe. His Holiness has placed me in the Belvedere, and made me guardian there. To-morrow my things will be carried thither, for a permanent establishment ; and I can place at your disposal a room with a bed and everything you want. You can even enter by the gate outside the city, which opens into the spiral staircase, and reach your apartment and mine without passing through Rome. From here I can let you into the palace, for I keep a key at your service ; and what is better, the Pope comes every day to visit us. If you decide on the

---

[1] Gotti, ii. 75.   Benvenuto was the son of Lorenzo della Volpaia, the famous mechanician and clockmaker of Florence. Gotti regards this letter as belonging to 1531 ; but I think it probable that Volpaia used the Florentine style, and that it therefore belongs to 1532. At any rate, Sebastiano del Piombo, writing on February 8, 1532, mentions that he has met Volpaia, who spoke of having prepared rooms at the Belvedere for Michelangelo. *Les Correspondants,* p. 80.

Belvedere, you must let me know the day of your departure, and about when you will arrive. In that case I will take up my post at the spiral staircase of Bramante, where you will be able to see me. If you wish, nobody but my brother and Mona Lisabetta and I shall know that you are here, and you shall do just as you please; and, in short, I beg you earnestly to choose this plan. Otherwise, come to the Borgo Nuovo, to the houses which Volterra built, the fifth house toward S. Angelo. I have rented it to live there, and my brother Fruosino is also going to live and keep shop in it. There you will have a room or two, if you like, at your disposal. Please yourself, and give the letter to Tommaso di Stefano Miniatore, who will address it to Messer Lorenzo de' Medici, and I shall have it quickly." [1]

Nothing came of these proposals. But that Michelangelo did not abandon the idea of going to Rome appears from a letter of Sebastiano's written on the 24th of February.[2] It was the first which passed between the friends since the terrible events of 1527 and 1530. For once, the jollity of the epicurean friar has deserted him. He writes as though those awful months of the sack of Rome were still present to his memory. "After all those trials, hardships, and perils, God Almighty has left us alive and in health, by His mercy and piteous

---

[1] Tommaso may have been the son of Michelangelo's old servant, Stefano di Tommaso, the miniaturist.

[2] *Les Correspondants*, p. 36.

kindness. A thing, in sooth, miraculous, when I reflect upon it; wherefore His Majesty be ever held in gratitude. . . . Now, gossip mine, since we have passed through fire and water, and have experienced things we never dreamed of, let us thank God for all; and the little remnant left to us of life, may we at least employ it in such peace as can be had. For of a truth, what fortune does or does not do is of slight importance, seeing how scurvy and how dolorous she is. I am brought to this, that if the universe should crumble round me, I should not care, but laugh at all. Menighella will inform you what my life is, how I am.[1] I do not yet seem to myself to be the same Bastiano I was before the Sack. I cannot yet get back into my former frame of mind." In a postscript to this letter, eloquent by its very naïveté, Sebastiano says that he sees no reason for Michelangelo's coming to Rome, except it be to look after his house, which is going to ruin, and the workshop tumbling to pieces.

In another letter, of April 29, Sebastiano repeats that there is no need for Michelangelo to come to Rome, if it be only to put himself right with the Pope. Clement is sincerely his friend, and has forgiven the part he played during the siege of Florence.[2] He then informs his gossip that, having been lately at Pesaro, he met the painter Girolamo

---

[1] Menighella was a painter from the Valdarno, who amused Michelangelo, as Topolino used to do, by his oddities and buffooneries. See Vasari, xii. 281.

[2] *Les Correspondants*, p. 38. See above.

Genga, who promised to be serviceable in the matter of the tomb of Julius. The Duke of Urbino, according to this man's account, was very eager to see it finished. "I replied that the work was going forward, but that 8000 ducats were needed for its completion, and we did not know where to get this money. He said that the Duke would provide, but his Lordship was afraid of losing both the ducats and the work, and was inclined to be angry. After a good deal of talking, he asked whether it would not be possible to execute the tomb upon a reduced scale, so as to satisfy both parties. I answered that you ought to be consulted." We have reason to infer from this that the plan which was finally adopted, of making a mural monument with only a few figures from the hand of Michelangelo, had already been suggested. In his next letter, Sebastiano communicates the fact that he has been appointed to the office of Piombatore; "and if you could see me in my quality of friar, I am sure you would laugh. I am the finest friar loon in Rome." The Duke of Urbino's agent, Hieronimo Staccoli, now appears for the first time upon the stage. It was through his negotiations that the former contracts for the tomb of Julius were finally annulled and a new design adopted. Michelangelo offered, with the view of terminating all disputes, to complete the monument on a reduced scale at his own cost, and furthermore to disburse the sum of 2000 ducats in discharge of any claims the Della Rovere might have against him.[1] This seemed too liberal, and when Clement was informed of the project, he promised to make better terms. Indeed, during the course of these negotiations the Pope displayed the greatest interest in Michelangelo's affairs.[2] Staccoli, on the Duke's part, raised objections; and Sebastiano had to remind him that, unless some concessions were made, the scheme of the tomb might fall through: "for it does not rain Michelangelos, and men could hardly be found to preserve the work, far less to finish it." In course of time the Duke's ambassador at Rome, Giovan Maria della Porta, intervened, and throughout the whole business Clement was consulted upon every detail.

Sebastiano kept up his correspondence through the summer of 1531. Meanwhile the suspense and anxiety were telling seriously on Michelangelo's health. Already in June news must have reached Rome that his health was breaking down; for Clement sent word recommending him to work less, and to relax his spirits by exercise.[3] Toward the autumn he became alarmingly ill. We have a letter from Paolo Mini, the uncle of his servant Antonio, written to Baccio Valori on the 29th of September.[4] After describing the beauty of two statues for the Medicean tombs, Mini says he fears that "Michelangelo will not live long, unless some measures are

[1] See Lettere, No. cdvii.
[2] See the letter of June 16 about Michelangelo's health and unremitting industry, and that of July 22. *Les Correspondants*, pp. 50–56.
[3] Ibid., p. 50.   [4] Gaye, ii. 229.

taken for his benefit. He works very hard, eats little and poorly, and sleeps less. In fact, he is afflicted with two kinds of disorder, the one in his head, the other in his heart.[1] Neither is incurable, since he has a robust constitution; but for the good of his head, he ought to be restrained by our Lord the Pope from working through the winter in the sacristy, the air of which is bad for him; and for his heart, the best remedy would be if his Holiness could accommodate matters with the Duke of Urbino." In a second letter, of October 8, Mini insists again upon the necessity of freeing Michelangelo's mind from his anxieties. The upshot was that Clement, on the 21st of November, addressed a brief to his sculptor, whereby Buonarroti was ordered, under pain of excommunication, to lay aside all work except what was strictly necessary for the Medicean monuments, and to take better care of his health.[2] On the 26th of the same month Benvenuto della Volpaia wrote, repeating what the Pope had written in his brief, and adding that his Holiness desired him to select some workshop more convenient for his health than the cold and cheerless sacristy.[3]

In spite of Clement's orders that Michelangelo should confine himself strictly to working on the Medicean monuments, he continued to be solicited with various commissions. Thus the Cardinal Cybo

---

[1] Mini mentions in particular headache, chronic cold, and giddiness.
[2] Bottari, *Lett. Pitt.*, vi. 54.　　　[3] Gotti, i. p. 211.

wrote in December begging him to furnish a design for a tomb which he intended to erect. Whether Michelangelo consented is not known.

Early in December Sebastiano resumed his communications on the subject of the tomb of Julius, saying that Michelangelo must not expect to satisfy the Duke without executing the work, in part at least, himself.[1] " There is no one but yourself that harms you : I mean, your eminent fame and the greatness of your works. I do not say this to flatter you. Therefore, I am of opinion that, without some shadow of yourself, we shall never induce those parties to do what we want. It seems to me that you might easily make designs and models, and afterwards assign the completion to any master whom you choose. But the shadow of yourself there must be. If you take the matter in this way, it will be a trifle ; you will do nothing, and seem to do all ; but remember that the work must be carried out under your shadow."

A series of despatches, forwarded between December 4, 1531, and April 29, 1532, by Giovan Maria della Porta to the Duke of Urbino, confirm the particulars furnished by the letters which Sebastiano still continued to write from Rome.[2] At the end of 1531 Michelangelo expressed his anxiety to visit Rome, now that the negotiations with the Duke were nearly complete. Sebastiano, hearing this, replies : " You will effect more in half an hour than I can do in a whole year. I believe that you will arrange everything after two words with his Holiness ; for our Lord is anxious to meet your wishes." [1] He wanted to be present at the drawing up and signing of the contract. Clement, however, although he told Sebastiano that he should be glad to see him, hesitated to send the necessary permission, and it was not until the month of April 1532 that he set out. About the 6th, as appears from the indorsement of a letter received in his absence, he must have reached Rome. The new contract was not ready for signature before the 29th, and on that date Michelangelo left for Florence, having, as he says, been sent off by the Pope in a hurry on the very day appointed for its execution. In his absence it was duly signed and witnessed before Clement ; the Cardinals Gonzaga and da Monte and the Lady Felice della Rovere attesting, while Giovan Maria della Porta and Girolamo Staccoli acted for the Duke of Urbino. When Michelangelo returned and saw the instrument, he found that several clauses prejudicial to his interests had been inserted by the notary.[2] " I discovered more than 1000 ducats charged unjustly to my debit, also the house in which I live, and certain other hooks and crooks to ruin me. The Pope would certainly not have tolerated this knavery, as Fra Sebastiano can

---

[1] *Les Correspondants*, p. 78.
[2] Lettere, No. cdxxxv. p. 489. Written in October 1542, when the tragedy of the tomb was entering upon its final phase.

bear witness, since he wished me to complain to Clement and have the notary hanged. I swear I never received the moneys which Giovan Maria della Porta wrote against me, and caused to be engrossed upon the contract." [1]

It is difficult to understand why Michelangelo should not have immediately taken measures to rectify these errors. He seems to have been well aware that he was bound to refund 2000 ducats, since the only letter from his pen belonging to the year 1532 is one dated May, and addressed to Andrea Quarantesi in Pisa. In this document he consults Quarantesi about the possibility of raising that sum, with 1000 ducats in addition. " It was in my mind, in order that I might not be left naked, to sell houses and possessions, and to let the lira go for ten soldi." [2]   As the contract was never carried out, the fraudulent passages inserted in the deed did not prove of practical importance. Della Porta, on his part, wrote in high spirits to his master : [3] " Yesterday we executed the new contract with Michelangelo, for the ratification of which by your

---

[1] According to this contract, Michelangelo acknowledged to have received 8000 ducats in various payments, and promised to finish the tomb at his own expense, disbursing in addition 2000 ducats, in which sum his house at the Macello de' Corvi was included. Lettere, pp. 702, 703.

[2] Lettere, No. cdx. It is possible that the words written upon the back of a drawing at Oxford, *Andrea abbi patientia—A me m'è consolatione assai*, may have been drawn forth from him by the anxieties of this year.

[3] Vasari, xii. 380. The despatch is dated April 30.

Lordship we have fixed a limit of two months. It is of a nature to satisfy all Rome, and reflects great credit on your Lordship for the trouble you have taken in concluding it. Michelangelo, who shows a very proper respect for your Lordship, has promised to make and send you a design. Among other items, I have bound him to furnish six statues by his own hand, which will be a world in themselves, because they are sure to be incomparable. The rest he may have finished by some sculptor at his own choice, provided the work is done under his direction. The Pope allows him to come twice a year to Rome, for periods of two months each, in order to push the work forward. And he is to execute the whole at his own costs." He proceeds to say, that since the tomb cannot be put up in S. Peter's, S. Pietro in Vincoli has been selected as the most suitable church. It appears that the Duke's ratification was sent upon the 5th of June, and placed in the hands of Clement, so that Michelangelo probably did not see it for some months. Della Porta, writing to the Duke again upon the 19th of June, says that Clement promised to allow Michelangelo to come to Rome in the winter, and to reside there working at the tomb. But we have no direct information concerning his doings after the return to Florence at the end of April 1532.

It will be worth while to introduce Condivi's account of these transactions relating to the tomb of Julius, since it throws some light upon the sculptor's private feelings and motives, as well as upon the falsification of the contract as finally engrossed.[1]

"When Michelangelo had been called to Rome by Pope Clement, he began to be harassed by the agents of the Duke of Urbino about the sepulchre of Julius. Clement, who wished to employ him in Florence, did all he could to set him free, and gave him for his attorney in this matter Messer Tommaso da Prato, who was afterwards datary. Michelangelo, however, knowing the evil disposition of Duke Alessandro towards him, and being in great dread on this account, also because he bore love and reverence to the memory of Pope Julius and to the illustrious house of Della Rovere, strained every nerve to remain in Rome and busy himself about the tomb. What made him more anxious was that every one accused him of having received from Pope Julius at least 16,000 crowns, and of having spent them on himself without fulfilling his engagements. Being a man sensitive about his reputation, he could not bear the dishonour of such reports, and wanted the whole matter to be cleared up ; nor, although he was now old, did he shrink from the very onerous task of completing what he had begun so long ago. Consequently they came to strife together, and his antagonists were unable to prove payments to anything like the amount which had first been noised abroad ; indeed, on the contrary, more than two thirds of the whole sum first stipu-

[1] Condivi, pp. 54–57.

lated by the two Cardinals was wanting. Clement then thinking he had found an excellent opportunity for setting him at liberty and making use of his whole energies, called Michelangelo to him, and said : 'Come, now, confess that you want to make this tomb, but wish to know who will pay you the balance.' Michelangelo, knowing well that the Pope was anxious to employ him on his own work, answered : 'Supposing some one is found to pay me.' To which Pope Clement: 'You are a great fool if you let yourself believe that any one will come forward to offer you a farthing.' Accordingly, his attorney, Messer Tommaso, and the agents of the Duke, after some negotiations, came to an agreement that a tomb should at least be made for the amount he had received. Michelangelo, thinking the matter had arrived at a good conclusion, consented with alacrity. He was much influenced by the elder Cardinal di Monte, who owed his advancement to Julius II., and was uncle of Julius III., our present Pope by grace of God. The arrangement was as follows : That he should make a tomb of one façade only ; should utilise those marbles which he had already blocked out for the quadrangular monument, adapting them as well as circumstances allowed ; and finally, that he should be bound to furnish six statues by his own hand. In spite of this arrangement, Pope Clement was allowed to employ Michelangelo in Florence or where he liked during four months of the year, that being required by his

Holiness for his undertakings at S. Lorenzo. Such
then was the contract made between the Duke and
Michelangelo. But here it has to be observed, that
after all accounts had been made up, Michelangelo
secretly agreed with the agents of his Excellency
that it should be reported that he had received some
thousands of crowns above what had been paid to
him ; the object being to make his obligation to
the Duke of Urbino seem more considerable, and
to discourage Pope Clement from sending him to
Florence, whither he was extremely unwilling to go.
This acknowledgment was not only bruited about
in words, but, without his knowledge or consent,
was also inserted into the deed ; not when this was
drawn up, but when it was engrossed ; a falsification which caused Michelangelo the utmost vexation.
The ambassador, however, persuaded him that this
would do him no real harm : it did not signify, he
said, whether the contract specified a thousand or
twenty thousand crowns, seeing they were agreed
that the tomb should be reduced to suit the sums
actually received ; adding, that nobody was concerned in the matter except himself, and that
Michelangelo might feel safe with him on account
of the understanding between them. Upon this
Michelangelo grew easy in his mind, partly because
he thought he might have confidence, and partly
because he wished the Pope to receive the impression I have described above. In this way the thing
was settled for the time, but it did not end there ;

for when he had worked his four months in Florence and came back to Rome, the Pope set him to other tasks, and ordered him to paint the wall above the altar in the Sistine Chapel. He was a man of excellent judgment in such matters, and had meditated many different subjects for this fresco. At last he fixed upon the Last Judgment, considering that the variety and greatness of the theme would enable the illustrious artist to exhibit his powers in their full extent. Michelangelo, remembering the obligation he was under to the Duke of Urbino, did all he could to evade this new engagement; but when this proved impossible, he began to procrastinate, and, pretending to be fully occupied with the cartoons for his huge picture, he worked in secret at the statues intended for the monument."

VII.

Michelangelo's position at Florence was insecure and painful, owing to the undisguised animosity of the Duke Alessandro. This man ruled like a tyrant of the worst sort, scandalising good citizens by his brutal immoralities, and terrorising them by his cruelties. "He remained," says Condivi, "in continual alarm; because the Duke, a young man, as is known to every one, of ferocious and revengeful temper, hated him exceedingly. There is no doubt

that, but for the Pope's protection, he would have
been removed from this world.   What added to
Alessandro's enmity was that when he was planning
the fortress which he afterwards erected, he sent
Messer Vitelli for Michelangelo, ordering him to
ride with them, and to select a proper position for
the building.   Michelangelo refused, saying that he
had received no commission from the Pope.   The
Duke waxed very wroth; and so, through this new
grievance added to old grudges and the notorious
nature of the Duke, Michelangelo not unreasonably
lived in fear.   It was certainly by God's aid that
he happened to be away from Florence when
Clement died."[1]   Michelangelo was bound under
solemn obligations to execute no work but what
the Pope ordered for himself or permitted by the
contract with the heirs of Julius.   Therefore he
acted in accordance with duty when he refused to
advise the tyrant in this scheme for keeping the
city under permanent subjection.   The man who
had fortified Florence against the troops of Clement
could not assist another bastard Medici to build a
strong place for her ruin.   It may be to this period
of his life that we owe the following madrigal,
written upon the loss of Florentine liberty and the
bad conscience of the despot:[2]—

---

[1] Condivi, p. 51.   Compare Vasari, xii. 215.   See Varchi, *Stor. Fior.*,
iii. 43, for the commencement of this fortress, the foundations of which
were laid upon the 27th of May 1533.

[2] Rime, p. 25.

Lady, for joy of lovers numberless
   Thou wast created fair as angels are.
   Sure God hath fallen asleep in heaven afar
   When one man calls the bliss of many his !
   Give back to streaming eyes
   The daylight of thy face, that seems to shun
   Those who must live defrauded of their bliss !

Vex not your pure desire with tears and sighs :
   For he who robs you of my light hath none.
   Dwelling in fear, sin hath no happiness ;
   Since, amid those who love, their joy is less,
   Whose great desire great plenty still curtails,
   Than theirs who, poor, have hope that never fails.

During the siege Michelangelo had been forced to lend the Signory a sum of about 1500 ducats.[1] In the summer of 1533 he corresponded with Sebastiano about means for recovering this loan. On the 16th of August Sebastiano writes that he has referred the matter to the Pope.[2] "I repeat, what I have already written, that I presented your memorial to his Holiness. It was about eight in the evening, and the Florentine ambassador was present. The Pope then ordered the ambassador to write immediately to the Duke ; and this he did with such vehemence and passion as I do not think he has displayed on four other occasions concerning the affairs of Florence. His rage and fury were tremendous, and the words he used to the ambassador would stupefy you, could you hear them.

[1] Lettere, No. cdvii. Was this perhaps levied for his contumacy in the flight to Venice ?
[2] Les Correspondants, p. 112.

Indeed, they are not fit to be written down, and I must reserve them for *viva voce*. I burn to have half an hour's conversation with you, for now I know our good and holy master to the ground. Enough, I think you must have already seen something of the sort. In brief, he has resolved that you are to be repaid the 400 ducats of the guardianship and the 500 ducats lent to the old Government." [1] It may be readily imagined that this restitution of a debt incurred by Florence when she was fighting for her liberties, to which act of justice her victorious tyrant was compelled by his Papal kinsman, did not soften Alessandro's bad feeling for the creditor.

Several of Sebastiano's letters during the summer and autumn of 1533 refer to an edition of some madrigals by Michelangelo, which had been set to music by Bartolommeo Tromboncino, Giacomo Archadelt, and Costanzo Festa. [2] We have every reason to suppose that the period we have now reached was the richest in poetical compositions. It was also in 1532 or 1533 that he formed the most passionate attachment of which we have any knowledge in his life; for he became acquainted about this time with

[1] "Li ducati 400 del pupillo." Perhaps this sum had been lent to the Ufficiali dei Pupilli. See Capponi, vol. i. p. 648. With regard to the Pope's rages, we may remember what Cellini says of him : " Veduto io il papa diventato così *una pessima bestia.*" Lib. i. cap. 58.

[2] *Les Correspondants,* pp. 108-112. Compare Lettere, No. cdxv., in which Michelangelo acknowledges the receipt of them. Gotti, vol. ii. pp. 89-122, publishes an interesting essay on this music by Leto Puliti, together with the score of three madrigals.

Tommaso Cavalieri. A few years later he was destined to meet with Vittoria Colonna. The details of these two celebrated friendships will be discussed in another chapter.

Clement VII. journeyed from Rome in September, intending to take ship at Leghorn for Nice and afterwards Marseilles, where his young cousin, Caterina de' Medici, was married to the Dauphin. He had to pass through S. Miniato al Tedesco, and thither Michelangelo went to wait upon him on the 22nd.[1] This was the last, and not the least imposing, public act of the old Pope, who, six years after his imprisonment and outrage in the Castle of S. Angelo, was now wedding a daughter of his plebeian family to the heir of the French crown. What passed between Michelangelo and his master on this occasion is not certain.

The years 1532-1534 form a period of considerable chronological perplexity in Michelangelo's life. This is in great measure due to the fact that he was now residing regularly part of the year in Rome and part in Florence. We have good reason to believe that he went to Rome in September 1532, and stayed there through the winter.[2] It is probable that he then formed the friendship with Cavalieri, which played so important a part in his personal history.

---

[1] See Ricordo in Lettere, p. 604.

[2] Angelini's letter indorsed "le lettere de dugento ducati" (see Appendix), Norchiato's about a translation of Vitruvius (date Dec. 7, 1532, Arch. Buon., Cod. x. 582), Stephano's about the lantern of the Sacristy (Arch Buon., Cod. xi. 713), lead to this conclusion.

A brisk correspondence carried on between him and his two friends, Bartolommeo Angelini and Sebastiano del Piombo, shows that he resided at Florence during the summer and early autumn of 1533. From a letter addressed to Figiovanni on the 15th of October, we learn that he was then impatient to leave Florence for Rome. But a *Ricordo*, bearing date Oct. 29, 1533, renders it almost certain that he had not then started.[1] Angelini's letters, which had been so frequent, stop suddenly in that month.[2] This renders it almost certain that Michelangelo must have soon returned to Rome. Strangely enough there are no letters or *Ricordi* in his handwriting which bear the date 1534. When we come to deal with this year, 1534, we learn from Michelangelo's own statement to Vasari that he was in Florence during the summer, and that he reached Rome two days before the death of Clement VII., *i.e.*, upon September 23.[3] Condivi observes that it was lucky for him that the Pope did not die while he was still at Florence, else he would certainly have been exposed to great peril, and probably been murdered or imprisoned by Duke Alessandro.[4]

Nevertheless, Michelangelo was again in Florence toward the close of 1534. An undated letter to a certain Febo (di Poggio) confirms this supposition.

---

[1] Lettere, pp. 470, 604.

[2] I shall print all Angelini's letters in the Appendix. Angelini's last dated letter is Oct. 18.

[3] Lettere, No. cdlxxxii., written in May 1557.

[4] Condivi, p. 51.

It may probably be referred to the month of December. In it he says that he means to leave Florence next day for Pisa and Rome, and that he shall never return.[1] Febo's answer, addressed to Rome, is dated Jan. 14, 1534, which, according to Florentine reckoning, means 1535.[2]

We may take it, then, as sufficiently well ascertained that Michelangelo departed from Florence before the end of 1534, and that he never returned during the remainder of his life. There is left, however, another point of importance referring to this period, which cannot be satisfactorily cleared up. We do not know the exact date of his father, Lodovico's, death. It must have happened either in 1533 or in 1534. In spite of careful researches, no record of the event has yet been discovered, either at Settignano or in the public offices of Florence. The documents of the Buonarroti family yield no direct information on the subject. We learn, however, from the Libri delle Età, preserved at the Archivio di Stato, that Lodovico di Lionardo di Buonarrota Simoni was born upon the 11th of June 1444.[3] Now Michelangelo, in his poem on Lodovico's death, says very decidedly that his father was ninety when

[1] Lettere, No. cdxx. Milanesi assigns it to the year 1533. But the date of Febo's answer makes this impossible. Besides, we have seen above that he must have gone to Rome at the end of Oct. 1533.

[2] This letter I shall print in the Appendix. It will be fully discussed in chapter xii.

[3] Libro 3 delle Età, in the Arch. delle Tratte, fol. 109, and Libro 2, p. 92, *tergo.* This information I owe to the Cav. G. Biagi.

he breathed his last. If we take this literally, it must be inferred that he died after the middle of June 1534. There are many reasons for supposing that Michelangelo was in Florence when this happened. The chief of these is that no correspondence passed between the Buonarroti brothers on the occasion, while Michelangelo's minutes regarding the expenses of his father's burial seem to indicate that he was personally responsible for their disbursement.[1] I may finally remark that the schedule of property belonging to Michelangelo, recorded under the year 1534 in the archives of the Decima at Florence, makes no reference at all to Lodovico.[2] We conclude from it that, at the time of its redaction, Michelangelo must have succeeded to his father's estate.[3]

The death of Lodovico and Buonarroto, happening within a space of little more than five years, profoundly affected Michelangelo's mind, and left an indelible mark of sadness on his life. One of his best poems, a *capitolo,* or piece of verse in *terza rima* stanzas, was written on the occasion of his father's decease.[4] In it he says that Ludovico had reached

[1] See Gotti, ii. p. 81.

[2] It is published by Gaye, ii. 253. No other extant documents throw much light on the matter.

[3] It only remains to add that, considering Michelangelo left Florence for good at the end of 1534, and that Lodovico must have died before that date, two letters written to Giovan Simone (which Milanesi assigns to 1532, 1533) were probably sent at the end of 1534. They are Lettere, Nos. cxviii., cxix. Both refer to Mona Margherita, an old servant, who had been left to Buonarroti's care by his father on his deathbed.

[4] Rime, pp. 297-301.

the age of ninety. If this statement be literally accurate, the old man must have died in 1534, since he was born upon the 11th of June 1444. But up to the present time, as I have observed above, the exact date of his death has not been discovered. One passage of singular and solemn beauty may be translated from the original :—

Thou'rt dead of dying, and art made divine,
    Nor fearest now to change or life or will ;
    Scarce without envy can I call this thine.
Fortune and time beyond your temple-sill
    Dare not advance, by whom is dealt for us
    A doubtful gladness, and too certain ill.
Cloud is there none to dim you glorious:
    The hours distinct compel you not to fade :
    Nor chance nor fate o'er you are tyrannous.
Your splendour with the night sinks not in shade,
    Nor grows with day, howe'er that sun ride high,
    Which on our mortal hearts life's heat hath rayed.
Thus from thy dying I now learn to die,
    Dear father mine ! In thought I see thy place,
    Where earth but rarely lets men climb the sky.
Not, as some deem, is death the worst disgrace
    For one whose last day brings him to the first,
    The next eternal throne to God's by grace.
There by God's grace I trust that thou art nursed,
    And hope to find thee, if but my cold heart
    High reason draw from earthly slime accursed.